THE SHADOW OF THE UNATTAINED

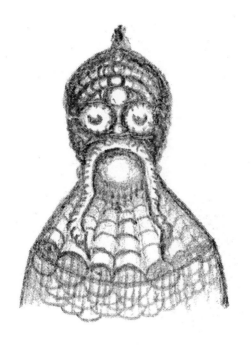

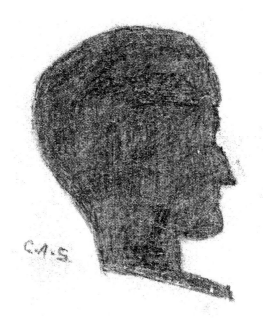

SILHOUETTE OF G.S.

THE SHADOW OF THE UNATTAINED

THE LETTERS OF GEORGE STERLING
AND CLARK ASHTON SMITH

Edited by David E. Schultz and S. T. Joshi

Hippocampus Press
New York

Published by Hippocampus Press
P.O. Box 641, New York, NY 10156.
http://www.hippocampuspress.com

Cover art by Philip Fuller.
Cover design by Barbara Briggs Silbert.
Hippocampus Press logo by Anastasia Damianakos.

First Edition
1 3 5 7 9 8 6 4 2

ISBN 0-9748789-3-6

Contents

THE NAIAD

C.A.S.

INTRODUCTION

It is likely that George Sterling (1869–1926), in the early days of his mentorship of Clark Ashton Smith (1893–1961), felt something akin to *déjà vu;* for his nurturing of the incandescent poetic prodigy surely evoked memories of his own tutorship under Ambrose Bierce a decade and a half before. All three poets were devoted to the ideal of "pure poetry"—poetry free of social or political propaganda, whose *raison d'être* lies in its creation of crystalline beauty as evoked by the glory and tragedy of the universe through skillful use of symbol, image, and metaphor—and all variously suffered from the misfortune that such poetry could be appreciated only by a select few. Smith and Sterling doggedly attempted to seek wider readership for their verse, but perhaps they knew that the undertaking was futile.

Smith tells us that it was an Auburn schoolteacher, Emily J. Hamilton, who urged him to send some of his poems to George Sterling. Given Sterling's current obscurity, it is difficult for us to imagine how bold this act must have seemed to Smith: Sterling not only was a widely published poet (even though most of his books until late in life were published by a San Francisco bookseller, A. M. Robertson); he was also the acknowledged leader of a California literary colony that included such figures as Jack London, Mary Austin, Nora May French, James Hopper, Upton Sinclair, and many others, including for a time the young and then unheralded Sinclair Lewis. That an unknown and unpublished would-be poet would have the temerity to send his work to such a celebrity would have seemed the height of presumption. But Smith took that step in early 1911, and his life was transformed thereby.

We lack Smith's earliest letters to Sterling, but Sterling's surviving responses make it clear that he immediately recognized in Smith both poetic genius and a consonance of poetic ideals. The degree to which Smith's early cosmic poetry was directly influenced by Sterling's own forays in that vein—notably *The Testimony of the Suns* (1903) and "A Wine of Wizardry" (1907)—will always remain a matter of debate; one senses that Smith would have written very much as he did even had he not read these masterworks. In any event, Sterling's earliest letters contain meticulous criticisms of Smith's verse on the smallest levels of diction, rhythm, and nuance—exactly as had Bierce's letters to him.

The lives of Bierce, Sterling, and Smith came tantalizingly close to converging in 1911–12. In July 1911 Sterling showed Bierce Smith's "Ode to the Abyss," eliciting a favorable response in a letter. And just as Bierce spent years trying to place "A Wine of Wizardry" with a standard periodical, Sterling undertook to market Smith's poem, although he quickly gave up after a few rejections. The gregarious Sterling may actually have met Bierce in the early 1890s, before corresponding with him (he tells of how he first met Bierce in the summer of 1893,[1] but the first extant letter between the two dates to 1896), but it was a year and a half before Sterling could pry the shy and reclusive Smith out of his fastness in Auburn. Their first meeting occurred in June–July 1912, when Smith spent a full month with Sterling at Carmel; this was exactly the time of Bierce's last trip to California (he had settled in Washington, D.C., in late 1899), but

---

1. GS, "The Shadow Maker," *American Mercury* 6, No. 1 (September 1925): 11.

evidently Smith was too diffident to meet with the intimidating old firebrand. Smith also passed up several opportunities to meet Sterling's best friend, Jack London, before the latter's death in 1916.

Despite Sterling's early involvement in Smith's budding career, the first publication of Smith's poetry was not without problems. Sterling had quoted Smith's "The Last Night" in an interview with Edward F. O'Day in the San Francisco weekly, *Town Talk*, on 15 April 1911; Smith himself published little (aside from the short story "The Mahout" in the *Black Cat* for October 1911) for another year and a half.[2] But as early as December 1911, Smith informed Sterling that on a recent trip to San Francisco he had met with A. M. Robertson, who had asked Smith to submit some of his poems with a view toward book publication. The news caught Sterling by surprise, so it certainly cannot be said that it was Sterling who arranged for the publication of *The Star-Treader and Other Poems* the following year. Robertson was no doubt aware of Sterling's good opinion of Smith's work, and in any event Sterling soon took over many of the particulars of the project, meeting with Robertson (who, in another parallel with the Bierce-Sterling relationship, wanted Sterling to "boom" Smith in the papers just as Bierce had done with Sterling's "A Wine of Wizardry"), conferring with Smith as to which poems should go into the book, and taking him in hand very much as Bierce had done with the publication of Sterling's first book, *The Testimony of the Suns and Other Poems* (1903).

But at this juncture the redoubtable Boutwell Dunlap enters—or, we should say, re-enters. It was Dunlap, a San Francisco lawyer, who had brought Smith to meet with Robertson in late 1911, and it was Dunlap who, in August 1912, proclaimed Smith as a boy genius to the San Francisco papers, claiming Smith as his own discovery. Both Smith and Sterling knew that Sterling's interview with O'Day long preceded Dunlap's involvement with Smith; indeed, that interview had alerted Dunlap to Smith's existence. The matter was put right shortly thereafter by various letters and articles published in *Town Talk* (whose editor, Theodore Bonnet, seemed particularly keen on reporting the doings of Sterling and his coterie), although Robertson was irked that the Smith boom was occurring months before *The Star-Treader* could appear. Bierce also was caught up in the fracas: having been misquoted in the papers over his views of Smith, he wrote a tart letter to *Town Talk* in which he publicly asserted Smith's talent and expressed sympathy that Smith was being "thrown to the lions of reaction."

The Star-Treader and Other Poems did create a sensation, and its sales were surprisingly robust. There is some doubt as to exactly how many copies were sold: a year after publication Smith notes that between 500 and 600 copies had been disposed of; less than a year later he is claiming that 900 copies have been sold, but in April 1917 he reports that figure as probably erroneous. Nevertheless, given that the book went through two printings and was selling well into the 1920s, it is likely that as many as 1400 copies ultimately were sold—a remarkable figure for a first book of poems issued by an unheralded publisher. Smith's sudden celebrity seemed to have little effect upon his general situation—his life in a remote village in the foothills of the Sierras, tending to two increasingly ailing parents with little money for travel, books, or even basic necessities. It was probably his poverty, and painful shyness, that prevented him from visiting Sterling for more than a year and a half after their initial contact; even so, that

---

2. In 1910, before becoming acquainted with Sterling, Smith had published two poems and two short stories in the *Overland Monthly* and a poem in *Munsey's*.

first meeting was facilitated by travel fare supplied by Sterling (who was not exactly flush with cash himself).

As aesthetically and philosophically in tune as the poets seemed to be, tension between them occurred as early as September 1912, when Sterling criticized the apparent predominance of cosmic themes in Smith's verse. Smith strongly rebutted the assertion ("To my imagination, no other natural event seems half as portentous as the going out of a sun"), and even more vigorously defended himself three years later when the subject resurfaced, refuting the implied charge of being a Johnny one-note by declaring: "I've no intention of playing a 'harp of one string.'" In 1913 Sterling also warned Smith about excessive morbidity in his verse: "If posterity ever notice me at all, I may be censured for not trying to get you away from such subjects, too morbid to occupy more than a line or two of the artistic spectrum." Smith does not appear to have defended himself against this charge, which more than a decade later re-emerged in a different context. One can only wonder at Smith's response to this censure, mild as it was: he acknowledges in memoirs that his reading of "A Wine of Wizardry" (a "horror" poem far more than a "cosmic" poem) was one of the defining moments of his youthful aesthetic life. But Sterling's own poetry was tending toward the elegiac and the human, in such works (praised by Smith) as "The Master Mariner" and "Willy Pitcher." Perhaps Sterling was hoping that his protégé would follow his example.

Sterling's poetic palette certainly had broadened, in an uncharacteristic direction, in the fall of 1914: almost immediately upon the outbreak of World War I, he began the writing of numerous war poems that were widely published in the newspapers. Sterling would later join the Vigilantes, a loose organization designed to advocate pro-American propaganda. There seems no doubt of the sincerity of Sterling's patriotism, but one wonders how he reconciled it with his ideal of "pure poetry." For his part, the war seemed to leave Smith entirely unaffected, even upon the United States' formal entry into it in April 1917. He did not volunteer for military service, as had his later friend H. P. Lovecraft, and when the draft was instituted later in the year, Smith was found medically unfit to serve. Smith continued in his reclusive isolation, squeezing out a few poems and dutifully submitting them to Sterling's arbitration. He resisted Sterling's urging to attend the Panama-Pacific International Exposition in the fall of 1915 until Albert Bender, a wealthy businessman and patron of the arts, provided the funds.

It was, indeed, at this time that Sterling, Bender, and other well-wishers began having increasing concerns about the state of Smith's health. The cause of Smith's general malaise from the period 1913–21 remains a mystery: Sterling believed it to be tuberculosis and continually urged Smith to have himself examined by the quack doctor Albert Abrams, whom Sterling naively believed capable of miracle cures of t.b., cancer, and other diseases; Smith referred to it variously as nervous troubles, indigestion, and an overriding concern over finances. In late 1916 Smith finally was persuaded to have himself checked by Abrams, the results of which are not entirely clear. A little later Sterling made the bold proposal to have Smith stay at a hospital, then at a private sanatorium, for several months, he or others paying expenses and also providing Smith's parents with funds to live on. After much pondering of the generous offer, Smith declined: the idea of staying away from home for months at a time and being regarded as a "patient" apparently was quite distasteful to him, and he asserted (perhaps in a spasm of wishful thinking) that his health was slowly improving. The likelihood is that Smith did indeed have a mild form of tuberculosis, but that the dry climate of Auburn and the vigorous physical activity in which he engaged (wood-chopping, fruit-picking, and the like) caused it go to into remission.

Smith maintained to Sterling that his real trouble—and the true cause of a worry that might lead him to depression or a nervous breakdown—was purely financial. Saddled with a mortgage on their property on which they could barely meet the interest payments, the Smiths could do little but live from month to month, with no chance to set up a business that could bring in income. In 1917 Smith suggested to Sterling that he try to encourage his many wealthy friends in the Bay Area to give him a lump sum of $1500 or $2000 to set up a chicken ranch. Sterling didn't think he could raise such a large sum of money, but he did attempt to persuade some wealthy socialites to give the Smith family a monthly stipend. One of the first to do so was Mrs. Celia Clark, the wife of a mining magnate, who (perhaps in conjunction with others) agreed to supply $75 a month. This stipend appears to have lasted until the spring of 1920, when Mrs. Clark inexplicably stopped giving (perhaps she merely forgot about the matter in planning for an upcoming tour abroad). Sterling then attempted to find a series of benefactors who could contribute $10 a month; but it appears that the sum total of donations rarely exceeded $40 a month, whereas Smith would have been more comfortable with $60.

The sale of poetry was not likely to augment the Smith family income significantly. Both Smith and Sterling bombarded the standard magazines with submissions, Sterling having quite a bit more success than Smith. In 1912, both writers had managed to land a few poems in the newly founded magazine *Poetry,* but its editor, Harriet Monroe, soon made it clear that she preferred the avant-garde poetry of Ezra Pound and his congeners, and Smith and Sterling quickly concluded that their work would not be welcome. In 1918 Sterling, having struck up a correspondence with H. L. Mencken, sent him Smith's prose poem "Ennui" for consideration in the *Smart Set,* the magazine that Mencken would edit from 1914 to 1923. Mencken accepted the work readily, and this set the stage for several more appearances by Smith in the highly regarded but poor-paying magazine. Smith, however, complained that Mencken only accepted those of his works submitted by Sterling rather those submitted by himself.

But it was the absence of a new book of poems to follow up the success of *The Star-Treader* that most troubled Smith: as the years passed and no book bearing his name appeared, the prodigy of 1912 seemed likely to appear to the general public, and even to Smith's friends, as a mere nine-days' wonder. As late as 1921, Smith observed wryly: "My inability to publish puts me in a false position, and disappoints the few people who care for my work. It has even affected my last love-affair—the lady accused me of being a failure!"

There is virtually no discussion in the letters of Smith's second book, *Odes and Sonnets* (1918), published by the Book Club of California. This is probably because the venture was largely the brainchild of Albert Bender, secretary of the Book Club. It was likely discussed during Smith's visit to San Francisco in late 1917, and in January of the following year Smith thanks Bender for "your efforts in regard to the Book Club volume."[3] The slim book (only 28 pages) contained four poems from *The Star-Treader* and eleven new poems, all of which would later be included in *Ebony and Crystal* (1922). At 300 copies, the volume did not make any especial impression upon the literary community as a whole, although any publication by the Book Club of California was sought

---

3. CAS to Albert Bender, 15 January 1918 (*SL* 37).

as a collector's item and constituted a feather in the cap of an author privileged enough to be published by this exclusive organization.

By this time, however, Smith was looking to assemble a much more substantial volume of his post–*Star-Treader* work, in both poetry and prose poetry (he had begun writing prose poems as early as 1913). After long debate Smith settled upon the title for the new book: *Ebony and Crystal: Poems in Verse and Prose.* Its chief component would be the 582-line imaginative epic, *The Hashish-Eater,* which Smith had begun in January 1920 and completed no later than the end of March. Sterling's belated response, in June, is noteworthy:

> "The Hashish-Eater" is indeed an amazing production. My friends will have none of it, claiming it reads like an extension of "A Wine of Wizardry." But I think there are many differences, and at any rate, it has more imagination in it than in any other poem I know of. Like the "Wine," it fails on the esthetic side, a thing that seems of small consequence in a poem of that nature.

What this tells us is that, in the two months since he received *The Hashish-Eater,* Sterling had sent the poem to a number of his associates—whose peculiar belief that the poem was merely an extension of "A Wine of Wizardry" was rightly rejected by both Smith and Sterling.

Smith's attempts to shop *Ebony and Crystal* to major publishers like Alfred A. Knopf, Boni & Liveright, and Houghton Mifflin seem doomed from the start: he was still a very obscure figure outside California, and the tendency in Anglo-American poetry was increasingly away from the metrically exact and gorgeously imaginative verse that Smith was writing. Smith eventually decided to arrange for the volume's publication himself. Luckily, in the summer of 1922 he found that his local paper, the *Auburn Journal,* was willing to print the book on credit. As soon as Sterling heard of the book's imminent publication, he at once lent all the assistance he could, reading proofs, arranging for reviews, and urging Smith to have the book appear well before Christmas so that it could take advantage of holiday sales. Smith failed in this last venture because of problems with the binders, so that initial sales of the book were perhaps disappointing. In the matter of reviews, Sterling did more than merely solicit them from local papers: he actually wrote one (in spite of having also written, at the last moment, a preface to the book, at the suggestion of Smith's printer) and had it signed by George Douglas of the *San Francisco Bulletin.* Sterling soberly writes to Smith: "I dare say you'll find parts of Douglas' review severe, but when you're fifty you'll realize their justice." Douglas himself, in a memoir of Sterling, alludes to the incident, saying that Sterling had brought in "a book of poems and a manuscript review" and stated: "Read the poems first and then the review. I am sure that I have spoken the truth, and some of it is just the truth that should be told, but I cannot tell it to him in person."[4] The gist of Sterling's review is that Smith's work was unduly imitative and that *The Hashish-Eater,* imaginative triumph that it is, nonetheless "fails of that terror it was the evident purpose to suggest" and at times becomes unintentionally comical. This is no doubt what Sterling was referring to in his letter when he said that the poem "fails on the esthetic side."

---

4. George Douglas, "Glimpses of George Sterling," *Overland Monthly* 85, No. 11 (November 1927): 333.

The printing costs for *Ebony and Crystal* came to more than $550, and by May 1923 a balance of only $180 remained; but Smith had difficulty settling his debt, and so he began writing "Clark Ashton Smith's Column" for the *Auburn Journal*, consisting of poems, epigrams, and other miscellany. In May 1924 Sterling sent some of the epigrams to Mencken, who had resigned from the *Smart Set* and begun the *American Mercury;* but Mencken's reaction was not favorable:

> Some of these Smith epigrams are excellent (particularly the ones inspired by Bierce!) and if I were still running The Smart Set I'd buy at least half of them, but I have a doubt that they would hold up if printed together in a formidable series. Too many of them run in obvious directions. I know only too well the art and mystery of making such things: I once wrote 88 in one day.[5]

Perhaps the most interesting of the contributions to "Clark Ashton Smith's Column" were his translations from Baudelaire—an endeavor he appears to have begun in early 1925. Dissatisfied with all previous translations, Smith resolved to translate the whole of *Les Fleurs du mal*, a task he nearly completed over the course of the next several years. The remarkable thing is that, as recently as 1915, he was admitting to Samuel Loveman (a poet with whom Sterling had put him in touch in 1913) that he did not know a word of French ("I've been too indolent to learn any language but my own").[6]

By the spring of 1925 Smith had assembled another book of poetry, *Sandalwood*, and was ready to shop it around. On Sterling's recommendation, he sent the manuscript to George Steele Seymour, secretary of the Bookfellows, a literary group in Chicago that published limited editions; the group would issue Sterling's grove play *Truth* (a revision of his 1923 poetic drama of the same title) in 1926. In a letter to Sterling, Smith suggests that Seymour summarily rejected the volume; but elsewhere he mentions that Seymour had said that "he can do nothing with it till next year. I am inclined to fear that he is emulating the courtesy of the Chinese!"[7] Whether Seymour was giving Smith a definite rejection or merely asking him to wait a bit, Smith felt he had no alternative but to resort again to private publication. Again the *Auburn Journal* printers were chosen, but this time Smith got financial assistance from an unexpected source—his recent associate Donald Wandrei, who subsidized the book. Once more Sterling rounded up the usual sources—sending the book out for review, urging local booksellers to carry it, and sending copies to select individuals who might promote it.

Sterling's own career had been progressing modestly for a decade or more. Smith had relished the poems in *The House of Orchids* (1911), which may well be Sterling's best and most balanced collection—unless that distinction goes to *Beyond the Breakers and Other Poems* (1914). *The Caged Eagle* (1916) contained a miscellany of work, including war poems that were augmented in *The Binding of the Beast and Other War Verse* (1917). Smith responded enthusiastically to *Sails and Mirage and Other Poems* (1921), the last original collection to appear in Sterling's lifetime. Sterling had managed to break into such difficult periodical markets as the *Atlantic Monthly, Harper's, American Mercury,* and *Scribner's,* and this led to Macmillan's offer in 1921 to issue a volume of his selected poems. Sterling, however, was not comfortable with the terms offered by the publisher,

---

5. HLM to GS, 17 May 1924 (*FBB* 200).

6. CAS to Samuel Loveman, 22 April 1915 (ms., Bancroft Library, University of California).

7. CAS to Donald Wandrei, 4 August 1925 (ms., Minnesota Historical Society).

but shortly thereafter he accepted Henry Holt's similar offer. The volume emerged in 1923, to mixed reviews: advocates of Modernism such as John Gould Fletcher heaped abuse upon it, but more conservative critics hailed it as a choice selection of the best that Sterling had written in more than two decades of work. Sterling later accepted Macmillan's offer to republish his scintillating verse drama *Lilith* (1919), with a preface by Theodore Dreiser; but his death prevented preparation of a new volume of lyric poems that Macmillan had also commissioned.

With the advent of the 1920s Smith and Sterling seemed virtual equals as poets, even if Sterling's general reputation was still the greater. As early as 1919 Sterling was admitting: "you are so much my superior in this kind of poetry [i.e., 'pure poetry'] that I'd regard any strictures on it as almost an impertinence on my part, excusable only by reason of my venerable years." With this sense of equality, however, came disagreements, as Smith became increasingly unwilling to accede to Sterling's judgments, either on himself or on other aesthetic or philosophical matters. In 1915 Smith had sent Sterling some of his drawings; Sterling's cool response to them ("The drawings you sent have not much value as art, as you know") did not dissuade Smith from persisting in the work, and he had his modicum of quiet revenge when, in the early 1920s, several art galleries in San Francisco and elsewhere exhibited his artistic work with some success. In 1923 there was a brief and highly amusing discussion of the merits of Smith's new colleague H. P. Lovecraft, whose story "Dagon" did not meet with Sterling's favor (the climax, in his opinion, was "all over in ten minutes, like a rabbit's amour"). Sterling then took the liberty of suggesting an absurd revision of the story. In 1925–26 the two poets disputed the merits of Robinson Jeffers, Smith finding him too tinged with the Modernist ethos to be much to his liking, whereas Sterling (who in a small way acted as Jeffers's mentor, although Jeffers really had little to learn from Sterling) defended him as a distinctive voice in modern poetry. Sterling even went to the length of writing an embarrassingly bad imitation of Jeffers, *Strange Waters* (1926), a poem about incest and lesbianism that was probably meant to evoke Jeffers's far superior poem about brother-sister incest, *Tamar* (1924).

But Smith and Sterling had their greatest disagreement when Smith sent his short story "The Abominations of Yondo" to Sterling. *Weird Tales* had rejected the story, and Smith expressed the hope that it might land in the *Overland Monthly*, to which Sterling was contributing a monthly column, "Rhymes and Reactions." Sterling, although managing to place the story in the *Overland*, wrote with magisterial disfavor:

> All highbrows think the "Yondo" material outworn and childish. The daemonic is done for, for the present, so far as our contemporaries go, and imagination must seek other fields. You have squeezed every drop from the weird (and what drops!) and should touch on it only infrequently, as I on the stars. The swine don't want pearls: they want corn; and it is foolish to hope to change their tastes.

Smith shot back: "I . . . refuse to submit to the arid, earth-bound spirit of the time; and I think there is sure to be a romantic revival sooner or later—a revolt against mechanization and over-socialization, etc. . . . Neither the ethics or the aesthetics of the ant-hill have any attraction for me."

If it now seems odd to us that Sterling could announce the death of the weird at the very time when Lovecraft and his colleagues were enlivening the pages of *Weird Tales* with their powerfully original material, we must take note that Sterling was specifically reflecting the opinions of "highbrows" (presumably he had shown "Yondo" to some of his colleagues just as he had done with *The Hashish-Eater*)—and, perhaps, of the mainstream magazines, which were indeed in the process of banishing the weird from their pages, except when written by such luminaries as Algernon Blackwood or Lord Dunsany. *Weird Tales,* struggling as it did in its first two or three years of existence, itself appealed in general to "lowbrows," as did all pulp magazines of the period; the fact that the weird was now relegated to such venues was a major reason for its ghettoization for the next half-century. And yet, Sterling himself fell into a contradiction in asserting that "the swine don't want pearls": now he is referring to those very lowbrows whose taste for weird, mystery, and science fiction supported the pulp magazines for decades.

Smith and Sterling's final contretemps, though relatively mild, concerned Donald Wandrei's laudatory article on Smith, "The Emperor of Dreams." Sterling correctly observed that Wandrei's effusiveness was the product of youth (Wandrei was eighteen when he wrote the article) and that it might actually cast Smith himself in a bad light; but he nevertheless felt it worth running in the *Overland Monthly,* where it appeared in the issue of December 1926—the month following Sterling's suicide on November 16.

Smith's noble prose tribute, "George Sterling: An Appreciation," is exceeded only by his poetic tribute, "To George Sterling: A Valediction"; the former appeared in the *Overland Monthly* for March 1927, the latter in November 1927—an issue filled with memoirs and elegies by a wide array of friends and colleagues, from Robinson Jeffers to James Hopper to Edwin Markham to Mary Austin. While valiantly defending the morality of Sterling's suicide, Smith elsewhere speaks poignantly of the effect Sterling's death had on him:

> I am desolate and heart-broken over the terrible news. George was easily the first of living American poets, and there is no one left now to carry on the classic tradition. His work, I feel sure, will outlive most of the verse that has been written in English since the beginning of this present century. Sooner or later, there is bound to be a reaction in favour of pure poetry.[8]

To Donald Wandrei he wrote:

> George's death was a great shock to me. We were intimate friends, and I have always had the highest admiration for his poetry. But I suppose he took the best way out. . . .
>
> I think his poetry (not the best of it, however) will come in for considerable appreciation now. "A Wine of Wizardry" had great influence on my own poetic development, and helped to confirm my flair for the fantastic. I think it is the longest poem that I know entirely by heart.[9]

To what extent Sterling's death—and the concomitant flowering of his relations with Lovecraft, Wandrei, and other writers of weird fiction—turned Smith away from poetry and toward the production of prose fantasy is difficult to gauge: it would be another three years before Smith would begin writing short stories in quantity. After *Sandalwood,* it would be a decade before another book of Smith's poetry would emerge, and that vol-

---

8. CAS to James D. Phelan, 19 November 1926 (ms., Bancroft Library).

9. CAS to Donald Wandrei, 6 December 1926 (*SL* 97).

ume, *Nero and Other Poems* (1937), was entirely a reprint collection. Smith did make efforts to market a book, *The Jasmine Girdle*, to various publishers, and in the 1930s R. H. Barlow planned to issue Smith's long-anticipated *Incantations;* but both ventures came to nothing. Smith has many devotees for his weird and fantasy tales, and also for his paintings and sculptures, but most fair-minded readers would judge his poetry to be his supreme aesthetic accomplishment; and in this body of work he gained so much from his mentor of fifteen years that, however much he surpassed his teacher, the two forever will be linked as a pair of writers who carried imaginative poetry to its outermost limits of expression. Their correspondence, surviving nearly intact, allows us a unique window into the workings of their minds and their hearts, and into the complex web of literary and personal associations that made the California of the 1910s and 1920s the dynamic cauldron of creative achievement that it was.

—S. T. JOSHI
DAVID E. SCHULTZ

A NOTE ON THIS EDITION

The manuscripts for nearly all the letters in this volume are in the Henry W. and Albert A. Berg Collection of English and American Literature, New York Public Library (New York, NY); a few items are in the John Hay Library, Brown University (Providence, RI); the Mills College Library (Oakland, CA); and the Dartmouth College Library (Hanover, NH). Letters not specifically identified as to their location are in the Berg Collection. The letters are published without alteration or abridgment. They have been annotated to clarify literary, historical, and other references; notes are placed following each annotated letter. The glossary of names at the end of the volume supplies information on persons frequently mentioned in the letters.

Some time after deposition in the Berg Collection, many of the poems or other works that each author included with his letters were removed and filed separately; some works remain with the letters, but in several instances their placement appears to be erroneous. The editors have attempted to identify, from the internal evidence of the letters themselves, the items sent with a given letter, but in many cases such identification is conjectural. We provide a listing of all the extant manuscripts by each author that accompanied the letters.

The Appendix contains relevant documents (poems, essays, or memoirs) by Smith on Sterling and by Sterling on Smith, along with Ambrose Bierce's letter on Smith in *Town Talk* (10 August 1912).

Abbreviations used in the notes are as follows:

AB	Ambrose Bierce
AJ	*Auburn Journal*
ALS	autograph letter, signed
ANS	autograph note, signed
AS	GS, *After Sunset* (1939)
AY	CAS, *The Abominations of Yondo* (1960)
BB	GS, *Beyond the Breakers and Other Poems* (1914)
BtB	GS, *The Binding of the Beast and Other War Verse* (1917)
CAS	Clark Ashton Smith
CB	Charles Baudelaire

CE   GS, *The Caged Eagle and Other Poems* (1916)
EC   CAS, *Ebony and Crystal* (1922)
FBB   *From Baltimore to Bohemia: The Letters of H. L. Mencken and George Sterling* (2001)
GS   George Sterling
HLM   H. L. Mencken
HO   GS, *The House of Orchids* (1911)
JHL   John Hay Library, Brown University (Providence, RI)
JL   Jack London
LO   CAS, *The Last Oblivion* (2002)
MMM   *A Much Misunderstood Man: Selected Letters of Ambrose Bierce*, ed. S. T. Joshi and
        David E. Schultz (Columbus: Ohio State University Press, 2003)
NYPL   New York Public Library
OS   CAS, *Odes and Sonnets* (1918)
S   CAS, *Sandalwood* (1925)
SL   CAS, *Selected Letters* (2003)
SM   GS, *Sails and Mirage* (1921)
SP   GS, *Selected Poems* (1923); CAS, *Selected Poems* (1971)
ST   CAS, *The Star-Treader and Other Poems* (1912)
TfS   GS, *Thirty-five Sonnets* (1917)
TMS   typescript
TS   GS, *The Testimony of the Suns and Other Poems* (1903)
ThS   GS, *The Thirst of Satan* (2003)
WT   *Weird Tales*
WW   GS, *A Wine of Wizardry and Other Poems* (1909)

    We are grateful to Mike Ashley, Scott Connors, Alan Gullette, Rah Hoffman, Derrick Hussey, Stuart David Schiff, Steve Sneyd, Thomas M. Whitehead of Temple University Libraries, Special Collections, and especially Donald Sidney-Fryer for their past work on Smith and Sterling or for their contributions to this volume. We are also grateful to the Bancroft Library, University of California, for permission to publish the letters and other works by George Sterling; to CASiana Enterprises, Inc., for permission to publish the letters and other works by Clark Ashton Smith; and to the libraries holding the original documents: the New York Public Library, Astor, Lenox and Tilden Foundations; the John Hay Library, Brown University; the Mills College Library; and the Darmouth College Library.

THE SHADOW OF THE UNATTAINED

In quest of visions half-forbid,
    My soul must put aside the screen,
    And walk in regions vaguely seen,
Round Mind's half-conscious borders hid,

As one who seeks a mystic bloom
    On ways beset with nightly chance—
    Circled with alien vigilance,
And rustling of the ghostly gloom.
              —*Clark Ashton Smith*

THE MUSE

C. A. S.

APOLLYON

CAS

CAS

werewolf

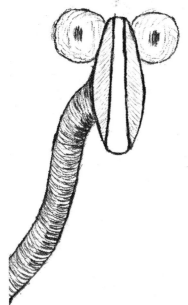

CAS.

[0a] CAS to GS [non-extant]

[Auburn, Cal.
c. early January 1911]

[Enclosure: "The Butterfly" and other poems.]

[1] GS to CAS [ALS]

Carmel, Cal.,
Jan. 31, 1911.

Clark Ashton Smith,
        Auburn, Cal.
Dear Sir:
        Your letter, addressed to my former residence at Piedmont,¹ has finally
reached me. It is not my custom to criticize the work of my fellow-poets, as I lack time,
ability and willingness in such matters,—the last, because it is my experience that "faint
praise" results in the undying hatred of the praisee.
        As your work is, however, so much above the average of what comes to me from
stranger and friend, I have ventured to make a few comments and suggestions, not to
be taken too seriously if you find many folk disagreeing with me.
        You are, I take it, still young. If so, I think a bright future awaits you. The poems
are rich in promise, and the "Butterfly" one qualifies as performance. Your work is
rather too delicate for the man in the crowd, but you will count that, I hope, no disadvantage.
        With best wishes for your success,
            Very sincerely,
                George Sterling.

1. GS lived at Piedmont from 1890 until 1905, at which time he built a house half a mile
from Carmel-by-the-Sea and took up residence there.

[1a] CAS to GS [non-extant]

[Auburn, Cal.
2 February 1911]
[Enclosures: "The Eternal Snows," "The Last Night," "The Moonlight Desert," "Nocturne," "The Voice of Silence."]

[2] GS to CAS [ALS]

Carmel, Cal.,
Feb. 24 / 11.

Dear Mr. Smith:
        Your letter, with poems, arrived safely, but I've been too busy to give
it proper attention, and must ask for a week or two more of your patience. At present

I'm planting several acres of potatoes, and am using all my time and energy at that. I'm to visit my friend London next week, and will probably write from there.

>Very sincerely,

>>George Sterling.

[3] GS to CAS [ALS]

>>>>>Carmel, Cal.,
>>>>>Feb. 28, 1911.

Dear Mr. Smith:

>I'm returning the poems that you've given me the pleasure of running over, with such comments as seem pertinent to me. Doubtless I should have given them, and your letter of the 2nd, attention ere now. But I've more duties and troubles than you'd expect, and am besides notoriously slow in replying to those kind (and unfortunate) enough to be my correspondents.

It has been to me a matter of sincere pleasure and great inter[e]st to examine these poems, and I do not think I err in saying that such work on the part of a youth of eighteen years is phenomenal, and an indication of true genius. If you go ahead at the rate normal to poets, you will not set any great value on any of these enclosed poems (good as some of them are), except in the case of "The Last Night." There is actual performance.

At least I *think* that will some day be your feeling toward this early work of yours. I find it so in my own case, and poems that once I looked on as matter for self-congratulation now arouse only a sad smile. We all grow, you see. There's no going back.

You are beginning your literary life with fine and high ideals—ideals such as once I had, and retain in part even now. Yet you will find their retention, as you grow older, by no means the simple matter that it once seemed to me and may seem to you. It is the tragedy of the man of thought to mistrust and under-estimate the value of his own work, as years widen his horizon and show him the giants who have preceded him to the "palace of art."[1] But youth is mentally antiseptic, and poets usually succeed in staying young till they're old.

By the way, let me recommend for you daily reading of Browning and the Old Testament, to counteract the "overmuch honeycomb" that is the young poet's first portion.

And I trust that you'll permit me to see more of your work, even if it seems to you below the standard of what I've already seen. And will you send me a copy of "The Last Night?"

Trusting I'm not leading your poetic steps astray, I remain

>Very sincerely,

>>George Sterling.

[Enclosure:]

1   I fear that use of that compound is impossible. It sounds most awkward to *me*.[2]

2   "Burnt-out" is rather too commonplace.

3   Capitals usually add a false emphasis. As one grows older one uses them more sparingly. I wish *I* had used fewer in my younger days.[3]

4   That "shine" seems *forced:* better use another word.

5   See 3.

6   "Swarthy" is rather too human and ugly a word to use in that context.

7   Take my advice and *never* use these three words: doth, wondrous and beauteous. They're jokes. That's a good ending to that sonnet. I'd like to see it end
And thro the rift I see Arcturus peer,
Like etc.[4]

8   I think "pinnacles" *implies* "keenly." I'd like to see it read "In snows insuperable" etc.

9   I don't like that "shine." As a noun it always sounds forced—as if you were stuck for a rhyme.

10   Make it "Drenches", and get rid of that "Doth." It is best, anyhow, occasionally to begin a line with a trochee, as you do in the 14th line of this sonnet.

11   Can't say I care for that verb.

12   You have "snows" (plural) so "thou" must be changed to "ye." You make your sonnets end well, which is half the trick.[5]

13   This is a fine sonnet—the best of these you send. That ending is sublime.
         Just a word as to compound words such as "fear-stricken." Bierce warns me against any great use of them, unless thereby unusual strength is attained. I didn't agree with him at first, but (as in most instances) begin to do so as I grow older. It seems to me that "shadow-slain" is an improvement on "darkness-whelmed."[6]

14 15   I'd certainly cut out all those capitals, especially since those below seem worth retaining.

16   This last line seems rather unpoetically expressed. Bierce warns me to avoid lines made up entirely of monosyllables. I begin to agree with him more and more.[7]

1. Alfred, Lord Tennyson, *The Palace of Art* (1833).

2. The poem referred to in comments 1–2 is "The Moonlight Desert." CAS changed the compound "darkness-mystified" to "dark-obscured" (l. 1); "burnt-out" occurs in l. 5.

3. Comments 3–5 refer to "The Pageant of Music."

4. Comment 6 refers to "Nocturne," l. 2; comment 7 refers to ll. 13–14. CAS's ms. (JHL) does not contain the suggested revisions.

5. Comments 8–12 refer to "The Eternal Snows." CAS's ms. (JHL) contains the suggested revisions., save that the verb "hieroglyphed" was not changed.

6. Comment 13 pertains to "The Last Night." CAS adopted the suggested revisions.

7. The poem referred to in comments 14–16 is "The Voice of Silence" (the TMs has a superior title that reads "*The Voice of Silence and Other Poems,*" but no such compilation ever appeared. Line 16 of the poem reads ". . . Ah, would that we the whole might learn!" Cf. AB to GS, 9 October 1910 (ms., NYPL) regarding *Lilith:* "I think it exceedingly good in plot (so far as that is developed) and in manner I have marked with an X a few lines of monosyllables, which ought not to be so. Please go on with it."

[3a] CAS to GS [non-extant]

[Auburn, Cal.
March 1911?]

[Enclosure: "Ode to Music," "The Last Night" (revised).]

[4] GS to CAS [ALS]

Apr. 13, 1911.

My dear Smith:

I've been meaning for weeks to write and tell you how much I like your beautiful music-ode. But I've been away from Carmel since Mch. 1ˢᵗ, mostly up at London's, and so the matter must wait till I can get back to Carmel, which should be by the end of next week.

I'm sending you a copy of my new book, just out.¹ Also I'm taking the perhaps unwarranted liberty of quoting your fine "Last Night" in a "Town-Talk" interview, a copy of which I'll send you on Saturday.² I don't think this will interfere with the salability of the sonnet. Should it do so I'll make the T. T. editor dig up. But you speak of its having been refused eleven times; so I infer that you've given it a rest from its journeying. *I* usually quit about the *fourth* time; but hope dies hard in the young.

I'll write you at much greater length in a couple of weeks, till when may the Lord be with you—but inattentive!³

Sincerely, your friend,
George Sterling.

1. *HO.*

2. "The Last Night" was quoted in full in Edward F. O'Day, "Varied Types: XVII—George Sterling," *Town Talk* No. 972 (15 April 1911): 8. The editor of *Town Talk,* a San Francisco weekly that frequently discussed GS and his circle, was Theodore Bonnet (1865–1920).

3. A closing that AB had used in his correspondence.

[5] GS to CAS [ALS]

Carmel, Cal.,
May 11, 1911.

My dear Smith:

Pray be patient with me! I'll get around to your fine poem soon. It's too good a thing to review hastily, and I've had very few spare hours since my return to Carmel, about ten days ago. In those ten days I've had to write dozens of deferred and urgent letters (my correspondence would stagger a maids' seminary!) and also write a grove-play for the midsummer Jinks of the Family Club.¹ *That's* done, thank Xt., but now, just as I thought I could get around to your poem and poems sent me by other poets, I find I must leave early tomorrow morning to attend a meeting of an enterprise in which I've the good or bad luck (so far it's uncertain) to be a director.

So it's farewell to letters and literature for a few days more. But I know you'll understand!

I had a fine letter from Markham yesterday—he wants me to correspond regularly with him. It's an honor, but a few more epistolary straws and the back of this camel will break.

Your brother-poet,
George Sterling.

1. GS wrote the play *The Vision of Portola* for performance at the Family Farm near Redwood City on 15 July 1911. This is not to be confused with the play *The Triumph of Bohemia*

(1907), or the later *Truth* (1926), which GS wrote for the annual High Jinks of the Bohemian Club.

[5a] CAS to GS [non-extant]

[Auburn, Cal.
c. 15 May 1911]

[6] GS to CAS [ALS]

Carmel, Cal.,
May 19, 1911.

My dear Smith:

You'll excuse, I know, this graphite, when I tell you it enables me to write out in a lovely nook among the sighing Carmel pines, with no one able to butt in on my meditations—which are sublime.

I'd have answered ere now; but since my return to Carmel I've had to write a grove-play for the approaching midsummer Jinks of the Family Club—also write the songs to go with it. So I've been pressed for time. Thank God, it's all off my hands now.

I've prayerfully considered your beautiful "Ode to Music," and want to express my utter amazement that a youth of your years is capable of such a production. It is pure poetry of a high order, and I wish *I'd* written it. To quote all its exquisite lines would be to quote most of the ode, but I especially admire

"Vales mist-implicated"
"Where Beauty is an echo and a dream"
"Eternal winds shall touch him with their wings"
"High melodies, like tears the angels weep"
"Of her moon-coloured robe"
"The moonlight foam round some enchanted isle"
"Flowers whose fragrances are melodies."
"Eve's solitary star."
(which is rather too reminiscent of "Eve's one star.")[1]
"As sunset storms the sight"

There are plenty of other fine lines, but I think those the best.

On separate sheets of paper I've indicated such changes as seem to me of value. Probably I'm not correct in all instances, but you'll make some of them, I know. When you've done so, may I not have a copy (signed) of the ode, to go among other poems that are sent to me occasionally by poet-friends? (By the way, you mustn't enclose stamps any more. That was all right for the first time. But now we're acquainted.)

I've not written any verse (except personal poems to men and women I care for) since January.[2] And it now looks as though I were to be laid on the shelf, poetically, till autumn, as my rich uncle[3] has invited me and my wife to spend several months with him at his summer home on Long Island, where I was born, and which I have not seen for 21 years, when I left it to come to California. I shall have to accept the invitation, though I'd rather remain in quiet Carmel, the more so because I was hoping to have you, and other gifted folk, as my guests here this summer. Well, we'll have to defer the pleasure for a while. I'll even miss my friend Porter Garnett's grove-play at the Bohemian Club's mid-summer Jinks—a thing I'm loth to do, indeed. He'll be furious at me, too.

I'm glad you cared for my new book—and you pick the best things in it. The or-chid-poem is probably the best thing I've ever done so far as art and beauty go. The Job thing is *greater*. "Duandon" is more readable, vital, human, coherent.[4]

Well, let me hear from you again—if possible with poems. Any first-class mail ad-dressed to me at Carmel will be forwarded.

Trusting all's well with you, I remain, as ever,
                    Yours very cordially,
                    George Sterling.

[Enclosure:]

1   I think I've never seen the word "unfound" used before. I'd not cut it out for that reason, however.
2   You'd better use "Seeking" in place of "Following." The latter breaks the rhythm too much.
3   I'd *certainly* say "unsure."
4   "That" is better than "the," on account of the vowel blending—"th*e* *a*ngels." Be-sides, "th*e*" and "w*ee*p" are synchronous.
5   Better "Then shall he."
6   Better, "The veils and outer barriers," which eliminates "Th*e* *ou*ter"—more vowels weakening each other.
7   I don't like that "And *even* catch." Get something like "And catch afar."
8   Harmony suppose[s] two or more sounds blending, which can't apply to a single voice. I'd say "her voice's *mystery*." For the "mystery" in the line a little preceding, you can say "splendor," so some equivalent word.
9   I'd use "startled" in place of "wakened," which is a trifle trite. You use "trees" just below: why not substitute another noun in this line?
10 I don't like "begemmed"—it's too young-ladyish. Why not use "enchased" or some other word?
11 How Keats has infected us later singers with his "magic casement" lines![5] But don't change this one: we're all dipped in the same iris, and your line is a beautiful one indeed.
12 I care for neither "silver" nor "radiant," both being commonplace. Why not "cav-erned", "quiet", "sinking" or some such adjective?
13 This line is somewhat overcharged with the consonant S—you might use "heart" for "soul."
14 You have "harmonies" just above. I suggest "As forms unlike (or diverse) ex-pressed in melody." It gives the idea of blending and reconciliation.
15 "Pomp" is not an especially admirable word. I'd much prefer the simpler and love-lier word "light."

1. From Keats, *Hyperion* (1820), 1.3.
2. "To Vernon L. Kellogg," "Charles Warren Stoddard," "To Ambrose Bierce," "To Hall B. Rand," all in *HO,* are examples of GS's "personal" poems.

3. Frank Colton Havens (1848–1917), real estate developer in Alameda and Contra Costa counties, CA, and also a member (1881–83) of Havens & Company, stockbrokers, San Francisco. GS dedicated *WW* to him.

4. GS refers to "The House of Orchids," "The Forty-third Chapter of Job," and "Duandon" in *HO*. The book of Job has, of course, only forty-two chapters.

5. Keats, "Ode to a Nightingale" (1819), ll. 68–70: "The same that oft-times hath / Charm'd magic casement opening on the foam / Of perilous seas, in faery lands forlorn."

[7] CAS to GS [ALS]

Auburn, California
May 21st, 1911.

Dear Mr. Sterling:

I've received your letter of the 19th, returning my "Ode to Music." You've certainly added something to the debt I owe you for praise and helpful criticism. I don't think the poem *will* ever receive a higher compliment than the one you pay it in saying you wish that you'd written it yourself. That is a whole lot more than the "Ode", or anything I've written or am liable to write, deserves.

I've adopted most of your suggestions as to changes, with a few more alterations that occur[r]ed to me. I am glad to enclose the copy that you asked for. That was another compliment, and I only wish the thing were more worthy.

Some of your suggestions have more than doubled the value of the lines in question, particularly the line: "Her forms divine expressed in melody", in which you suggested the substitution of *diverse* for *divine*, thus introducing the idea of reconciliation. And there are others, which wouldn't have occur[r]ed to me in a hundred years, and for which I can't thank you enough.

I think I write too hastily, and don't work hard enough over my things. I seem to have a "deadly facility["] for turning out verse,—of a kind.

I've been trying my hand at some cosmic verse lately, and a month's work, and a lot of spoiled paper have led me to the conclusion that your "Testimony of the Suns" is about the last word in that line, and that the subject is too big for me to handle, anyway. I'd better stick to butterflies and roses, etc. (I don't mean that these subjects are less worthy) instead of trying to wipe out half the constellations (on paper) and put the rest askew. This is about what I've done in four poems, varying in length from 112 to 56 lines.[1]

One of the things—an "Ode to the Abyss", has about all the sparks of originality in the collection. That's a deep subject, isn't it? (Forgive the rotten pun.) I'll send it to you, afterwhile, when I've pruned it a bit more, and sweated out as much of its crudity as I can.

I'm sorry to hear that you won't be able to write any more poems before Autumn. If it weren't for you, American poetry would hardly have the wherewithal to clothe its nakedness. Of course, there is Markham, but he doesn't seem to have done anything lately. At least, I haven't seen it. I hope his silence means that a long poem will be forthcoming.

I've written a few short nature lyrics during the last few days, treating simple subjects in the simplest manner that I can. They should be about the most saleable work that I have done. The "Ode to the Abyss", setting aside its length, is rather too tart for the magazines. It might "gall the kibes"[2] of the blatant optimists among their readers.

I think I'll quote you one of the lyrics. It is quite short, and rather better than some of the others, and it will serve to show the drift of my present work. Here it is:

The Messengers
Catching a little wind's unrest,
        The dandelion-crests dissolve,
        Where swooping wings of air involve
And lift them to a scattered quest.

Snared in the tangled zephyr-coil,
        They try the day to hidden ends—
        The messengers that Beauty sends
With words of waking to the soil.

That should be simple enough for the average reader, unless the A. R. disdains to apply his intellect to the understanding of poetry at all.

I hope you'll enjoy that eastern vacation. I hardly think that I could have come down to Carmel this summer, on account of my father's ill-health. It may be different next year, when I fervently hope to accept your kind invitation.

It's about time to put an end to this dissertation, and it might as well stop one place as another.

Yours, most sincerely,
Clark Ashton Smith

[Enclosure: "Ode to Music" (revised).]

1. CAS may be referring to "Ode to the Abyss" (75 lines; *ST*), "Ode to Matter" (56 lines), and other early odes.
2. Shakespeare, *Hamlet* 5.1.150. A *kibe* is an ulcerated chilblain.

[7a] CAS to GS [non-extant]

[Auburn, Cal.
May or June 1911]

[Enclosure: "Ode to the Abyss."]

[8] GS to CAS [ALS]

Sag Harbor, N.Y.,
July 13, 1911.

My dear Poet:
        What little energy has been mine during the past three weeks has gone entirely towards setting my unalterable curse on this devastating heat. I've had 21 years of cool, bracing weather, and this height of temperature is a matter of misery for me, coming on the heels of the years.

Both your letters have been forwarded to me from Carmel. How I long for that blue bay over the shoulder of the world! I'm on a blue one here, and go about on it in my uncle's large and expansive power-boats, but I can't write a line in this climate of Hell, and I miss all my friends—male and female created He them.[1]

"The Messengers" is a charming lyric. I especially love your exceedingly felicitous use of the verb "dissolve." But what roc's egg have you sent me with this lark? I don't believe you're 18 years old! You're 35, and have been stuffing yourself for eight years on Hyperion, Prometheus Unbound, Paradise Lost and (I say it as shouldn't) The Testimony of the Suns.[2] Your splendid "Ode to the Abyss" is fitted to rank, so far as quality goes, with the first three, and is better than the last. And I'm not inferring you're not original. Your work is slightly influenced by, but entirely independent of, all those four poems.

Well, perhaps you *are* eighteen. Genius *happens,* as Whistler wrote.[3] And he added that no hovel is safe from it and that no prince can command it. (That "safe" sounds rather cynical, don't you think?) One's age and one's opportunities for knowledge haven't a great deal to do with it. I must, am forced to, against my own sense of literary caution, consider that this amazing ode of yours is the most remarkable example of youthful (which isn't in the way of decrial) genius in the history of literature. Pope and Keats are nowhere in comparison. For the Lord's sake re-assure me as to your age, lest I make an ass of myself before Bierce![4]

And this ode is not merely very great as regards precocity, but as regards actual substance. Any poet, of any age, of any period, might well be proud of it. *I* am pretty particular about my contour, but I'd cheerfully give a finger-joint to have written it. I can find nothing to suggest in the way of improvement, though I not[e] that *you* have altered it only with happy effect. I would, however, substitute "forsaken" for "discarded."[5] That's a more poetical and stronger word, by odds. "Discarded" smacks a bit of poker.

I've been going over this ode for a month, wondering whether I could trust my wits, and waiting for a cool day to come, that I might be a little surer. It's here now, and I find my enthusiasm over your poem even more warm. It is a noble, majestic and thoughtful thing, and you must permit me to bring it to the attention of some magazine editor in New York—I'm likely to make a trip there next week. Whatever its value, it would be refused on account of its length, if you sent it by mail. When a *long* poem gets into a periodical, it's by virtue of personal interviews, influence, or fame of its author. I'm going to get this ode into print, with your permission, or leave a few contused (mentally) pates in my wake.[6]

Oh! it is great, *great!* And what a pleasure it is to be able to praise sincerely and unstintedly!

Write me as soon as you can. I'll be here till October, I fear. Next Nov. or Dec. you must come to Carmel.

> I am, dear Poet,
> Your sincere admirer,
> George Sterling

1. Gen. 1.27: "So God created man in his own image, in the image of God created he him; male and female created he them."

2. I.e., John Keats, *Hyperion;* Percy Bysshe Shelley, *Prometheus Unbound;* John Milton, *Paradise Lost;* GS, *The Testimony of the Suns.*

3. The actual quotation is: "Art happens—no hovel is safe from it, no prince can depend on it, the vastest intelligence cannot bring it about." In "Ten O'Clock" (1885), a lecture by American expatriate painter James McNeill Whistler (1834–1903).

4. AB spent at least a week with GS at Sag Harbor in mid-August 1911.

5. "Ode to the Abyss," l. 45.

6. The poem was widely quoted the first week of August 1912 (see below) but never appeared entire in print before *ST* was published. Of the poem AB wrote to GS (8 August 1911): "Kindly convey to young Smith of Auburn my felicitations on his admirable 'Ode to the Abyss'—a large theme, treated with dignity and power. It has many striking passages—such, for example, as 'The Romes of ruined spheres.' I'm conscious of my sin against the rhetoricians in liking that, for it jolts the reader out of the Abyss and back to earth. Moreover, it is a metaphor which belittles instead of dignifying. But I like it." Cited in *MMM* 225–26.

[8a] CAS to GS [non-extant]

[Auburn, Cal.
19 July 1911]

[Envelope postmarked Auburn, Cal., 19 July 1911.]

[8b] CAS to GS [non-extant]

[Auburn, Cal.
1 September 1911]

[Envelope postmarked East Auburn, Cal., 1 September 1911; forwarded to Sag Harbor, N.Y., 2 September 1911.]

[9] CAS to GS [ALS]

Auburn, Calif.
Sept. 5th, 1911

Dear Mr. Sterling:

Did you receive my letter, dated the 19th of July? Having heard nothing from you since, it has occur[r]ed to me that perhaps it went astray. The post office here is notoriously careless, and it won't be the first time I have had a letter go wrong. Of course there may be other reasons for your not having written before, but at any rate I'll repeat the substance of my former letter.

Your praise of my "Ode to the Abyss" is far higher than I had expected or dared hope for. Nor can I concede, after more consideration, that the poem deserves it. It does not seem possible to me that I can have written anything having the merit that you assign to this Ode. What has been written since Tennyson's death, barring your own work, and possibly some of Edwin Markham's, that deserves the praise that you give it?

But I can't express how glad I am that you like the poem, and think it so worthy. Even if you have greatly overpraised it, as I think, there must be some foundation for your judgement and this gives me much more confidence in myself than I have had for a long time—since my first-submitted manuscript came back with a blue rejection-slip.

To return to your criticism of the poem, I particularly cannot see wherein it exceeds your "Testimony of the Suns" in quality. It does not seem to *me* to at all approach your work except, possibly, in a few scattered lines and images.

It's altogether too good of you to offer to place the Ode, but if you wish to try it on some editor, I shall surely have no objection. But I hope you won't waste overmuch energy in trying to convince New-York magazine editors of the merit of my work. I don't know how I can repay you for the kindness, but if gratitude is of any worth to you, rest assured that I am not lacking in that coin, at least.

I'll send you a photograph of myself in a week or two, to resolve your doubts as to my age. I should have ordered one long before, had not the only photographer in this sink-hole of desolation been away.

Have you written anything lately? I'll be most glad to know what you are doing or planning to do. American poetry, as far as I can see, would be almost a lost cause were it not for your work. However, I see little contemporary poetry save what is published or quoted in some of the magazines. I was much struck by some extracts from Anna Hempstead Branch's work in the "Literary Digest,"[1] but otherwise I have seen nothing of late to arouse my interest. The principal trouble with the average poets nowadays, it seems to me, is lack of imagination, or, if they do have it, a fear of giving that faculty free range, lest they write something that would throw their intricate and minutely woven pattern a little out of proportion. Surely it is better to strike at a big idea and miss it, than not to strike at all.

Have I ever thanked you for advising me to read the Bible? If I haven't, let me do so now. All the books that I have read so far, amply repaid the reading, and the Book of Job, in particular, was like a "new planet" to me.[2]

Yours, with the most sincere gratitude,
Clark Ashton Smith

1. Two poems by American poet Anna Hampstead Branch (1875–1937), "The Wedding Feast" and "Ere the Golden Bowl Is Broken," were quoted in the "Current Poetry" column of *Literary Digest* 42, No. 21 (27 May 1911): 1060, 1062.

2. Keats, "On First Looking Into Chapman's Homer" (1816), ll. 9–10: "Then felt I like some watcher of the skies / When a new planet swims into his ken."

[9a] CAS to GS [non-extant]

[Auburn, Cal.,
mid-September 1911]

[Enclosure: photograph of CAS.]

[10] GS to CAS [ANS][1]

[Postmarked Carmel, Cal.,
3 October 1911]

Dear Smith: Am home at last, and will write soon. Thanks for the remarkable photograph. You *look* as though you could write so greatly.

I'll be a better correspondent from now on. In the East I found it almost impossible to find energy or time for letters. As ever, George S

1. *Front:* Main Street, Easthampton, L.I.

[11] GS to CAS [ALS]

Carmel, Cal.,
Oct. 5th, 1911.

My dear Poet:

I hope you'll not fancy me indifferent either to your talent—hear me! I mean *genius!*—nor your friendship, when you recall how long it is since I've written to you. The truth is that the eastern climate fairly *wilted* me, and though I could have found time for certain letters, I found no energy, no will for them. Now, back in Carmel the Blest, I'm quite otherwise: I feel like a mountain-lion, and have tackled a foot-high pile of neglected correspondence with fire in my eye. And your letter comes first.

I dropped you a postal thanking you for the photograph. I'll send you one of me some day. At present I want to thank you for this one, and say that I think it *shows* you are a poet—a sort of philosopher-poet. And it is otherwise quite charming, making our hearts go out to you instinctively. It's a pity you'll ever have to change!

I've just re-read your "Ode to the Abyss" for about the fiftieth time, and admire it more than ever. While in the East I gave a copy of it to Miss Cutting, the assistant-editor of the North American Review,[1] and should have heard from her by now. She hasn't written to you, has she? When you let me know, I'll "take further steps."

I read the Ode at Markham's, to sincere applause. I was there two Sundays. One Sunday he had about forty folk there to meet me, and it was then that I read the poem. *He* liked it, though the theme was a little beyond his mind.

Did I tell you that I thought you could further improve that line "The forms diverse expressed in melody" by changing the last word to "harmony?"[2] Harmony implies, of course, a blending of diverse sounds.

And did I say that I was delighted with your use of "dissolve" in that little lyric? I think I've said so.

I want to see your other "star poems," and trust you'll send them along soon.

I saw Anna Branch at Markham's. She's a weird-looking creature—a sort of sibyl; but she can write! Parts of her "Nimrod"[3] are better than most of "Paradise Lost."

I hope you'll be able to get down here some time between now and Christmas. Remember that the only expense you'll be put to is the fare. You may have to share my cabin with another young poet, though, if he keeps his promise of coming here from the East this autumn.

I didn't write a line while in the East (except a lot of love-sonnets, which don't count),[4] and so far do not feel like doing so. But this tonic weather will soon set me to sprouting pin-feathers, at least. We stopped over at the Grand Canyon, a terrific spot to which even an ode would be patronizing, and I wrote a *sonnet* to it![5] But I've enough decency to keep it to myself.

Well, let me hear from you soon. I've too much to say to you to put it into ink.

Faithfully,   George Sterling.

1. Elisabeth Brown Cutting (1871–1946), editor at the *North American Review*, 1916–25.

2. "Ode to Music," l. 65. CAS did not make the change suggested by GS.

3. In *Rose of the Wind, Nimrod, and Other Poems* (1910).

4. These were at least sonnets I–X of what was later published as *Sonnets to Craig* (1928), 102 poems (only two were not sonnets) ostensibly written to Mary Craig Kimbrough (later wife of Upton Sinclair), whom he met while in New York. GS wrote many more poems to Kimbrough en route to Carmel.

5. "At the Grand Canyon" (see letters 28 and 28). This, too, was sent to Mary Kimbrough.

[12] CAS to GS [ALS]

Auburn, Calif.
Oct. 6th, 1911

Dear Mr. Sterling:

Your card and letter at hand. I am glad you like the photograph, but really, it isn't a very good one. To me the eye of a camera always looks like the mysterious, murderous muzzle of a thirteen-inch gun, and *I* am apt to look like the enemy.

I have heard nothing from the North American Review. It quite knocked me over to hear that you had sent my "Ode to the Abyss" to such a big magazine. If it's accepted, I'll probably lose what little reason I have left.

How I wish I were down in Carmel with you! I am not at all certain whether I can get away this winter or not. If I do come, it probably won't be before December. I am so tied down that the way is not at all obvious now. I'd rather be able to accept your invitation than have the "Abyss Ode" accepted—even by the "high and mighty" North American Review! Auburn is nothing but a cage, and with little gilding on the bars at that.

I am enclosing some more poems, which you must consider at your leisure. Don't worry about my feeling "neglected" if they are not returned for a month or two. I really do not know what you'll think about the "Star-Treader."[1] It was written in a mood of midsummer fantasy, and altogether to suit myself. It is frightfully irregular, both in thought and form, and probably a little obscure. I have begun to doubt the propriety of such a lack of regular form in a narrative or semi-narrative poem, but this was the way it presented itself to me, and I have not the courage to try working it over.

The "Song From Hell" is a subject that it would take Browning to do rightly. I do not remember to have seen anything of the kind before. I think you will admit, after reading these two poems, that I do not lack courage in attacking difficult subjects!

I have several others as good, or for aught I know, better than the poems enclosed, but I lack the nerve to load any more upon you.

Here are a couple of lyrics which I am sure you will like. They are too slight to enclose separately:

Wind-Ripples
Did Beauty's unseen spirit pass
    With tread unstayable and fleet?
Surely I saw the crested grass
    Bow 'neath supernal feet!

A Live-Oak Leaf
How marvelous this bit of green
    I hold and soon shall throw away!
Its subtile veins, its vivid sheen,
    Seem fragment of a god's array.
In all the hidden toil of Earth,
    Which is the more laborious part—
To rear the oak's enormous girth,
    Or shape its leaves with poignant art?

I am glad that Mr. Markham liked the "Abyss" thing. The poem must be fearfully esoteric if *he* did not quite grasp the theme. It seems quite plain enough to me, but I have had others (people who read and understand most poetry) own up to being puzzled by it. I am astonished to find how few really grasp the sublimity and vastness of the stars and star-spaces. One acquaintance did not think such things suitable for poetic treatment, and from the indifference or bewilderment with which most who have seen it regard my cosmic work, I must regard those fitted to understand such things as being very rare.

Your younger-brother-poet,
Clark Ashton Smith.

[Enclosures: "A Song from Hell," "The Star-Treader."]

1. "The Star-Treader" is the title poem of CAS's first book. Cf. Robert Browning's epitaph on Shelley in *Pauline* (1833): "Sun-treader, light and life be thine for ever" (l. 151). CAS had first titled the poem "The Sun-Treader."

[13] CAS to GS [ALS]

Auburn, Calif.
Dec. 12th, 1911

My dear Mr. Sterling:

This isn't to remind you that you haven't reported yet on the poems that I sent you in October, for I am sure you have some good and sufficient reason for that. But I write to enclose a sonnet which I want you to accept as a tribute to your poetical genius. I only wish it were better, but whatever defects it may have, I wish you to believe that it is sincere. It's about my first attempt at a personal poem.

I presume that my "Ode to the Abyss" is still on the road (unless you've grown weary of having it rejected.) Do you think that you had better try continuing to place it? The poem does not seem salable to me, and besides, you've taken enough trouble on my account, anyway, for which I hardly know how to thank you. Of course, you're to keep the copy that you have.

I was in San Francisco for a couple of days in Nov. as the guest of an Auburn friend, and while there met your publisher, Mr. Robertson, who invited me to submit some of my work. I understand that if he undertook to publish it that he would assume all the losses,—and take all the profits, should there be any. What do you think of the plan? I have submitted nothing yet.

It does not seem possible that I can come to Carmel this Winter; though if wishing could get me there, I'd have been down long ago. But I'll get down next Summer, (providing your invitation holds) if I have to ride on a box car.

Believe me, yours most sincerely,

Clark Ashton Smith

[Enclosure: "To George Sterling."]

1. CAS wrote several poems on GS; the one referred to here begins: "What questioners have met the gaze of Time." See Appendix.

[14] GS to CAS [ALS]

Carmel, Cal.,
Dec. 16, 1911.

Dear Clark:

You must think I'm a barbarian! I am, in spots. Have been away from Carmel since Oct., and did not feel like letter-writing.

Well, I'll write you at length in a day or two.

Most sincerely,

George Sterling.

[15] GS to CAS [ALS]

Carmel, Cal.,
Dec. 21st, 1911.

My dear Poet:

I know I'm a slug and a sloth—don't remind me! But the more seriously I take a person, the harder it is for me to write him a letter, for I always get "that inadequate feeling."

But I would have written to you over a month ago, had not I been up at London's: I spent most of November at his thousand-acre ranch in Glen Ellen. And I don't write letters while I'm visiting. Result, a pile of them, slowly decreasing, before me now. And Sara Teasdale, Gen. Foote, Yone Noguchi, Samuel Loveman,[1] a convict-poet (I forget his name) and one or two others have sent me volumes of their poems, and I had to read them discreetly and make some intelligent comment on them—God help me!

But Loveman is all right. He is only twenty-three (not as good a poet as you, however), and expects to leave his home in Cleveland this month and come to Carmel. I'll be able to have decent company yet!

About the poems you send: you might almost put my silence down to envy! I wish to hell I'd written the "Star-Treader!" It's a magnificent thing wonderfully put, and (to me at least) not at all obscure, though it will be far over the heads of the many. I hardly know how to express myself about it, as I like one part about as well as another. But I *can* say that it's *great poetry*, and that you are unquestionably the most phenomenal example of precocious genius in the history of literature—and I'm not forgetting Rossetti and Bryant.[2] God knows how far you are to go: it makes me worry to think about it, for I'd say at a guess that you'll probably die in a couple of years. Well, you must come to Carmel and let me give you physical-culture lessons.

But the poem is wonderful, wonderful! The "Song from Hell" is powerful and well-handled, but (to me personally) distasteful, by reason of its subject-matter being inherently and fundamentally untrue: "hell is the only thing that can't be," as I once said to a priest-friend. For the same reason "Paradise Lost" always has for me a taint on its sublimity. I may seem captious and hypercritical to you; but the world is going to pay more and more attention to that point, as it grows in intelligence and sensitiveness.

I'm sorry you can't get down here this winter, as Carmel is lots warmer than Auburn. But I'll see if I can't get you down here in May, our finest month. Would it interfere with your studies?

About the "Ode to the Abyss:" I've written to the woman to whom I "submitted" it. She was the sub-editor, and away on her vacation. She has not replied yet, and, as she is rich, may be in Europe (she mentioned some such plan). But I hope to hear from her in a week or two more. It was only to the "N. A. Review" that I gave the ode, and I've been attributing their silence to hesitation, usually a good sign in that least of God's mercies, the editor. But maybe she merely mislaid and forgot the poem: it would be the natural thing to happen to anything so great!

About Robertson: I am surprised that he offered to publish your poems—not because they're not very much worthy of publication, but because he told me he was going to bring out no more poetry for several years, having been "stung" on several of his ventures. I advise you by all means to accept his proposition: if you wish I'll talk it over with him. You cannot expect to make money out of a first book of poems, and a publisher is always lucky to get his money back from a volume by an unknown author. *I* have never had any money from Robertson, nor even a statement of how we stand. He's welcome to what he can make out of my work for the coming few years, if only he keeps it in print, so I can get copies to give away.

But you must first allow me to go over any manuscripts you think of letting him print, as I think I can be of use to you in that way. Bierce has done the same thing for me, to my no small advantage.

I don't know how to thank you for the fine sonnet—Heaven knows I wish I were worthy of it! It is good all through, tho' improving as it goes on, as a sonnet should. But Fame! I'm beginning to have my doubts of it! As Bierce once wrote me: "There's no longer any room, even at the top. One may gain foothold there only by crowding some one else off!"[3] The bars are down, the herd is in the song-pastures, and all the old values and criteria are changing and becoming meaningless. What folks seem to be clamoring for to-day is poetry about machinery, sky-scrapers, etc.,—good enough material if they *would* make poetry of it. But they *don't!* It's all muck to *me*. Material things seem to need "Time's purple" to become adequate matter for poetry.

The "lyrics in little" that you send are exquisite: I advise you to do more of such work, even though it's just about what the magazines want. And do send me the other poems that you speak of! They can't come too fast for *me!*

It's heavenly to be back in Carmel, after the city and the dentist thereof! I've written nothing yet but a "Christmas poem" for the Bohemian Club (by request), which they probably will not use, as it's pretty strong meat for those amiable hedonists. However, as I'm on the water-wagon, I hope to be able to "turn loose" before long. I go gunning about every afternoon, and get so many birds that I have to give them away. Abalones also interest me: it's hard on the local butcher. But even poets have to eat occasionally. And as for their wives!

Well, I trust you'll return good for ill and let me hear from you soon. I hope too you'll pass a pleasant holiday season. A gang is to motor down from the city to make *me* liven up!

Faithfully you friend,   George Sterling.

1. Sara Teasdale (1884–1933), American poet. Lucius H. Foote (1826–1913), American diplomat (US consul to Chile) and poet. GS later wrote an essay on him, "The Poems of General Lucius H. Foote: A Brief Appreciation," *Town Talk* No. 1086 (14 June 1913): 7. Yone Noguchi (1875–1947), Japanese poet who wrote both in Japanese and in English. He spent much time in California, becoming friends with Joaquin Miller and other local poets. Samuel Loveman (1887–1976), American poet whose *Poems* had been published in 1911.

2. Cf. GS, "Preface," *S*: "At that [CAS's] age Pope had a certain hard cleverness (little more), and Rossetti had written, though not perfected, the beautiful 'Blessed Damozel.'" William Cullen Bryant (1794–1878) wrote the first draft of "Thanatopsis" at the age of seventeen.

3. Cf. AB to GS (21 October 1903; ms., Univ. of Pennsylvania): "Poetry is a ladder on which there is now no room at the top—unless you and Scheff [Herman Scheffauer] throw down some of the chaps occupying the upper rung. It looks as if you might, but I could not."

[15a] CAS to GS [non-extant]

[Auburn, Cal.
January or February 1912]
[Enclosure: "The Song of a Comet" and unidentified sonnets.]

[16] GS to CAS [ANS][1]

[Postmarked Carmel, Cal.
9 February 1912]
Dear Poet: I'm back here at last—had to go to Oakland last month to attend the funeral of a brother-in-law.[2] Am going to get at your poems to-day, and will write very soon. Saw A. M. Robertson about them, too, and think it will be all right. Don't bother to write till you hear from me again.

Sincerely,   Sterling.

1. *Front:* Cypress at Point Lobos, Carmel, California.

2. GS had six sisters. It is not known who is referred to here.

[17] GS to CAS [ALS]

Carmel, Cal.,
Feb. 11th, 1912.

My dear Poet:

At last I've had leisure and impulse enough to give to your poems some appreciable fraction of the time and consideration necessary, and herewith return them, defaced by a few inadequate words of praise and such suggestions as seemed pertinent to me.

The "Comet" ode is a big thing, and of the same rank as your great odes "To the Abyss" and "The Star-Treader." All the sonnets are good, too. But I've indicated my preferences below them. Some day when we're together I want to take your poems one by one, and tell you how much I like them, and why. It is hard to do so with the pen, as it takes so long.

I enclose a letter from the N. A. Review lady, and if you'll return it to me with a new copy of "To the Abyss," I'll see she has to go on record about the thing. You'd better send me a copy of "The Star-Treader" too, as she'll be more likely to care for and accept that. I have, however, no very high estimate of her taste—there seems to be a taint on all editors. Perhaps that's why they're editors.

While in San Francisco, I had several conversations with A. M. Robertson about bringing out a volume of your poems, and it seems to me he is far from averse to the proposition. But he wants *more* than you sent him, and I think that he is correct in so wishing. Will you not send me revised copies of everything that you care to have go in the book (omitting, if you wish, those lyrics of which you write), and send them to me? There was at least one poem in the collection Robertson had that seemed to me quite outclassed by its companion poems. If I can get all these poems together, I'll then better be able to "talk business" with Robertson, who is a miracle in the line of unthrift and procrastination.

To refer to some of the things in your letter: I'm glad you are not the pale ascetic that your picture somehow seemed to proclaim you. I suppose it's that tremendous forehead of yours that makes one think you're all brain and no muscle. But if you're addicted to that severest of exercises, sawing wood, you must be all right. "Let the good work go on," but don't overtrain.

As to comparing "The Star-Treader" with "The Blessèd Damozel" and "Thanatopsis," I didn't intend to do so to the discredit of those two last poems. Your ode does not outrank nor even equal them in charm and poetical quality (especially "The Blessèd Damosel"), but it is a *greater* poem, I think, because far sublimer, and pregnant with thought of a vastly higher order, which postulates a higher precocious mentality. I am aware that I'd find but few to agree with me, for a taste for and comprehension of the cosmic is a rare gift. But I'm standing by my guns.

Yes, "The Star-Treader" would be an excellent title to the book. I see no improvement.

As to my writing more "cosmic poems," I have to say that I fear anything of any length I might write would be too much of an anticlimax to "The Testimony of the Suns." I put into that about all I had to say of the stars,[1] and now refer to them only *en passant,* as any poet might do, and until I wrote "The Testimony," *did* do. No—I've "blazed the way," and now you other star-treaders may parcel out the kingdom among yourselves. *You* are doing it so thoroughly that I fancy your successors will find "small pickings." We'll be a duumvirate.

That's a great title, the "Epitaph to the Earth!" See that you use it!

It will be good to have you here in May—if *I* am here. My future movements are mightily uncertain. My wife refuses to remain in the comparative stagnation of Carmel, and has gone to Oakland to live at the Key Route Inn (a hotel owned by my millionaire uncle) with her recently-widowed sister. I don't know yet whether she means to leave me for good: if she does, I'll probably hike out to see some more of the world.

I can't exactly blame *her* for not caring to live in this scandal-bed. But I can't afford to live in a city, nor, for that matter, am I able to write in one any more, it would seem. They gossip frightfully about me here, as Auburn "old-cats" did about Bierce (I've seen the satire),[2] and for the same reason. All country-towns are alike in that respect, nor can women justly be censured for gossiping. It's usually their highest (almost their only) form of pleasure. They're welcome to my bones; and I know they'll leave them nice and white.

Our weather here is heavenly. I still go hunting, to the horrible joy of my cat. Last night I got three rabbits. He likes the heads and innards. Have you ever been much near the sea? I mean where it's clear—not adjacent to San Francisco. You'd love it.

But talofa!

As ever,

George Sterling.

1. But cf. "Pleasure and Pain," written Feb.–Mar. 1923, a pessimistic essay on humanity and the cosmos, influenced by Schopenhauer and AB. It remained unpublished in GS's lifetime; see letter 305.

2. GS refers to AB's acerbic poem about Auburn, "The Perverted Village" (*Wasp*, 5 July 1884). AB lived in Auburn for much of 1884–85.

[17a] CAS to GS [non-extant]

[Auburn, Cal.
c. February or March 1912]

[18] GS to CAS [ALS]

Carmel, Cal.,
Mch. 10, 1912.

Dear Poet:

Don't give me up entirely—I'm spreading your enormously-deserved fame north and south, at the awful expense of my own!

I've been in the city for a week, and have to return to-morrow. It's all right about Robertson—he's to give me your proofs soon (next week) and then we'll launch you a career of disillusion and mis-spelt words. But to-day I'm answering letters from all the Lords of Thought and crowned heads of Petaluma, and insist on saving you up. So please comprehend and forgive!

Faithfully,   George S.

[19] GS to CAS [ALS]

Carmel, Cal.,
Mch. 22, 1912.

My dear Poet:

As usual, I've been a scan'lous time getting around to an answer to your last letter. But I've had to spend most of the past thirty days in Oakland and San Francisco, where correspondence comes too hard to me to be more than feebly spasmodic. Now I'm "home" again, and can turn to cleaner heavens.

Robertson gave me all the MSS you turned over to him, as he wants me to pass on it. I'm going to get at it right away—and you know in advance what I'll tell him about it. I would have done so a few days ago, but have had to go over a bushel of London's proofs—a job that falls to me when he's out of the country. And even these proofs I've neglected for over a month!!¹

I'm returning the last batch of poems you sent (thanks for the new copies of the great Odes!), though I've no especial changes to suggest. I like them, but some of your other work so overshadows them that I'm only mildly enthusiastic about them—you know yourself how *that* is.

I think we'd better *not* send anything to the N. A. Review, as they're unlikely to accept anything (it's over their heads), and if they did it certainly *would* interfere with getting out the book.

I wasn't in the least offended by your sending the MSS to Robertson—how could I be? Besides, a correspondent so dilatory as I has no rights anyhow!

I'm alone down here, as Mrs. S. refuses to live in Carmel, and I can't afford to live anywhere else. Her rich sister is taking care of *her*. I hope you'll be able to get here in the summer, but not from July 25th to Aug. 10th, as I'll be up at the Bohemian Grove *then*.

My sterile mood still prevails, and I've written very little for over a year. Did I send you copies of three sonnets I wrote in January? "Kindred," "The Muse of the Incommunicable" and "The Coming Singer"? The last was suggested by *you*. By the way, the Muse doesn't love you for "forgetting the existence" of so wonderful a sonnet as "Wharf of Dreams." Neither do I.

I must go hunting now, if only for my cat's sake. Pray let me hear from you soon!

As ever, faithfully,   George Sterling.

[P.S.] Will forward those poems to-morrow—no large envelope.

1. These were for the story collection *Smoke Bellew* (1912).

[20] CAS to GS [ALS]

Auburn, Calif
March 24th, 1912

My dear Friend:

I've just received your letter, at the end of a day of tussling with inveterate boulders, and an even more stubborn ploughman, who has a prejudice against doing anything except in his own way. He likes to plough straight lines, and insisted on taking in a nest of half-ton cromlechs in one corner of the field. So they had to be removed from his lordly path. I'll have to write an "Ode to a Boulder" to get even. . . . Really, though, it should be a good subject, when you think of the cosmic evolution that every stone of the earth must have passed through. The big black brute that persisted in rolling back into the hole every time I got a good leverage upon it, may at one time have formed part of the inmost core of some forgotten sun.

I am rather at a loss to understand the previous note you wrote to me. You said in that (at least so I understood) that Robertson was to give you the proofs on my book in a week or so. But from your last letter it seems that it was only the poems in Mss.

I did not receive copies of the sonnets you speak of; but I hope you'll send them to me soon, if it's convenient. "The Muse of the Incommunicable" sounds particularly good. That's the kind I have to wrestle with most of the time . . . I talk your poetry to every one I can get to listen to me, and am glad to say that I have made three converts, which is pretty good for Auburn. You'd appreciate my efforts if you knew the place. It's peopled with particularly impenetrable (and impenitent) Philistines, whose Goliaths are Bierce's "champions of offended dulness."[1] I'm to tackle a bunch of them, who form a debating-club, with a paper on "The Philosophy of Literary Criticism."[2] It will be rather a hot tamale for them, I expect, and then should be some good fun. This paper is about all that I have had time to write lately. I have any number of ideas for poems, but neither time nor strength to work them out.

I am extremely sorry to hear that you have written so little of late. Aren't you going to have a try at Mitchell Kennerly's "Lyric Year" Competition?[3] That $1000 sounds pretty good, particularly to me, who am as poor as a Scotch mouse. But of course I can't get even a smell at it. Was there ever a contest in which the prize was rightfully awarded? I am especially suspicious of this one. William Stanley Braithwaite, who is announced as one of the judges, writes critical eulogies on Richard G. Badger's publications, and a man who will do that is capable of anything. I suppose a review by Braithwaite, in "Poet Lore", is part of the contract Badger gives to his victims.[4] I can always tell when one of my poems has appeared in the magazines, by the resultant letter from Badger, asking me to submit some of my work.

It's a devilish age for poets, this, with the sharks of publishers on one hand, the lions of critics on the other, and such part of the public as is not away at the nearest baseball park, sitting around trying to look Romanesque while they watch the battle. Don't think that I'm beginning to squeal, though. I'm going through with it now, and have no present intention of taking Nora May French's method of escape.[5] By the way, can you tell me who publishes her poems, and also the title and price of the volume? I intend to add it to my little collection of present-day poetry as soon as I can. Besides your books, I already have Alfred Noye's [sic] "Drake" and a volume of Bliss Carman.[6] By the way, what do you think of "Drake?" It seems to me to be a great poem. Second to you and Markham. Noyes appears to me to be the foremost living poet who writes in English. Stephen Phillips hardly ranks with him.[7]

I'm enclosing a "Dedication" which you might add to my poems if you think it good enough. That sort of thing is particularly hard to write: even Tennyson fell down on it. Mine has a certain merit—its briefness.

I won't quarrel with you about the "Wharf of Dreams." To keep the peace, I'll admit that it is a great poem; and I know it by heart now. But I have read so much poetry in the last three years that I have to forget some of it, at least temporarily—or bust. If "The Harbor of Dead Years"[8] is in the collection you have, I give you full permission to throw it out.

Please forgive this slipshod, fag-end letter; and send me your sonnets. You don't know how much I'd appreciate them.

Most sincerely, as always
Clark A. Smith

1. From AB's "An Insurrection of the Peasantry," *Cosmopolitan* 44, No. 2 (December 1907): 222. The essay was a rebuttal to attacks on GS's "A Wine of Wizardry" (*Cosmopolitan*, September 1907) and AB's own essay on the poem, "A Poet and His Poem," published in the same issue.

2. CAS refers to the Monday Night Club, a group that included several of his friends, including the poet Harry Noyes Pratt and Emily J. Hamilton, the teacher who introduced him to GS. CAS delivered his address on "The Philosophy of Literary Composition" on 25 March 1911. Notes for CAS's address survive on the typescript of his poem "Copan" (JHL).

3. The publisher Mitchell Kennerley offered a $500 first prize and two $250 second prizes, and published the 100 best poems in an anthology, *The Lyric Year*, ed. Ferdinand Earle (1912). GS's "Ode on the Centenary of the Birth of Robert Browning" received one of the second prizes.

4. William Stanley Braithwaite (1878–1962) was a noted African-American critic and anthologist who served as literary editor of the *Boston Evening Transcript* and editor of the annual *Anthology of Magazine Verse* (1913–29). Richard G. Badger was a publisher in Boston, known for publishing the work of poetical novices.

5. Nora May French (b. 1881) committed suicide at GS's home in Carmel on 13 November 1907 at the age of 26. Her *Poems* was published by GS, Harry Anderson Lafler (who edited it), Porter Garnett (who printed it), and Arnold Genthe (who provided a portrait).

6. Alfred Noyes (1880–1958), *Drake: An English Epic: Books I–XII* (1906–08). Bliss Carman (1860–1929), American poet; CAS owned his *From the Book of Myths* (1902).

7. Stephen Phillips (1868–1915), British poet and dramatist.

8. Edwin Markham, "The Wharf of Dreams," in *The Man with the Hoe and Other Poems* (1899). CAS may be referring to his own "The Harbour of the Past" (ms., JHL).

[20a] CAS to GS [non-extant]

[Auburn, Cal.
24 March 1912]

[Envelope only: Postmarked Auburn, Cal., 24 March 1912.]

[21] GS to CAS [ALS]

Carmel, Cal.,
Apr. 10, 1912.[1]

My dear friend and poet:

As usual, my letter's a belated one: I have to spend so much of my time in the bay cities, and have so many duties when "home" again, that a letter a month is about as good as I can do for any mere male. But I've read your poems, as handed to me by Robertson, at least half a dozen times, and if they're *not* the most striking example of precocious genius in literature, then I want (to use London's phrase) to sit down and bite my wrists. It's incredible—but here are the spacious poems to speak for themselves.

I too thought that R. was to give me proofs; but the MSS seemed to have been what he had in mind. If he gets you out by next October it will be a wonder: a paralyzed snail has him nailed to the road-bed. And he agrees to bring you out only on condition that I start about you in the S. F. newspapers some such boom as Bierce gave me when "The Testimony" first appeared. And he's right there, as it's the only way he could get enough advertising for the book to get his money back on it. Publishers aren't such sharks as you think: most books of verse are a *loss* to them. It always surprises me when a publisher can be found for one.

I thank you a thousand times for the fine sonnet to me, for the dedication, and for the dedicatory poem.[2] I can't, however, accept *any* of them, as it would interfere too seriously with what I'd have to say about your work when the time comes. "Logrolling" is a term that comes too effectively to hand now-a-days, and *my* dedication of "The Testimony" to Bierce took a good deal of the "kick" out of his comments.[3] So, greatly and sincerely as I appreciate the honor you would do me, I must ask you to defer to my wider experience and allow me my own way in this matter. And this I know you'll do when you come to realize that I am acting solely in *your* best interests.

You may, if you wish, give me the dedication of your second book; but this one would far better go to your parents, or one of them.

I've sent the MSS back to Robertson, saying to him about what I've said to you in regard to your genius. When next I go to S. F., which should be in about ten days, I'll try to make him get a move on.

To revert to certain things in your letter: here are two of the sonnets of which I spoke. Another two I've no copies of, but shall soon have them made. I don't own a typewriter: I'd save lots of time if I did. Thanks for your efforts to advance my fame in partibus infidelium; but you would better stick to your boulders. They'd move more easily, I fear.

I don't intend to enter the Kennerly Marathon. No "competition" in mine! The old Greeks fell for it; but *they* had audiences not so sadly porcine. No—that prize may go to the girl who'll get it, and I'll stick to my highway robbery.

I am going into one thing, though: the "symposium" of poets on the Browning centenary. Your friend Braithwaite wrote asking me, and as Markham, Carman and other real poets were to indulge, I thought that *I* might as well have a lick at it. But as usual I've been very busy and so have done nothing as yet.

I'll send you one of Nora May's books soon. Don't bother to buy one.

I don't follow you at all as to Noyes. I've not read *all* of his "Drake," but have read *much* of his other work, and must say he seems greatly inferior to Phillips to me. Noyes is orthodox, you know, and by dint of his conformity and a flood of patriotic verse expects to be made the laureate when Austin dies.[4] But the English, who are mostly pretty radical now, are on to his little game, and I imagine that it will fall through. (My friend Scheffauer writes me this from London, where he now lives).

Well, I must turn to other affairs. Let me beg once more that you realize that I'm aware of the honor you would pay me by your dedication, and give it up *only* with the intent of being able to appear more disinterested when the time comes for me to say in print what I think of your work. I regret that such a necessity should be; but the public is a suspicious and malignant beast.

Write soon to me and say that you understand, and will do as I suggest.

Most sincerely yours,

George Sterling.

[Enclosures: "The Coming Singer," "The Muse of the Incommunicable."]

1. This responds to CAS to GS, 2 March 1912.

2. It is not clear what poem is being referred to. Perhaps it is another of CAS's poems on GS (see Appendix).

3. GS's *TS* opens with a "Dedication: To Ambrose Bierce."

4. Alfred Austin (1835–1913), mediocre British poet who provoked ridicule when he was named Poet Laureate of England (1896–1913). The poet who succeeded him was Robert Bridges (1844–1930).

[22] CAS to GS [ALS]

Auburn, Calif.

Apr. 12th, 1912

My Dear Friend:

I must first thank you for your lovely sonnets. I blush to think that "The Coming Singer" is meant for me, for I have not the courage to hope that I may fulfil such a prophecy. Nothing could be more sublime than the ending of that sonnet and I think it the better of the two, though the last lines of "The Muse of the Incommunicable" have been chanting themselves in my ears all day, to a ghostly music.[1] You are one of the few masters of the sonnet.

I am extremely sorry that you think it necessary to withdraw the Dedication and the personal poems. But I understand the situation well enough, and have observed the temper and characteristics of the "many-headed beast". Only I had not expected that you would be required to act as my press-agent—and I don't like the idea any too well. But as you, in your friendship and kindliness, have offered to do so, I cannot be so ungrateful as not to accept it. The only way that I can repay the debt will be by living long enough to pass it on to someone else.

Of course, I understand how it is with Mr. Robertson—and I am not including him among the "sharks." But I have one remark to make on publishers in general: Their principal defense is that they must give the public what it wants—but are they not in many ways responsible for the taste of the public—are not they, in company with the periodicals, theaters, etc, largely the creators of the present depraved standards? If all were to band together to refuse the publication of the torrents of wish-wash—and worse—that are rotting the appreciation of anything *better* in so many minds—could they not educate their readers (and audiences) to something higher? Most people are neither better nor worse, mentally or any other way, than their environment—and literature and its counterparts are a potent part of environment. Perhaps, though, I am overestimating the latent capacities of the public, perhaps it's as imbecile as the publishers seem to think it is. If it is imbecility, it's a dangerous and violent form. But its present literary diet must be having some effect on the Beast, if only to impair its digestion. There is not a volume of Ambrose Bierce among the two thousand-odd in the local Carnegie Library—and I suppose Auburn is average enough in its tastes. I told a local debating-club that Bierce was the greatest living American of letters, and they were too much surprised, I suppose, to dispute me. Possibly they thought it safer to humor the lunatic! But what's the use? Demoralization has the stronghold, and you and I and a few other eccentrics to whom no one pays attention, are on the outside.

I do not care so much for "Drake" on re-reading it. The faults are all painfully evident, but still I think it notable work. I have not read much else of Noyes. I spoke of Phillips from a reading of three plays—"Nero", "Ulysses", and "Paolo and Francesca."[2] I thought "Nero" much the best of the three. If Noyes is "playing to the gallery", it counts a great deal against him. I fear I speak of current poetry from too little knowledge. I have to depend too much on "Current Literature" and "The Literary Digest[']," for I can't afford to buy much, and the books are most unobtainable here otherwise.

As you suggest, I shall transfer the Dedication of "The Star-Treader" to my parents. But my second book will certainly be dedicated to you—and I shall try to write a better poem to go with it.[3]

Who is Mr. Ross? He was in Auburn some time ago, and introduced himself to me as a friend of yours and of Mr Robertson's. He talked mostly on political economy.

> In all sincerity and gratitude,
> Your friend,
> Clark Ashton Smith

1. "Beauty and death her speechless lips assign, / Where silence is, and where the surf-loud feet / Of armies wander on the sands of doom" (ll. 12–14; *TS* 94).

2. Stephen Phillips, *Paolo and Francesca* (1900), *Ulysses* (1902), and *Nero* (1906).

3. The volume was in fact dedicated only "To my mother." CAS dedicated his fourth book, *S* (1925), to GS.

[23] GS to CAS [ALS]

> Carmel, Cal.,
> Apr. 21, 1912.

My dear Poet:

I've just replied to a letter from our fellow-singer Neihardt, with whom I'm trading books, and now I'd like to have a letter to you go out in the same mail.

I heard from Robertson, yesterday, on a personal matter, and in the letter he said he would write about *you* soon. I replied that I was going to S. F. next Wednesday, so he'd not have to bother about writing. You can trust me to make him "stick," if there's any stick in him. He has been faithful enough with *me*, I must say.

Ross is a man whom I once met at the Bohemian Club's midsummer "Jinks," up in Sonoma County. I don't recall him; but some time ago I got a letter from him urging me to write Socialistic verse. I have been too busy to answer the letter, and probably shall not. He's a "well-meanin' cuss."

This is only a note—all I've time for. I enclose those two other sonnets.

Turner[1] and I got seven curlew on the beach yesterday. He has my bungalow now (as he has a wife and child) and I'm living in my cabin. Very snug, though.

As ever.   Sterling.

[Enclosures: "Respite," an unidentified sonnet ("Kindred"?).]

1. I.e., John Kenneth Turner.

[24] CAS to GS [ALS]

Auburn, Calif.

Apr. 28th, 1912.

My Dear Friend:

Many thanks for your sonnets! Both are good, and I can't criticize except to say that I like "Respite" a little the better of the two. If it isn't ungrateful of me to say it, I think that you would better be writing poems of your own than reading and criticizing my out-put. You are writing altogether too little (This is putting it mildly!)

Your friend Ross was after me to write Socialistic verse, too; but I can't see it. The chief trouble is that it wouldn't be anything but verse—and to make it at all effect[ive] one would have to write down to the straitest capacity of that economically-brained animal, the Mob. Edwin Markham is an example of what it leads to[1]—and there are others. I have a poet-friend on a San Francisco newspaper who is going the downward path.[2] Besides, what's the use, anyway? Even if one could advance the cause of socialism, (which I theoretically believe in), the tides of things are so regulated that everything would swing back afterwhile, and be all the worse for the added momentum. The thing called civilization, as the history of the past shows conclusively enough, is only a dog chasing its own tail. As Bernard Shaw points out, there is an accumulation of inventions and mechanical knowledge (the work of exceptional men, but not requiring exceptional men for their appliance) and this gives the illusion of progress—this, and the wave-like integrations of material wealth—, which by their own excess, tend to become disintegration. The history of nations is the same as that of worlds and individuals—birth, youth, maturity, age, and Death—or, more scientifically, integration and disintegration.

To get back to the starting-point, I don't see that I owe anything to the mob anyway. Bierce says that the present state of things is all the crowd's own fault; but I suppose one might go further back and lay the blame on the law of gravitation, which is as good a place to let it rest as any. In either case, I don't see that I'm "obligated" to attempt the amelioration of the muddle by the composing of Socialist rhymes. It won't matter so very much, anyway, whether I did or didn't, in the days when the world begins to bleach and shrivel, and the sun is blotched with death. Socialist and Individualist, they'll all be a little dirt lodged deep in the granite wrinkles of the globe's countenance. (There's nothing like a cosmic perspective for cheering one up!)

I am doing a certain amount of work, but it doesn't seem to me that I am putting much inspiration into it. Most of my best work has been done in the months between May and September. I have finished a narrative poem entitled "Saturn", dealing with the fall of the Titans, which runs to about 250 lines. It's rather an experiment, and I don't feel very sanguine about it. I have also written a dramatic monologue, "Nero",[3] which is even more of an experiment. It's the emperor's soliloquy after he has watched the burning of Rome. I suppose one has to do a lot of inferior work to pay for the privilege of writing something really good on occasion. I am trying another poem, "The Shadow of the Unattained", but it doesn't seem to take shape at all easily. Sometimes I get clear lines like these—

> "Fainter than winds that breathe
> The folds of twilight's drapery."

and, again—

> "Beauty, whose lyric laughters hold
> A sadder music learned of old,
> An echo from the halls of Death"—[4]

but, on the whole, what I have done so far is rather unsatisfactory.

I entered the Kennerly contest, and got paid for my temerity. The editor told me that if I'd re-write the poem I sent in,[5] according to his notions (he was so kind as to send me a version of his own to work on!) he might use it. I spent the most of one perfectly good Sunday trying to re-write the poem without undue violence to my own conception of it, but I take it from what the editor said that I'll have to be one of the goats omitted from the Kennerly fold. Why is an editor? Perhaps like red motor-cars, church-bells, mosquitoes, and the saltatory flea, they are sent upon us as a judgement for our sins.

> Most sincerely, your friend,
> Clark Ashton Smith.

1. CAS alludes to Markham's "The Man with the Hoe" (1899), which had led AB to sever relations with Markham in the belief that the poem was political propaganda.
2. Ernest Jerome Hopkins (1887–1973), later known as a Bierce scholar.
3. CAS appears to have read Steven Phillips's play *Nero* only weeks previously.
4. There appear to be no extant poems with these lines.
5. CAS had submitted "Nero" to the contest.

[25] GS to CAS [ALS]

> [Hotel Del Monte
> Del Monte, Calif.]

May 13th, 1912.

My dear Poet:

This will introduce you to Mr. Robert Haven Schauffler, the poet and writer, who is out here for the Metropolitan Magazine. I've been talking *you* to him, and he'd like to know you better. I'm sorry he's going to see you before I do.

> Fraternally yours,
> George Sterling.

[26] GS to CAS [ALS]

Carmel, Cal.,
May 25th, 1912.

Dear Poet:

After our years (or year?) of letter-writing, you've doubtless too few illusions left to expect a prompt reply to your good letters. About one a month seems to be my limit, and as a rule I can't reach even that.

Robert Haven Schauffler, the poet, musician and all-round literateur, spent the 13th with me. He's out here for the Metropolitan Magazine, "doing" the Missions and other scenery for it. Just now he's at Yosemite. I showed him your "Abyss" and "Star-Treader," and he was immensely interested. Asked for a letter to you, and will get off the train, if he has time, on his way east, and put in a few hours with you. His book, "Scum o' the Earth,"[1] has some fine work in it. And he's a fine fellow.

I'm enclosing the "symposium" page of the Boston Transcript. My ode must be better than I thought, as Dr. van Dyke[2] and Braithwaite and a few others have been kind enough to write me in a laudatory vein about it.

I've been "home" here since the 9th, have been on the wagon, answered some dozens of letters, and even written three or four "poems,"—none worth while. Incidentally, we've had some good hunts for abalones and wild-strawberries. So life has not been all in vain. We're planning a week's trip "down Coast" of the middle of June, when there'll be some very low tides.

Our old lion, Ambrose Bierce, will be in Oakland about the 25th of next month. I wish you could meet him.

John Neihardt sends me his three books—there's big stuff in all of them.[3] The poor devil lives in Nebraska!

I'd like to see that "Nero" of yours, if you've a spare copy. The lines you quote from your other poems are *very* good. I've heard nothing further from Robertson; but I've already warned you that he's toad-slow.

My friend Heron here has sent twelve poems to The Lyric Year contest. Heaven send that he lands one!

Good hunting to you! Write with the spirit moves.

As ever,   George S.

1. Schauffler, *Scum o' the Earth and Other Poems* (1912).

2. Apparently Henry van Dyke (1852–1933), an American poet and journalist.

3. By this time Neihardt had published *The Lonesome Trail* (1907), a collection of short stories; *A Bundle of Myrrh* (1907), a poetry collection; *Man-Song* (1909), a long poem; *The River and I* (1910), a travel book; and possibly *The Dawn-Builder* (1912), a poetry collection. Neihardt had probably sent GS his three books of poetry.

[27] CAS to GS [ALS]

Auburn, Calif.
May 26th, 1912.

My dear Friend:

I've just received your letter, and the clipping from the Transcript. Your ode seems to me by all odds the best of the lot; the first two stanzas of it are particularly great, and all of it, indeed, is good. Markham's sonnet is good, too, but I don't care much for the others. I don't like to say that you have overinformed your subject; I like Browning, and think he is a great poet. But to me (perhaps I don't understand him well enough) it seems that he is not a poet of the very first rank, like Poe, Milton, and Keats. I measure a poet largely by his imaginative powers; and to me, "human interest" is not in the least essential. Most people who see my work complain that it lacks the human note; but that is something I have not tried to put in it. Perhaps imaginative insight into human life (like Browning's) is just as valuable as the more sidereal kind; but I don't see it that way. For that reason, there are stanzas in your "Testimony" that seem to me to outweigh in poetic value any whole poem that I have ever read of Browning's. However, my reading of him is rather limited, so I won't pass absolute judgement.

I am almost afraid to send you "Nero". About four-fifths of it is prose, and not particularly good prose at that. However, I'm sending it. I hope you're not expecting too much of it. It has psychological value, I suppose; pathological might be a better word. The human interest (if it has any of what is usually meant by that term) is sinister and abnormal. It has a few great lines (according to my tests) such as "The vampire Silence at the breast of worlds",[1] but I am not at all hopeful about it.

I have been trying other poems; but the "Uncontrollable" (as someone has called it) does not seem to be on the job. Consequently, it's been slow and painful work for me to piece any thing together at all. It's unpleasant, to say the least, to *want* to write some thing with all your might, but not to be able to do it. The state is not unfamiliar to me, though; I don't think I've ever had more than three or four straight, clean attacks of inspiration. One of them was when I wrote the "Abyss Ode;" I did practically all of it at a sitting . . . My nerves, too, are giving me hell as usual; it's a sort of musical toothache.

I, also, have heard nothing from Mr. Robertson. I understood, a month or so ago, that he was to send me a contract soon; but nary a word. I suppose he'll dump the proofs on me without warning some day when the mercury is trying to climb out of sight.

You mention Neihardt. I have seen some of his work, and it's certainly fine stuff. I hope he'll do some yet that's even better; I think he has the power.

I saw something of Shauffler's in Current Literature awhile ago. I think it was a plea for the European immigrants—the "scum of the Earth", which is about what most of them are. I don't think he has a very good case.[2] It's the low European, the anarchist and King-ridden, who is going to bring about America's downfall, and that at no very distant day, either. The criminally insane and viciously imbecile thing called American civilization can't stand many more of the breed. They're like rats gnawing at the foundations of a rotten barn. Well, let it go with the rest,—with these "tribes of slaves and Kings"[3] that have kept the world's dust astir for awhile. It won't affect the "cost of living" in the worlds around Antares and Canopus, I suppose—this collapse of a pseudo-republic, built mostly of paper, and mortared with ink. They won't even know about it in the other planets of *this* system, unless they have rather better telescopes than ours. It seems of importance here, though; I suppose that the social upheavals of the ant-hill are of importance to the ants, too. But all colors will look alike in the night of Death. In the meanwhile, the race goes merrily on. I think the motor-car should be the symbol of American civilization, with the motto, "speed, dust, noise, and stink." Joy-riding, if it's kept up long enough, and fast enough, generally has but one end.

I wish I could meet Bierce when he comes out; but I don't suppose it will be possible. Possibly he wouldn't care so much about meeting me.

Well, I must close. May the muse attend you!

Ever your friend,

Clark Ashton Smith

[Enclosures: "Nero," "Saturn"?]

1. "Nero," l. 58.

2. Schauffler's poem "Scum o' the Earth" appeared in the *Atlantic Monthly* (November 1911) and was reprinted in *Current Literature* (January 1912).

3. CAS may be misquoting GS's lines from "'Omnia Exeunt in Mysterium'": "Slaves, seamen, captains, councillors and kings, / Gone utterly, save for those echoes far!" (ll. 9–10).

[28] GS to CAS [ALS]

Carmel, Cal.,

June 6th, 1912.

Dear astounding comrade:

This is the last time I'm going to make you wait long for an answer to a letter: you are too big a proposition to "vex with delay."[1] It is odd to note you decrying Nero, and speaking of it as half prose, when as a matter of fact I rank it higher even than your great odes. It has a maturity, a vertebration, a pertinency and grasp beyond those other poems, and I'd give a reasonably-sized slice off one of my ears to have done anything so great for this many a year. Ah! yes! it's a tremendous thing—I wonder where you're going to wind up, with such a beginning as you are making!

You mustn't feel discouraged if your periods of inspiration are not more frequent. The wonder is that you have any at all at your age. As time ripens your powers and expands your possibilities you'll find quite as much as will be good for you. I'll not forget Miller's wail to me: "Ah! It's not the quantity but the quality!" I've a notion he was silently comparing his bulky volume with Poe's slender one—or Coleridge's, or Keats'.

I've just received a most interesting letter from Schauffler in regard to you. I'm so glad he spared the time to call, as his words seem to draw you nearer to me and make you less of a mythical being. His poetry is not of as fine a quality as I wish it was; but he's an excellent chap and has a very good mind—a bit too orthodox. He is a graduate of Princeton.

His visit to you brings to mind another matter: I want you to visit me, soon. I'll take great pleasure in paying your fare, both ways—you may regard it as a loan of indefinite term if you prefer it on that basis. When here you will have *no* expenses, though you may have to sleep in a very small tent or share my little cabin with me, as I've loaned my house to a financially-embarrassed friend who has a wife and child. You'll not have to bother about clothes, either, when here, as I've a partially-worn outing-suit that will fit you all right, with golf-stockings and tennis-shoes, which also I have.

I'd like to have you remain at least a month, though perhaps your parents will object to being deprived of your society for so long: I don't want to make them dislike me. Tell them it's all for their good as well as yours, as I hope that this visit will lead to something substantially to your advantage, once I've had a talk with you and seen what you most want to do.

Now please don't disappoint me in this, but write at once and tell me what the fare is between Auburn and S. F. (I know what it is the rest of the way) and how soon you can start—the sooner the better. I will go to Monterey and meet you at the train; there's an auto-bus to Carmel.

I've been fairly busy for over two weeks, and have ground out several "poems," none of which I like well enough to send to you. I'll enclose, however, a sonnet that I may not have sent you, and a lyric into which I've tried to put something of the dove's voice, by using the vowels o and u frequently.

I'll see that you meet Bierce, who'll be out here this month, to remain for quite a while. Your economic views, by the way, are more in accord with his than with mine or my associates—but that only makes you the more interesting.

You'll like it here; it's never hot, like Auburn, and isn't as cold as S. F., while the natural beauty is beyond anything you've ever seen.

Write soon, my dear poet, and tell me you'll come.

As ever, George S.

[Enclosures: "At the Grand Canyon," "The Voice of the Dove."]

1. Thomas Brewer (fl. 1624), "Drowsy sun, why dost thou stay?," ll. 7–9: "Then vex'd with delay, /Away she flung and, lisping, said: / Prithee, prithee, let's go to bed."

[29] CAS to GS [ALS]

Auburn, Calif.,
June 9th, 1912.

My dear Friend:

I think *you* are the "astounding comrade." I'm sincerely surprised by your judgement of Nero, even though I find, on re-reading it, that it doesn't seem as bad as I thought it was . . . I had to work so hard getting the thing into any kind of shape, that I suppose no possible achievement could have seemed to me commensurate with the effort. I aim too unattainably high, I fear. Keats was dissatisfied with Hyperion, I believe (don't suspect me of thinking there's any point to the analogy beyond the dissatisfaction.)

It's very kind of you to offer to loan me carfare (of course it *is* a loan, and I hope to repay it soon.) And I fear I'll have to accept. But I can't come down, it would seem, for perhaps two weeks yet. My father is not at all well at present, and there is some work that has to be done before I can leave this impested haunt of Philistines and rattlesnakes.

The fare to San Francisco from here is $3.65. But why couldn't I come straight through via Niles and Santa Cruz? The total fare that way is $5.85. I want to visit San Francisco on the way back, but I don't care about passing through it twice.

Many, many thanks to you for the lovely volume of Nora May French's poems. They're all wonderful, and some of them have stirred me more than anything I have seen, in many a day. I love them all . . . And that wonderful face! I think this little book should live, if the love of poetry survives the materialistic smother of the present age.

And I'm glad it's so well gotten out, in this day of meretriciously bound and cheaply printed books. There's no discord between the cover and the contents.

I like your "Grand Canyon" sonnet. The sestet is great, particularly the last two lines. And I fancy it conveys the impression of the place pretty well. Your "Voice of the Dove" haunts one, and I think you've succeeded in echoing the call. I wish you'd try something longer—another narrative poem like Duandon, or an Ode like that on the Browning Centenary, which is a big thing —

I have begun a narrative poem entitled "The Titans Triumphant", but I may not do much more with it at present. It will inevitably be rather Miltonic. After I've had a good look at the sea, I think of attempting a poem on the voyage of Magellan. It should be a good subject, and I do not remember having seen it touched on in poetry, though Columbus has had rather more than his due.

I like Schauffler. He's a fine, inspiring sort, and I enjoyed his visit a good deal. He *is* a bit orthodox, though, as you say. I fear he was very much shocked by my views on suicide, and some other subjects, such as European immigration. He's recovered from his college education better than most do, I think.

As ever, Your friend,
Clark Ashton Smith

[30] GS to CAS [ALS]

Carmel, Cal.,
June 11th, 1912.

My dear boy:

I'm glad to see you bow to the inevitable and tell me you'll come to Carmel for a while. I'm surprised at the fare, having a notion it was about $12. I enclose check, and hope you will be able to come in two weeks. Let me know a day or two ahead of time the day you're leaving, and I'll meet you at the Monterey station. I think that's a good plan of yours to come via Niles and San Jose (*not* Santa Cruz), as it must be quite a bit shorter, and the trip here is tiresome, at its best.

When you return, I'll be wanting to go to S. F. myself. So we can go up together and I can show you the Bohemian Club, and my picture facing the bar!

I knew you'd like Nora May's poems. She wrote in crystal, and I'm sure the writing will endure. The book was well gotten up because we her friends published it. I've thirty of the books here in my cabin, which once she occupied.

I had a good letter from Bierce in the same mail as yours. He reaches Oakland June 26th, and will be up around Tahoe from July 1st to 17th. Then he'll be in Oakland again, where you and I will run him to earth. He likes my Browning ode, by the way, though he doesn't like Browning.[1]

I sold a "poem" on the coyote to the Sat. Even. Post[2]—can you beat it? I'll be butting in to the Atlantic Monthly if I'm not careful.

Have you anything more to send me? "Nero" improves on acquaintance, something not to be said of its original.

Fraternally yours,
George S.

1. Cf. AB's "With a Book": "Words shouting, singing, smiling, frowning— / Sense lacking. /Ah, nothing, more obscure than Browning, / Save blacking" (*Collected Works* [Washington, DC: Walter Neale, 1909–12], 5.170).
2. "Father Coyote."

[31] GS to CAS [ANS, JHL][1]

[Postmarked Carmel, Cal.,
18[?] June 1912]

Dear Clark: Just got back from hunting trip and have not the time for a long letter. Hope you can show up on the 23rd or 24th. Let me know date and train (morning or afternoon).

Yours ever,

George Sterling.

1. *Front:* Dunes and Point Carmel, Carmel, Cal. CAS gave this postcard to R. H. Barlow.

[32] GS to CAS [ALS]

Carmel, Cal.,
June 26th, 1912.

Dear Clark:

I'm uncertain, from your letter, as to when you're coming, for you write it on a Sunday and say "the latter part of *next* week," which would make it after the 4th. Now, I want you to be here by the night of the 2nd, at the worst, so as to take in the Forest Theatre. Likely enough you mean to come the latter part of *this* week. At least I'm hoping so.[1]

Yours in haste,

George S.

1. CAS spent the following month in Carmel with GS. See Ferlinghetti and Peters, *Literary San Francisco*, p. 47, for a photo from the occasion. During this time, CAS participated in the annual grove play.

[33] GS to CAS [ALS]

July 30, 1912.

My dear Clark:

Here are some negatives, and Miss Conti[1] will send you two fine enlargements of a couple of them. Gee! but you were feeling sad (it would seem) when you "sat" that day.

I'm still treading the primrose path down here in our bad grey city, but will get off to the Grove by Saturday, I think. There I expect to recuperate. Crossed the bay with Lafler this morning: he wants to be "remembered" to you.

Can you send me (here) fresh copies of "Nero" and "Saturn?" These hounds here borrow my copies when I'm drunk, and I forget to whom I entrusted any of them.

This can be only a note, as I must go downstairs at once to keep a luncheon engagement.

Don't let Auburn and the Philistines thereof oppress overmuch thy spirit. Be patient, and we'll extricate you from the place—you and yours.

Had a fine time with A. B. yesterday. He was sorry to have missed you.

As ever, affectionately, G.

1. Bianca Conti had photographed CAS in 1911 and again in 1912. Presumably the portrait referred to here is that used as the frontispiece of *ST*.

[33a] CAS to GS [non-extant]

[Auburn, Cal.
c. early August 1912]

[34] GS to CAS [ALS]

Aug. 2nd, 1912.

Dear Clark:

No doubt Dunlap will have sent you copies of to-day's "Examiner" and "Call," so I'll send you only a few copies of "Town Talk", as soon as I get a little leisure.[1] I deeply deplore Dunlap's action in "springing you on the public" so far in advance of Robertson's publication of your book, as the public, on whom a publisher has to rely in order to pay expenses, will have forgotten all about you by November. My "puff" of you in "Town Talk" could have done no harm, as it was gossip rather than news. But now you're "news" no longer to the newspapers.[2]

I went to see Robertson this morning, and found him rather sore; but I've persuaded him to stick to his guns. We can probably re-hash the news as soon as the book is for sale.

I'm not blaming Dunlap extremely. The poor fellow was evidently jealous of me and fearful of losing the honor of "discovering" you—a thing to which he was entirely welcome. But he seems to have been thinking more of himself than of you—certainly of Robertson, and I don't advise you to fall into his hands any farther than necessary.

Thanks for the poems. I'll take care not to lend these new copies. As to sending anything to England, that's all right, for it would in no way interfere with book-publication here. Take all the free advertising you have thrust upon you: never *seek* it. (I know you don't). However, I'd like to know in advance what you'd send to England: you might be misadvised. I'm so afraid you are going to be exploited by persons anxious to shine by reflected glory. In my case, you would know in advance that I neither desire nor need anything of the sort.

Since writing the above, I've had to talk to Robertson over the 'phone. Dunlap had just rung him up to apologize, in a fashion. D. also wants to have a talk with me, but I've postponed the pleasure until I feel a trifle less vexed. D. is perhaps feeling the pangs of a guilty conscience, so we mustn't be hard on the poor fellow.

I've two fine "enlargements" of you by Miss Conti that I'll be mailing to you this afternoon. You really *have* that expression, Clark; but it's a good expression to have, in the case of a young poet.

Your quotation from "Shadows" is anything but insane.

Your regards shall go to Bierce and Lafler. Here's mine!

Affectionately,   George.

1. See the unsigned articles, "Auburn's Precocious Genius" [by "The Spectator," i.e., Theodore Bonnet], *Town Talk* No. 1041 (3 August 1912): 9; "Sierra Teaches Poetry to Boy of Its Peaks . . ." *San Francisco Examiner* (2 August 1912): 5; "Boy Is Poetic Genius . . ." *San Francisco Call* (2 August 1912): 1–2.

2. GS refers to his initial discussion of CAS in his *Town Talk* interview in 1911 (see letter 4, n. 2).

[35] CAS to GS [ALS]

Auburn, Calif.
Aug. 4th, 1912.

Dear George:

So far, Dunlap has had neither the nerve to write me an apology, or to send me the papers you speak of. However, I've seen the thing in Friday's Call, and also a yarn in the Chronicle of the same date. But I could find nothing in that day's Examiner. Was it in Thursday's issue?

Have you seen the Chronicle story? If you haven't, for Allah's sake take a look at it. They've got my name George Ashton Smith to begin with, and they say, along with other statements of a similar discernment, that my work ranks with that of Milton, Dryden, and Pope.[1]

It does look as if Dunlap wanted to hog all the credit of my "discovery". As a matter of fact, he didn't discover me. You've got a title to that antedating Dunlap's by six months or so. In fact, it was through your quoting a poem of mine in "Town Talk" that he came to know about my work at all.[2] When it comes to the last analysis, I think I should be given a little credit for discovering myself—surely no mean feat in the midst of a circular and orbicular encompassment of Auburnites. However, we won't say anything more about the matter. The milk of free advertisement is spilt and there's no use writing imprecatory letters about it.

What's that in "Town Talk" about your going to Glen Ellen to live? You never said anything to me about it. Is that a fair example of the reliability of Town Talk's statements? . . . What a putrid, stinking lot the San Francisco papers are, anyway—quite on a par with nearly everything else in the city that's a stench to the nostrils of Alcyone, and a howl of abomination in the ears of Altair. Even Auburn, in my sight, is preferable to S. F., for the simple reason that there's so much less of it.

How I wish that you were with me, or I with you—even in S. F.! I'm awfully jealous of all your friends down there . . . And Auburn has even fewer mitigations than usual, at this season. I'm not in the "society" of the place, you know. To most of the people here, I'm only a crazy chump who imagines he can write poetry. I don't especially resent being "out" of things here; only I'd have a better chance at the girls of the place if I weren't such a pariah. The only one available at present is a divorceè; and she lives about three miles away, on the other side of town,—too far to walk in this hellish temperature.

Affectionately,
Clark.

1. [Unsigned], "California Youth Is Hailed by Critics as Poetical Genius: George [*sic*] Ashton Smith, Aged 19, Writes Poems Pronounced Literati as Ranking with Best of Keats and Byron," *San Francisco Chronicle* (2 August 1912): 6.
2. See letter 4, n. 2.

[36] GS to CAS [ALS]

Aug. 5th, 1912.

Dear Clark:

I'm glad to learn that the local newspaper brass band has not lost you your ear-drums. Otherwise it will do you no especial harm. Dunlap promises to re-hash the thing when the book comes out; so Robertson will not be particularly a loser by reason of the premature explosion.

Of course what D. was after was the credit of discovering you. I'm glad to know he's a Doc Cook.[1] I had a conciliatory talk with him, in which he was profuse with locks to the empty stable. He hadn't sent you copies of the papers, so I made him promise to do so. If he doesn't, let me know. The "outside the city" edition of the Examiner didn't carry the article.

I go to the Jinks to-morrow, Christ be praised, and will be spared some cacophony and stench for a few days. Address me next at "Bohemia, Sonoma Co." After next Saturday I'll be at Glen Ellen, at London's, for a week. Then I hope to get back to "that dear Carmel." Nothing in that "Town Talk" statement of my giving Carmel up. And I hope to get you there for keeps before Hell is finally frozen. So keep your spirits up.

Affectionately,   George.

1. GS refers to Frederick A. Cook (1865–1940), American physician and explorer who claimed to be the first person to climb Mt. McKinley in 1906 and to reach the North Pole in 1909; both claims were subsequently found to be false.

[36a] GS to CAS [non-extant]

[San Francisco, Cal.
c. 5 August 1912]

[Envelope: postmarked San Francisco, Cal., 6 August 1912 (3 A.M.).]

[37] GS to CAS [ALS]

Aug. 6, 1912.

Dear Clark:

Here's the latest. I was present at its concoction a few days ago, in Dunlap's office, and said that about Keats—to which I adhere.[1]

Bierce was, however, somewhat vexed at being misquoted, as he has been in all the other papers, and said he['d] have to send a few lines to "Town Talk" disavowing praise so extreme.[2] So if you see some such letter, pray do not feel put out, as he admires and feels kindly toward you—only, he naturally doesn't care to have the newspapers "quote" him in any terms that seem pleasing to them.

The "Bulletin" reporter was named Hopkins[3]—a pleasant chap. He'd met you, and wanted to be "remembered" when I wrote.

Don't feel irritated at all this newspaper gush. It can't hurt you if you keep your present modesty, and otherwise will be of ultimate benefit. Remember that your publisher (especially in a poet's case) has his rights.

Don't feel that you have to answer all my letters. I know that your hands will be full for a while yet.

Affectionately,   George.

1. In the *Town Talk* article of 3 August 1912 (see letter 34, n. 1), Theodore Bonnet (presumably at GS's insistence) wrote of CAS: "Here is a youth hardly more than half educated who is said to be writing poetry as remarkable for its beauties as some of the finest of the early performances of John Keats . . ."

2. See "Letter from Ambrose Bierce" dated 6 August 1912, *Town Talk* No. 1042 (10 August 1912): 10–11. See Appendix.

3. See letter 24, n. 2.

[38] CAS to GS [ALS]

Auburn, Calif.
Aug. 8th, 1912.

Dear George:

Many thanks for the pictures: they're very fine and artistic work, I think—infinitely better than any others that have been taken of me.

I was afraid that Bierce had been misquoted in the papers. The statements they've been attributing to him didn't sound quite like the old boy. I'm very glad to hear that he does think well of my work. Personally, I don't think it's quite all the papers have been saying it is. Keats and Shelley are in the first rank of greatness; and I'm only in the second rank, at best.

Dunlap came up here Monday, with a lot of prolix explanations. He put up rather a large and ample bluff about not being to blame; but he looked guilty, and I think he was afraid I didn't quite believe him. He said it was your thing in "Town Talk" that started the whole avalanche of newspaper stories. However, it's all right, anyway, except for a slight ringing in my ears.

I met the Bulletin man, Hopkins, while he was teaching in a private school up here, near Auburn. He's a poet himself, and has written some rather good things. But, alas, he's married now, and a reporter—a hellish combination for a poet, especially a small one.

I'm not as busy as you seem to think I am. I'm not bothered with visitors, and my correspondence isn't very extensive. I've received only two letters from strangers since the papers began to discuss me; and one of them was from a lady-astrologer.

Yours ever, affectionately,
Clark.

[39] GS to CAS [ALS]

Glen Ellen, Cal.,
Aug. 16, 1912.

Dear Clark:

I'm still here at London's, recuperating from the Jinks and the days preceding it. After five days on the wagon I'm beginning to feel almost myself again—last Sunday I was all in.

I'll have to be here till next Wednesday, as Bynner is coming up. But by the Saturday after that I hope to reach Carmel the Blest, and turn to something worth while, if it's only hustling my pitch-pine logs for next winter, a task (or play) confronting me.

It's very enjoyable here, of course. There was seven or eight of us, and we take walks in the morning and ride (Jack has 8 saddle-horses) or drive in the afternoon. Evenings go to cards or "arguments," tho sometimes Jack reads to us from his last novel,[1] not yet sold. 172000 words—think of it! I am glad I'm not a novelist, as I haven't the energy, at least mentally.

He's having a big stone barn-foundation wired over, & when the job's done, we're going to release a fox, jackrabbit, 2 snakes and three coons in it. I'm wondering what'll occur. Mrs. London is down in Oakland. Has had another miscarriage, poor woman! Bierce is there too—he doesn't care enough for London's "views" to put in a few days here. London, by the way, wants you to visit him this coming November, when I'm here. You'll find it well worth while, and you'll like him very much.

Well, be good; but not too good, for—"the good die young."

Affectionately,

George.

1. *The Valley of the Moon* (1913).

[40] CAS to GS [ALS]

Auburn, Calif.
Aug. 18th, 1912.

Dear George:

I haven't done much since my return here, except to read the surprising newspaper accounts of myself. Robertson's just sent me one from a Stockton paper, which describes me as being nine years old, and as having written poetry ever since I was eight.[1] This advertising has had one good effect, though: Robertson tells me that he's going to get my book out about the middle of September, instead of in November, as he originally intended.

Thank Mr. London for his kind invitation.[2] I sincerely hope that I'll be able to accept it; but I'm not sure that I can.

We're enjoying rather lukewarm weather here just at present—a surprising mercy for a Placer County August. It's really quite cool—but still a little warmer than Carmel, on the average. I cut wood in the morning, walk to the post office in the afternoon, and go out again to murder a cottontail or two in the early evening, besides miscellaneous other walks. I've written hardly anything since my return, except disconnected lines in my note-book. My inspiration seems to be working in fragments at present—a sure sign that there'll be something more doing later.

I saw Bierce's letter in "Town Talk." The old boy treated me pretty well, under the circumstances. It must be maddening to be misquoted as he has been. I don't think he's the only sufferer, though. Schauffler was quoted in the San Francisco "Post" as saying that I was the greatest American poet to date;[3] but he never said anything of the sort to me.

We had a forest-fire near here the other day—just across the American River in El-Dorado Co. I went out and watched it from the canyon edge in the evening. It was something of a sight—a long line of flaming trees that seemed to move over the hills like the swaying torches of Titans, and behind it a great burnt-over space blue with twilight and a low haze of smoke, through which scattered glowing fires made me think of your line about the "coals of Tartarus".[4] They were like the strange red constellations of some imagined firmament.

Ever yours, affectionately,
Clark

1. "9-Year-Old Poet From the Sierras." *Stockton Record*, 35: 98 (5 August 1912): 2.

2. See JL to GS, 30 January 1913. In *The Letters of Jack London: Volume Three: 1913–1916*, ed. Earle Labor, Robert C. Leritz, III, and I. Milo Shepard (Stanford:, CA: Stanford University Press, 1988), p. 1119.

3. Sophie Treadwell (1890–1970), "Makers of Books and Some Recent Works," *San Francisco Post* (10 August 1912): 12, quotes Schauffler as referring to CAS as "the greatest poet ever produced in America." Treadwell also reviewed *The Star-Treader* (*San Francisco Evening Post*, 23 November 1912): magazine section, p. 2.

4. From "A Wine of Wizardry," l. 29.

[41] GS to CAS [ALS]

Carmel, Cal.,
Aug. 27th, 1912.

Dear Clark:

I've been chasing around at too lively a gait to have had a chance to reply till now to your letter. Got back here (thank God!) night before last, and am sleeping twelve hours a day, trying to catch up. It's good to be here, but a pile of neglected correspondence is a dilution to my happiness.

I saw Robertson in S. F., and he'd going to send me proofs of your book as fast as they come out. I'm to make comments on them and then forward them to you. I hope that arrangement will seem best to you, as it saves time.

I'd no chance to see that "Town Talk" with Bierce's letter in it till I got back to S. F. last Friday. "Town Talk" handled Dunlap a bit roughly, and I imagine he's a bit ruffled. But he's a Hun.

Bierce was *very* easy on you—for Bierce. It was a harder rap he gave me, and I don't thank him for it, as I had already asseverated that I was misquoted in the papers as to what I'd said he'd said. Well, he's a peppery old gentleman, and I suppose he thinks he's acting with vast restraint.

I showed him "Nero" and "Saturn," early in August, and he made certain comments on them (nothing radical) with which I agree. They are as follows:

He doesn't like the title "Nero," thinking that the title should suggest more the fact that Nero is speaking, a thing one isn't sure of for a while.

He doesn't like "bind" Dull Matter's mouth.[1] I forget why; it seems all right to me.

He says "toward" is accented on the first syllable. I'd suggest "that reach" or something similar—and better.[2]

Of course it should be "Of time *or* faculty." You have it "nor" in my copy.[3]

He doesn't like "*crouching* at the back of Time." I agree with him in thinking that "crouching" has too much connotation of fear or feebleness. "Lurking" is better, and there's probably a better word than that.[4]

He doesn't like "silentness," and I think he's right in thinking that "the stretched silence of the blinded gulfs" is decidedly stronger. "Silentness" is a weak sort of word.[5]

In "Saturn" he objects to "*fed* with victory," saying that as a soldier he knows victory doesn't feed. "Fed" is a miserable sort of word anyhow—"drunk" is much stronger, tho' it may have been used before. I'd change "fed," at any rate.[6]

He'd never seen "rivelled," and thought the word too archaic to be suitable. I don't know whether to agree with him or not. It's a good word in itself.[7]

He thought (as do I) that "weighty" isn't a very poetic word, and that some such word as "vast" is greatly preferable.[8]

That's all, and it's mostly very good advice, even if a trifle meticulous.

No more now, as I'm swamped with letters. I hope to go up to London's in late October, and shall expect to see you there too. You'll enjoy all of it.

I hope those proofs will soon begin to appear.

Affectionately yours,   George.

1. No longer extant in "Nero."
2. "Nero," l. 24.
3. "Nero," l. 32.
4. "Nero," l. 56.
5. "Nero," l. 91.
6. "Saturn," l. 79: "Nor the foe newly filled with victory?"
7. "Saturn," l. 111.
8. Possibly "Saturn," l. 206: "In vaster disarray, with vanguard piled . . . "

[42] CAS to GS [ALS]

Auburn, Cal.
Aug. 30th, 1912

Dear George:

That's a good plan (for me) that the proofs should go to you first. Give 'em hell while you're about it—at least as much as A. M. will stand for.

I agree with some of Bierce's criticisms (not all, though). I think "Nero" is title enough. Browning gives some of his most dramatic lyrics similar titles. And I must hasten to defend my use of "rivelled". The verb "rivel" is an intermediate word between "shrivel" and "wrinkle", and is defined as meaning, "to contract into wrinkles." I'd like to thank Bierce, though, for some of his other criticisms.

Dunlap is as unmanageable as a sore elephant about the thing in "Town Talk." He seems to think that he really was my "discoverer", basing his claims chiefly on the assertion that he saw a poem of mine in a magazine sometime back in 1910. The magazine was "Munseys",[1] which has a circulation of 500,000 or so. I've had a sort of break with him because I wouldn't write a letter to "Town Talk" acknowledging him as my "discoverer". He's carrying the matter to rather ridiculous lengths, I think.

I've written some more blank-verse lately—a thing called "The Titans in Tartarus", but I won't be sending it to you for a long time yet. I'm not sure that it's much good, but I am sure that it needs some whole-hearted and hard-handed revision.

I've got a beastly cold that makes me feel as if my head were screwed up inside. Also a slight headache and a monumental grouch. Every time I see an Auburnite, I want to bat him over the mazzard with his own jaw-bone. Everyone I meet has the gall to "congratulate" me on my "notoriety". Even the children (incipient little Bromides!) know I'm a poet, and make an objectionable and vociferous use of their knowledge.

I've recently secured a copy of "Rose of the Wind", and have been re-reading the book very carefully. I don't see much to the title-poem, but "Nimrod" still impresses me as it did at my first reading. I can see where it's a bit over-wrought in places, though. I think Miss Branch rather overdoes the personification of words and thoughts, effective as it is. But for a' that,[2] I think (as I may have said to you before,) that, next to you, she's about the foremost American poet.

By the way, when you write to me again, I wish you'd give me the address of the publisher of Moody's "Masque of Judgement;"[3] also the price, if possible. It's the next book that I want to add to my collection.

I both dread and desire the sight of those proofs. Deal not at all gently with them, I pray you.

Yours, affectionately,
Clark

1. "The Sierras."
2. Robert Burns (1759–1796), "For A' That and A' That" (1795).
3. William Vaughn Moody (1869–1910), *The Masque of Judgement* (1900), a poetic drama.

[43] CAS to GS [ALS]

Auburn, Cal.
Sept. 7th, 1912

Dear George:

What's the use? The current "Current Literature" quotes and praises your coyote-poem; and in "Town Talk", Witter Bynner says that he regards it as a hopeful sign in your poetical development.[1] Don't you feel like going out and kicking a jack-rabbit? I would, if I had such things said about me. It should be a warning to you not to write such verse, or at least not to publish it. That kind of work will make you famous, if you aren't careful.

I've just finished an "Ode on the Placer County Roads."[2] It isn't quite as bad as the roads, though it's pretty poor doggerel. I'll show it to you when you come up here, and have been over the road which I walk every day into Auburn. Perchance you'll appreciate it then.

The newspapers are still going it with me, it would seem. I received a mash-letter from Minneapolis today.

That's a slightly cryptic sling that Binner [*sic*] took at me in saying that my work shocked him. If he means what I'm pretty sure he means, I don't feel very kindly toward him for it. Does he think I'm the human equivalent of a five-legged kangaroo?

As ever, with affection,

Clark

1. Edward F. O'Day, "Varied Types: XC. Witter Bynner," *Town Talk* No. 1046 (7 September 1912): 7, 21. Bynner had said: "It's shocking to me to see such a young man write poetry which might be written by Sterling. . . . as Harry Lafler says, two are less than one." Bynner referred to GS and CAS as "the Star Dust Twins." Regarding Bynner's statements about GS, GS wrote to him: "Don't worry, O wandering faun! as to how I took your flippant remarks in 'Town Talk:' there was a rhinoceros among my immediate ancestry. But I think you might have spared that poor boy on the Auburn ranch. He wrote me a rather pathetic letter on the subject, saying that you evidently mistook him 'for the human equivalent of a five-legged kangaroo.' The child has a sense of humor, but not about himself." GS to Witter Bynner (11 September 1912), "George Sterling's Life at Carmel: Sterling's Letters to Witter Bynner," *Markham Review* 4, No. 1 (October 1973): 12.

2. Apparently non-extant.

[44] GS to CAS [ALS]

Carmel, Cal.,
Sept. 8, 1912.

Dear Clark:

I've gone over your proofs (to me a nerve-racking job) three times in as many successive days. But such is the instinct of the memory to supplant the eye that I'm not sure that I've caught all the errors. So be very careful yourself when R. sends these proofs to you.

I'm returning them, as per *his* request, to him to-morrow, if the express-office is open. He in turn will forward them to you—probably by express. I found but one poem in the lot that seemed to me (and I may be wrong) of much less merit than the others. Print it or not, as the fancy may seize you. Also I note that "Saturn" is not there. You'll supply the omission, I'm sure.

It's interesting, and not absolutely pleasing, to see (when one has your poems in bulk) how you are (or were) obsessed by the vision of the death of worlds and suns. I mean that you've insisted on it rather too much in the substance of your work. Also you "overwork" such words as "gyre"—even as *I* am partial to a lot of other words.

This is merely to put you on your guard for future poetry. I'd advise you to leave the abysses for awhile, and turn to the gentler aspects of nature—if only for rest & change in your own art. But if the inspiration point too directly otherwise, follow that and not my well-meant advice. "Art happens."[1]

I would have replied long ere now to your letter, but wanted to finish first with the proofs. I advise you to stand firm in the Dunlap matter. The man is evidently "impossible," and will only be a nuisance and a detriment to you in the long run. It is evident he wants to

"Ride your fame as monkeys ride a goat."[2]

Such a personality can succeed, however good the intent, only in making you absurd. See what he has done already!

I don't envy you your swanhood among the geese of Auburn. But you must grin and bear it until we can find some way out of that town for you. We must first have your book to "go by."

You can order what books you want through Robertson, with whom your credit will now be good. Make him sign a contract with you for "The Star-Treader," and don't make it for more than five years. By the way, I'd put "Nero" first in the book. Otherwise I've no suggestions as to the order of the poems. "Suit yourself."

Several persons have suggested that you drop the "Smith" from your name. I consider it a good idea; but wouldn't it hurt your father's feelings?

Houghton Mifflin & Co. are Moody's publishers. R. can get you any book you order without having to know the publisher's name, unless it's a very recent book.

I've put in lots of time hunting, since my return, as we're "a broken community" here. Got 14 rabbits near the river, early this morning. Turner will move over to his mother's house in a few days. I'll be pleased to be alone again.

I've had a week to myself, after attending to my correspondence for a week, and have written six poems already. Will send you copies of them when Mrs. S. has made them.

Please write Miss Conti what you thought of the pictures: you owe it to her.

Note the "Poetry" letter.[3] You ought to "get in" on that. Don't return *any* enclosures.

And let me hear from you before long!

Affectionately,   George.

1. See letter 8, n. 3.
2. AB, "Authority" (1889), l. 21; *Collected Works* 1910), 4.233.
3. GS refers to the founding of the Chicago magazine *Poetry,* edited by Harriet Monroe, the first issue of which appeared in October 1912.

[45] GS to CAS [ALS]

Carmel, Cal.,
Sept. 10, 1912.

Dear Clark:

You'd not mind what Bynner said if you had met him. He's a flippant critter, and doesn't mean a third of what he says. I had an apologetic letter from him yesterday, saying that he sounds like a damn fool to himself, in the interview.

I was as sure that Cur. Lit. would re-print the coyote-poem as I was sure they'd *not* re-print the Browning ode. What's the difference?

Yours ever,   George.

[46] CAS to GS [ALS]

Auburn, Cal.
Sept. 11th, 1912.

Dear George:

It's tremendously good of you to have corrected my proofs for me—rather more than I'd have had the nerve to ask you to do. I surmise that they were an awful job. To get even with me, you'll have to let me take a turn at the proofs of your next book.

It's queer that "Saturn" wasn't in the bunch. I sent a copy of it to Robertson several weeks ago, after receiving it back from the "Atlantic." The editor said it was "an interesting poem".

The amount of work in my book descriptive of the death of suns and worlds, is, I confidently expect, the chief thing the critics are going to slam me for. I was surprised myself, the other day on going over a lot of copies of my stuff, to find how much work of that nature I really had written. Not that I at all regret the writing and publication of these poems. But I'm conscious that they'll lay me open to some unfavourable criticism. I'll get the reputation of being a sort of cosmic decadent—a sidereal Baudelaire.

To my imagination, no other natural event seems half as portentous as the going out of a sun. I admit that I have been, and still am, obsessed by visions of stupendous dooms—of blotching suns and whitening worlds hushed and slow in the black night of space. But I agree with you that I'd best quit writing about such things, at least for awhile. I think I shall make a few ventures into the realms of wonder and terror; also, of course, I shall write some nature-verse.

I'm very glad to hear that you're at work again; and I'm eager to see the poems you speak of sending me. "The Master Mariner", which you enclose, is good, but I don't think it's goodness surpasses the point of salability. I'd like to see you writing some more lyrics like "White Magic," and "The Gardens of the Sea," or sonnets like "Of Yesterday", and "The Sibyl of Dreams." I've never lost the first, fresh sense of wonder that these poems gave me. They're "a garden of eternal dews".[1]

I'm glad to hear of the new magazine devoted to poetry. It's encouraging that such a thing should be possible.

I shall write to Miss Conti. I'm glad you reminded me of it. By the way, have you a picture of yourself that you could send me? I haven't any regular one, except some clipped from magazines several years old.

That's a tremendous bag of rabbits that you speak of getting. I couldn't nail that many here in a week. The hunting (of all kinds) is rather sparse around Auburn.

Affectionately,
Clark

1. GS, "Justice," l. 51. In *HO*.

[47] CAS to GS [ALS]

Auburn, Cal.
Sept. 15th, 1912.

Dear George:

I received the proofs Friday afternoon, and have been wrestling with them most of the time since. I've been over them twice, and found more errors the second time than I did the first. I shall go over them again, and make a separate inspection of each letter, I think. Thanks to you, though, I found the worst errors all corrected, and several of my faultiest lines already remedied. However, I've found enough others that needed changing, and a sufficient number of printer's errors, to be able to sympathize with you when you speak of the task as nerve-racking. The worst of it is, that I fear I haven't detected them all yet.

"Lineage" is a good sonnet. It's all good, though some of the lines in the octave seem especially admirable. "Babylon"[1] contains rather more truth than poetry. It should sell to Collier's Weekly, which I don't mean altogether as a slam. The poem is striking and effective, especially in form.

It's interesting that you should have picked out "The Wind and the Moon" as the poorest poem in the book. It's an earlier poem than any of the others, and was written rather more than two years ago. To me it seems that there are several others in the collection just as inferior, if not more so. I'll leave them in as measuring-sticks for the excellence of the better poems.

I shall stick to the "Smith". You're right in thinking that my father would feel hurt if I dropped it. Really, I don't see why the name shouldn't prove rather an asset, in the long run. No one of that name has become especially famous in poetry so far.

"Saturn" is to go into the book, but the proofs aren't ready yet.

I read my "Ode to Music" before a local woman's club yesterday,[2] where I was the only male person present. It was an interesting, and possibly amusing, experience, though I was too tired from a morning of proof-correction, and too nervous anyway, to feel very appreciative at the time. And the audience was mostly lemons.

Yours ever, with love,
Clark.

1. CAS refers to GS's poem "In the Market-Place," in which each stanza begins with a variation of the line "In Babylon, high Babylon."
2. See *Placer County Republican* (26 September 1912): 1.

[48] GS to CAS [ALS]

Carmel, Cal.,
Sept. 15, 1912.

Dear Clark:

I suppose that by now you've received your proofs, and found that I've not been especially severe in my comments or suggestions. And you'll doubtless find that I've overlooked more than one printer's-error.

Sorry, but I've no picture of me, yet. The Contis were too busy to take me when I passed thro' S. F. on my way home, as they'd just returned from a three-weeks vacation. But I'll have some taken the next time I am in S. F., and of course will send you one.

No news here—everything is dull and quiet; even the skies are overcast, and the wind a very shy prowler. We had a spell of hot weather last week, though. I couldn't write a line while it lasted.

Here are a few poems. Mullgardt, architect of the South Court of the Panama-Pacific Exposition, wants me to write a play for it.[1] There should be big money in it, but I fear I can't descend to what would be a popular success. Which isn't meant as a brag.

I'm going for some mussels soon.

Affectionately,   George.

[Enclosures: "Finis" (original title for "'Omnia Exeunt in Mysterium'"), "The Golden Past."]

1. Louis Christian Mullgardt (1866–1942) was a leading California architect who designed the Memorial Museum in Golden Gate Park, many private homes on the Pacific Coast, and the "court of Ages" of the Panama-Pacific International Exposition. GS did not write a play, but did write an *Ode* (1915) for the exposition.

[49] CAS to GS [ALS]

Auburn, Cal.
Sept. 20th, 1912.

Dear George:

Thanks for the new poems. They're all good, but I think I like "Finis" perhaps the best of the lot. I much prefer the second sonnet of "The Golden Past", to the first, some lines of which I think might be re-written to advantage, notably the sixth. In the sestet, I think "enormities" would be slightly better than "atrocities", though the suggestion may be hypercritical. That's an awfully expressive line at the end of the second sonnet.[1]

I shall have some poems to send to you after I've seen my book through the press. I understand that I'll have to go over the final proofs; and I haven't yet received the first proofs of "Saturn." Have they been sent to you yet?

I think I'll write another dramatic lyric, somewhat like "Nero", with "Satan Unrepentant" for the title and subject. I've only the vaguest idea as to what it'll be like; but the subject seems rather promising. I certainly shan't present the conventional conception of Satan, nor the terrors of a "fire-and-brimstone" inferno. I've the impulse to make something out of it that'll frizzle the untonsured sections of a few priestly pates, if I can do this without any sacrifice of poetic beauty or sublimity.

Is the edition of Nora May's book all sold out yet? I've the impression that you told me it was; but I'm not sure. Some people here have been asking me about it.

Yours ever, with affection,
Clark

1. "The Golden Past," 2.14: ". . . Welded in dumb convulsions of delight."

[50] GS to CAS [ALS]

Carmel, Cal.,
Sept. 24, 1912.

Dear Clark:

By now you'll have received the "Saturn" proofs. Robertson in his last letter to me said that he expected to have the book out in "about three weeks." But you never can tell, with Robertson.

I've "wasted" the last two weeks in various follies. Hope to be well enough to do some more work in a day or two. I rather expect Bynner here this week, which will mean some more mis-spent days.

About Nora May's book—there were a few copies still on sale @ $1.²⁵ some months ago. I have quite a number of them that I'll sell @ $1.⁰⁰ to anyone with enough sense half-way to appreciate them.

I seem unable to sell any more of this year's poems, and suppose they're either too long or too gloomy. Magazines do not want sonnets, anyhow, as the swine who make up 90% of their clientele think sonnets are "high brow." Lord help us poets! I suppose I'll have to take to the road-agent business.[1]

Yours affectionately,   George.

1. *Road-agent* was a slang term for a highway robber.

[51] CAS to GS [ALS]

Auburn, Cal.
Sept. 26th, 1912.

Dear George:

I've gone over the proofs of "Saturn," and have returned them to Robertson, with a few changes. For the last line, to which you objected, read: "Against their march, with the diminished stars."

The weather here has been uncomfortably warm for the last few weeks, though the housefly, in his swift and musical multitude, doesn't seem to mind it at all. My inspiration seems rather sodden under the influence of the weather, and the cold that's been hanging to me ever since I returned here from San Francisco. The latter has sapped my vitality a bit, I suspect.

I sent a bunch of poems to the new poetry magazine, and have just received a letter from the editor saying that she intends to accept several of them. That's one rift in the grey, at least. Also, the Board of Education here has decided to put my book in the libraries of all the schools of the county. Doesn't that appeal to your funny-bone? I'm not altogether without honour here, otherwise: one of the local citizens was heard to admit lately that I might be able to write if I had a good education ... They can't get over the fact here that I never attended High School.

I feel tempted to do a little road-agenting myself. The Sacramento motor-cars that I have to pass every day, make me feel like a red anarchist; and the blatant optimism of the Bromide is an unctuous and unremitted offense to my nostrils.

I wish there were a hall for magazine-editors and their public, in which, for a few hundred thousand years, they could be made to see themselves as you and I see them.

I'm enclosing a couple of new poems, the best of the few that I've written lately.

Lovingly,
Clark.

[Enclosures: "A Fragment"(= "The Last Goddess"?), one other poem.]

[52] GS to CAS [ALS]

Carmel, Cal.,
Oct. 4, 1912.

Dear Clark:

Thanks for the poems, one of which I return with a suggestion. I have none to make on the other, so am keeping it. It's a beautiful thing, tho "nenuphar" is a bit puzzling[1]—I had to look it up in the dictionary.

All's well along the Carmel, tho' I'm a bit lonesome. I've written a few negligible verses lately, but have as yet no copies to send you, as Mrs. Sterling seems to have struck a lazy streak. I don't feel so very much like writing, this fall.

I've received the first number of "Poetry," but wasn't greatly impressed by the contents, except in the case of Moody's poem, which had some fine passages.[2]

Witter Bynner is to visit me "most any day" now. I'm wondering how he'll like my cooking! But we'll eat otherwhere, mostly.

Have been here six weeks, and have no prospects of leaving. This is my tenth letter to-day, so it must be a short one.

Affectionately, as ever,   George.

[P.S.] Don't use "Mr." with my address. It's insulting![3]

1. CAS uses the word in "Echo of Memnon" (sent to GS, 30 December 1912) and "The Last Goddess" (subtitled "A Fragment"), both in *EC*.

2. William Vaughn Moody's "I Am the Woman," was published in the first issue of *Poetry* (October 1912).

3. Ironically, GS opened his letters to AB, from 1903 until as recently as 1911, with "Dear Master," which AB said "makes me wince a little."

[53] CAS to GS [ALS]

Auburn, Cal.
Oct. 5th, 1912.

Dear George:

Here's a new poem, "Satan Unrepentant", which owes a certain deductible debt to John Milton, but is a somewhat more direct justification of the devil than "Paradise Lost." It might have created a row fifty years ago; but I hardly think it would to-day. Still, such a poem seems to me worth writing, for I'm not aware that anything exactly of the same kind has been done.

I'd like to know if you advise submitting the thing anywhere. I think of trying it on the English Review.

I've no especial news, except that "Nero" (a newspaper copy of it, I suppose) is being studied as a classic in the local High School. I hadn't counted on winning the hatred of Young America quite so soon!

I wish that book of mine were out, and done with. Robertson is slower than an anemic tortoise.

Write to me when you feel like it.

Yours, affectionately,
Clark.

[Enclosure: "Satan Unrepentant."]

[54] CAS to GS [ALS]

Auburn, Cal.

Oct. 13th, 1912.

Dear George:

I've just sent my last batch of final proofs back to Robertson. So I suppose the book will be out ere "old age shall this generation waste".[1] A. M. says, in about two weeks—which means the first of November at the earliest.

Have you seen the crack that "Current Literature" took at me in its last issue?[2] The "blue King owl" who runs the "Poetry Column", said about what I expected he'd say. He evidently thought it his duty to whittle me down a bit from the magnitude given me by the S. F. newspapers.

I've seen the first issue of "Poetry," and like Moody's poem; also "The Mexican Garden"[3] thing; the others didn't amount to much. I've a letter from Miss Harriet Monroe accepting four of my things,[4] and have found the fly in this particular honey-pot; which is, that "Poetry" doesn't pay until publication; and not at such a superlative rate even then (about ten dollars a page).

The Bromide, couchant and rampant, still maintains his pestiferous abundance hereabouts. He's at his worst when most thickly disguised, sometimes, as in the case of a certain horrid old humbug, on whom I made a semi-annual call the other day. He has written books (one of them a romance) and is a shrewd-looking little monkey who has accumulated money (not from the sale of his books) and a handsome wife.

I've been reading a volume of Lafcadio Hearn lately, and the poems of William Watson.[5] I never get tired of Hearn. "Gleanings from Buddha-Fields", the book I'm reading, contains, with other excellent things, a tremendously cosmic essay on "Dust". I rather like Watson; "Lachrymae Musarum", an elegy on Tennyson, seems to me a noble poem, and much the best of his that I've read.

Yours ever, affectionately

Clark.

1. Keats, "Ode on a Grecian Urn" (1819), l. 46.

2. In the "Recent Poetry" column of *Current Literature* 53, No. 4 (October 1912): 473–74, CAS's poems "The Abyss Triumphant" and "Nero" were quoted. The poetry editor (unidentified) wrote that "a reading of the poems in question, while it reveals a genuine talent and a mastery of words remarkable in so young a writer, fails to justify the superlative praise which has come from some of the California newspapers" (p. 473).

3. Grace Hazard Conkling, "Symphony of a Mexican Garden," *Poetry* (October 1912).

4. *Poetry* published "The Sorrow of the Winds" [as "Sorrowing of Winds"], "Remembered Light," "In the Wind," and "Fire and Snow." In reviewing *ST*, Harriett Monroe stated: "In spite of the sophomoric quality in many of these poems we have here a rare spirit and the promise of poetic art" ("Recent Poetry," *Poetry* 2, No. 1 [April 1913]: 32).

5. Lafcadio Hearn (1850–1904), *Gleanings in Buddha-Fields: Studies of Hand and Soul in the Far East* (Boston: Houghton Mifflin, 1897); Sir William Watson (1858–1935), British poet; *Lachrymae Musarum* (1892).

[55] GS to CAS [ALS]

Carmel, Cal.,
Oct. 15, 1912.

Dear Clark:

Your "Satan Unrepentant" seems to me a great and noble poem, and one which I would certainly force the magazines to refuse or accept. Send it to any English periodicals that seem "possible," and at the same time, on this side of the sea, to the "Atlantic," "Scribners," "Century" and "Forum," in the order named.

Forgive me for not writing till now. I've had considerable company, a combination that always knocks out my letter-writing. I'm keeping this copy you send, as I want one very much, and have but one suggestion to make. That's on the word "rumored:" it's excellent onomatopoetically, but hardly satisfies one's *mind*. There are better words, I think: try for one.[1]

Thanks for the Visiak bit—a hair-raiser![2] I'll keep that too unless you want it. Imagine trying such a poem on any of the magazines noted above! Except possibly the "Forum."

Yes I saw the "Cur. Lit." effusion. "What can you expect from a pig but a grunt?" They evidently rank my "coyote poem" far ahead of "Nero!" I wish they'd had to [*sic*] decency to run the latter unmutilated—they were not fair to you.[3] But you'll have to expect that, and worse, so long as you write poetry, and especially long poems. However, you'll grin and bear it.

I've not tried to write lately. The quail law goes off to-day, and in the afternoon Turner and I are to have a grand massacre.

Here is a negligible sonnet. I've a dozen things about ¾ finished. "Not yet but soon."

As ever, affectionately,   George.

[Enclosure: unidentified sonnet.]

1. "Satan Unrepentant," l. 72: "With rumored thunder and enormous groan . . ."
2. E. H. Visiak (1878–1972), British poet and novelist; author of the classic weird novel *Medusa* (1929). The poem in question was possibly "The Skeleton at the Feast," in *The Phantom Ship and Other Poems* (1912).
3. *Current Literature* had quoted ll. 1–10, 38–52, and 76–96 of the 96-line poem.

[56] CAS to GS [ALS]

Auburn, Cal.
Oct. 18th, 1912

Dear George:

Thanks for the new sonnet, which is by no means "negligible." I'm eager to see some of the others you speak of.

I enclose one ("Namelessness") out of a bunch of brief lyrics that I've written lately. It seems to me to stand out of the average. Don't ever return any poems that I send you unless you have a number of criticisms to make.

There's one slight alteration for "Satan Unrepentant": In the general sense in which I used the word, "apocalyptic" shouldn't have been capitalized. I don't think of any likely substitute for "rumored" just at present.

There's some compensation (for having to live here) in the prolonged sunsets and gorgeous twilights that we've been having lately. I wish you could see them: they last for half an hour, I should judge, and go through a rapid graduation of changes—saffron, red-gold, umber, pale crimson, and scarlet, and diffuse at last into a violet afterglow that covers half the sky. I noticed olive-green and glaucous clouds one evening . . . The condition is probably due to the amount of smoke in the air from extensive forest fires in this and the neighboring county, El-Dorado. There's a terrific one on the rampage just across the river from here, now. It'll be a spectacle for Nero to-night, if it can keep it up.

> Yours, affectionately,
> Clark.

[Enclosure: "Namelessness."]

[57] GS to CAS [ALS]

> Carmel, Cal.,
> Oct. 26, 1912.

Dear Clark:

Your lyric is a delicate and beautiful one. I've no suggestions to make about it, except a half-wish that you'd add another verse and make it a little less tenuous.

I've not written anything of late. Have just had Witter Bynner here for five days. We put in part of them at Harry Leon Wilson's. Read his serial in the Sat. Even. Post:[1] it's well worth it.

And read Masefield's "Dauber" in the English Review for Oct.,[2] if your library takes it. It's a tremendous poem, and makes my own work seem so dead and artificial by comparison that I feel like a pretender, and am more than tempted not to write any more verse. He weds beauty to life as it has never been done before.

I have my hunt almost every afternoon. Got 2 ducks, 4 rabbits and a quail, yesterday, then sliced a fore-finger cleaning them,—a revenge the poor creatures would doubtless think inadequate.

I've several letters to write, so farewell!

> Affectionately,   George.

[Enclosure: "From the Mountain."]

1. Wilson's *His Majesty, Bunker Bean* was serialized in the *Saturday Evening Post* (12 October–14 December 1912). It appeared in book form in 1913.
2. John Masefield (1878–1967), *Dauber, English Review* 12 (October 1912): 337–89, a long poem about a sailor who aspires to be an artist.

[58] CAS to GS [ALS]

> Auburn, Cal.
> Oct. 29th, 1912

Dear George:

Thanks for the new lyric ("From the Mountain"). It's good, and, it seems to me, especially musical. The form is effective; I don't remember seeing just such a stanza used before. Here's a list of the other poems that you've sent me since my return here: "In the Market-Place", "Discord", "The Golden Past", "Finis," "Lineage", "The Setting", and "The Master Mariner." I'll be awfully glad to have the omissions you speak of.

I'm rather surprised to hear anything good of Masefield. The English Review is totally unobtainable here, so I've no way of seeing the particular poem you speak of. But I've seen extracts from other "poems" of Masefield's, and hardly a line of his that struck me as being much better than doggerel. I'm incredulous that anyone with real poetic power or conscience should have the unadulterated gall to try to pass such stuff off as poetry. It isn't especially objectionable in itself, but when it becomes possible for such work to be confounded with poetry—well, it's about time for another Deluge, or a revolution.

But if Masefield is doing such work as you say he is, I think I'll give up trying to write, too. I don't seem to be getting ahead much. In my present mood, my stuff sounds like a tinkling of tin when I compare it with Milton or Poe. I'm being forced to the belief that no one else has ever written, or ever will write, blank verse comparable to that of "Paradise Lost". I think Milton has been equalled for sublimity and imagination; but not for his tremendous and consummate mastery of blank-verse rhythms. I remember someone calling his verse-structure Gothic; that describes it better than any adjective I can think of myself.

I'm enclosing "The Titans in Tartarus," which won't prove very startling to you. I've begun another thing, "The Titans Triumphant", which may run to 200 lines or so. It should be better than the poem I enclose. I shall give the old gods a well-earned rest after I've finished it; and I think I'll leave off blank verse for awhile, too.

As ever, affectionately,

Clark.

[Enclosure: "The Titans in Tarturus."]

[59] GS to CAS [ALS]

Carmel, Cal.,
Nov. 11, 1912.

Dear Clark:

How the days hurry past! I've been here *over* eleven weeks now—my longest stay here. I'm going up to Berkeley, tho', for Thanksgiving, in either one week or two: I'm waiting for the Heron baby to arrive. Any day now.

I've not written a line in two months—simply don't feel like it. Harpers took my "Night Sentries," on condition of my cutting out two stanzas, so they could get it all on one page!

Jimmy Hopper's in New York now, but will be out here by January, when we expect to put in three weeks or so at London's, at which time *you* must come there. I'd like to drop in on you, but see no likelihood so far. I'm eagerly awaiting your book. It seems incredible that anyone should be so slow as R.

I guess I've sent you all my latest verses, except possibly the enclosed sonnet. Your own "Titans in Tartarus" I like, for there are some big lines in it, and the whole visualization is sublime. But it is not nearly as good as your poem on the marching Titans—I forget its exact title. I especially like

"Left to the barren and devouring dust,"
"And phantoms pointing at eternal gulfs," and
"All iris that enchants the sunset foam."
I should have "copped" that last one.

Some of what you say about *some* of Masefield's work is "true," as things seem true to you and to me. But his "Dauber," while characteristic of him, is far greater than his other work, in not being squalid and in having a far greater element of beauty. The scene is on a ship going around the Horn, you see, and he knows his ocean wonderfully, as London has already written me. I'll send it to you when I can.

I still hunt a good deal, and lately got 10 mallards in two shots—a record! Turner expects to go to Mexico soon. I don't envy him.

My sister Avis was married Saturday, I believe. Affectionately,
George.

[Enclosure: unidentified sonnet.]

[60] CAS to GS [ALS]

Auburn, Cal.
Nov. 13th, 1912.

Dear George:

I've just received several copies of "The Star-Treader["] from Robertson, and am sending you one of them. It's a relief to have the book out at last, for I've had it hanging over my head ever since September, the first date that Robertson set for bringing it out.

The poems read rather better to me in book-form. The binding is surprisingly good—much more beautiful than I really expected it to be. I found only one error persisting in the text—"contrained["] for "constrained" in "To the Sun["].[1]

Thanks for your good sonnet. It is good—but not very, very good.

Your remarks on "The Titans in Tartarus" are entirely just. The thing is decidedly inferior to ["]Saturn["]. However, I believe I shall do some better work presently.

I wish you *would* drop in on me, before January. Really, why can't you? I'd like to have you here for Christmas. Believe me, my father can make an English plum-pudding that's worth while.

I got up at half-past six this morning, and saw a good sunrise over the Sierras—a long rose-red sky above a hundred odd miles of indigo mountains. It looked like the Judgement Day climbing over the outermost rim of things. I wish you could have seen it.

Now that I'm laid open to the critics forevermore, I wonder how many of them will damn "The Star-Treader." It might be interesting to know—to a crank on statistics ... I shall watch the poetry columns of "Current Literature" with a rapt interest, though, to see if the editor says what I'm quite sure that he will say.[2] I'll bet you a bone collar-button that he'll quote "Averted Malefice" and "The Medusa of the Skies," and let the book go at that.

Affectionately,
Clark.

1. 1. 13 (the reading is correct in *SP*). CAS corrected by hand this and other errors in "Nero" (*close* for *bind* in l. 13) and "Ode to the Abyss" (*indivisible* for *invisible* in l. 16).
2. See letter 74, n. 4.

[61] GS to CAS [ALS]

Sunday A.M.
[postmarked 17 November 1912]

Dear Clark:

I'm up here for a week or two of debauchery, and have your letter in my trunk. I'll reply to it soon: this is just to tell you to ignore the rather mean and entirely stupid comments of "Town Talk."[1] I'll drop in on that bunch in a couple of days and give them Hell. The worst of it is, that in the case of a book so far above the heads of the majority, you are in for remarks even more crass and idiotic.

I got the book, and was glad to see that R. had given your poems so pretty a dress. The stuff seems even better, in book-form. I'm going to get a good many folk to buy it during the two or three weeks I'm here. I am usually pretty well bored by persons, and so am inscrupulous in asking them to spend their money as I see fit.

Carmel was lovely when I left. Did I tell you that Mrs. Heron had her child, a fine 8 lb. boy? "Mother and child are progressing as well as could be expected." The kid is so healthy that it rarely cries.

I fear I'll have no chance to see you at Christmas time. It is then that I have the least to say as to my movements, owing to friends, relatives & other enemies.

Keep a stout heart and do not mind the buzzing of the gnats.

Affectionately, George.

1. "The Spectator" [Theodore Bonnet], "'The Star Treader'" [review], *Town Talk* No. 1056 (16 November 1912): 12–13.

[62] CAS to GS [ALS]

Auburn, Cal.
Nov. 19th, 1912.

Dear George:

I don't especially mind the thing in "Town Talk:" For the most part, it seems a rather dull and silly attempt to be funny at my expense; otherwise, it's merely nasty. I'll be extremely lucky if I receive no worse treatment. In fact, I've already received worse treatment, and from one of the Auburn papers, too, which, in attempting to praise me up, said things that were in even poorer taste than some of "Town Talk's" remarks.[1]

"Town Talk" is a stinking rag, and no mistake, but it did me good service last Summer in "manhandling" Dunlap. I'd have had some trouble "shaking" that Hun, if it hadn't been for their little write-up of the affair. Dunlap blamed it all upon you and me, and was extremely wroth because I wouldn't re-establish him as my "discoverer." I've had no communication with the man since.

I'm very sorry to hear that you can't come up next month. But perhaps you can make it later.

Yours, affectionately,

Clark.

1. [Unsigned,] "Junior Poet of the Sierras," *Placer Herald* (16 November 1912): 4. This was followed by "Book of Poems by Local Poet," *Placer County Republican* (23 November 1912): 1

[63] GS to CAS [ALS]

Carmel, Cal.,
Dec. 9, 1912.

Dear Clark:

I've been up in the city for three weeks' dissipation, so am behind with my correspondence.

I trust you're not being offended by the inevitable idiocies of the critics. Garnett's review[1] was not nearly as bad as I expected it to be. I've seen no others, so far.

The book *has* been well bound and printed. I've given away several copies so far, and have been the cause of many others being bought. Robertson told me the book was selling well. Of course he meant "well" for a book of poems.

It's good to be back in Carmel. As soon as I've disposed of about thirty letters, I'm going to buckle down to a few poems, as I have orders for some. I'd like to be up your way about Christmas time, but see no chance for it, as I have to be with Mrs. S. then. I want you to be at London's with me and Hopper some time in Jan. or Feb. I'll arrange for your fare.

It's rather cold here, as there has been no rain for so long. I still go hunting afternoons, usually in the river and marsh, as there are ducks there now. I got four and Turner three, a day or two ago. And of course one can always get plenty of rabbits.

I suppose you saw in the last Friday's "Examiner" that I got one of the second prizes in "The Lyric Year" contest. (Of course I didn't make most of the remarks attributed to me in the interview). The $250. almost paid up my debts! I've read the book, and find much good work in it, tho' few great lines. The first prize was justly given to Johns.[2] Many of the poems in the book should never have been accepted. It makes me sick to think of some that they took in place of your great "Nero" and Heron's fine "Departures." But when it comes to editors and critics, I throw up my hands and quit—or vomit.

I got the prize on two "second choice" votes by E. J. Wheeler (Current Lit.) and Braithwaite. Ferd. Earle (the book's editor) didn't even give me a third mention. It was he who dug up the $1000.

Well, write soon, and tell me that the stupidity of critics is tending but to your own illumination.

Yours ever,   George.

1. Porter Garnett, "Notes & Book Reviews—Comments: A Young and True Poet," *San Francisco Call* (1 December 1912): 6.
2. "Second Avenue" by Orrick Johns (1887–1946) won the Lyric Year contest.

[64] CAS to GS [ALS]

Auburn, Cal.
Dec. 13th, 1912

Dear George:

I rejoice to say that I survive all onsets of the critics to date. If the reviews on this coast are a fair sample, the dictionary will be rather well de-boned for verbs of abuse, by the time the eastern cohorts of critics are through. One reviewer, in the San Josè [*sic*] *Mercury*, speaks of the "sinister" and "ghoulish" qualities of much of my work, and particularly of the "vicious spirit" animating the sonnet, "Retrospect and Forecast."[1] I've seen only one really decent review so far,—one by Herbert Bashford in the "Bulletin" for Nov. 30th[2] . . . I feel sorry that so many who are doubtless otherwise quite inoffensive citizens, should be led to make such blatant exhibitions of themselves, in ill-advisedly attempting to criticize my work. But even the ass and the zebra have opinions, I suppose, and must bring them out to air on occasion.

Congratulations on the prize! I rather think you should have gotten the first one, though. I saw some things quoted from the "Lyric Year" in "Current Literature," but wasn't greatly impressed by them.

I enclose a rather fantastic experiment, in which I've tried the irregular repetition of lines and phrases, and a desultory rhyming of words with themselves. I don't remember seeing it done this way before—only in an arbitrary stanza, as in Poe. I don't know that I've succeeded in making anything of it. However, the experiment may interest (or amuse) you. I've given it an improvised Latin title, in desperation at not being able to find a suitable English one. If my Latin is incorrect, I wish you'd tell me. It should be correct, tho, if there's any truth in dictionaries.

Yours, with affection,
Clark.

[Enclosure: *"Luna Aeternalis."*]

1. John Jury, "*The Star Treader* [*sic*]: A Book of Verse by Clark Ashton Smith." *San Jose Mercury and Herald* (8 December 1912), magazine section: 2.
2. Herbert Bashford (1871–1928), "The Latest in Literature: Clark Smith's Poems. Wonderful Lyrics Deserve Recognition with World's Best," *San Francisco Bulletin* (30 November 1912): 14.

[65] CAS to GS [ALS]

Auburn, Cal.
Dec. 16th, 1912.

Dear George:

The enclosed money-order is for a copy of Nora May's book. I believe you told me that you'd sell the copies you have for a dollar each; and I've found someone here who wants one.

I've seen no reviews of my book lately. I can't afford to subscribe to a clipping bureau; perhaps it's just as well that I can't, if the other reviews are like the ones that I've seen.

On looking over the poem that I sent you the other day, I find several changes suggesting themselves. I've altered the first line to read: "On the way of a vain dream driven," and the seventh to "That, cloven to shadow and sheen, upsprang." The old seventh line was pretty ambiguous; and perhaps I haven't got the meaning entirely clear yet. The "dull iron" is the dark half of the moon. I've also changed the beginning of the second stanza to read thus:

> "Self-shadowed half, upstood the moon,
>   Yea, tarnished half; but soon
> Had her soft light stilled the stars to croon,
> Had her low light, etc."

> Yours, ever,
>   Clark.

[66] GS to CAS [ALS]

Carmel, Cal.,
Dec. 18, 1912.

Dear Clark:
    Thanks for the order for the book. I'm sending it by "even mail."
    The improvements that you make in the poem are all excellent ones. The poem itself should (or might) have been discovered in one of Poe's old trunks—if the poor fellow had any. In fact, it's so absolutely an echo of Poe that it's more of a curiosity than a credit to you. But soon you will be beyond the "derivative" stage.
    I don't subscribe to a clipping bureau either—it's not worth it. But Robertson does, and you can see your reviews there, as I've seen many of mine. Once will probably be enough for you, as it was for me. I didn't find the "San Jose Mercury" one so *very* unjust. Jury is a good deal of a Christian, and writes from a peculiar point of view. Lend me the "Bulletin" review: I'd like to see what the toadlike Bashford had to say. I thought he'd knock you, as he and I do not get on well together.
    I think I was very lucky in getting even a 2nd prize in that contest. There were kicks as to the decisions in the last "N. Y. Times Book Review."[1] As Mrs. S. knew of the award, the money had to be applied to my debts: I had devised pleasanter ways of disbursing it.
    Your Latin title is all right, I suppose: I'd a dim recollection that the adjective was aeternus-a-um, but suppose my memory's at fault. The poem is very weird, poetical and impressive. It's only fault is the "too much Poe." His exact spirit, in fact.
        Affectionately,   George.

1. See Jessie B. Rittenhouse, "The Lyric Year," *New York Times Review of Books* (1 December 1912): 746. In the article Rittenhouse delivers a mixed but on the whole favorable verdict on GS's poem.

[67] CAS to GS [ALS]

Auburn, Cal.
Dec. 20th, 1912

Dear George:
        Enclosed find the Bashford review, which you wished to see. I'd like you to return it to me though, when you've read it.

You're quite right about "Luna Aeternalis". The thing is very much like Poe—far more so than I realized when I wrote it, and than I consciously intended it to be. It should be excellent material for a hoax if I had the inclination, and the facilities for "pulling it off."

I think I understand how I came to write the poem. For a long while I've had the inclination, or desire, to try my hand at something very weird and musical. I'd no definite idea—only occasional lines and phrases which had come to me at odd times,—when I sat down to the composition of the poem. But my subconsciousness, obedient to the desire of the conscious mind, seems already to have shaped the poem, and I had little difficulty in writing it, though I did not really know, when I wrote down the first two lines, what the third was to be about. That the thing is so much in the spirit and manner of Poe, must of course be due to the fact that when I first conceived the desire to compose such a poem, I (more or less consciously) had Poe's work in mind as the ideal, or perfection of the weird in poetry. My subconsciousness, like a good and faithful, but over-zealous servant, went to work accordingly.

Yours, affectionately,
Clark.

[68] CAS to GS [ALS]

Auburn, Cal.
Dec. 30th, 1912

Dear George:

A thousand thanks for the copy of "Shapes of Clay!"[1] You could scarcely have picked anything to please me better . . . Bierce is a much finer serious poet than almost anyone gives him the credit of being.

There's no news here of any moment. Indeed, I might say that things are a wee bit monotonous. The stillness of the tomb stalked forth long ago to claim Auburn; so there's little to be hoped for from that quarter, in the way of diversion. An attack of biliousness, in close league with the hammering demons of headache, is about the only diversion I've had lately.

I sold a poem the other day, to a magazine called the "Yale Review."[2] I enclose a copy of the poem, which I don't think I've sent you before; and one or two other late lyrics of mine. I hardly think they'll startle you. I've been pretty slack and negligent these latter months, and haven't forced myself to write much. I should write all the better this coming year, for the rest I've been giving myself. I've a feeling that I may do something even better than "Nero," before next Summer. I seem to write best in the months when the earth is returning toward the sun.

The "English Review" recently acquired the distinction of refusing "Satan Unrepentant." The thing is in the hands of the "Atlantic Monthly" at present. Schauffler wrote me (after I'd mailed "Satan Unrepentant") that he'd gotten the editor of the Atlantic interested in me, and that I'd better send in something . . . I'm a-wondering . . .

I shall go on with "The Titans Triumphant" presently. It's a thing I began several months ago. It should be better than "The Titans in Tartarus," anyway, for the action that I shall put into it. You'll easily see the possibilities of that kind in the idea.

Yours, affectionately,
Clark

[Enclosures: "Dream-Mystery," "Echo of Memnon," "The Nereid."]

1. See CAS to Herbert Bashford, 15 January 1913, *Selected Letters*, ed. David E. Schultz and Scott Connors (Sauk City, WI: Arkham House, 2003), p. 18.
2. "The Nereid."

[69] GS to CAS [ALS]

Jan. 4 / 13.

Dear Clark:

Your letter received, but it's over in Berkeley, so I'll not try to answer it until I return to Carmel—about the 9th. This is only to ask you to autograph a book of yours I'm sending by even mail. Please write in it

To Albert M. Bender, from his friend

Clark Ashton Smith

if you don't mind relaxing to that extent. You met him, you'll remember, when here. And he has bought several of your books to give to his friends.

Yours ever,   George.

[P.S.] A happy new year to you and your parents!

[70] CAS to GS [ALS]

Auburn, Cal.
Jan. 6th, 1913.

Dear George:

I'm returning you the book which you sent me, autographed according to directions. I've pleasant memories of our friend Bender.

It's been colder than an Eskimo hell here for the last few days,—something really phenomenal in the way of temperature. The glass was down to about fifteen above zero last night—pretty chilly for a country that's been extensively advertised as an orange-growing belt. The Sierras look like a stranded fleet of icebergs armored with putrefied snow, and the gale that's blowing off of them feels as if it had been refrigerated in the cellars of the North Pole since the days of the Patriarchs. The weather is all right otherwise—clear as a dome of crystal; but the cold is a matter of discomfort to me.

Yours ever, with affection,
Clark.

[71] GS to CAS [ALS]

Carmel, Cal.,
Jan. 11, 1913.

Dear Clark:

This unprecedented cold is bothering me too, tho' probably in a less degree than it does you. Some of my vines and plants seem to have died, and there's snow on the mountains to the south and east—tho' not to compare for an instant with the view you must have of the great Sierras.

Thank you for inscribing Bender's book. I'll return you the Bashford review as soon as Garnett returns it to me. He is certainly "strong" for you—and his natural tastes are not along your "lines" at all. Why don't you write and thank him for the review?[1] It was the old custom, and I occasionally revert to it, in the case of an unusually kind review.

If you sell anything to the "Atlantic" you'll do more than I've ever been able to do—and I've sent them most of my best stuff. The paper seems to be run by a gang of old women.

Your "Echo of Memnon" is a fine and impressive lyric, and your "Dream-Mystery" is beautiful indeed. But above and beyond them both is this exquisite poem "The Nereid." I wish I could do as well before I die; but I guess I've done my best work. Anyhow, I can see the perfection in that of others, thank Fate!

I'm not going to send you any more of my weak stuff. It's no fair return. I've no corrections to suggest as to these three lyrics—you seem to have found a very straight path to beauty.

I have a bird-dog now, and go hunting every afternoon. So life has its compensations.

Hopper will be out here by Feb. 1st. We may go up to London's during that month, and then I want you to run over for a week.

I still owe a score of letters, Heaven pity me!

Affectionately,　George.

1. AB, *Shapes of Clay* (San Francisco: W. E. Wood, 1903), a book of poetry largely financed by GS. The same publisher brought out the first edition of GS's *TS* in the same year.

[71a] CAS to GS [non-extant]

[Auburn, Cal.
January 1913]

[72] GS to CAS [ALS]

Carmel, Cal.,
Jan. 21, 1913.

Dear Clark:

I've been down the coast at Wilson's for several days, loafing when I should be at work. But I finished a short-story just before I left.[1]

That *is* a high compliment that the editor of the "Atlantic" paid you. I have at last succeeded in selling them a poem—"Willy Pitcher." guess I've sent it to you. I'm sorry no better magazine than the "Yale Review" took the beautiful "Nereid." And I fear you'll get little or nothing for it.

This last poem you send is one of the finest things you have ever written. Evidently you don't think so; but you will some day. It's the very spirit of poetry, and weird beyond Poe's work, even. I'll write further of it when I've got it back from Mrs.

S., to whom I sent it, to have her make me some typed copies (I suppose you don't mind my showing it to the discerning).

The weather here is moderating, thank God! I expect to go down for abalones in an hour or so. And the salmon have begun to run up the Carmel. Several men (mostly Mexicans) are always watching at the river-mouth with spears.

I've not written a poem for a week, and only one since my arrival here two weeks ago. I sent you my sonnet, "The Thirst of Satan," I guess, in December.

To what magazines did you send "Nereid" before the Y. R. took it? It will be interesting to know—the bats and moles!

Lots of letters still be [*sic*] reply to, so good-bye!

Affectionately,   George.

1. In the early months of 1913, GS wrote six short stories which appeared in *Popular Magazine* between 1 February and 15 April 1914 under the general title "Babes in the Wood."

[73] GS to CAS [ALS]

Carmel, Cal.,
Feb. 1, 1913.

Dear Clark:

Thank you for the lyrics. They are **beautiful,** tho' in a way so vague as rarely to mean anything except to you who have written them. I do no entirely agree with the "Atlantic" man, and yet I can see the justice of his point of view. Just compare such things with the compact vitality of your "Nero," and you'll see that it's like contrasting jelly-fish with jewels. And yet the jelly-fish have a life and beauty of their own. I dunno! I guess I'll give up. I'm afraid I've reached the calamitous age where thought outweighs form. You'll get there too, but by then I'll be dead and beyond our mutual sympathies.

But "The Nereid" and "Hecate" (that's a three-syllabled word as you know; few persons besides you, Bierce and I seem to know that much)—your "Hecate" and "Nereid" are exquisite things.[1] You ought to be afflicted with chilblains for not sending the "Nereid" to the big magazines. One of them would have been pretty sure to have taken it.

When you write to folk who don't admire you as much as I do, spell it "Nietzsche."

Many things in "The Lyric Year" were awful. Earle must have warts on his cerebrum. Imagine taking "Pat" in place of "Nero!"

I'm enclosing Shaemas O'Sheel's review of your book, in the "Times Review of Books."[2] I'm hoping the first of it will not hurt you; and yet you are very sensitive. Remember that toward the last he pays you a fine tribute.

It's oddly reminiscent of my first reviews, to the extent that they usually complimented me & took a fling at Bierce. Now Shaemas lams me. The Lord bless the joyous Mick!—*I* don't care.

Your "Bulletin" review turned up finally: here it is. Bashford has risen several degrees in my estimation, tho' he has no use for Bierce.

I've been on another story, tho' I've found time to write a few poems. Will enclose what I've copies of.

Have been out in the open most of the time lately, and have acquired many ducks, rabbits, mussels, fish and abalones. I send most of them to the city, Berkeley, Oakland, etc. Had a hard fight with a big octopus two days ago. The row terminated by my presenting him, alive, to the Pacific Grove "museum!"[3]

Your affectionately   George.

[Enclosures: "Scrutiny," "The Thirst of Satan," one unidentified poem.]

1. No known copy of "Hecate" exists.

2. [Shaemas O'Sheel], "A Young Poet: He Has Quality, But Also the Faults of Youth," *New York Times Review of Books* (26 January 1913): 38.

3. An inaccurate account of this incident appeared in the *San Francisco Examiner* (6 February 1913): 5. GS hooked the octopus while fishing, clubbed it with an oar to subdue it, and took it home, where he kept it in a bathtub in his back yard.

[74] CAS to GS [ALS]

Auburn, Cal.
Feb. 3rd, 1913

Dear George:

I like "The Thirst of Satan" best of the three poems that you enclose. It's a strong sonnet. And I like the thought of "Scrutiny" . . . You're right enough, I suppose, about the things I sent you; there isn't much thought-content in them.

Thanks for the "Times" review. It isn't so bad, except for the generally flippant tone and the execrable English. How can a poet be a "note in a symphony of arts"? A poet isn't an *art*. And is the phrase "caressing hills" a bit of the Celtic mysticism recommended to my study? The phrase is mystic enough, I'll confess. I'd like to find a way to put a crimp in the self-satisfaction of such critics. But there isn't any way. And the English language has few champions these days, to protect her.

I've just read "The Land of Heart's Desire," by W. B. Yeats.[1] I've heard it praised highly; but I can find little in it. I rather prefer Anna Branch's "Rose of the Wind", which is similar to the Yeats poem.

I've also been reading "The City of Dreadful Night," by James Thomson.[2] It's a tremendous thing in its way, and rather different from anything else that I've read. The thing is about the last word in the literature of despair and pessimism.

Who wrote a book called "The Ape, the Idiot, and Other People?"[3] Someone who wrote to me mentioned it among several books which she thought had influenced my work. The title sounds like Bierce; but I've never heard of the book before.

"Current Literature" has just noticed my book, quoting two poems from it.[4] I suppose you've seen it, too. I think there are forty or fifty better things in the book that they might have quoted from.

I'd like to have been there when you caught that octopus!

Affectionately, Clark.

1. W. B. Yeats (1865–1939), *The Land of Heart's Desire* (1894), a poetic drama.

2. James Thomson ("B. V.") (1834–1882), *The City of Dreadful Night* (1874), a long poem, with some fantasy elements, reflecting pessimism.

3. W. C. Morrow (1854–1923), *The Ape, the Idiot and Other People* (Philadelphia: J. B. Lippincott Co., 1897). Morrow was a friend of AB.

4. "Recent Poetry," *Current Opinion* (formerly *Current Literature*) 54, No. 2 (February 1913): 150. The article quotes "Cloud Islands" and "Retrospect and Forecast" from *ST.* The reviewer ponders whether CAS or the other poet reviewed, Edna St. Vincent Millay, would be the more celebrated in the future.

[75] GS to CAS [ALS]

Oakland, Cal.

Feb. 14, 1913.

Dear Clark:

I'm up here for a few days—have to attend Mrs. Sutro's gipsy-fête in S. F. to-night, and stay up all night: curses![1]

I saw the "Current Lit." review. They usually select with poor taste, and you've fared no worse than we others.

"The Ape, etc." is by the Californian writer W. C. Morrow, and contains some very good stories, rather on the Bierce model. I have it at home, and will lend it to you when I return. Damn this pen!

No more now, as I hear the train by which Jimmy Hopper is coming to see me—at last.

Good luck!   Affectionately,   George.

1. Rose Newmark Sutro, wife of prominent San Francisco lawyer Alfred Sutro (1869–1945).

[76] CAS to GS [ALS]

Auburn, Cal.

Feb. 19th, 1913

Dear George:

I'll be glad of the loan of "The Ape, the Idiot and Other People." I wish you'd come along with it.

There's absolutely nothing happening here. I haven't even received a manuscript back from a magazine for ever so long—Is there no way of getting back at an editor who holds a poem for three months, and then returns it?

I enclose a couple of sonnets—about all I've written of late. No doubt they're pretty punk. They're likely to be, considering my present mood and state of health. I've any amount of work planned, but no strength and little inclination for going ahead with it. One of the things that I've planned is "The Ghoul, the Cypress, and the Grave"—a three-cornered dialogue among the entities of the title. The ghoul comes to claim the grave, and finds his rights disputed by the Cypress, which is already "on the spot". They have an argument, at the end of which the Grave also speaks. The idea is ghastly enough for Bierce, don't you think?

I shall write it out sometime, in short trochaic verses (for a light, "tripping" effect) and send it to the "Atlantic."

Affectionately, as ever,

Clark.

[Enclosure: "The Land of Evil Stars," two other poems.]

[77] GS to CAS [ALS]

Carmel, Cal.,
Mch. 5, 1913.

Dear Clark:

I've had the Hoppers and other friends here for a fortnight, and have had no time for letters. But I'm "alone at last."

These are two somber and powerful sonnets that you send. Bierce would like them more than I do, as he would that terrific "Ghoul, Cypress, Grave" thing that you contemplate writing. If posterity ever notice me at all, I may be censured for not trying to get you away from such subjects, too morbid to occupy more than a line or two of the artistic spectrum. But since your genius runs in that direction at present, I can't see that I'm called upon to deflect its course. You'll come out into the sunlight when you have matured.

As to magazines keeping back one's poems, one can only be patient. The Century has kept two of mine since Dec. 10th.

I'll send you Morrow's book, as soon as I find time in which to wrap it up. But I owe a whole stack of letters. I've not written a line of verse in over 6 weeks, either.

My mother and youngest sister are up at Pine Inn, to stay a week or so. Alice is all run down, poor kiddie. They're on their way to Catalina Island.

I enclose a snap-shot of me and my dog. We're both in our hunting-costumes. It's a glorious day outside—truly summer weather. We need a big rain, however. Later in the day I'm going down with a friend and try to get some mussels, though a high surf is running.

I expect to go to London's about the second week in April. Can you go there for a few days about the third week? We'd arrange for the tickets.

In the mean while I must "get busy."

Affectionately yours,

George.

[P.S.] Keep the Morrow book as long as you please, but kindly return the copy of yours before long, inscribed. If you don't mind, write in it

"To Mrs. Augusta Dolph
with the compliments of
Clark Ashton Smith."

She's one of my friends.

[78] GS to CAS [ALS]

Carmel, Cal.,

Mch. 17, 1913.

Dear Clark:

      I'm sorry to say that I made a mistake about the book I sent you: Mrs. Coryell's[1] name should have gone in it, and not her friend's. So I must bother you to autograph one more copy.

      Please write:

For

Mrs. J. B. Coryell,

with the best wishes of

Clark Ashton Smith.

And the date and place, of course.

      I should have written ere now, but have been chasing around altogether too much. These are three fine poems you send me. The sonnet is a noble one, though the words "That these may know not" are rather ambiguous. I like also the clean, terse lyric; and there is much beauty in "The Land of Evil Stars," though it has a pretty strong flavor of Poe.

      I've done very little for two months, but shall enclose a poem or two. I'm on a short-story at present.

      The Hoppers have settled down here for eight months (they say) and Jimmy and I have a good walk about every afternoon. I expect to be here for over three weeks.

      By the way, if you'll mail the book direct to Mrs. Coryell at Menlo Park, Cal., it will save me six cents.

      No news. We need rain greatly here. I got 3 full sacks of mussels Saturday, and sent one to London. We've had some fine surfs lately.

      Sorry you can't come to Jack's. But you must come here next summer, anyhow. I hope to have Mrs. Sterling here by then.

Affectionately,

George.

[Enclosures: "The Hunting of Astarte," others?]

1. GS dedicated "The House of Orchids" to "Mrs. Joseph B. Coryell." She and her husband were longtime friends of GS in San Francisco.

[79] CAS to GS [ALS]

Auburn, Cal.,

March 21st, 1913

Dear George:

      I've inscribed the book, and forwarded it to Mrs. Coryell as you desired.

      There's no news here—except that it's raining at present, to the vast relief of the local horticulturists. It's the first rain we've had for a month.

Your "Hunting of Astarte" is beautiful, tho I don't like the form very well. Some of the lines toward the last seem to me rather hasty and vague.

I enclose a poem or two, which I'm almost ashamed to send. But they're about all I've written of late. You don't have to praise them.

Someone has sent me Henri Bergson's "Creative Evolution,"[1] which I'll tackle when I've mustered sufficient courage. It's a formidable-looking book.

I'm returning "The Ape, etc" by the same mail with this. Do you mind loaning me your translations of Baudelaire and Verlaine?[2] I enclose what is probably sufficient postage for the two small volumes.

I enclose a story of mine from "The Black Cat" which you may like to compare with Morrow's tale, "His Unconquerable Enemy."[3] Mine isn't half as good, of course. I may have to take to story-writing again, tho I don't like the idea very well.

> Yours, affectionately,
> Clark

[Enclosures: "The Clouds"; an unidentified story.]

1. Henri Bergson (1859–1941), *L'Evolution créatrice* (1907); tr. A. Mitchell as *Creative Evolution* (1911). The French philosopher was experiencing a vogue in England and America at the time.

2. Paul Verlaine (1844–1896), possibly *Poems,* selected and translated, with an introduction, by Ashmore Wingate (London: Walter Scott Publishing Co., [1905]). CAS ultimately translated about fifteen poems by Verlaine.

3. Either "The Mahout" or "The Raja and the Tiger." "His Unconquerable Enemy" is a grim *conte cruel* in *The Ape, the Idiot and Other People.*

[80] GS to CAS [ALS]

> Carmel, Cal.,
> Apr. 8, 1913.

Dear Clark:

Thanks for inscribing the book for Our Lady of Orchids. I meant to have written ere this, but have been in S. F., and very much occupied while here, as Mrs. Sterling is here a few weeks' visit.

I sent you the B. & V. books, hoping they'll not influence your poetic mood very much: you have enough of that tendency already. I liked your story; Morrow's is merely suggestive of it. I agree with you that it's a better one; but wait till you catch up with him in years!

I could weep to think of you reading that rot of Bergson's—a "mystic mush" compounded of the drool, bones and garbage of outworn superstitions. I can't understand the vogue of the man, except from the point of view that "civilized" folk will fall for anything.

I enclose a letter to which I assented, asking that the names of the authors be withheld. Please return it. (But I'd like to see the discarded poems: from what I've seen of college-critics, I'll bet the winner is among them!)

I don't think I've any poems on hand I've not already sent to you. I've been working on prose of late, trying to earn a dishonest living. Have just given three unsalable sonnets to the "International."[1]

My trip to London's has been again postponed, as Hopper has thrown his knee out, and will be bedridden and on crutches for over a month. And I guess he needs my society. He did it helping me team in two loads of pitch-pine (which I sold to Bechdolt),[2] so I feel he's on my conscience. Shall enclose a snap of him (the runt), my friend Fenelon,[3] myself and my "animal." That's the lagoon in the background.

Well, summer will soon be here again, and I'll be expecting you at Carmel once more. It will be livelier this time.

> Affectionately,   George.

1. "The Thirst of Satan," "'That Walk in Darkness,'" and "Respite."
2. Frederick Bechdolt (1874–1950), writer of Western stories and novels.
3. Gene Fenelon, friend of GS and JL.

[81] CAS to GS [ALS]

> Auburn, Cal.
> April 12th, 1913

Dear George:

I received your volumes of Verlaine and Baudelaire and have been reading them. Verlaine I don't get much out of; but I like some of Baudelaire's things very well, tho I draw the line at "The Corpse." The poem is *horrible*, while such things as "The Remorse of the Dead"[1] are *terrible*—to my mind an all-important distinction.

I've succeeded in getting through a hundred-odd pages of Bergson's "Creative Evolution"—but only with wading-boots. The man seems to have become so entangled in a jungle of philosophical abstractions that he doesn't know a figment from a fact. His book is too much of a mess for my stomach; but the "cultured" human oyster will swallow nearly anything, I suppose.

Such work as I have written lately seems rubbish to me; I see no use in inflicting it upon you. I might do something if I didn't have such a hellish cold in the head. It's been with me for months and months, and seems rather worse than usual at present. I get a new idea for a poem about once a day, but I don't seem to make much out of them.

I've a borrowed camera, and have been taking a few pictures around here, mostly of trees. There's a lot of character in the twisted grey pines of these foothills; hardly any two of them are alike.

The enclosed is Stanley Braithwaite's review of my book, in the Boston Transcript.[2] The tag at the top doesn't mean that I'm subscribing to a clipping-bureau: The Komicke firm keeps sending me samples, along with an invitation to subscribe. This is the third or fourth that they're sent; and I think that you'll admit that it's a prize. Think of getting a hundred such for only five dollars! (the subscription price) Don't return the thing.

Stephen Phillips recently gave me rather brief mention in the English "Poetry Review," at the end of a review of Robert W. Service's latest book of doggerels. He quoted my quatrain "The Sunset", with the comment that it wasn't by any means contemptible considering my age![3] And then he had the gall to send me a copy of the number containing this "review". This, and the Braithwaite review, both forced upon my notice, are all the criticism that I've seen in months. But they're enough.

> Affectionately,
> Clark.

1. "The Corpse" ("Une Charogne") and "The Remorse of the Dead" ("Remords posthume") are two poems in *Les Fleurs du mal.* CAS eventually undertook to translate the whole of *Les Fleurs du mal.*

2. William Stanley Braithwaite, "Our Modern Poets," *Boston Evening Transcript* (2 April 1913): 24.

3. See "Voices from Overseas," *Poetry Review* 2, No. 4 (April 1913): 139–41. In fact, the review (unsigned but presumably by Stephen Phillips, editor of *Poetry Review*) covered three books, by G. Herbert Gibson, Robert W. Service, and CAS.

[82] GS to CAS [ALS]

Glen Ellen,
May 8, 1913.

Dear Clark:

I've been chasing around the country for quite a while, or I'd have replied ere now to your letter of last month. Now Carrie and I have come to anchor here at London's, for the rest of the month, I hope, and I've a stack of letters to answer. It's raining outside, so I don't mind so much.

I saw Phillips' review, and thought it a damned skimpy one. But an English poet always thinks it a great condescension even to mention an American one. So you did better than you think.

I too don't get much out of Verlaine. Baudelaire is a far bigger fellow, disgusting as he is at times.

I managed to answer Herman Scheffauer's letter (written last Sept.) the day before I left Carmel. It took me a whole morning! He wants to see your book, and I wish you'd inscribe one and send it to him. He can give you some good advertising. His address is

Bank Point, Jackson's Lane,
Highgate, London.

I'm enclosing a rather neat roast (by Viereck)[1] of the complacent Noyes. He (N.) needed it badly—only a hotter one.

On second thought, I'm *not* enclosing it, as it's in Carmel, unless I've sent it to Scheffauer or some other friend.

We spend four days, before coming here, up on the Russian River, at the home of Albert Bierce, Ambrose's elder brother. I'm sorry to say he's a far more lovable man than Ambrose, being free from the latter's intolerance. His home is at Montesano, only a couple of miles from the grove of the Bohemian Club, which we visited. It seemed strange without tents in it—a great improvement, of course.

While at Montesano, we picked lots of ripe wild-strawberries, *big ones.* The wild-flowers were profuse and beautiful, too. But there are as many on this ranch, though I've not seen any strawberries yet. London now has 1500 acres, mostly beautiful wood-lands. The ranch runs from Sonoma Creek to the crest of Sonoma Mountain. The woods are mostly madrono, maple, oak and redwood—also spruce. There's lots of game there, including deer.

He has bought a flock of Angora goats, to eat away the undergrowth. Their kids are cute little cusses, but not as cute as some pigs that were born a day or so ago.

I've written nothing for two or three weeks, but hope to write at least a story before long. I trust your cold is better by now, so you will not have that handicap on your productivity. But then you don't have to feel in any hurry. Suppose you were 43!

Tell me if you think you can get down to Carmel again in July. Mrs. Sterling will be there then, and she is a good cook. You may have the cabin.

Yours affectionately,   George.

1. George Sylvester Viereck (1884–1962), German-born American poet, novelist, journalist, and essayist. The article referred to might be an unsigned and untitled discussion of Noyes in *Current Opinion* 54, No. 4 (April 1913): 315, presumably written by Viereck, one of the editors of the magazine. No signed article by Viereck on Noyes has been found for this period.

[83] CAS to GS [ALS]

Auburn, Cal.
May 11th, 1913

Dear George:

It doesn't seem likely, at present, that I can come to Carmel, in July. I've too much on my hands for one thing—plans for a score or so of poems which I'd like to at least draft out before I forget them. And the early summer is my best time for work. I'd rather come down in the fall, anyway, if it's all the same to you. It'll be quieter then. Your saying that Carmel will be livelier this summer, is no inducement to *me*: You know I don't care much about meeting people.

I'd love to see Veirick's [*sic*] remarks on Noyes. Noyes has an almighty gall, it seems to me—coming over here to tell us that Whitman and Emerson are better poets than Poe! and that he "heartily disapproves of the decadent and pessimistic schools of poets in America". And he was so kind as to add that he wouldn't mention any names!

I don't suppose you'd care for the few things I've written lately. Here are some of the titles: "The Medusa of Despair," "Gothic Nightmare,"[1] and "The Doom of America." The last is a sort of Bible prophecy, in about fifty verses. I don't suppose it's poetry. It's a sort of round-up of all my grudges and kicks against the present age. I even took a swat at the suffragettes. I'm glad it's out of my system.

I've some prose-poems planned; the idea of one of them is about as perfect a nightmare as I ever got hold of: it's to be a description of the carnivorous, half-animal plant and tree-life of an imaginary world—huge jungles of rooted serpents and vampire orchids, and things, monstrously luxuriant in the ghastly and exuberant light of some vast green sun. There's no reason why there shouldn't be such things, in the worlds of other systems; but think of being caught in the octopus-like tentacles of some enormous plant—and slowly absorbed by its innumerable leech-like mouths! I shall call the thing "The Forest of Strange Horror."[2]

Just before receiving your letter, I returned the French translations which you lent me, to Carmel. I suppose you'll get them all right, tho.

Yours, affectionately,
Clark.

1. I.e., "Nightmare."

2. CAS produced a prose poem ("The Flower Devil"), a poem (*The Hashish-Eater*), and a short story ("The Demon of the Flower") that all use this setting and imagery.

[84] GS to CAS [ALS]

Glen Ellen,
May 14 / 13—

Dear Clark:

It will be, of course, just as well if you go to Carmel in the autumn. If you care for quietness you'll certainly find it more prevalent there then.

I'm writing this out by Jack's swinery. He has seven baby pigs that are a pure joy to the soul (especially when they all suckle at once), and in a near-by corral are 13 kids—pretty little cusses.

I wish you'd kindly inscribe one of your books and send it to Samuel Loveman, 7206 Harvard Avenue, Cleveland, Ohio. He is a young poet (22, I think) of whom I expect great things—after his own style.

You must have these books I keep asking you to send to poets charged to me by Robertson. Tell him to charge me only what he would charge you, however. Each of these poets will do something to advertise the book.

I may find that roast of Noyes down in Carmel, when I get there next month. Here's a good one by John Neihardt which I may not have sent you yet. Pound is another sassy brat that needs a spanking.[1]

I went out before breakfast to-day and slew three jack-rabbits. One of them was too big to eat, and will go to the dogs and cats.

I've written three poems in the last four days, but have no copies to send you. One is only some nature-muck anyhow. About cotton-tails.[2]

I won $3.55 from Jack at pedro, last night; but I don't imagine that the Fates will allow me to be that far ahead of the game for long.

Your idea for "The Forest of Strange Horror" is *great!*

Affectionately,   George.

1. Neihardt's article apparently is "The Chances for Poetry," *Minneapolis Journal* (6 April 1913): Women's Section, p. 5. GS also refers to American poet Ezra Pound (1885–1972). AB and GS had debated the merits of Pound's poetry in 1910 (see *MMM* 199, 201).

2. Probably "The Plaint of the Cottontail," in *BB*.

[85] CAS to GS [ALS]

Auburn, Cal.,
May 16th, 1913.

Dear George:

Thanks awfully for lending me the roast of "Poetry", which I'm returning. I don't think that magazine will come to any good end under the present management.

That's a very true thing that Neihardt says about the "new" tendencies in art being part of the world-tendency toward democracy and the consequent spilling-over into anarchism.

It's all right about the books you asked me to send to Scheffauer and Loveman. I *won't* have Robertson charge them to you; but we'll let the amount go on that ten I owe you, if you like.

I've written two or three moderately rotten sonnets of late. I may enclose one of them (as a sample) Here are some subjects that I have in my note-book: "The Music of Evil", "The Discord of the Spheres", "A Vision of Satan", and "Uriel." I don't quite know what the last will be; but I'm rather attracted by the idea of using Uriel as the chief character of a short narrative poem. First, tho, I shall do the prose poems of which I spoke, if I'm permitted so much strength and inspiration. I've a thing in prose, "The Demon, the Angel, and Beauty," about two-thirds drafted out.

Affectionately,
Clark.

[Enclosure: "The City of the Titans."]

[86] GS to CAS [ALS]

Carmel, Cal.,
June 6, 1913.

Dear Clark:

We've been back a week to-day, in which time we've got "settled," cleaned the house, and got to work—I writing and Carrie typing my stuff.

I've answered a lot of letters, leaving yours till the last, as it came last, and have completed my sixth short-story. I have had to cut out the Muse, though. "Why wasn't I born rich?"

Here's that Viereck-Noyes article: please return it. I like the sonnet you sent very much, especially the strong ending and that great adjective "thunder-named."[1] The titles you want to use for poems also strike me as unusually good, especially "The Music of Evil."

I spent a day in S. F. on my way back from London's, and ran into Dunlap. He was rather stiff, but evidently lacked the nerve to show his hostility, if indeed he felt any.

It's rotten weather here, what of seven straight days of high fog. I've gone hunting for rabbits lately, as there are hundreds along the river. One can get ten in an hour, ¾ grown ones, very good to eat. And what we don't eat we give away.

Affectionately yours,   George.

[P.S.] Do you know the address of "Youth's Companion?"

1. "The City of the Titans," l. 8.

[87] CAS to GS [ALS]

Auburn, Cal.
June 8th, 1913—

Dear George:

Thanks for the lovely roast of Noyes, which I return herewith. Everything in it seems well-deserved, to me . . . I suppose Noyes will get the laureateship now, unless it's given to Masefield!

I had a nice letter from Samuel Loveman the other day. His "testimonial" was worth the book.

I enclose a number of miscallaneous [sic] productions, some of them in prose. I rather think the prose-poems are the best of the batch. I've given up the vers libre of which there's so much in my book, so when I feel like doing something of that sort now, I write it out as honest prose. I know you won't agree with the views set forth in "The Doom of America," but I expect you'll like some of the rhetoric in the thing. The writing of it eased my mind a lot. Keep all these poems, etc, that I send you; but you needn't praise or even comment upon them unless you want to. It's well that you should have copies of most of my things.

I'm beginning a short narrative poem, "Uriel", the story of the compassionate angel who intercedes with God for the wretchedness of Man, and rebels because of God's equivocal answer. It's rather a new idea, I think.

I wish I could get out of this infernal atmosphere. Auburn gets less fit to live in, or even near, all the time. The local trustees and school board are trying to oust the principal of the high school, who is the only intelligent man in the place, and the only worthwhile friend that I have here. Someone else wants his job, I understand, and is willing to pay to get it. How's that for graft? A bunch of meddlesome females calling itself the Auburn Improvement Club, is assisting in this task of expulsion. They've an itch for running the morals of the community by clock-work, and because of a few sex-scandals among the high-school pupils, they're complaining that Engle's discipline is lax! Apparently they want a combination of gum-shoe detective and member of the W.C.T.U.[1] in his place.

The weather here has been rather infernal, too, with thunder-clouds hanging over the mountains, and the consequent oppression of humidity. We've had some pretty displays of lightning over the Sierras, tho.

Affectionately yours,

Clark

P.S. "The Palace of Jewels" is an old poem of mine, written about the time of "The Star-Treader." I've just exhumed it, and think you might like to have it. It's peculiarly in your line.

[Enclosures: "The Demon, the Angel, and Beauty," "Desire of Vastness," "The Doom of America," "The Medusa of Despair, "Nightmare," "The Palace of Jewels," "The Peril That Lurks among Ruins," "The Refuge of Beauty," "The Years Restored."]

1. The Woman's Christian Temperance Union, founded in 1874.

[88] GS to CAS [ALS]

Carmel, Cal.,
June 22, 1913.

Dear Clark:

At last I have time to re-read the poems, etc. that you sent me, though I may not be able to finish this letter to-day.

If you don't want me forever to be owing you a letter, wait a week before replying to mine. That won't offend, but give me the comfortable feeling, for a space, of not being in your debt as to letters!

We've been here 25 days now, in which time I've written one or two more stories and poems. I'll try to get a copy of one of the latter, one about swimming, as it's a bit out of my ordinary vein.[1]

But as to the poems you send: I think the "Demon, Angel and Beauty" a fine thing, thoughtful and lovely. Have you tried it on any periodical? I would, even though it *is* too good for them. "The Peril etc." is good too. "Incubi," not "incubi*i*," though. The "Doom of America" is also a magnificent thing, even though, like my "Job" stuff, it's an echo of the Bible. Personally I've quit what Scheffauer called "marching under Ambrose's black banner of despair," and think America is getting more intelligent and decent yearly, though I've neither leisure nor inclination to discuss the matter with pen and ink. And if she has only the sun's dying to fear there's no cause for immediate worry, of course.

"Nightmare" is good too, especially its tremendous ending. "The Years Restored" is a fine thing. I like particularly the line

"The gold long dim in Herculaneum."[2]

"The Refuge of Beauty" is strong, though the clash between "escape" and "Hate" jars me. "Desire of Vastness" is big too, and with a *very* good ending. Its octave is pretty obscure: I get it, but fear that few others will.

"The Palace of Jewels" *is* "a gorgeous thing![*"] I like it all except that "intermittently" applied to rubies. It seems to me that the ruby's light is peculiarly steady and *un*intermittent. Especially felicitous are

> "Deep sapphires, clouded to the core with blue."
> "with spears
> In sunset dipt."
> "Across the gloom their irised swords unite."
> "The balas-ruby's orange ire."
> "What dawns and sunsets march from room to room!"

But biggest of all is this great "Medusa of Despair," a truly terrible sonnet. It's clearer than most of your sonnets, too, and ends wonderfully. I dislike "Ensuant," and don't care for "cognate,"[3] though the latter might be hard to find a substitute for. But it's a big sonnet. Have you tried it on the "Atlantic?"

I'm not sending any more verse to "Scribners," as a friend who was in the office writes me that they have enough poetry on hand to last them for the *next four years*. No wonder I've never disposed of anything to them!

Everything's quiet here. We've had over two weeks of perfect weather, but it's overcast and cool to-day. I've been on the wagon since last month. Do a good deal of hunting and quoit-pitching. I got 13 rabbits in an hour, yesterday at sunset time. Turner is back again, his fortunes improved. He has a new automatic shot-gun, a beauty. Cost only $35., too.

As I owe a good many other letters, I guess I'd better answer a few of them. So good-bye!

Yours affectionately,

George.

1. Apparently "Beyond the Breakers" (called "Past the Breakers" in letter 89).
2. l. 8.
3. Neither word is in the poem; see letter 92.

[89] CAS to GS [ALS]

Auburn, Cal.
July 1st, 1913

Dear George:

I think I've delayed sufficiently in answering your last letter. But you needn't worry about owing me letters: I'm never offended by that, for I know you've much less time for correspondence than I have.

I like your "Past the Breakers", tho I don't think you're so successful with the three-syllable meters as with the iambic. I'm even less so—That's an especially fine line, "The hissing ridges ran like dragons driven by gods—"

I'm surprised by your judgement on "The Medusa of Despair." I hadn't thought so much of it myself. Personally, I'm getting a wee bit sick of the introspective element which so dominates modern literature. So many present-day writers are like the diseased beggars at the gates of Eastern cities, exposing their sores to public pity and benevolence. There's a frightful lack of dignity and reticence, so that the public seems even to resent these qualities when it does find them. That's one reason why people accuse my work of wanting "human interest", I suppose. Another reason is that I've no soothing-syrup for 'em.

I've a new poem or two, but shan't send them now. "The Witch in the Graveyard" is the title of one. 'Tis a sweet subject, as I'm sure you'll agree.

Miss Monroe of "Poetry" has just returned a bunch of my late things with a gentle intimation that she doesn't think much of 'em. What do *you* think of that editor and that magazine, by the way? "Poetry" seems to be getting badder and badder, what with the Whitmanesque Hasidu in the last number.[1]

I received five dollars for "The Nereid," from the Yale Review the other day. The editor spoke of the check as a "modest honorarium (!)"

I agree with you as to the desirability of the changes which you suggest, in the "Medusa" and the other poems. But I've no suitable alternatives at present.

Affectionately yours,
Clark.

1. CAS refers to "Poems," a series of 14 poems in prose and verse by Indian poet Rabindranath Tagore, published in *Poetry* 2, No. 3 (June 1913): 81–91. They employ the long lines and proselike rhythms made popular by Walt Whitman. Tagore was awarded the Nobel Prize in literature in 1913. It is not clear what *Hasidu* refers to.

[90] GS to CAS [ALS]

Carmel, Cal.,
July 30, 1913.

Dear Clark:

I'm going up to the Grove on the 4th, so am replying first to a lot of letters, beginning with yours.

I suppose it's been hot up your way, and that you've not felt much like writing. Here the weather has been mostly overcast, but I've put in on prose what time I've not "wasted" on sociability. As I expected, there has been a large and lively crowd here this summer, and we have scores of callers. To-night its a "rag" in honor (?) of that gnome Burgess,[1] who is here for a few days. I'll not be sorry when it's winter

"Collier's" took my "swimming" poem, for the stupendous sum of $30. They're worse in their degree than the Yale Review, as *that* doesn't *make money*. I've also sold poems to the Bookman and Smart Set,[2] but haven't had much luck (that's about all it is) generally speaking.

As to "Poetry," I agree with you that it keeps getting worse. Miss Munro[e] has been "infected" by Ezra Pound, who is rabid for a "new form," and she is letting *poetry* go by the board. It's all that could be expected from putting a magazine, however humble, in the hands of a woman, for there's not one of them that's not more the echo of a man (or several) than she is herself. They have neither originality or courage. If "Poetry" were not subsidized, it would cease publication in a very few months, as it represents only a clique of no-poets, *now*.

We've just put on "Fire" at the Forest Theatre here. I suppose you saw accounts of it in the Examiner, as well as pictures of me and Opal. I surely looked fierce![3] She was **great!**

Thank Heaven the thing is over! But it was the only success that ever went on here, and we even cleared $200. instead of ending with a deficit—a thing that has much impressed the local peasantry (the "Toad" gang)[.]

Carrie, Mrs. Hopper and one or two others are going down the coast while I'm at the Grove. I sha'n't be away long this time, but expect to return on the 12th. Usually I stop over at London's for a few weeks; but I must go home and "get busy." One's expenses are trebled when there's a woman around.

No news worth the ink, so here's good-bye and good-luck!

Affectionately,

George.

Hopper has thrown his knee out again, and is going to S. F. to have it X-rayed. Poor Jim!

1. [Frank] Gelett Burgess (1866–1951), author, illustrator, and friend of GS. Author of "The Purple Cow."
2. "Afterward" and "The Master Mariner."
3. Mary Austin, *Fire* (1913), performed at the Forest Theater on 26 July. A photo of the event in Ferlinghetti and Peters, *Literary San Francisco*, p. 117, shows GS dressed in an animal skin and bearing a club.

[90a] CAS to GS [non-extant]

[Auburn, Cal.
c. July–August 1913]

[Enclosures: "Cyclopean Fear," "Neptune," "The Sea-Gods," "The Witch in the Graveyard."]

[91] GS to CAS [ALS]

Carmel, Cal.,
Aug. 19, 1913.

Dear Clark:

Since writing last to you, I've been to the Jinks and, lately, on a deer-hunt way up the Carmel. And too little sleep and too much of other things have lost me my writing mood. But probably I can write letters.

The sonnet "Neptune" you sent me is a fine thing, especially (as should be) the sestet. "Cyclopean Fear" I cared less for. "The Sea-Gods" is a beautiful thing. My only suggestion is that you don't repeat the first stanza, but write a new one that will be even better than the rest.

>"Their eyes like changing emeralds gleam"

And

>"From foam left grey by sunset's rose,"[1]

are lovely lines.

"The Witch in the Graveyard" is grimly impressive. I'd have been wild about it twelve years ago. Now I rather deplore seeing so much imagination wasted on such a theme. But there's great work in it.

I'd advise you to "go slow" on "horror" poems, and see your best energies along the lines of sheer beauty. You do best then. You could have used much of the material in this poem to make something *weirdly* beautiful instead of repulsive, however impressive. But it may be wiser for you to follow your natural bent. All anyone else can give you is a resumé of his own tastes or prejudices.

About that adjective: seems to me I'd put it:

>"Enough! 't will be a night made infamous
> By commerce etc."

Or, "cavernous (for)," "poisonous," "ominous" or "sibilant."

I'm sorry to say I can't find the one book of Davidson's I used to possess.[2] It was one of his tamest works, anyhow. Ask me for something else.

My friend Fenelon, who occupies the cabin this summer, is now building us a sleeping-porch. It hitches on to the bed-room on the west. A Londoner named Miles, a bright chap, is in the tent.

My Airedale pup must have run into an old coon night before last. We had to have twelve stitches put in her ear! But she's cheerful enough now.

It has been a bright summer here—very little fog, comparatively. The grove-play was, scenically, the best we've had. It was worthless as literature.

I've no poems worth enclosing, and don't seem able to sell what I have. Hope the same isn't true of you!

Affectionately,   George.

---

1. "The Sea-Gods," ll. 9, 16.

2. Presumably a book by the British poet John Davidson (1857–1900).

[92] CAS to GS [ALS]

Auburn, Cal.

Aug. 23, 1913

Dear George:

The temperature here is 104° to-day, with a wind like the sigh of Hell blowing straight from the north. Also we've the prospect of a visit from some relatives in the near future. So you'll not envy me.

I've written hardly anything since the enclosures of my last letter, and have lost all heart for submitting my work to the pismires who edit magazines. The money that I've gotten from magazines (for poems) has hardly paid for my postage-stamps; and I fail to see that there's any *glory* in magazine publication. "So what's the use?"

I had a letter from Hermann Scheffauer some time ago. I gather from the tone in which he writes, that he has been manhandled by a certain class (or group) of English critics who think themselves the supreme court of literary appeal. He seems inclined to disparage American poetry, and says that "practically all our more ambitious work is derivative" (as if all poetry weren't more or less derivative!) In his comments on my work he praises the "Forsaken Gods" highly; but neglects to mention "Nero" or "Saturn", or the other really important poems (except the "Abyss.")

Here are some alterations for the lines to which you objected in "The Medusa of Despair:" "Depart, and curse more kindred things instead," and "Triumphant o'er what realms of elder doom." They're the best I can do at present.[1] I've changed the line in "The Witch in the Graveyard" to read thus: "Enough! [']twill be a prosperous night, methinks, for gossip", etc. One of your suggestions ("sibilant") was very good, but I'd have had to change the sense of the last two lines to use it.[2]

I enclose the only poem that I've written this month—a sonnet for which I've taken one of your phrases as title.[3] It's purely intellectual.

I'm sorry you've nothing of Davidson's. I like what I've seen of his work very much, and have been trying to get hold of some more of him. I don't suppose that Davidson is very popular.

Have you any good books on demonology? That's a subject in which I'm interested at present. If you haven't, you might send me up any volume of Bierce, except the poems, "In the Midst of Life," and "The Shadow on the Dial," all of which I've read. I'll pay the postage (or express)[.]

Affectionately yours,

Clark

[Enclosure: unidentified sonnet.]

1. CAS rewrote the first line quoted (l. 7, and rhyming lines 2, 3, and 6) as "Get hence! the dark gods languish on their throne," and the second line quoted (l. 9) as "Regressive, through what realms of elder doom."

2. "The Witch in the Graveyard": "Enough! 'twill be a prosperous night, methinks, / For commerce of the demons with the dead," ll. 64–65.

3. CAS's poem "The City of the Titans" derives from the line "As tho' a city of the Titans burned" in GS's "Duandon" (l. 99); however, CAS had sent that poem to GS earlier (letter 85).

[93] GS to CAS [ALS]

Carmel, Cal.,
Sept. 16, 1913.

Dear Clark:

We got some of your Auburn weather here, yesterday, and to-day it's even hotter. So I feel like anything but work, and guess I'll reply to a few letters.

No especial news, however. The Sutros took us and the Harry Leon Wilsons to Tassajara Hot Springs on Saturday. We returned Sunday. It was a long and rather hazardous trip for a motor-car, but unusual and beautiful, scenically.

I've not given much time to verse this month, and what I have done wouldn't appeal to you. The damned "Collier's" has not yet run my swimming-poem, though they managed finally to pay me for it. But if they intend to keep the thing till next summer, I shall ask them to sell it back to me.

I'd not let any of Scheffauer's opinions carry very much weight with me. He belongs to a "school" that's hunting for something that can't be found—something "new." To attain it they resort to formlessness. They are folks who can't write much real poetry; and such little as they do write *is* "derivative!" Ezra Pound's "Goodly Fere," for instance.[1] Some of his other stuff would give a she-baboon the erysipelas. Scheff. was practically certain to praise some of your "least good" work and ignore the best.

The sonnet you sent is a big one, especially the ending. I don't like that word "aidant," though. Seems to me I'd sacrifice thought to beauty in that instance.

I don't like to trust any of my Bierce set to the mail or express—usually the corners of the book get blunted; and I want to keep that set in A.1. condition.[2] Isn't there any other book I can send?

I hear that Kipling is going nutty; also that he takes dope. I don't take any stock in either rumor, though. Probably you read of the burning (incendiary) of London's new house.[3] He figures he's out over $25000. But he makes that much every six months.

"Current Opinion" and the "Literary (?) Digest" re-printed my "Master Mariner" from "Smart Set." But I couldn't *give away* my "Thirst of Satan!" The "Smart Set" astonished me by taking my "Last Monster," however.

I don't remember sending you a copy of the enclosed circular. But I think I sent you the sonnet "That Walk in Darkness."

Affectionately,   George.

---

1. Pound's "The Ballade of the Goodly Fere" (*English Review*, October 1909; in Pound's *Exultations*, 1909) is the poem that engendered the controversy between AB and GS over Pound's merits. AB (to whom the poem had been sent by Pound's father) maintained that "it seems to me an admirable ballad, as it is given a modern to write ballads" (*MMM* 201); GS replied: "I suppose I *don't* rightly value 'The Goodly Fere'—probably because I've never been 'stuck on' ballads" (AB to GS, 21 March 1910; ms., NYPL).

2. GS refers to his copy of AB's *Collected Works* (1909–12; 12 vols.).

3. JL's Wolf House burned down on the evening of 22–23 April 1913, the day it was completed, at a loss of $80,000. The fire was probably set by a disgruntled workman.

[94] CAS to GS [ALS]

Auburn, Cal.
Oct. 3rd, 1913

Dear George:

I've delayed answering your letter longer than is usual with me, chiefly because there's been nothing here to write of. I haven't written a poem since early in August, or received a returned manuscript since an even prior date. I wish I had a pole long enough to reach across the continent: I should find a mighty satisfaction in discomforting the dorsal regions of certain editors.

The adjacent counties have been full of forest-fires—a most uncommon number of them—during the last month. But the weather is rather pleasant than otherwise, except for the north wind—a wind that always makes me restless, and exasperates my nerves.

I see by to-day's *Town Talk* that you've recently sold a bunch of your short stories. Congratulations! To what magazine did you sell them?—The T. T. didn't specify. I shall have to "pitch in" myself, presently.

You *didn't* send me your sonnet, "That Walk in Darkness." I'd certainly like to see it, if you can spare a copy. I've nothing to send in exchange just at present—for which you should be thankful. However, I'm incubating a number of ideas—one of them quite the biggest that I'm ever likely to get hold of. If I manage to handle it with any measure of success, it will dwarf all my past work, and (I fear) will make anything subsequent in the line of the sidereal seem rather tame and anticlimactic. The title will be "Demogorgon," and the poem a sort of one-act drama in which the suns gather and take council against God, whom they regard as their common enemy—an invisible, tremendous God who alters and destroys them at will, or sends forth plagues of comets, etc. I shall give "speaking parts" to the principal suns, such as Antares, Rigel, Betelguese, [*sic*] and Vega, and have choruses of constellations and galaxies. I shall fill the speeches of thee stars with the most Titanic blasphemies of which my imagination is capable—and I think you'll admit that there are opportunities for what is usually termed blasphemy, in the idea.

Yours affectionately,
Clark.

[95] GS to CAS [ALS]

Carmel, Cal.,
Oct. 19, 1913.

Dear Clark:

The hot north wind you speak of has been a frequent visitor here of late, and interfered with even my correspondence. It's even too hot for hunting! But the ducks haven't appeared yet: we must first have a storm.

"Town Talk" got rather too excited over those stories. I sold only three, for only $50. each, and to the "Popular" at that. Thro' an agent. They were cave-boy stories, childish affairs of mere plot.

As you've been getting "Town Talk" for a year, why not *give* them another poem, for a new annual subscription? I always do that—something unsalable, of course.

Your scheme for a new "sidereal" poem is a huge one. I had the same idea, almost, once. (See my interview with Ashton Stevens. A "Litany of the Suns.")[1] I finally concluded that one incursion into space was enough.

Yes, the idea is very big, so big that I hate to have you treat it in your adolescence, for you'd handle it much more firmly in the thirties. Often I wish I had "The Testimony" to do all over again. Now it's too late!

Editors are always late in returning MSS in the summer and early autumn, as vacations cause a depleted office-force. The Century has been keeping my "Menace" for over three months! One can only grin and bear it, being (financially at least) at the mercy of these termites.

Have lately sold a poem to Harper's Weekly,[2] but can report no other ray in the gloom. It's odd, but the better class of magazines are the only ones to take my work. The more squalid ones never do (I mean in poetry).

Would like to ask you to come down, but Mrs. S. is rather tired of having guests, and expects one of her sisters here, too. I imagine she'll return to Oakland when the rains begin, if they ever do. Perhaps you'll not mind visiting me *then*. I predict the worst for this state in the matter of rain (or rather drouth): they've cut down too many forests and had too many forest-fires. The years will get dryer and dryer, I fear.

Here are a couple of sonnets, absolutely unsalable, of course. I sent the Lilith one[3] only to "Smart Set," and even they returned it. No use to send the other one *anywhere:* it's far too gloomy. Good-bye!

> Affectionately yours,   George.

[Enclosures: "That Walk in Darkness" and one unidentified sonnet.]

1. Ashton Stevens, "Ashton Stevens Interviews George Sterling, Poet," *San Francisco Examiner* (24 January 1904): 48.
2. "Then and Now."
3. I.e., "That Walk in Darkness."

[95a] CAS to GS [non-extant]

> [Auburn, Cal.
> c. October 1913]

[Enclosure: unidentified prose poem.]

[96] GS to CAS [ALS]

> Carmel, Cal.,
> Nov. 14, 1913.

Dear Clark:

I've had an energetic spell, or fit, rather, for two weeks and have committed a couple of stories and finished two poems. You may like the sonnet a bit, so I'll enclose it.

I'm sorry to learn you continue to be depressed and disgusted with life. Life is pretty bad, but most dissatisfaction with it is a physical matter. You matured too swiftly, I think, both ways, and your vitality will probably take a few more years in which to "catch up" with the rest of you. If you can stick it out until then, you'll go very far, and life in at least some of its aspects will seem fairly endurable. The trouble is, we start in expecting too much of life. Remember, you might be working in an office, as I had to for fifteen and more years, the best of my life.

The prose-poem you send is very good, so good that one doesn't forget it. It is prose in form only.

If I'm here in Jan. or Feb. I'll be glad to see you. My home seems breaking up again, this time for keeps. If it does I may go to New York for a time. I'm sure of nothing yet, but shall know more after Thanksgiving.

We've had abundant rainfall lately, and the countryside has turned green almost over-night. I'm still on the hunt. Turner and I have invested in a second-hand rowboat, and used it on the lagoon yesterday, for the first time. We got no ducks, though, as four Dagoes were there from Monterey, shooting mudhens to sell to the Chinese at 10¢ each, and the noise they made kept the game out at sea.

I had a bum poem in the "Call," called "The Path of Portola." It made a hit with the proletariat, and I also received $50. for it. I know just how a whore must feel!

Well, if they'd take, any of them, my best work, I'd not have to do such things. For instance, I can't sell *any* of my sonnets, not even the Lilith one.

Do you recall "Old Pop" Gates here? He died of apoplexy a few days ago. Funeral this afternoon, in S. F.

A friend has sent me the MS of a book of indifferent verse to revise, and write a preface for![1] So my cup is full.

It's good for him that I'm his *friend!*

Affectionately,   George.

[Enclosure: unidentified sonnet.]

1. Unidentified. GS does not appear to have written a preface for any such book at this time.

[97] GS to CAS [ALS]

Carmel, Cal.,
Dec. 1st, 1913.

Dear Clark:

I'm still of the opinion that a few more months will see me in N. Y., etc., at least for a while. Carrie has once more left me, this time for ever, I fear. She says it's neither my fault nor hers; if it's anyone's it's mine, as I'm sure I should have written more and drunk less. Damn poets marrying, anyhow!

I guess the news will come out in the papers to-day or to-morrow. I only hope they put all the blame on me, as she deserves none.

I wanted you to come here for the week in Dec. that you've suggested. But now I'm "all up in the air," and am so uncertain as to when I can be in Carmel that I don't dare ask you to come here. Wait a bit and see how things shape themselves—then it'll be surer.

If "Town Talk" doesn't run your "Medusa" soon I'll get after them. I'm almost certain, however, that they're keeping it for their Christmas number. I've sent them the poem I call "War" for that number, tho' not sure they'll fancy it.

All's quiet here now. I've written little but a ballad for over two weeks. My mind's in too much of a turmoil to settle down to work, and even letter-writing comes none too easily to me. It's a heart-troubling thing to break up an intimacy of twenty years' standing. Such things send their roots very deep & wide.

I suppose it's no use to warn you not to marry unless you're rich—and not even then.

Affectionately,   George.

[98] CAS to GS [ALS]

Auburn, Cal.
Dec. 7th, 1913

Dear George:

I've been practically laid up for the last week with a desperate cold, and have done nothing but sit around and cough and curse alternately. Nearly everyone here seems to have a cold: there's an epidemic in this blasted real-estate Paradise every time the north wind blows down from Alaska or Eskimoland.

It seems improbable at present that I can come down during December, anyway. I seem stuck here indefinitely, with everything, even my work, at a standstill. I've several ideas for prose-poems, but, with this cursed cold, have scarcely felt like doing much with them so far.

I hear indirectly that Robertson has already sold between five and six hundred copies of "The Star-Treader." That's a surprising number, don't you think? I should have some royalties coming presently (I'm to receive 10% on each copy sold, after the first five hundred.) But I don't expect to get rich very soon.

I'm hellishly sorry to hear that you're having trouble. The newspapers were rather flippant about it, I thought. The American public would die of ingrowing curiosity, I suppose, if they weren't told all about the affairs of their betters.

I seem to have unusually little to write this time, and I've no poems to send you— I wish I could see you: I seldom think of the things I really want to say, when I sit down to write a letter.

Affectionately yours,
Clark.

[99] GS to CAS [ALS]

Carmel, Cal.,
Dec. 20, 1913.

Dear Clark:

I hope you're over that cold by now. I've had one, actually, myself; but it's getting less.

Doubtless you've read of my approaching divorce. She has relieved me of most of what remorse I had, by making her "complaint" quite unjust and needlessly harsh. I admit to a little dissipation, but she always shared it, and frequently drank too much herself.

I supported her, and wasn't "profligate" nor especially idle. Twelve short stories and over twenty poems, this year, bear witness to *some* industry. And I was improving every month.

It surprises me to hear that Robertson has sold so many of your books. I've not sold that many of any of my editions, yet. He drove a hard bargain with you in giving no royalty until after the 500th volume. It is after the 250th in my case. And to offset that I make him pay me $25. down! Make him do that with your next book.

I've written nothing for a month. Am not sure when I'll go to N. Y., but expect it will be late in March.

Affectionately,   George.

[100] CAS to GS [ALS]

Auburn, Cal.
Jan. 5th, 1914.

Dear George:

I've delayed answering your last letter these many days, or rather weeks, thro an uncommon lack of subject-matter: Everything in my life seems fallen flat and stagnant during these latter months. I've a number of unanswered letters on my desk, besides yours, and have just rallied sufficient energy for an effort toward the relief of my epistolary conscience.

I read "War" in the Christmas "Town Talk", and liked the idea, and many of the images. The poem, tho, on the whole, struck me as being less musical than most of your work.

I've no poems to send you. I seem to lack even the impulse toward literary con-centration, not to mention the energy. Doubtless I need a change of scene and envi-ronment, together with a thorough stirring-up of all my stagnant energies. But I don't see my way to it at present.

I wish I might see you. Will it be entirely out of the question for you to "stop over" a few days, on your way to New York?

Yours affectionately, as ever,
Clark.

P.S. Have you ever seen the picture of Poe which I enclose? If not, you may like to have it. There's a tragic intensity about it, beyond that of the other pictures extant.

[101] GS to CAS [ALS]

Jan. 12, 1914.

Dear Clark:

I'm marooned in this particular section of the Vale of Tears while Mrs. S. is in Carmel, engaged in packing up some more of her possessions. But I hope to be able to leave for "home" on Friday. I've been here since the 3rd, I believe.

Your comment on "War" is quite just. You'll note I was correct in surmising they were keeping *your* poem for the Christmas number. I've just *given* them three pretty good poems,[1] as I'll have them in a book by May or June, and it would be too late to send them to magazines.

I've seen this picture of Poe. It's a good one. Am returning it, for you to pin on the wall of your den.

I'd like to drop off and see you when I leave for New York in March. I'll see if the railroad will let me do it conveniently. But is there no chance of my meeting you in S. F. instead?

I've sold five poems to the "Call" and two to "Sunset," as I ask only $10. per for them![2] My fool "cave-boy" stories have begun to appear in the "Popular."

But I've not written a line in almost two months.

Affectionately yours,   George.

1. "'Tidal, King of Nations,'" "Discord," and "The Secret Room," all rpt. in *BB*.

2. Only one poem, "The Abandoned Farm," has been found in the *San Francisco Call and Post* for this period. Only one poem, "'On a Western Beach,'" appeared in *Sunset* at this time; GS may have purchased the other back because it had not appeared in the magazine before its inclusion in *BB*.

[102] CAS to GS [ALS]

Auburn, Cal.,
Jan. 27th, 1914.

Dear George:

I hope you'll be able to arrange the "stop-over". I *must* see you soon; and I fear there's little likelihood of my being able to meet you in San Francisco.

I've no news worth mentioning. I continue, I am sorry to say, in my usual frame of mind—dispirited, and a prey to the most abject doubt and self-distrust. I am unable to write a line; peace of mind is one of the prime necessities in poetic composition; and mine is a divided kingdom.

This pestilential climate has been exceeding even itself of late, in the way of rain and wind. Consequently, I've been kept indoors a great deal. Today, I think, is the first really clear day in weeks. There's a cold wind blowing, tho,—a wind that seems to have been refrigerated in some iceberg-cavern for the last thousand years.

The thirteenth of the month was my twenty-first birth-day. I was born on a Friday, too, by the way, and under the influence of the planet Saturn. A rather ominous combination, don't you think?

Affectionately as ever,
Clark.

[103] GS to CAS [ALS]

Carmel, Cal.,
Feb. 5th, 1914.

Dear Clark:

I'm back here in Carmel at last, thank Heaven, and in a mood to reply to many neglected letters, yours coming first.

I'm damned sorry that you're in so dispirited a state. Surely it's all physical, for you are as yet only on the threshold of life and art, and have a solid fifty years ahead of you in which to size things up, "make good," be happy, go to the devil, or otherwise dispose of yourself. I don't see why you should waste any time in doubt or self-distrust. Let your work go for a year (you can easily spare that much) and tell yourself that only physical culture will be worth while for the year 1914. Then, in 1915, you can turn to poetry with fresh energy, and, perhaps, a new view-point. Do not feel as though you had to write just so much every year. Take your art easy, if it'll let you. Don't be hag-ridden, even by the Muse.

I've done nothing for about eleven weeks. As soon as I've cleaned up my corre-spondence, I'm going to write a grove-play for the Family Club, and get together the material for my next book.[1] Robertson can't bring it out till June 1st, though.

I think I can get away by Mch. 20th. Before I go I'll run up and pay you a brief visit—I don't like the "stop-over" idea.

Carrie is living up at the Key Route Inn, where also my mother and a few of my sisters live. I hear to my grief that she's unhappy. May Time make her less so! As for me, I don't care especially *what* becomes of me. I feel "all adrift," and have no use, yet, for my new, and strange (to me), freedom. It was crowded on me, anyhow, as you are aware.

It's beautiful here—soft and sunny. The willows are budding and the woods are full of wild-flowers. The surf was so great on our beach last month that ledges are ex-posed of whose existence no one here was aware. The river overflowed, and damaged fields and roads to a considerable extent. I'm wondering if cottontails can swim: lots of them must have needed to!

I sold some poems to the "Call" for $10. each, and *gave* "Town Talk" three or four. It became too late to send them east.

Well, good hunting! And a lighter heart! Affectionately, George.

1. The play was *The Flight,* performed by the Family Club in early September. The work is unpublished (ms., Bancroft Library). The book was *BB.*

[104] CAS to GS [ALS]

Auburn, Cal.,
Feb. 27, 1914.

Dear George:

Several wasted weeks have passed since I received your last letter, and have found me without the energy to attempt an answer. As you know, I am not usu-ally such a sluggard in my correspondence. But, in the name of all the damned, how is one to make a decent letter out of nothing? I feel duller than—a dead codfish, for ex-ample—and have been able to write nothing. I've started half-a-dozen poems since the first of the year, but have finished none of them, with the exception of a rather indif-ferent prose-poem. I begin to think that the Muse is a jade, like most of her sex.

Have you any of the poems of Lloyd Mifflin?[1] I'd like you to lend them to me if you have. An unknown correspondent "detects" his influence in my work; which is very interesting, as I've never read any of the man's poems, with the exception of a few sonnets in an anthology—

I suppose you're right about my depression being due to physical causes. My di-gestion has been rather disordered for over a year,—ever since I was in Carmel, to be exact. Also, I've not been taking my usual amount of outdoor exercise.

I'm praying for good weather during your visit here in March, so that we can take some long walks. Some of the scenery is worth seeing, tho by no means equal to that on the Coast. There's a lot here that I've not seen myself. I don't feel much incentive to walking-trips, unless I've someone to go with me, which isn't more than once in a green moon.

I shall be inexpressibly glad to see you; and selfishly so, too, to some extent, I suppose. I feel the need of someone to assure me that I'm sane, or even alive. I doubt both, half the time. I've been living off here on the edge of nothingness too long, I think, and am haunted by the fear that I may slip over some day.

Let me know the day of your arrival, and the train, if possible, so that I can meet you. I live over a mile from the town, and you'd find my place rather difficult to locate without a guide, on account of the multiplicity of cross-roads.

As ever, Affectionately,

Clark.

1. Lloyd Mifflin (1846–1921). American poet best known for his sonnets and his imitations of Greek poets. Houghton Mifflin published a few of his books.

[105] GS to CAS [ALS]

Carmel, Cal.,

Mch. 11, 1914.

Dear Clark:

I've been up in S. F. for ten days, or you'd have heard from me ere now. I'll stay here about ten days, I guess, and then go to the city for good. Hope to visit you about the 23rd.

I've none of Mifflin's books, though I've read many of his sonnets. Some are excellent. I believe he writes in no other form, and has written several hundred. He's a relative of the publisher.

All's well along the Carmel, except that I have to stay indoors this soft, blue morning and write a dozen letters. So be forgiving if this one is a short one.

As usual, I'm writing nothing, though I got that grove-play done and was paid $250. for doing it. I'm getting the material in shape for my book now, as Robertson is getting impatient.

I suppose you saw the indecent ruction as to my engagement. It was grossly exaggerated—what Miss T. said. In fact it was *all* wrong except the possibility that we may get married some day.[1]

Affectionately,   George.

1. GS refers to his girlfriend Estelle Tuttle; for *possibility* he had initially written *fact*.

[106] GS to CAS [ALS]

Mch. 24, 1914.

Dear Clark:

I'm off to-day on a visit to London, Albert Bierce, and you. I have only five days in which to see you all, so I'll be able to put in only 2 nights with you (and part of a day) as I must be back in S. F. by Sunday noon.

I've made no enquiries as to trains yet, but shall try to get one that gets to Auburn Friday afternoon some time.

I'm not giving you much advance notice, nor even a chance to head me off if the time isn't propitious. But if you've guests on hand I can stay at an Auburn hostelry, and we can have a walk and a talk, anyhow.

Just turned my MSS over to Robertson. They'll make a book of about 170 pages. He promises to get right to work on it. But, as you know, he's a sluggish cuss.

Hoping to see you on Friday, I am, as ever,

Yours affectionately,   George.

[107] GS to CAS [ALS]

Glen Ellen,

Mch. 25, 1914.

(57th day on water-wagon.)

Dear Clark:

I'll not be able to get to Auburn before Saturday. There's a train leaving S. F. about noon-time, and I'm going to catch that, probably at Vallejo Junction.

I can't get to Guerneville before to-morrow evening, and Old Man Bierce will feel hurt if I stay there only over night. I can be with you Sunday, however.

Go to *absolutely no* "fuss" on *my* account! It would make me feel bad.

Affectionately,   George.

[108] GS to CAS [ALS]

Bancroft, Neb.,

Apr. 17, 1914.

Dear Clark:

I've finally escaped from the dentist and got as far as Nebraska—which is more than half way in point of time, even if *only* half way in respect to distance.

I'm staying here at John Neihardt's, whom you know, I think, as a true poet. He is book-reviewer for the Minneapolis Journal, a paper of some consequence, and if you'll send him one of your books he'll give it a good review. I wish you'd do this, whether you care for the review or not, for he's a fine fellow, and greatly interested in you from what I've told him of you.

I'll return to Omaha this afternoon, and catch a night train to Chicago, with the hope of being in Ann Arbor by to-morrow evening. It's a big nuisance having to stop over *so much*—I'm not regretting *this* visit; but I should really have been in N. Y. weeks ago.

Auburn and its environs looked beautiful as I passed through, Monday afternoon. I waved a final good-bye in the direction of your home. I'm glad that you live in Placer County instead of Nebraska. Talk about monotony! You'd go crazy here. One eternal expanse of brown, rolling plain.

My address in N. Y. will be

The Lambs

130 W. 44th St.

Affectionately,   George.

[109] CAS to GS [ALS]

Auburn, Cal.
Apr. 25th, 1914

Dear George:

I've forwarded a copy of "The Star-Treader" to John Neihardt, as per your instructions. I don't care much for reviews, as you know, but I'd certainly value one from Neihardt. There's little trustworthy criticism to be had, since Bierce quit writing. Literature seems to be sharing the general demoralization of the age. And criticism, always the most pestiferous of parasites, appears to grow fatter and more offensive upon its corruption. It's a pity that Whitman, the prophet of Chaos—chaos on earth—isn't alive at this day to see the fell effect of his doctrines upon literature,—particularly in Miss Monroe and her crew of poetic I.W.W.'s.[1]

As usual, I've no news. I've written nothing, and done nothing, save to curse the leaden flight of unprofitable time. I don't mind things as much when I can write. But my brain seems as sterile as any of the moraines you'll remember seeing hereabouts.

I enclose a couple of "snaps", which you may like to have—one of my parents and myself together, and one of me standing in a rocky field.

Do you think you could place any of my prose-poems in New York? I've several, as you'll remember, and hope to write a few more presently. I've just amassed the nerve to send "The Demon, Angel, etc" to the Atlantic Monthly, but scarcely expect that they'll take it. The form is so unusual in English literature, that I'm doubtful as to whether the magazines would consider it.

Nebraska must be a hashish-dream of a place—a sort of infinity rolled flat. I'd rather live in Hell—the infernal scenery has more variety, if Dante and Dorè are to be trusted as geographers.

As ever, affectionately,
Clark.

1. The Industrial Workers of the World, a radical labor organization.

[110] GS to CAS [ALS]

[The Lambs
130 West 44th Street
New York]

May 6, 1914.

Dear Clark:

I've had little time to myself in roaring Gotham, or I'd have given attention ere now to yours of the 25th. But I'm usually belated with letters, anyhow.

I don't like N. Y., and suppose few folk really do. There are some fine chaps here, though, and I've met some of them already. It's a cruel, sensual city, and will serve to make S. F., in the future, seem young and gentle.

I went to a meeting of the Poetry Society last week, and saw Kilmer, Wheelock, Cawein, Viereck, Scollard and other poets there.[1] C. and S. seem rather venerable. There is a picnic of the Society up the Hudson, Saturday, and I hope to go and see several other singers. Ella Wheeler is apt to be there![2]

I had luncheon with Witter Bynner at the Players this noon. He's a fine chap, tho' not just our kind of a poet. Saw Burgess too.

I feel pretty homesick for Carmel, and lonesome, despite more and better friends than I deserve. However, the feeling should wear off after a while. Anyhow, I'll try to stick it out here for a year. I can at least make a living.

You'll hear from young Hyatt soon.[3] Be nice to him. He's your age, and a poet, tho' far from your poetic stature. He means very well.

It must be nice in Auburn now. Here one would hardly know "country" existed. A stone inferno.

> Affectionately,   George.

1. GS refers to the American poets Joyce Kilmer (1886–1918), John Hall Wheelock (1886–1978), Madison Cawein (1865–1914), and Clinton Scollard (1860–1932). For Viereck see letter 83, n. 1.

2. Ella Wheeler Wilcox (1850–1919), American poet and newspaper columnist whose platitudinous prose and verse AB and GS frequently ridiculed.

3. Norbert Hyatt. At about this time, GS had written to JL that Hyatt "wanted me to go around the world with him" and to John Neihardt that Hyatt is "quite a poet."

[111] GS to CAS [ALS]

> Sag Harbor, N. Y.,
> June 4. 1914.

Dear Clark:

I've escaped from the City of the Damned for a few months, and Sag Harbor will, I hope, be my address till late in October. There's a certain amount of hectic excitement about the metropolis, and I met some fine folks there, as well as a lot of useful editors, etc. But I've the country too deep in my nature to be happy for long in a city, even San Francisco. But I expect to pass the winter in N. Y. or Bermuda, and return to California next Spring.

This old town where I was born is a sweet old place, with long, bent streets made cavernous with big elms and maples. There's a freshness and tenderness that California never quite gets. But it pays for that in winter—the East does.

I'm rather lonesome here, so far, as my relations here are old and conventional; and I've outgrown such old friends as still infest the town. But the Upton Sinclairs may come here for the summer, soon; and Hyatt says he's coming early in July.

I live at the hotel here, and find it comfortable. I've never had to be alone this way before: always there have been close fiends and a sweetheart. Can't say that I like the change!

It's night, and raining hard. I've been reading till I feel stuffy, and have also sorted over some sea-shells I'm sending to the Neihardt kiddies, in monotonous Nebraska. I've not got down to work yet, in any serious way, though I've several poems and stories in mind, and orders for them all.

"The Orchid of Beauty" is very much to my taste. *I* don't find it obscure, nor have I any alterations to suggest.

I don't intend to live in my uncle's house here, as the bill for water would be too high. I'm to have his smallest gasoline boat, though to knock around in. It's a late

Spring here, and too cold for swimming yet—at least for me: the kids go in to some extent.

I got the galley-proofs of my book, but so far the book-proofs haven't appeared. Robertson is notoriously slow, however; and a printers' strike has been on for some time, I think.

I saw Markham, Carman, Cawein, Viereck, Wheelock, Kilmer, O'Hara, Mrs. Wagstaff, Zoë Akins[1] and many other poets in N. Y. Markham will have a book out soon.[2] Three of us took him to dinner one evening last week, and the old gentleman got quite "lit up" on table-claret, and was a joy to us and the neighbors. But that is between you and me.

"Write to me when the spirit moves."

Affectionately,   George.

1. Bliss Carman (1861–1929), John Myers O'Hara (1870–1944), Blanche Shoemaker Wagstaff (1888–?), Zoë Akins (1886–1958), American poets.

2. *Children in Bondage* (1914), a landmark in the crusade against child labor.

[112] CAS to GS [ALS]

Auburn, Cal.
June 23rd, 1914

Dear George:

Here's another delayed letter; but as usual, I've not had a blessed thing to write about, which you'll admit is a most excellent excuse for silence.

I suppose you've read about the volcanic activities of Mt. Lassen? The peak is not visible from here, on account of a range of intervening foothills; but I saw the smoke from it drifting down the Sacramento Valley several days ago—a thin brown ribbon a hundred miles or more in length. We had a slight earthquake last week; *I* didn't notice it, doubtless being out-of-doors at the time, but others in the vicinity did.

The leopard-lilies, which grow in the canyon near by, are in blossom now. I've an enormous bunch of them—almost an armful,—in front of me on the table as I write. I found one stem, well-nigh as tall as myself, which held sixteen of the huge and gorgeous blossoms. My hands were brown with the cinnamon-like pollen when I reached home with the lot.

My mood of laziness and sterility seems to continue. I enclose nearly all the work that I've done during the month—a lyric and a brief prose-poem, both of them fantasies of a rather mortuary nature. I don't know that you'll care for them; however, they're about as good as I can do without inspiration.

By the way, I've had no acknowledgement from John Neihardt of the copy of my book which I sent him nearly two months ago, at your request. I wish you'd ascertain, when you write to him, as to whether or not he's received it.

Affectionately yours,
Clark.

[Enclosures: "A Phantasy of Twilight," "The Sun and the Sepulchre."]

[113] GS to CAS [ANS][1]

[postmarked 30 June 1914]

Dear Clark: I have your letter, and shall write soon. Too hot here now for correspondence.

Am at work again, but it's a case more of quantity than quality.   George.

1. *Front:* Rome—Tomb of John Keats.

[114] GS to CAS [ALS]

Sag Harbor, N. Y.,
July 14, 1914.

Dear Clark:

I fear I've less even than you *say* you have, to impart in the matter of news. But here is your *excellent* poem to comment on, which I'll venture to the extent of saying I like it very much, but am of the opinion that it's first line is too suggestive of that which begins "The Rubaiyat."[1] Also I think you could find a far better adjective than the rather banal (to me at least) "important." Say "portentous," or something like it. The third stanza is especially fine: I wish I were doing work as good.

I've been industrious enough, but one takes a lower key in the debilitating eastern climate. I've written sixteen poems, a 6000 word story and 2000 words on another tale, within a month; none of the poems have sold yet, and the story is not yet typed, so poverty impends. But I shall make out well enough. Still, I'd be happier in Carmel, though that home of the termite is now given over to the horrors of amateur theatricals.

But I'll stay east for the winter, anyhow, I'm thinking. There are some things I want to do in New York then. I want to get better acquainted with the d—— editors, also. That helps, though they won't admit it.

I wish I could have seen that leopard-lily. We used to call Ina Cowdery "Panther-lily!"[2] I didn't know there was a "leopard" one.

You may have heard from Neihardt by this time. I owe him *two* letters, and shall mention your book when I write him.

The thought in "The Sun and the Sepulchre" is splendid. I wish you'd put it into metre, though. It's *too good* for prose, even your prose-poetry.

Hyatt is here with me now, and mild, conventional little chap, too good, conservative, and a practising Presbyterian! He may remain all summer. He's no bother, though.

Here is my picture; here are two of my solemn poems.
                    Affectionately,   George.

[P.S.] I guess you *mean* "important" to be a rather "chesty" word. Correct!

[Enclosures: "Autumn" and one unidentified poem.]

1. Cf. "A Phantasy of Twilight," l. 1: "Ere yet the soaring after-fire was flown." See further letter 115.
2. Ina Cowdery Beckman, one of three sisters whom GS knew during his years in Carmel, all strikingly beautiful.

[115] CAS to GS [ALS]

Manzanita Springs,
Weimar, Cal.
July 27th, 1914.

Dear George:

I'm staying for a few days with some English friends of mine, on their ranch twelve miles or so above Auburn. The country is quite different here, considering the smallness of the distance, and the temperature is a few degrees cooler. The scenery is much wilder, and is full of ravines which are deep and steep enough to be called canyons. I'm told that there are rattlesnakes in the vicinity. But I've neither seen nor heard one during the five days that I've spent in scrambling up and down the manzanita-covered hills roundabout. And the genus homo is well nigh as scarce as the rattlesnakes.

You're quite right about the resemblance of the first line of my poem to the one in the Rubaiyat:—"Before the phantom of false morning died," which begins the second quatrain of that poem. It's strange that I'd not noticed the reminiscence before. I've not thought of a new line, so far.

Thanks for the picture—Lord, but you do look doleful! And have you really grown so thin as that? Or is the lens of the camera to blame?

I like the "Autumn" poem the best of the two you send. The other is excellent, too, but it doesn't appeal to me so much.[1]

I've done very little, myself, and marvel at your industry. My health is to blame, I suppose: I can't digest anything, it would seem, and have been suffering from the curse of constipation to boot.

I shall enclose a prose-poem that I have with me, if it seems good enough on re-reading. My faculties are too relaxed for composition in verse.

I wish you could see this place. The scenery is not unlike some of the Carmel country, tho steeper, on the whole. There's rather a variety of conifers—the sugar pine, the spruce, the cedar, the yellow pine, and a sort of fir whose name I forget, besides the common grey and green pines. The golden-rod is beginning to appear, and there are a few other flowers. I found some columbines in the canyon the other day—a flower that I've never seen before. The only objectionable thing is the omnipresent tar-weed: one's shoes become fairly coated with the tar from walking thro whole fields of it.

Don't address me here when you write: I shall probably return to Auburn before the middle of the present week.

Affectionately,
Clark.

[Enclosure: unidentified prose poem.]

1. A poem entitled "Autumn" appears in HO, but it is unlikely that this is the poem sent to CAS. Perhaps the poem is "In Autumn" (in CE).

[116] GS to CAS [ALS]

Sag Harbor, N. Y.,
July 29, 1914.

Dear Clark:

Do you care to help me with the enclosed story?[1] You see I don't know my Sierran scenery at all well, nor the method of staking out claims. And as your father is something of a miner I suppose *he can* describe the conventional procedure.

So I'm hoping that you'll not mind re-writing parts of this indifferent tale and getting in a bit more "atmosphere" anon the legal way to stake out a claim. I don't know even the town where the filing should be done, as I don't recall just what county the railway goes through along the crest of the Sierras. I dare say your father will find much to criticise in the story.

But if you've the time to give to "touching it up" I'll be grateful, and will do the right thing financially by you when the story "sells." I suppose it *will* sell, eventually.

No news here. I'm hard at work now.

Affectionately,   George.

1. Unidentified; possibly not completed or published.

[117] CAS to GS [ALS]

Auburn, Cal.
Aug. 5th, 1914.

Dear George:

I'm returning your story with only a pencilled comment or two on the margin. Your scenic description seems correct enough to me, and I think you've worked in sufficient "local color" for so short a story. *I* couldn't do anything better with it. Your "claim-staking" is all right, too: there's nothing more to it than the putting up of signs at a certain distance—150 feet, I think, on each side of the ledge. Auburn, as the capital of the county, is the place where any claim taken up in the mountains near the railroad would have to be filed: Placer extends to the border of the state, and the S. P. runs thro it all the way—Ophir (the place you named,) is a dead mining town, below Auburn, and not even on the railroad.

Do you think there's enough plot in the story? It doesn't seem to me that it's likely to sell as it stands. You should have something at once more probable and more interesting. I wish I could suggest a new plot; but my mind seems entirely sterile, and capable of nothing but negative criticism.

By the way, here's an idea which you might use as the germ of a story: An alienist catches the contagion of insanity from the lunatics under his charge. I don't remember to have seen the conception used before. There should be possibilities in it.

There's nothing new. Even the devil seems to have forsaken this town of the perambulating dead, and has left such souls as are available hereabout, to rot within (and before) their bodies. He's wise not to waste his time in foraging for such wretched hell-fuel as the Auburnites are likely to make.

Affectionately, Clark

P.S. My father tells me that a Californian quartz-claim is 300 feet in width and 1500 in length,—the length being, of course, parallel with the ledge. Signs denoting ownership are set up at each of the four extremities.

[Enclosure: unidentified prose poem.]

[118] GS to CAS [ALS]

Sag Harbor, N. Y.,
Sept. 10ᵗʰ, 1914.

Dear Clark:

I find a letter from you in a stack of the letters (I've always kept yours by themselves) and fear that, like those others, it hasn't been answered. Do forgive the oversight! I'd been expecting to hear from you, and now know why I haven't.

Thanks very much for going over my bum story. I agree with all you say; but pot-boilers don't have to be good.

Now that autumn is on us, I'm hoping that you're feeling more like work. The summer here has been unprecedentedly cool, and I've managed to write five stories, such as they are, and over sixty poems. From Aug. 5ᵗʰ to Sept. 1ˢᵗ I wrote war-sonnets, sometimes two a day, as I've 36 on hand.[1] I've done little since then, however, having had to be in N. Y. seeing old friends from California. I have to go up again, this after-noon, to see James Hopper, but hope to get to work by day after to-morrow. I'm mak-ing a living, but no more. I suppose I'm lucky to do even that much.

The prose-poem you send is a beauty—and big in thought. You have a peculiar faculty for such work. They'll make a great book some day.

Robertson has been incredibly slow (as usual) with mine. It should have been out last spring, but all the time he intended to make it a "fall" book—and me a "fall guy." For had he been frank with me I could have gone on sending lots of the poems in it to magazines insteady [sic] of job-lotting them to the measly "Call." I figure I'm out $100. on his reticence, to call it by no harsher term.

My book is probably out by now, and I'll send you a copy as soon as I get one. It's a long ways from being as good a book as the third one, as *you* know.

Autumn is on us too, and its coolness makes me wild with energy, the water-wagon and a *girlless* life also assisting, no doubt. I expect to stay here till late in October, though. Then N. Y. I suppose I can stand it till Spring.

Affectionately,   George.

1. Many were gathered in *BiB*.

[119] CAS to GS [ALS]

Auburn, Cal.
Sept. 17th, 1914

Dear George:

Your war-sonnets are very much superior to anything else on the subject that I've seen—which isn't paying them so very high a compliment. The last of the three is the best, I think. You'll perhaps have noticed by now that the Literary Digest quotes your sonnets with praise unusually just, considering the source.[1]

I fear I've done nothing at all to compare with the fruits of your incredible industry. The trifling and not overly well-executed lyric, and rather solemn sonnet which I enclose, are all that I've brought to completion of the numerous poems that I've intended to write, and the few that I've begun. Ideas come to me often enough; but I've neither the strength or courage to wrestle with them. It's a matter of health, I suppose.

I'm very glad to hear that you're so well, and that you're exempt from the visits of what De Quincey calls "the formidable curse of taedium vitae."[2] I wish I could say as much for myself. But no one can be really well with a stomach that's forever starting Mexican revolutions. It's more than a metaphor when I say that I've no stomach for anything at present.

Ever yours, affectionately,
Clark.

[Enclosures: two unidentified poems.]

1. Three of GS's sonnets "To Germany" appeared in *Literary Digest* 49, No. 11 (12 September 1914): 465, as "To Europe." They had first appeared in *New York World Magazine,* 16 August 1914, p. 2.

2. From the preface to *Confessions of an English Opium-Eater* (1821–22) by Thomas De Quincey (1785–1859).

[120] GS to CAS [ALS]

Sag Harbor, N. Y.,
Oct. 4, 1914.

Dear Clark:

As usual, I'm in arrears to you for a good letter; but I have to write so many, including one or two a day to my fiancée in S. F. Also I've been up in N. Y. most of the past two weeks, as the guest of one person or another. And N. Y., whatever its faults or merits, surely doesn't put one in a letter-writing mood.

I'm still here by the inland sea, but expect to go to N. Y. for the winter in a couple of weeks, or when a dentist has done something for some teeth of mine. I imagine I can make a living there, though so far I've not done so, and were it not for $250. that Barbour Lathrop gave me, I'd be in quite a hole.

The 36 or so war-sonnets I wrote don't sell; and I've only just turned my stories over to Paul Reynolds, the literary agent. I've sold three sonnets to the Sunday World, and of other poems (?) two to the Delineator, two to the Youth's Companion, and two to the squalid Munsey's,[1] whose editor is a friend of mine, apparently.

I'm sorry that your health should be such that you do not feel more like clothing the thoughts that come to you. But what you do do you do well. There is much beauty in the lyric you send, tho' I don't like "sunshine smile." And the sonnet is admirable, especially the *great* sestet. Bierce would have exclaimed over that. I hear that the "Departments at Washington" think that Villa had him shot.

The autumn is fairly on us here, and the cold drives me wild with energy. Being on the wagon helps, too. I've a lot of poems in mind, especially one on a caged eagle in the Bronx Zoo. But I *should* be giving all my time to prose, damn it!

The swimming is over here, and that is the main attraction of the place. I suppose I can do better in N. Y. financially. So I'll have to go back to paved walks ere long. I forget what poems I've sent you, but—here's one!

Affectionately,   George.

[P.S.] Tell your father that the sufferers from rheumatism here get relief from cutting out starchy food from their dietary.

[Enclosure: "Bombardment."]

1. See letter 131, n.1 for the sonnets sold to the *World.* The two poems sold to the *Delineator* are "The Seasons" and "Henri"; "The Fish Hawk" is the only poem that appeared in *Youth's Companion;* "After Vacation" and "Night Sounds" appeared in *Munsey's.*

[121] CAS to GS [ALS]

Auburn, Cal.
Oct. 16, 1914.

Dear George:

I see by to-day's issue of "Town Talk" that your new book is out at last. They (Town Talk) give you a very good notice, but can't forbear crowing over the fact that you've "come down to earth" in some of your magazine poems. You'll have seen the notice, tho, I suppose, by the time this reaches you.[1]

I've just received a letter from Robertson,—the first I've had from him for over a year—enclosing a fifty-dollar check to cover the first royalties on "The Star-Treader." I'm very much surprised that the book has done so well. Robertson doesn't say *how* many copies have sold, but the number must be close to nine hundred, since I was to receive no royalty at all on the first five hundred.

I'm glad to get this money, since I'll at last be able to repay the ten dollars which I owe you. I shall enclose a postal money-order with this letter.

The sonnet ("Bombardment") which you send, is good, tho I'd rather see you use another word than the cliché, "screaming." Why not "hurling", which can be used intransitively? There's enough about sound-effect in the preceding line, it seems to me.

I've little to send you in return, I fear, except the fragment of an "Ode to Beauty," which I've not had the strength to complete. I may try to finish it some day, if you think it worth while.

My father and I are sinking a shaft on our land at present—ostensibly for water.[2] But I hope to hell there'll be more at the bottom of it than that. Poverty grows monotonous after a time; and for me, it would seem, the only way out leads thro a gold-mine. We may strike "bedrock" before so very long.

Did you ever use a quill-pen? I'm writing this letter with one—the wing-feather of a hawk. It moves more easily and lightly than a steel pen—

Affectionately,
Clark.

[Enclosure: "Ode to Beauty" (fragment).]

1. Theodore Bonnet wrote an unsigned review of BB in *Town Talk* No. 1156 (17 October 1914): 12.

2. In April 1961, CAS was compelled under court order to fill the shaft.

[122] GS to CAS [ALS]

43 Washington Square, *South*
New York,

Nov. 16, 1914.

Dear Clark:

I should have answered your letter before this, but moved from Sag Harbor soon after it came, and have had all my time since then taken up in visiting friends and in getting settled in this now abode of mine. It's a big rear room on the second floor of one of the old, old houses on this picturesque and historic square, and is large (27 × 18, and 14 in height!) and well-lighted. But I had to install a stove, for winter is here now. But the stove is a wonder!

I've not got down to any literary work yet, even to selling any, but shall as soon as I've caught up with my correspondence. I *feel* like work, and hope that *you* do by now. The piece of ode you sent me is beautiful, so far as it goes, and I hope you've gone on with it.

Other poets here know of you, and often ask about you. Poets seem to keep track of one another.

Thanks so much for the $10.! I think I took at least two of your books and had them charged to you. So get some of my last from Robertson and have them charged to *me*. I sent you an inscribed copy, no doubt. It's not so poetic as the third book, tho R. may sell more copies of it. I saw the review you mention. They *meant* well, so I can't complain. In the "Literary Digest" of Nov. 7th is another rather too kind review. Joyce Kilmer wrote it. I've seen only those two notices.[1]

I'm so glad your book sold so well! You have a right to feel fortunate. I've sold no more of any one edition of *my* books, with all the free advertising I've had, and a long "head-start." You'll have a job getting any precise statement from R. He means well, but is inefficient in that way, and an incurable procrastinator.

I wish you all sorts of luck with that shaft. It would be *great* if you "struck it!"

The conclusion of this letter is lost.

[Enclosure: "Conspiracy."]

1. GS refers to a notice of BB in the *Literary Digest* 49, No. 19 (7 November 1914): 903.

[123] CAS to GS [ALS]

Auburn, Cal.,
Nov. 30th, 1914.

Dear George:

I've not seen your new book as yet, but am writing to Robertson for a copy. You must be mistaken in thinking that you sent me one. I've seen no review of it save the mention in Town Talk; but that's not surprising, as I've about ceased reading the periodicals. There's nothing in them but mediocrity and vulgarity; and I'd rather not risk the insidious contamination of such a mental atmosphere.

As usual, there's no news worth recording; and I find myself faced with the necessity of manufacturing a letter out of nothing. What *is* there to write of, in the dreary procession of days that forms my life? What, indeed, save a list of the things I have *not* done,—of sterile thoughts, and poems that never passed the stage of conception?

However, I shall at least *try* to do something before long. [[There's a great deal in effort, in arousing a dormant inspiration.]][1] The mere effort of composition often helps to arouse a dormant muse.

I like the conception of the poem you send ("Conspiracy"), but I wish it were more musical. You've rather too many monosyllables, I think. Several lines are made up entirely of such.

We've had but little rain as yet, and the autumn still smoulders in these inland valleys. The day is overcast with a high fog, thro which the sun looks as cold and dull as a disk of beaten lead.

I hear that Robertson is publishing an Anthology of California poets. Have you seen it? It's amusing to note (judging from a review that I read) how few of the poets included are Californian. But I suppose there'd be little to include, if only selections from native writers were chosen. [2]

Affectionately, as ever,

Clark.

1 CAS has crossed out this sentence.

2. Augustin S. Macdonald, ed., *A Collection of Verse by California Poets from 1849 to 1915* (San Francisco: A. M. Robertson, 1914). The volume contains CAS's "A Dream of Beauty," p. 54, and GS's "Night Sentries," pp. 87–88.

[124] GS to CAS [ALS]

43 S. Washington Square,
New York,

Dec. 15, 1914.

Dear Clark:

It's very strange that I didn't send you my last book—you should have been among the very earliest to receive it. Somehow I forgot. Forgive me.

I too have seen few reviews of it, but don't care if it receives none at all. Reviews are fatuous things. I couldn't help, however, being pleased by the "boost" the book got in the "Literary Digest" of Nov. 7th. Joyce Kilmer, himself a poet, wrote it.

I don't blame you for not reading the magazines! They are truly awful, and get worse every month, if such a thing is possible.

I'm sorry you find life so dull. Probably you'll have to "grin and bear it" for a while yet. When I return to California, I'll try to take measures that may make things brighter for you, and for your parents. But I'm going to stay here for the winter, I think. I'm not at all successful, but don't mind that, so long as I can exist and "size things up."

The poem "Conspiracy" isn't one I should *care* to have "musical." Preferable to its spirit is the funereal tolling of monosyllables, and if you'll observe again, you'll find I've done it rather well, without *over*-doing it. I've just written the poem for the B. C.'s Christmas Jinks, a job I detested, and was long in performing.

Yes—Macdonald's wretched "Anthology" was sent to me. You should see the three *things* of his in it! I'll send it to you when I've examined it more leisurely. He used your "Dream of Beauty," by no means representative of your work. He's a white worm, all right!

It's cold here now—20° above. I'll not mind it so long as I can buy coal.

Yours ever,   George.

[125] CAS to GS [ALS, Mills]

Auburn, Cal—,
Jan. 4th, 1915.

Dear George:

I've had a copy of your new book by me for some time, and have just been re-reading it carefully to verify or correct my former impression. Many of the poems are new to me, among them "The Last Monster" which is one of the strongest in the book, at least in point of thought. The conception is impressive and memorable.

The Browning Ode is, of course, one of your greatest poems; it's nearly all excellent and contains a number of marvellous single lines, such as "The indomitable laughter of the race", and "The hidden azures of eventual skies", not to mention others which seem to me nearly as admirable. No one but you could have written such lines, containing as they do a fine and original thought expressed in a diction as pure as rock-crystal. "War", "The Thirst of Satan", "Lineage", "The Coming Singer", "Said the Wind", "The Sleepers", "Discord," please me most among the briefer poems. The sestet of "The Setting", and the octave of the first sonnet of "Omnia Exeunt in Mysterium", linger in my memory for their peculiarly clear and graphic sententiousness. They're as quotable as anything in Pope's "Essay on Man"—and fifty times more poetical. I like also that bit of rollicking cynicism, "You Can Never Tell", and the coyote poem, which is better than any of the verses about animals that Kipling includes in his "Jungle Books."

I've nothing of my own to send you as yet; but I feel my ambition quickening once more, and, to use a poetical image, may gird myself before long to wrestle with the Angel of Art. I'm attaining a clearer sense of my faults, and promise myself that I will be continually vigilant against them in my future work. I wish you'd criticize everything that I send you, for harshness of rhythm or phonetic sequence, and overvague or merely conventional phrases and epithets. These I conceive to be my worst technical faults. They're thicker than thorns on a blackberry vine in most of my work; and even my best poems impress me on re-reading them, as hasty and inconsidered.

You'll have seen, by last week's "Town Talk," that some of your work is attracting attention and praise in London. It's good to think that your reputation is percolating even into the fog-invested citadel of insular prejudice.[1]

As ever, affectionately,

Clark.

1. See "The Spectator" [Theodore Bonnet], "London Discovers Sterling," *Town Talk* No. 1167 (2 January 1915): 10, telling of discussions of GS's work in the British magazine *New Age*.

[126] GS to CAS [ALS]

43 Wash. □
Feb. 4th, 1915.

Dear Clark:

I've been out of town, and writing an ode (on the exposition) for the "Examiner," and otherwise dissipating, and my correspondence has suffered in consequence.

I've sent them the ode—258 lines, for which I get 50¢ a line. There's more socialism and less exposition in it than they expected; but I suppose they'll not greatly mind. It's not so very poetical, but *says something*. So I'm not sorry to have it in print. It has pleased many of my friends here, too.

Thanks for all your kind words about my last book. I can respond with some that should please *you*. Lafler says of your "Harlot of the World," "What a tremendous sonnet! It says the last word. How does that lonely boy ever *get* such stuff?"

He wants to be of some help to you, in the matter of companionship, if he can, and wonders if you'd care to spend a couple of weeks with him at his home in Oakland (he lives with his mother). Should you care to, let me know, and I'll have him write to you.

I saw the "New Age" issues (got them at Brentano's) that spoke of me.[1] I don't attach any great importance to the matter, and don't care anyhow. Give me a warm room, a warm girl, a few dollars in hand, and all I ask of the world is that it leave me alone. Its plaudits are a joke and its attention a nuisance.

The winter of the east is with us at last, and I'm laughing at myself for imagining I'd ever mind the cold. I really don't seem able to feel it, I'm in so fine health and have so good a circulation. Snow has been falling since Sunday, to my joy, but 40000 men are wildly thrusting it into the sewers and rushing it away in wagons. The square opposite will always be beautiful, however, I think.

Turner is in N. Y. now, for a few weeks. I see him daily, as he's lonesome. Scheffauer writes he's likely to return to America soon. I suppose England is becoming too warm for so intense a Germanic sympathizer.

Here's an article that may interest you.

I hope you've felt like writing since Jan. 11th, and that you've something to show me. I've only the ode, and no spare copy of even that. You're not missing much, anyhow.

Affectionately,   George.

1. The following items regarding GS appeared in recent months in *New Age:* [Christopher Murray Grieve], "Rheims," 15, No. 14 (15 October 1914): 583 (as by "Pteleon"); G. R. Malloch, "George Sterling," 16, No. 3 (19 November 1914): 79; [Christopher Murray Grieve], "George Sterling," 16, No. 5 (3 December 1914): 134; D. G. Bunting, "George Sterling," 16, No. 6 (10 December 1914): 159; Henry Danielson, "George Sterling," 16, No. 6 (10 December 1914): 159; [Christopher Murray Grieve], "George Sterling," 16, No. 8 (24 December 1914): 207 (as by "Pteleon"); Upton Sinclair, "The Poetry of George Sterling," 16, No. 10 (7 January 1915): 261–62; Max Hereward, "The Poetry of George Sterling," 16, No. 12 (21 January 1915): 327; E[rnest] A. B[oyd], "American Notes," 16, No. 14 (4 February 1915): 377. One additional item appeared after GS had written to CAS: Gertrude Dix, "George Sterling," 16, No. 16 (18 February 1915): 439.

[127] CAS to GS [ALS]

Auburn, Cal.,
Feb. 16, 1915.

Dear George:

As usual, I find myself put to the task of manufacturing a letter out of nothingness, or of spinning it from myself, like the spider. Nor have I anything to send you except the prose-poem enclosed, a "Psalm to the Desert" in my usual vein. It's rather rough and hurried, and dismal even for a Bible parody. I'm sorry that I've nothing more cheerful to send; my mood for ripping up the universe seems to continue.

It's very, very kind of Mr. Lafler to invite me to visit him, but I fear that an acceptance is hardly possible at present. I wonder if he'd care to visit *me*, sometime in the spring when the weather is more pleasant; I should be delighted to see him, if he isn't too much of a sybarite for the accomodations [*sic*] which I'm able to offer. In the meantime, you must prefer him my thanks for his invitation; tell him to write to me if he will.

I have just read Macdonald's anthology. What a miserable collection of real-estate doggerels it is! There are *some* good things in it, tho, and the editor's own are so absolutely abominable that they're really an achievement of their kind. By the way, I thought Lafler's sonnet "Wireless" one of the best poems in the book.

I think of writing some psalms, and shall try to make them a little less dismal than the one I enclose. I may even write something of the kind in regular anapests. The repetitions of the Biblical style would greatly increase the sonority of such verse. You'll have noticed that this trick of repetition and redundancy is one of the secrets of Swinburne's volume of sound. Indeed, his whole style seems to me based on that of the Old Testament. He has even written rhymed paraphrases of some of its chapters . . . I shall probably take the mountains and the sea for subjects. One can hardly be anything but pessimistic about the desert.

As ever, affectionately,
Clark

[Enclosure: "Psalm to the Desert."]

[128] GS to CAS [ALS]

43 S. Washington Square,
New York,
Mch. 6th, 1915.

Dear Clark:

It's snowing heavily outside, and makes me think of that morning at your home. I think Lafler too would be glad to visit you, but doubt if he'll have the time. He always seems so "rushed." As to accomodations, [*sic*] you need not worry, as he has to do with far less when he's on his precipitous ranch below the Sur.

Your "Psalm to the Desert" has much imagination and sublimity in it, as has so much of your work. Even at that, I'm hoping you'll turn to other themes before long. The Abyss obsesses you overmuch. Still, who could ever "write it out?"

I keep on with my enjoyable life here, but find it so little conducive to writing that I intend to return to S. F. late in April, if I can raise the fare. I'm not selling much verse, though I had poems (?) in the "American Magazine" and "Delineator" for March.[1] But I got $125. from the "Examiner" for my exposition ode.

No one thought to send it to me, and the edition was sold out that day (Feb. 20th), so I suppose I'll never know just how it looked in print, nor how many errors the linotyper succeeded in making.

My young friend Hyatt asks me about orange culture in California, as he wants to buy a ranch there, plant it to oranges and hens, and put a Kansan friend (a school-teacher) in charge. I'm telling him to write to the Auburn Board of Trade (I hope there is one!)

Well, I wish it was April!

                    Affectionately,   George

[Enclosure: "The Caged Eagle"?]

1. "At the Last" and "Henri."

[129] CAS to GS [ALS]

                                Auburn, Cal.,
                             March 11th, 1915

Dear George:

      I hope you'll be able to stop over and visit me for a few days on your return. You'll come in the height of the season here, when the flowers are all out, and the months of long sunlight are assured. I want to see you, and have a long, long, leisurely talk with you—something that I seem never to have had.

Your "Caged Eagle" is a noble poem, as was also the Exposition ode, which I saw in the Examiner. I'll hunt up a copy of the latter, if I can find one, and enclose it with this. I think I can get the paper from the files of the local library—they give away old newspapers for the asking.

Your comments on "The Psalm to the Desert" are quite just. Still, why shouldn't the thing be written? It's quite true, and even original, since no one ever wrote anything really like it on the subject before, to my knowledge—Why shouldn't the Abyss be the dominant theme of my work? Other poets have made their main work a series of expatiations on some central subject, and no one has risen up to rebuke them for monotony or self-repetition. Poe really had but one theme—the death of a beautiful woman. And how about Rossetti and Swinburne, whose work deals mainly with passion, and sexual passion at that? However, it may be well to vary the images and symbols a bit, and I shall write less about the gulf for awhile. I've plenty of other themes, tho the ideas of change and death and evanescence will continue to be the ground-tones of my work. I shall write other things, tho—a "Psalm to the Sea" considered as the source and reservoir of all planetary life, and a few poems illustrative of certain of the less-handled Greek myths, such as that of the god Somnus . . . I think of doing a "Psalm to the Moth and the Worm", as the ministers of time and change, who liberate the atoms in decaying bodies, and deliver them over to the processes of new life. I shall tell of how these atoms dance and sing, and weave strange harmonies from dissolution—of how they jubilate in their freedom from the broken bonds of form—

Here are a few alterations for the Psalm to the Desert, which I sent to you in a rather crude state: For the sixth verse read: "Thy breasts are fallen from roundure, they are flat and rivelled: marah is all the milk thereof." In the eleventh, "terrible sighing of voidness." In the thirteenth, "a ban is proclaimed." And for the 15th, "Thy womb shall conceive but of death, the teeming thereof shall be dissolution, and the seed of corruption." You'll note that these changes simplify the grammar and help to explicate the sense.

I enclose a few short poems—nothing very good, I'm afraid. My main conceptions seem to hang in the air as yet.

I've been corresponding a good deal with Loveman of late. He's an odd genius—which I mean in the most complimentary sense,—and seems to have an inexhaustible supply of books (he sends me something with nearly every letter) and a treasury of praise to lavish on the few trifling poems that I give him in return—

Affectionately, as ever,

Clark

[Enclosures: "Inheritance," "Memnons at Midnight."]

[130] GS to CAS [ALS]

43 S. Wash. □ ,
New York,
Apr. 14, 1915.

Dear Clark:

I'm still here in neurasthenic Gotham, but hope to pull out by April 30th, as I'd have to dig up another month's rent if I don't. It's unlikely that I can stop over at Auburn, but as soon as I've seen the Exposition and something of Carmel, I expect to go to Yosemite for a month, and shall be able to see you en route. I suppose it's only a two or three days' journey from Auburn.

Of course if you want to file your first poetic claim on the Abyss, go ahead and do so. For that matter, you already have. Only, I didn't want you to play a "harp of a single string."

Don't bother about a copy of my ode: several friends have sent me copies.

Loveman is *all right*, and has written some real poetry. It's a pity he hasn't more time to devote to his art, for he has big possibilities in him. I'm glad you two correspond.

Have been living a very quiet life lately. My best friend here, Mrs. Putnam,[1] went to Bermuda for a rest, and was there operated on for appendicitis. So she'll not be back till next week. I'm expecting Hopper to return from Paris, any time now. He has been in the front trenches twice, and ought to be satisfied.

The poems you sent are all good—that "slow to leave the tavern of thy brain"[2] is terrific. But I like best the sonnet "Memnon at Midnight." The sestet of that is sublime. Send it to Loveman.

I've been absolutely sterile myself, so far as poetry is concerned, though I've done some prose work. New York seems to inhibit poetry in me. I'll do a lot of work this summer and autumn, however, so I'm not worrying. Long periods of rest are good for most any poet, I imagine.

I spent the last week-end out at the country-home of Mitchell Kennerley, the publisher. He gave me a lot of fresh eggs to take home with me! I'm not fond of the cold-storage variety that is New York's "one best bet."

It will be damned good to be back in California once more! I'm glad I spent this year in N. Y., since it taught me it has nothing I want. I left S. F. a year ago yesterday.

Just sold my "Witch" poem to "Munsey's."[3] I wish a better magazine had fancied it.

Affectionately,   George.

1. Nina Wilcox Putnam (1888–1962), American novelist.

2. "Inheritance," l. 16.

3. Apparently "The Slaying of the Witch."

[131] CAS to GS [ALS]

Auburn, Cal.,
Apr. 23rd, 1915.

Dear George:

I'm sorry that you can't stop over on your return. The country won't be nearly so inviting a month or so from now, because of the drying-up of the grass, which usually begins to "turn" early in May. However, I'll be hellishly glad to see you, anyway.

I've little enough that's worth recording. I have just answered a letter from Loveman, who speaks of being a bit "under the weather." I've had a touch of Spring fever myself, but have managed to write a few things—three or four prose-poems, and a few indifferent verses. I'll not bother to send them now—you can read them all when you're here, and I'll have more and perhaps better things to show you by that time. I seem to do most of my writing in the months between May and September.

The flowers are past their prime now, tho the Mariposa lilies are still to come— also the leopard lilies. I wish you could be here in time to see them. They're a gorgeous, barbaric blossom.

I've sold nothing at all to the magazines, and gave my "Harlot of the Generations" to Town Talk.[1] It was "impossible", I suppose, for any of the respectable eastern publications. I'll probably have to write some stories before long—it seems imperative that I should make a little money in some way or another. Damn the planet, anyway—it's fit only for the habitation of hogs, who enjoy rooting.

I've no intention of playing a "harp of one string." There'll not be nearly so much of the spacial element in my second book as in the other. Most of the things I plan are in the vein of the gorgeous or the ghastly,—anything but the ordinary, conventional type of nature-verse, for which I've come to realize that I don't care a whoop. But no more about that—we'll have time enough for literary argument when you're here.

Have you heard anything about Bierce? I've seen stories in the papers both affirming and denying his re-appearance. Loveman, who met him just before his departure for Mexico, seems to think that he may have disappeared merely for purposes of mystification.

Affectionately,
Clark

1. I.e., "The Harlot of the World."

[132] GS to CAS [ALS]

June 17th, 1915.

Dear Clark:

I suppose I'm in debt to you for a letter, since I've not heard from you for so long. The middle of June finds me still marooned in this (after N. Y.) very likable city, as I can't get off to Yosemite till the Nat. Supt. of Parks has returned from his vacation, and he returns to-morrow. So I'll perhaps be able to get off by next Tuesday.

If I do, it will have to be on a pass, I'm so poor. And that way, I'll not be able to go through Auburn. However, I'm promising myself a glimpse of you, and more, after our Jinks is over, as my friend Bender wants to have you see the Exposition, and will finance you here for a week, if you don't mind. *I*'d not mind.

As usual, I've written nothing for months—I never feel like writing in a city. Sent a letter off to Loveman to-day. He wanted a MS of Nora May's, but they're more scarce than hens' teeth, I'm afraid.

I hoped to go by motor to Yosemite (and Auburn too), but my friend's doctor won't let him go that way; so he has fled to Del Monte. London is still in Honolulu, but leaves for Cal. on July 13th, I think.

Markham is here. We're to have our Exposition poems brought out in the same booklet, as soon as he has completed his.

Yours ever affectionately,   George.

[133] CAS to GS [ALS]

Auburn, Cal.
June 19th, 1915

Dear George:

I'm deucedly sorry that you can't stop off on your way to the Yosemite,— we seem destined not to meet again. However, you won't miss very much, since the country is looking its worst—a desert of dry grass and "stickers". Also, my demons have been riding me hard of late, and you'd find me anything but amiable or entertaining.

Mr. Bender's offer is very kind, but I fear it's impossible for me to accept it. I feel too savage and morose to take favours from anyone, even your friend, of whom I've a very pleasant memory.

I enclose a few sonnets, for which I dare say you'll not care much. They're all that I seem inclined to write—a "safety-valve" for alternate fits of depression and devilishness ... Mandragora (as you may or may not know) which I've mentioned in more than one of the sonnets, was reputed an aphrodisiac at one time. Few will get the full force of the lines in which I've referred to this.

I'd like to get away from here for awhile, but I don't care about coming to San Francisco. Auburn seems worse than a desert, since it's full of bores and unattractive women. I don't go near it any oftener than I have to.

I've ceased to submit any of my work to the magazines. No respectable periodical would publish any of the four sonnets that I enclose. What hope is there for American literature as long as it's presided over by a lot of superannuated virgins?

Well, no more of this—I seem in too splenetic and exasperated a mood to write a decent letter. I suppose I'll see you before the year is out—you'd be welcome at any time, as you know. Or I may be able to get away from here, by some miracle.

> Affectionately,
> Clark—

[Enclosures: four unspecified sonnets: "Love Malevolent"? "Duality"?]

[134] GS to CAS [ALS]

July 27ᵗʰ, 1915.

Dear Clark:

After about a month wandering, I've anchored here again for a while, and shall try to catch up with my correspondence.

I was only two weeks in Yosemite, by which time I became so lonesome for my girl that I let a Bohemian friend, Barbour Lathrop, take me to Del Monte in his machine. He had three other Bohemians along, one of them Darrach, who is greatly interested in you.

We stayed at Del Monte for three days, before motoring up to S. F. That hotel bores me. Then I left for Carmel, to help the Herons over their summer madness of private theatricals, doing their house-work while they acted.

I managed to grind out a poem-to-order—nothing fit to send you. The *ode* is too long to copy, and has also a socialistic flavor that you'd dislike.

As to the four sonnets that you sent, I don't see why you should think I'd not like them. I think they're splendid! The two with the touch of passion interest me most. That's a new element in your work, and I hope you'll go on and develope [*sic*] it. Yes, they are four beautiful sonnets, and almost flawless.

I too have about ceased to send anything to the magazines. They're impossible. It isn't the editors' fault so much as the public's, however. The public hates real poetry; and the editor has to conform to its tastes, if he wants to live.

I'm going up to the Jinks next week, and after that to the London ranch for as many days as I can endure away from Stella. After that, I hardly know what to do: may take a newspaper job, in preference to starvation. It's not much better.

My beautiful sister Marian is coming up from Honolulu soon. I wish you could see her. I'm sorry you do not feel like accepting Bender's invitation. The exposition could do no especial good to a person of your great imaginative powers; but we could have some fine dinners together. Do you care to visit the Londons when I'm there?

My friend Hyatt gets here from San Diego to-morrow—a fortunate youth. What a hell of a lot money means, especially to the artist! He has the makings of a poet in him, too.

Did you ever write anything about Nora May French? And if not, do you care to? Lafler thinks of getting out a book comprised of various prose & poetical "tributes" to her. Loveman says he's on an elegy to her now. Lafler's beautiful "Pearl" was to her; and *I* have two or three things, as you know.[1]

Get your library to buy "Contemporary Portraits," by Frank Harris, if you want to read an interesting book. It's from Kennerley. $2.⁵⁰. He has Davidson, Wilde, Browning and several others in it.[2]

I live at Stella's now, but spend a good deal of time here in the Club. One can even work, in the library. But I've not felt (really) like work for over a year. Old age coming on, maybe?

Just had a letter from John Neihardt, who has finished a 3000+ word narrative poem that he has been two years at. "Hugh Glass," an epic of the old Nebraskan frontier. MacMillans are bringing it out, this autumn.[3]

Affectionately yours,   George.

1. The volume was never published, but CAS did eventually write a poem, "To Nora May French" (see letter 220). GS's poems on French include "The Ashes in the Sea" and "Nora May French." It is unknown if Loveman wrote his elegy.

2. Frank Harris (1856–1931), *Contemporary Portraits: First Series* (1915), a collection of critical essays.

3. John G. Neihardt, *The Song of Hugh Glass* (1915), the first of four epic poems on the American West.

[135] CAS to GS [ALS]

Auburn, Cal.
Aug. 16, 1915

Dear George:

It's good to write you a letter after so long. As usual, I've delayed thro lack of subject-matter, and, it would seem, might delay till doomsday for the same reason. Also, I've nothing to send you, except some prose-poems, and I've no extra copies of these, since my typewriter is temporarily out of order—However, you won't miss much.

I'm addressing you at Jack London's, since I presume you've reached there by this time. I fear it's impossible for me to join you, for I'm poorer than a Scotch mouse, and, even if I weren't, could scarcely find the time.

I'm glad you liked the sonnets. I plan to write some more presently, in a similar vein.

Here are some of my attempts at drawing. I hope they don't bore you. I like to draw, but really know very little about the art, and, I fear, have no very conspicuous talent for it. I've drawn a number of things in the vein of the weird and the grotesque, and will make copies of a few of them for you presently. There's one of a ghoul that you'd probably like—everyone thinks it too horrible to have around. "The Lich,['] "The Red Death," "The Vampire," "Abaddon," "The Abyss"—these are a few other titles.

Things have been even duller than usual this summer. I've not visited the local town in weeks, and have been too indolent to shave. Can you fancy me with the beginnings of a beard ala Swinburne?

You ask if I've ever written anything on Nora May French. I'd like to, but I fear I've no talent for personal or memorial verse. I've long intended to write an ode in honour of Poe, but have done nothing with it.

Please return good for evil, and write to me before so very long. Here are the drawings, among them a silhouette of yourself that I've drawn from memory. It may interest you.

As ever,

affectionately,
Clark.

[Enclosures: "The Blindness of Orion"?, "From the Crypts of Memory," "The Statue of Silence."]

[135a] GS to CAS [non-extant]

[San Francisco, Cal.
c. 18 August 1915]

[136] CAS to GS [ALS]

Auburn, Cal.,
Aug. 20th, 1915.

Dear George:

I wrote to you at Glen Ellen a few days before your card came. Perhaps the letter will have been forwarded to you by this time. However, there was nothing of importance in it.

All is "well" enough with me, I suppose—in a negative sort of way. My health, on the whole, seems better than it has been. It should be, since I've done no work to speak of, in months. I feel restless, even feverish at times. Do you think I'm in love? It seems to me that I am, in a general, collective way. I've all the symptoms of it.

"Work," as you use it in your card, is a most appalling sort of word to me. Do you really mean that you'll have to take a position in the city? It's hard for me to imagine you sweating away in that cheap inferno of brick and steel. I feel like swearing whenever I think of it. (Damn this pen!)

Tell Mr. Hyatt I'll be glad to see him, if he cares to stop off at Auburn. Anyone who has been with you will be welcome to me. Tell him to let me know the date, and I'll try to meet him at the train. He might have difficulty in finding me, otherwise.

My father and I are working on our shaft at present. The gravel looks good, but there's no telling. I *do* hope there's something at the bottom of it. If there isn't, I may find myself confronted with the disagreeable necessity of earning a living. I'm really as ill-prepared for that as if I had been brought up in affluence.

I'll try to enclose a prose-poem or two with this. I don't feel in the least like work. I seem unfit for anything but pleasure, and precious little of that ever comes my way.

I wish I might see you, but I fear it's impossible at present. I feel lonelier than ever, and more isolated from my friends. Mine, it would seem, is the fate of Alastor, tho I've hardly the temperament of the Poet of Solitude. Like Shelley himself, it seems to me that I desire affection more than anything else.

Write to me soon, if you can. Perhaps we'll have better news for each other, some day.

Affectionately,
Your friend,
Clark.

[Enclosure: "The Garden and the Tomb."]

[137] GS to CAS [ALS]

Aug. 21, 1915.

Dear Clark:

Both your letters are safely "at hand," as the business termites say, and I hasten to reply. I was at London's only for week-ends—twice lately. Of course if you'd signified a desire to be there I'd have sent you the fare. Perhaps you could "make it" next month. I may be there from Sept. 4th to 13th, as Stella has a vacation then.

The drawings you send have not much value as art, as you know; but the weird ones are imaginative, and I'd like to see you doing more of the sort. Cut out the females, and send me some spiders, hell-cats and octopi of the nether deep. I want to see "The Ghoul," "The Vampire" and the rest of that disturbing band, too. You *can* write a little elegy for Nora May, and you ought to. Don't try to force yourself, but just put the suggestion up to your subconscious mind every evening, as you drop off to sleep, and some day, the daemon will make its lyrical report to you.

I know just what it's like to feel restless, indifferent to work, and hungry for pleasure. It's one of an artist's most normal and familiar moods. I'm d—— sorry that you can't gratify it. Woman is about the only pleasure worth having, and when you're older she'll slam herself at your head in platoons. As you are now situated, all you can do is, I fear, to wait in patience. You've everything of *that* sort coming to you, if you'll only take your time and go on writing.

The shaft-work interests me greatly. Do stay with it! Who knows, you might hit it rich and become a patron of poets, myself (I *insist*) included. As for the work I may tackle here, don't worry—it would be nothing less agreeable than running a semiliterary "section" on one of the evening papers, and would be an easy living if I could land it. I have to be here, for love's here, and I'm bored to distraction without it.

If I had that "section" I could run some of your prose poems occasionally. They're always good. By the way, Robertson seems willing to bring out another book of poems for you, in a year. He thinks the P.P.I.E. is going go put him on his financial feet. I've enough for a new book, but he'll not be able to handle it till 1916.

"The Blindness of Orion" is good stuff—a few more unbroken lines than I fancy. That

"heard the ascending eagles hail the sun"[1]

is *great*. I've one or two references to eagles in the ode I wrote in Yosemite.[2] None so good as yours. I'd send this "fragment" to some of the monthlies, preferably the Century, the Forum and the N. A. Review. And I'd change "green" to the less lovely "blue," as the Mediterranean is the bluest of the oceans and seas.

"The Statue of Silence" is damned good, but I'd end it with "doom" instead of "judgement." Let the words go in increasing force—query, oracle, judgement, doom.

"From the Crypts of Memory" is beautiful. I'd cut down a few of the longer words, and use fewer ones ending in "able." It's too fine not to have it finer—Poe would have been delighted with it.

It's "metropol*es*," isn't it? And "to infinitely outnumber" is a split infinitive. And "simulachra" is better than "simulachres."

The Jinks was pretty good. I won $25. from London and Harry Leon Wilson at poker. I was there only four days. Had thirty drinks, one afternoon.

I'm going over to see Margaret Anglin act "Medea", in the Greek Theatre, this evening. She wants me to write her a sonnet about it. I wish she'd let me write her a dramatic poem—my "Lilith." I intend to take up the matter with her.[3]

Hyatt is still here, but won't be much longer. I'll give him your message. He's a queer little cuss, but knows it. He bought $55. worth of old books from me, some of them autographed. I owed him the money. Maybe that's why he took them.

I'm sorry you don't take up Bender's proposition to see the P.P.I.E. It's well worth it, and would feed your imagination—not that you can't imagine better; but the sub-consciousness needs real food. I'm doubtful if you've any right, as a poet, to refuse such opportunities. Try to put yourself into a mood for accepting the offer some time in Oct. or Nov. It'll do you good.

I had some "snaps" taken at the Grove, and will send you some soon. Don't be in any haste to answer this letter, if you're mining rock of Auburn or Parnassus.

I have to go down to Our Lady of Orchids to-morrow. Dead orchids, but she is almost as lovely as ever. It is to weep.

My love to you and your parents!

George.

1. 1.12.

2. *Yosemite: An Ode.*

3. Margaret Anglin (1876–1958), Canadian-born stage actress hailed as one of the finest in her day. GS wrote a poem to her, "To Margaret Anglin: In the Greek Tragedies."

[138] CAS to GS [ALS]

Auburn, Cal.,
Sept. 9th, 1915.

Dear George:

Please pardon my long delay in answering your letter. I've had nothing of importance to communicate, and haven't now, for that matter. "Everything is about as usual"—you know what that means. However, here are some more of my bum draw-ings; and I'll try to find a poem or two for enclosure with them. I've done next to noth-ing for months, except a little outdoor labour, and the idle picture-making which has become my chief amusement. I hope the same isn't true of you.

I'm a bit surprised that Robertson should be ready to publish another volume of my work so soon. Do you think he will let me include prose-poems in a rear-section? Otherwise, I'll have hardly enough work for even a very small volume. I've done very little that I care to preserve. Do you think the "Orion" good enough to include? The poem is too "tame" for my taste.

I'd certainly like to write an elegy for Nora May French; but I mistrust my ability for occasional verse. I've long planned memorial odes on Poe and Swinburne; but I've done nothing with them as yet. At any rate, I'll make an attempt at the elegy. I **must** get to work before so very long. I've no end of material for poems, and even have a few short-story plots. I ought to be able to do something with them, if I try hard enough. I'm convinced that the whole thing is largely a matter of will-power.

Here are a few poems that I've raked up from my drawer. Do you think any of these worth keeping? I may or may not have sent you my prose-dialogue, "The Corpse and the Skeleton." At any rate, it isn't very good. I dare say a hyena would weep at some of my humour.

Please return good for evil, and write me before so very long.

As ever, affectionately,
Clark.

[Enclosure: "Moon-Dawn," "The Mirrors of Beauty," and other unidentified poems.]

[139] GS to CAS [ALS]

Oct. 1st, 1915.

Dear Clark:

You needn't ever apologize to me for not replying promptly to my letters, for I'm much worse, as a procrastinator, than you'll ever be. I have to write many letters, and have ambition for only just so many a month.

All the short poems that you enclose in this last letter seem good to me, especially "Moon-Dawn" and "The Mirrors of Beauty." I wish I could be as enthusiastic about your sketches, but though they're interesting because *you* made them, I'd hardly admire them as the work of another.

I don't think Robertson could bring out another volume for you before spring, as he has rashly undertaken to publish, separately and expensively, my Yosemite and Exposition odes. I'd rather he brought out a new book by you, but he thinks he can make me popular! Poor Alec!

I'll send you copies of the books when they appear (Oct. 15th & 20th). The Yosemite ode will be in Saturday's "Call." I'll send you a copy of that too, though you'll like it only in spots.

I was at luncheon with Albert Bender yesterday, and he expressed his sorrow at your unwillingness to accept his offer to see the P.P.I.E., and asked me to try to induce you to reconsider your decision. He says he makes the offer only in the interests of poetry—of the effect of the Exposition on your imagination—that you'll be under no obligations to him, and that you'll not even have to *see* him.

Personally, I strongly advise you to come down, if only for a day and night. Parts of the Exposition are very beautiful, and would "feed" your subconsciousness richly. It may be we shall never see such architecture again in our lifetimes. And architecture, as you know, *is* an Art.

It would give you a chance to see Robertson, too, if you came—not to mention my girl Stella. I'd have you meet Lafler too. Just to see Stell would be worth the trip—and I can't see why you should have any pride against accepting B's generosity. *I* accept it, as I'd accept anything from anyone (almost) if it seemed best for my art. *I'd not think I had any right to* **refuse.**

Hyatt has gone back, in haste, to Ann Arbor. He hung to the last hour, as I was marking for him the *poetry* in his various books of verse. He paid me $1.25 an hour! It was too good to last. He'd have stopped over to see *you*, but feared you'd not care for an intrusion.

Now that autumn is on us again, I suppose you'll feel more like writing. I know *I* always do. Summer is usually a sterile season for me, though last summer wasn't.

I've no poems to send on. But please send me anything *you* may have written. A poet can't always trust individual judgement. There are some **fine** things in this last batch of yours:

> "While the red moon, a demon's ark
> Is borne along the mystic lands."[1]
> (I'd make it "demon*s*").
> And "the black crystal of the eyes of Death."[2] *Great!*

Affectionately,   George.

[P.S.] You didn't send me that prose-dialogue—I can't make out the name.

[P.P.S.] Yes—"Orion" is all right. And of course you could use the prose-poems.

1. "Moon-Dawn," ll. 7–8. CAS made GS's suggested revision.
2. "The Mirrors of Beauty," l. 14.

[140] CAS to GS [ALS]

Auburn, Cal.,
Nov. 8th, 1915

Dear George:

This is merely a note, to say that I have accepted Mr. Bender's offer,[1] and expect to be down Wednesday, on the morning train (No. 33, which leaves Auburn at 7.42) Can you meet me at the Ferry Building? I'd like you to, if it's possible.

Please pardon my long silence. I've had nothing to write, and no poems to send you. I've not felt equal to the attempt, even. Nervous ill-health and despondency have conspired to sap such creative energy as I ever possessed. You can never understand (since such a mental state would be impossible for you) the psychasthenia, the morbid miseries and worries, that I am forced to contend with.

As ever, Affectionately,
Clark.

1. See "The Spectator" [Theodore Bonnet], *Town Talk* No. 1213 (20 November 1915): 10–11, one section of which ("A Poet Sees the Fair," p. 11) describes CAS's coming from Auburn to see the Exposition, at the urging of GS and Albert Bender.

[141] GS to CAS [ALS]

Dec. 22nd, 1915.

Dear Clark:

Bender tells me that you are feeling better and getting your weight back, so I think the cold must be good for you after all, even if you *don't* like winter. As for me, I'm just the same. Have done quite a bit of writing lately, but most of it is on stories. However, I've just finished a ten stanza poem I call (so far) "The Soul of California." Wrote also a sonnet for "Sunset," not good, from our point of view, tho Field will like it.[1]

My poem "The Evanescent City" has been made into a Christmas book, with nine of Bruguiere's photographs, which are what really make the book sell. Robertson says he is disposing of several hundred a day.

I have a scheme to write some prose-poetry about all the missions, to go with a book of photographs of them. It ought to be a big seller, at least out here, and it would not be hard to write.[2]

I can't think of anything to get you for Christmas, so use the bill enclosed and get something you really want.

A merry Christmas to you and your parents!

Aff.   George.

1. "The Soul of California" was published as "California." The sonnet in *Sunset* is unidentified; GS had no poem in the magazine between December 1915 and April 1917. GS refers to Charles Kellogg Field (1873–1948), the editor of *Sunset*.
2. The work was never undertaken.

[142] CAS to GS [ALS]

> Auburn, Cal.,
> Dec. 27th, 1915

Dear George:

Many, many thanks for your letter, and the $5. I didn't deserve the letter, since I've not written to you for so long. As usual, I've had so little to write about, that I've kept putting it off from day to day.

My health seems much improved, partly, as you suggest, from the cold weather, and partly, perhaps, because I have made an effort to break my habit of morbid worrying. I haven't entirely succeeded, but at least there's *some* improvement, and my physical health is beginning to show the benefit. Worry is the deadliest of poisons, as you know.

I feel like working a little, now, and may have something new to send you in my next. I enclose a copy of "The Corpse and the Skeleton", which I've probably not sent you before. It isn't very good, but the mixture of ghastliness and ribaldry is perhaps a bit novel. "The Memnons of the Night" is an old prose-poem that I've forced myself to finish lately, by way of discipline. I've gotten into the habit of leaving too many things unfinished.

"The City Evanescent" is beautifully gotten up,—better even than the others—and the photographs are splendid. It certainly ought to be a seller. . . . I like your idea of a volume of prose-poetry on the old missions. The subject is poetical enough, certainly.

I think of writing a volume of fantastic fables and fairy tales, after my next book is off my hands. I may have to do a good deal of my work in prose. It seems necessary that I should make a little money; and of course, there's none in any verse that I've written or could write.

By the way, what sort of magazine is "The Lantern"? Do you think the editors would care to use any of my poems or prose-pieces? I'd give them away to anyone [who] would print them.

I hope Stella received the box of mistletoe that I sent her. I ought to have sent it earlier, perhaps, to avoid the usual jam in the Christmas mails.

Give my love to Stella, and my regards to Harry Lafler and the others. Tell Lafler that I'm planning an ode on Nora May French. I'll send him a copy, if I succeed in making anything out of it.

> Affectionately,
> Clark.

[Enclosures: "The Corpse and the Skeleton," "The Memnons of the Night."]

[143] GS to CAS [ALS]

Jan. 4th, 1916.

Dear Clark:

I write with the hope that you've not been snowed in nor blown into the American River! And I'm glad to know you are in better health and spirits.

Stella received your timely gift, and is grateful for it. Also she has twice reminded me to remind her to write and thank you. So far, we've both fallen down on the job!

"The Lantern" is run by the editors of "Town Talk," and can't afford to pay for poetry. Your notion of writing fables and fairy tales seems to me a good one, and I hope you find time for it. (The mine must be too full of water to work at now!)

My friend Roosevelt Johnson[1] has actually had a letter from Bierce, who was then in some small town in England. So the old war-horse is alive after all: I'm surprised that he let anyone know it.

Your "Corpse and Skeleton" is arresting enough in its way, but hardly to be compared with the powerfully beautiful "Memnons of the Night." That's a big thing, in my opinion, and I'm glad to have it. By the way, you have a "Memnon" sonnet that I'd like to have another copy of. It seems to me a very strong sonnet. I've just finished one on a mummy, the one in the club library.[2] I'll send you a copy in my next letter.

A happy new year to you!   George.

1. Roosevelt Johnson, GS's boyhood friend from Sag Harbor, followed GS to Oakland in 1890. At about that time Johnson introduced GS to the work of Ambrose Bierce.
2. "To the Mummy of the Lady Isis."

[144] CAS to GS [ALS]

Auburn, Cal.,
Feb. 3rd, 1916.

Dear George:

I find that I've let your last letter remain unanswered for nearly a month—a month of the worst weather that I've ever seen in a lifetime. The repeated snow-storms, the rain, fog, and drizzle that we've had almost without intermission throughout January, seem without precedent, even in the memory of the oldest inhabitant. I've suffered more from the cold than from anything else, tho—also from having to stay indoors a great deal. I can't work in such weather, and it always affects my health and spirits. Physically, at least, I'm not so well as when I wrote you last. Still, I'm almost the only person in the county who hasn't had an attack of influenza, pneumonia, or something.

I'm very glad to hear that Bierce has been heard from at last. Somehow, I've always had the feeling that he wasn't dead. But what a disappointment for his obituarists!

I enclose a transcription of "Memnon at Midnight". I never cared very much for the sonnet, myself. I'm glad you like "The Memnons of the Night"—Loveman thinks it the best of my prose-poems. Sam, tho, always inclines to the superlative in his opinions of my work.

Are you familiar with the prose of Oscar Wilde? I've just been reading "The Picture of Dorian Gray," and the fairy tales and prose-poems. "Dorian Gray" is full of the most tremendous epigrams, and the fairy tales are very beautiful and subtle. On the whole, I like Wilde's prose much better than his verse—it seems richer-coloured and more original. The epigrams are marvellous, and I like even the more paradoxical ones—a paradox often presents an unfamiliar aspect of the truth.

The 13th of January was my 23rd birthday. How is that for a combination of unlucky numbers?

I'll do some more writing in the Spring—I've always done the bulk of my work in the months between March and September. A long spell of wet or cold weather absolutely inhibits my inspiration. I hope it isn't the same with you.

Write when you can, and don't forget the sonnet to a mummy, of which you speak in your letter.

> Affectionately,
> Clark.

[Enclosure: "Memnon at Midnight."]

[145] GS to CAS [ALS]

Feb. 26th, 1916.

Dear Clark:

Our hard winter seems over at last, and I hope you're feeling more like work now. I've been rather busy myself, though mostly at stories. None of them has sold yet!

That was a canard about Mr. Bierce. Johnson, when drunk, got hold of a postal Bierce had written him two years before!

Thanks for the "Memnon at Midnight"—a great sonnet, with the sound of all the seas in it.

Yes—I've read about all of Wilde's prose, most of which is better than his verse, except a very few poems. Of all his work, I like best "Salome."

I've no copy of that mummy sonnet, but you'll see it in my book, which R. will publish in April.[1] It'll be a rather gloomy book, so such a sonnet won't be out of place.

I was down in Carmel for last week-end, and found it as lovely as ever, and the little Herons all well. It saddened me, though, to see how that high wind had prostrated hundreds of big oaks, pines and cypresses. But thank God! the "ostrich tree," the tourist's pride, went down!

Stella often mentions you—seems to have a bit of a case on you, and says she's sorry she didn't kiss you more when she had a chance! Bender also speaks often of you.

Just had an accounting with Robertson: we stand about even, at last.

Good luck!

> Affectionately,   George.

1. *CE.*

[146] CAS to GS [ALS]

Auburn, Cal.,
April 5th, 1916

Dear George:

I seem to have left your last letter unanswered for even longer than my usual period of procrastination. It isn't often that the calendar steals such a march on me!

However, you haven't missed much through my not writing. There's little or nothing for me to put on paper, excepting trivialities.

I've done a little gardening lately,—we're going to have a few pears, and strawberries, and other vegetables. I wish you could be here to eat some of them, in a month or so. Can't you remind Dr. Abrams of his plan for motoring up to Auburn with you in the Spring?

I'm eager to see your new book. By the way, I wish you would find out from Robertson when he will be ready to publish my next volume. I'd like it to come out in the autumn, if possible. I've not found a title for it as yet. I'd like something that would denote the mixed nature of the collection, if possible. "Ivy-Leaf and Orchid-Flower" might do, if floral titles weren't so common. I'd rather not use a title-poem, unless I have to.

I've had a few malarial symptoms lately, and haven't felt at all well—This eternal state of semi-sickness is a dreadful bore to me. I wish I could either die or get well—anything for a change.

Tell Stella that I wish she *had* kissed me a few more times! Kisses don't seem to come my way in Auburn.

Affectionately,
Clark.

[Enclosure: unidentified prose poem.]

[147] GS to CAS [ALS]

Apr. 28, 1916.

Dear Clark:

I'd have replied to yours of the 5th ere now, but have been off on a 1600 mile motor-trip, to see all the old Missions between here and Mexico. (I even invaded Mexico to the extent of ten feet, which was a plenty!)

Was gone about three weeks, and had a fine trip, though I missed Stella woefully. She and I are to have dinner with the Abrams to-night, and I'll sound him as to that trip he spoke of. He's darned busy, though, at present.

I'll speak to Robertson about the book, but fear he's not likely to do anything about it until the price of paper goes down—or stops going up. He has decided to give up the idea of my "old Missions" book till then; and he's going to print only 1000 copies of my "Caged Eagle" etc. We are paying for the war in more ways than one!

I'm sorry your health is no better; and malaria is "an hellish thing."[1] Have you written to Abrams about it?

I think "Cypress and Orchids" would be preferable to the longer title that you suggest. How is "Poppy and Cypress?" *I* don't mind flower-titles, if they're good ones.

The prose-poem you inclose is beautiful, like everything of that sort that you do. I've nothing to send in return, as you've doubtlessly seen my sonnets in "Town Talk"[2]—and I sent you, I suppose, my "White Logic." Harriet Monroe said of that that it was the "most awful arraignment of life she'd ever read or dreamed of." But Harriet as a critic is not one of my enthusiasms!

My book ought to be out in a couple of weeks, as I should have the "page-proofs" by to-morrow. I am not proud of it; but if some of the sonnets are a cause of pain to any of our hyphenated Americans, I'll be quite content. It'll grieve Viereck and Scheffauer, anyway. "Conspiracy," which you've seen, will be the best thing in it, by far. But how very few will like "Conspiracy!"

Well, here's hoping that you are feeling very much better!

Affectionately,   George.

1. Coleridge, *The Rime of the Ancient Mariner* 1. 91.

2. GS published six war sonnets—"Broadway, New York, 1916," "The Dream of Wilhelm II," "Earth's Anthem," "The Feast," "The Little Farm," and "The War-God"—in *Town Talk* No. 1231 (25 March 1916): 7. All are reprinted in *CE*.

[148] CAS to GS [ALS]

Auburn, Cal.,
June 15th, 1916.

Dear George:

As usual, I find it necessary to preface my letter with an apology for not having written before. You aren't the only one who has reason to complain, tho—my other correspondents don't fare any better, indeed, most of them fare worse. Considering the limited amount of my correspondence, I ought to hold the record for dilatoriness.

I've been expecting, from day to day, to hear that your book was out. But I've seen nothing so far. Robertson's procrastination seems to be constitutional.

I wish my next volume were off my mind—and off my nerves. I dread the ordeal of proof reading. "Poppy and Cypress," which you suggest, seems a much better title than the other.

I enclose a few things—nearly all that I have written of late. When one writes without caring to write, the result is not likely to be very good. I seem to have developed a deadly indifference toward my work, partly through my inability to please myself, but more through my increasing personal unhappiness. Misery is not a stimulant to me, as it is to some. With me, it has more the effect of a narcotic, of a deadly drug.

Some of the poems enclosed may interest you, since they are more personal than most of my work. Personal expression seems peculiarly difficult for me. I would prefer to write such things, if I could only do them well enough. . . . Love and death are the only things worth writing about.

Give my affectionate regards to Bender, and assure him that I'm not such a scoundrel as I seem. I'll write to him very soon.

Affectionately,
Clark

[Enclosures: "Arabesque," "Autumn Twilight," "Belated Love," "The Crucifixion of Eros," "Desolation," "Nocturne," epigrams.]

[149] GS to CAS [ALS]

June 17, 1916.

Dear Clark:

I was much pleased to hear from you, and even more pleased to have you send me such a fine bunch of poems. You may decry them as much as you please; but

I assure you they are extremely good. "Desolation" is a powerful and touching sonnet, and "Belated Love" and "The Crucifixion of Eros" are beautiful and moving things. I'm sincerely hoping you'll try them on the magazines. Editors are a purblind drove, but it seems to me impossible that these sonnets shouldn't find a home (such as it is) somewhere.

There is always a demand for very short lyrics such as "Nocturne" and "Autumn Twilight," and I'd send them out too. They're delicate and lovely. "Arabesque" is quite as good, but somewhat less salable, probably.

The epigrams are quite good, especially the second one, but I'd not give much time to that sort of thing.[1] The sonnets show a fresh and admirable phase of your genius, and if you can go on doing such splendid work you are sure of an audience, if you want one.

> "the gleam
> Of moons eternal on a land of stone!"[2]

That's great stuff! But "Belated Love" is harder to do—at least to us others.

My book is still promised from day to day; but the binders seem as lazy as they are mendacious, which is going some. However, it *will* be out next week, and I'll send you a copy as soon as I get some, though you'll not care especially for the book. It's not the kind of poetry that young poets like, except in certain spots.

As I think I've already told you, I fear that Robertson is too deeply in debt to the book-makers to venture publishing any more poetry this year, as his own expense. When he *is* able to do so, I shall see that your book gets the first opening. Don't see why you dislike to read proofs. I rather enjoy it, if they're *mine*.

I'm sorry you still feel so unhappy. I'd feel sorrier were you not so young. It's hard to do so, however, as things seem to be with you, as I cannot see you have a great deal to depress you, unless you are below par physically. You're still very young, you've a roof over you, you've an art to seek refuge in, you've friends interested in you, and you've even fame, not wide, but sure, and constantly increasing. Suppose you do have to stay up in Auburn for a few more years: it's a pretty spot, and lots of young men would gladly change fates with you. When you are forty-six, as I am, you'll hardly believe you were unhappy at your present age.

I've not been very busy of late, except at prose, but have written several poems to please *myself*. Here is one on Bierce, written because of much gossip as to his having committed suicide. And I've just finished one in which I hand it to Heinz for defacing the landscape with his signs. I call it "57."

Take your time about replying

    Ever affectionately,   George.

[Enclosure: "The Passing of Bierce."]

1. Unidentified (though some mss. are found in the GS paper). In 1923–24, CAS wrote numerous prose epigrams for the *Auburn Journal* under the general title "Clark Ashton Smith's Column."
2. "Desolation," ll. 3–4.

[150] CAS to GS [ALS]

Auburn, Cal.,
June 20th, 1916.

Dear George:

Your good letter came Sunday, and I'm going to surprise you by answering it with promptness. I treated you shamefully the last time, and there was really
no good excuse for it. To-day, I feel as if I'd like to make amends. It's the first time
that I've really wanted to write a letter in many months.

I like your poem on Bierce. Didn't Bierce write an essay on suicide?[1] It seems to
me that I remember reading something of the sort, in one of his books. At any rate, I
feel sure that his views on the subject were anything but orthodox.

I enclose a few more poems. "The Flight of Azrael," "The Mummy," and "Morning on an Eastern Sea" were written in 1915, but I don't remember having sent them
to you before. Probably I didn't think them good enough at the time. I don't feel sure
about them now; but, at any rate, they may interest you—

I feel rather relieved than otherwise, at postponing the publication of my next
book. In fact, I would be content to postpone it forever. If I could make money out of
my work, I might feel differently. As you know, I care little enough about money, but,
under the circumstances, I'd rather have it than fame. Fame isn't anything that one can
eat. I fear that all the reputation, or all the material benefits that the world could con-
fer, would do very little toward making me happy. My happiness would consist in other
things—things which, in my case, seem impossible. As to living in Auburn, I don't
mind that so very much. If I *could* get away, I'd hardly know where to go—indeed, I
would hardly care.

My health is better than it has been, tho not so very good. I've had a run of tooth-
aches, headaches, and neuralgia pains lately. Apart from these and malaria, there may
not be anything much the matter with me.

My father and I have been working on our shaft. We've reached a depth of about
65 ft, and may have to sink ten feet more before we touch bedrock. I hope there's
something at the bottom. If there isn't, we'll be rather up against it.

Has Loveman sent you any of his prose-poems? Some of them are very good, I
think. The conceptions are certainly original.

I began a poem on Nora May French some time ago, but haven't finished it yet.
I'll try to send it in my next.

As ever, Affectionately,
Clark.

[Enclosures: "Coldness," "The Flight of Azrael," "Morning on an Eastern Sea," "The
Mummy."]

1. AB, "The Right to Take Oneself Off," in *The Shadow on the Dial and Other Essays*, ed. S. O.
Howes (San Francisco: A. M. Robertson, 1909), pp. 245–49; rpt. *Collected Works*, 11.338–44
(as "Taking Oneself Off").

[151] GS to CAS [ALS]

July 8th, 1916.

Dear Clark:

I'll wind up the week with a few lines to you, the last of about twenty letters I've had to write within three days. You see, I've been up at Napa and down in Carmel, and my correspondence has suffered.

I was three days in Napa. Went there to see a girlfriend sing in "Pinafore." She was "Buttercup."

I saw Cale Rice and his wife (Alice Hegan) down in Carmel.[1] The Forest Theatre put on his play "Yolanda of Cyprus." It's not a bad play, but the acting was so bad that I quit after the 2nd act and went to bed (at Heron's; he's batching it now).

I was glad to see Hopper again, after nearly 2 years. He gave me an aeroplane arrow and some shrapnel, etc., that he'd picked up on the battle-field of the Marne.

My book's out at last, as you know (I sent you one, didn't I? I've sent out so many I've lost all track!)

I like these last poems you send. "The Mummy" is a pretty good sonnet, and "The Flight of Azrael" has more than a touch of the sublime. But I like best the lyric "Coldness," especially

"A dreaming crystal, clear and cold," and

"Thou knowest life and life's desire
As a bright mirror knows the moon."[2]

There may be a better adjective than that "bright," by the way.

Stella was greatly pleased at receiving the beautiful lilies, and said she was going to write and thank you. But if I know the sweet young cat she *won't* unless I prod her!

A friend of mine, Raine Bennett, is starting a biweekly paper he's calling "Bohemia." I'm giving him an indifferently good poem (all I had to spare) for his first number.[3] Do you care to let him have something of yours? He can't afford to pay anything just now, but may be able to do so when the thing gathers more momentum. (I'll see he pays *you* something, however inadequate, for your second contribution.) I'd like to see him succeed. It's a hard climb, at the best.

Yesterday I wrote some verses to be read at the French celebration of the Fall of the Bastille.[4] Nothing especially poetical.

Good luck, Clark!

Affectionately,   Geo.

[P.S.] I've managed to sell poems to Harper's ("Transmutation") and Bellman ("The Wind")

1. Cale Young Rice (1872–1943), American poet and associate of GS. Alice Hegan (1870–1942) was a popular novelist of the period.

2. "Coldness," l. 9 ("pure" for "clear" in the ms.) and ll. 19–20.

3. Apparently "The Passing of Bierce."

4. Unidentified.

[152] CAS to GS [ALS]

Auburn, Cal.
Aug. 7th, 1916

Dear George:

I ought to have written you a month ago, since I received your book some time in the early part of July. But, somehow, I've kept putting it off from day to day, till I feel very much ashamed of myself.

I like many of the poems, tho I agree with you that "Conspiracy" is the best. "The Caged Eagle" is very beautiful, and I've marked many others—"Shakespeare", "The Shadow of Nirvana", "The Fall of the Year", "The Gleaner," "Moloch"[,] the sonnet to Martinez, and several of the war-sonnets. The book ought to have an unusually good sale, on account of the latter.

I've nothing new to send you, of my own. My health is better, but I'm in anything but a creative mood. I've planned a volume of fantastic prose, among other things. I've ideas for a number of fables, allegories, and prose-poems, but I've no heart for literary work at present.

My parents are both "laid up"—my father with sciatica, and my mother with a bruised leg, so everything falls upon me—even the housework. I've been packing fruit, at odd times, to earn a little money.

I've sent out a number of my things to the magazines, but none of them have sold. I'm enclosing a copy of "Coldness," which you can give to the editor of "Bohemia," if you like. I don't know the address of the magazine, or I'd send it in myself, and save you the trouble.[1]

I wish I could see you. Can't you remind Dr. Abrams of his plan for motoring up to Auburn? September or October would be a good time, tho the weather isn't so very hot even now. We've had an unusually cool summer. I slept out-doors one night, and nearly froze before morning.

With much love to you and Stella,

As ever,
Clark.

1. "Coldness" appears not to have been published in *Bohemia*, but "Strangeness" and "The Exile" were.

[153] GS to CAS [ALS]

Sept. 11, 1916.

Dear Clark:

Thanks for that poem for "Bohemia." I hope that that magazine will some day be able to pay you; but at present it's in its raw and impoverished youth.

I wish I *could* get up your way, but am too poor to do so unless someone takes me in a machine. Abrams can't do so, as he has lately lost his wife (for the second time) and is all up in the air. He has to go east to a medical convention soon, also.

Odd that the weather isn't hotter up your way! I was at London's for two weeks following the Jinks, and most of the time it was hotter than I like it, except at night.

Thanks for your good words for my book. It's not having any great sale, even with those war-sonnets. A book of poems has to be pushed pretty hard to have much of a sale; and Robertson is an over-worked man.

I've not written much, lately, except a poem or two at London's, and a movie scenario (5 reels) last week. I *did* write several love-poems; but I don't count those! I always slack down in the summer—it takes cold weather to give me enough energy to write on.

Stella is as radiant as ever, and often mentions you. She's going to Fresno on the 20th, with some other girls, for a week's professional dancing, and is quite excited over her first real stage-work. She'll be less so after incurring the Fresno climate!

Had a pretty good time up at the Jinks. There wasn't much sleep in it. We played poker o' mornings, and I quit $30. ahead. London won over $150. And I didn't drink much.

I'm told they want me to write the 1918 grove-play.[1] I'd rather not, but shall have to if I'm asked. The 1917 one is already written, as the thing is allotted now nearly two years ahead of time, for the music-sire's sake.

My mother and most of my sisters are sick, but that seems to be the normal state of womankind. I hope your mother is all right by now—and your father. How's the mine progressing? If you could only strike it!

Affectionately yours,   George.

[Enclosure: unidentified.]

1. GS did not write the grove play for 1918, but did write songs for the play by Richard M. Hotaling and Wallace A. Sabin, *The Twilight of the Kings*.

[154] CAS to GS [ALS]

Auburn, Cal.,
Oct. 11th, 1916.

Dear George:

I'm ashamed to find that I've had your last letter lying by me unanswered for a whole month. I always have to preface my letters with an apology—so here's another one. But I'll try to do better next time.

There are beautiful lines and images in the poem that you enclose. The conception is very similar to that of something I had once planned to write. I've not much to send in return, excepting the draught of a companion poem for "Coldness." I've burnt most of my late work, and might do just as well to burn the rest. I write more to distract my thoughts than for any other purpose, and hardly care whether the result is good or bad. The intense technical preoccupation keeps me from thinking about things that I don't want to remember.

My mother is recovering very slowly, and may not be able to get around much for another month. My father is better, tho. We haven't been able to do much with our mine this year, and it will soon be too late, since the first heavy rain will fill the shaft with water.

My physical condition is better, temporarily at least. Abrams may have been right about my lungs—I've had more than one symptom suggestive of it.[1] However, the sort of life I lead is an ideal cure for lung trouble, so any tendency of the sort isn't likely to develop much.

My best friend here is very ill. She seems to have developed an attack of brain fever in addition to the consumption from which she has suffered for years. I don't know whether she will live or not. If she dies, I think I will go mad with grief and a guilty conscience.[2]

This isn't a very cheerful sort of letter, so I'll have to beg you to carry my troubles lightly. My life seems to be turning into a story of the sort that Poe might have written. I'm sure that some of the situations in it would have given him a gruesome delight.

Write before long, won't you? My love to you and Stella.

>   Affectionately,
>   Clark.

[Enclosure: "Strangeness."]

1. Abrams had diagnosed CAS as having tuberculosis.
2. CAS refers to a young woman with whom he was in love at the time named Mamie Lowe Miller; she died in November 1917 (see CAS to Samuel Loveman, 6 April 1918, Bancroft Library). CAS dedicated "*Requiescat in Pace*" to her (in *EC*, but dedication appears only in *SP*).

[155] GS to CAS [ALS]

Oct. 29, 1916.

Dear Clark:

I've had to declare this Sunday a day of work, and try to reply to a heap of letters, mostly from other poets. So I'll begin with you.

Nothing much has happened since I last wrote. The San Diego Exposition folk want to have a "day" in my honor (God knows why!), so I'm to appear there on Nov. 9th if I can raise the fare. Bender and Abrams both say they're coming too. Perhaps one of them will take me.

What in Hell are you burning any of your stuff for? I think that's most unwise! A few years from now you might have had a good opinion of that stuff. Don't burn things: just set them aside somewhere.

I like the lyric you send, decidedly. It's a jewelled thing. For some weird reason I've always hated the word "doth!" You'll not find it in any of my poems. But I've no good cause to dislike it.

It's a pity there's so much sickness up your way. I hope your mother and your friend are better now. *Some*thing has to be the matter with *every*one, always.

Stella has been away for two weeks, and will be gone for eight more. She's with nine other girls, doing classic dancing with a sort of vaudeville company called "A Night at the World's Fair." They're to be in Los Angeles for the next eight weeks, so I'll see her there after I've got through with the San Diego nonsense. I may stay there two or three weeks, as the Sinclairs and Herons are there, and want me as guest.

Stella loves (so far) that sort of life, and gets good pay—$25. a week, which is more than *I* can make! She "rooms" with three other girls.

I managed to sell another poem to "Scribner's"—"A Lost Garden." Did I send it to you? I don't write much any more, and it's not easy for me to get copies of what I do write.

I've owed Loveman a letter for about three months, and now I owe him another. Did he send you that discovery of his—two lines by Keats?[1] It's interesting.

Haven't seen Bender since weeks before last, but suppose the little man is as busy as ever, making money and then giving it away.

I wrote a movie scenario (it is going to sell) and expect to start another in a day or so.

Let me hear from you, at your leisure.

Affectionately,   George.

1. See Loveman's letter, "A Keats Discovery," *Dial* 63 (19 July 1917): 77–78; rpt. in Loveman's *Out of the Immortal Night* (New York: Hippocampus Press, 2004), pp. 199–200.

[156] CAS to GS [ALS]

Auburn, Cal—
Dec. 16th, 1916.

Dear George:

Bender wants me to come to the city, and be looked over by the doctor. I'll be down Monday, on the morning train (which leaves Auburn somewhere about 8.30) and would like you to meet me at the ferry, if possible. I feel like a fraud for coming to the city on any such pretext (since I've "picked up" a good deal during the last few weeks.) But I was really ill during November, and had to spend parts of several days in bed.

I'm ashamed of not having written before. My correspondence all went by the board during last month, and it seems difficult for me to pick it up again. However, I'll see you in a few days; and that will be better than a thousand letters.

I've a few new prose-poems and lyrics, and will bring copies of them with me. Also some new drawings, mostly of fantastic plants and flowers—black and green lilies, with tongue-shaped petals, serpentine orchids, and blue toadstools festooned with iridescent moss.

Affectionately,
Clark—

[157] GS to CAS [ALS]

Jan. 17, 1917.

Dear Clark:

How are you? Feeling any better? It's so damned cold here that I'm afraid it's a hardship for you to be out-doors all the time, though maybe it's warmer up in the foot-hills.

I've lately got back from Los Angeles, where I've been on account of this play. It was pretty much of a failure there.[1]

Do you care to come to S. F. and put in two or more months at the City & County Hospital here? It would cost you nothing for board or treatment, as one of my friends, Dr. Rathgin, runs the tuberculosis department. He is now using a serum there with startling success, and I think you'd better come try it.

As soon as I can get into touch with a certain rich woman hereabouts, I'm going to arrange for the future finances of you and your parents. I'm to have dinner with her on Monday evening. I've been trying to visit Mrs. Hearst, too, but sha'n't have a chance to do so at once, as I want to see W. R., her son, at the same time, and he won't be back till next month.[2]

Let me hear from you.

Yours affectionately (and in haste),   George.

1. GS refers to the play *Everyman* (1917), which he had translated. See further letter 159.
2. GS refers to William Randolph Hearst (1863–1951), publisher of the *San Francisco Examiner*, and his mother, Phoebe Elizabeth (Apperson) Hearst.

[158] CAS to GS [ALS]

Auburn, Cal.,
Jan 22nd, 1917.

Dear George:

I've had your letter lying on my desk for several days, tho I *should* have answered it immediately. Somehow, I haven't; but I shan't permit myself to delay any longer.

The long cold period seems almost without precedent in this section. The temperature is down to freezing half the time—we've had ice nearly every night since the first of the year. I suffer intense discomfort from the cold, even when I'm indoors; but I dare say it's good for me—the stimulation prevents one from tiring so easily.

As to my health, I hardly know—I feel pretty well at times—and more or less rotten between-whiles. However, that's a chronic state with me, so I can't say that I'm getting any worse. As to my going to the hospital,—that seems quite out of the question, and, as far as I can see, quite unnecessary. Besides, it would be very inconvenient for me to leave here at present.

If you succeed in getting hold of some money for me, I should like it to be in the form of a loan. Personally, I've no great scruples of pride in the matter; but my parents rather insist on this. Besides, with a little capital, my father could put our place on a paying-basis as a chicken-ranch; and in a few years, we would probably be in a position to repay the loan.

Affectionately,
Clark

[159] GS to CAS [ALS]

Napa, Cal.
Feb. 12, 1917.

Dear Clark:

I hope this warm weather has been of benefit to you: we certainly had an awful spell of cold.

I should have written before, but wanted to report results—and I've been unable to see the several persons I've had in mind. However, it's being arranged for me to meet at least two of their High Mightinesses, late this week. I think you are entirely wrong in imagining it is unnecessary for you to go to a hospital. This serum treatment is a big thing, and can do for you in six or seven weeks what six or seven months might not otherwise do. The greatest thing is, too, that you'd be absolutely comfortable there, have company, and feel that everything was all right otherwise; for of course I'd have made good arrangements for your parents.

I doubt if I could obtain the loan of enough money in a *lump sum* to help you with the chicken-ranch project, but an adequate monthly income, repayable when you were older, seems to me even better, since it would free you from worry as to the success of such a ranch. Besides, with such an income, you could build up a chicken business anyway.

But the main thing is to have you on our feet physically, and I hope you'll not be unwilling to give Dr. Rathgin's treatment at least a trial. It can't hurt you, even if maybe it shouldn't cure you. I think the "mental factor" in your case is a most important one, and I want to do all I can to save you worry. I only regret that the business seems to be so slow a one. It seems that everyone I wanted to see was in the east; and probably even *one* of them would have been enough. Anyhow, I'm to see Mrs. Charles W. Clark on Saturday or Monday.

I've written very little for some time. I lost about two months on "Everyman," and was deeply disappointed when Ordynski failed to develope [*sic*] enough courage to try it in San Francisco.[1] If he had, I'd have made a few hundred dollars, and could have been of some use to more than one person. It's just possible that he may put it on in N. Y. during Lent.

Take your time about writing to me. I hope to write again, within a week.

Affectionately,   George.

1. GS refers to Ryszard (Richard) Ordynski (1878–1953), a theatrical producer and actor, and GS's collaborator in the translation of *Everyman*. The play opened in Los Angeles in January 1917, but closed after a week.

[160] GS to CAS [ALS]

Feb. 23rd, 1917.

Dear Clark:

I have just arranged with the wife of a very rich man to have your parents taken care of while you are at Dr. Rochschild's sanatorium. He makes a specialty of cases like yours, and you will find your surroundings very pleasant. Of course all your expenses there will be taken care of by this lady. I've explained to her that you prefer to hold the financial assistance as a loan, and she will so assume it, thoroughly understanding.

Now I'm taking it for granted that you're not going to stand on any futile pride, or even dislike of leaving your home, and defer coming down very soon. Can you not get here early on Wednesday afternoon? Dr. R. is in his office on that occasion, coming up from his place at Belmont on Mondays and Fridays also. I'll be out of town on Monday, so if you can't come on Wednesday, wait till Friday.

Let me know as soon as you can how much your family will need per mensem. I'm assuming they'll need some one to do the chores, etc. And here's $50. for you to get what things you'll need.

If you have one of your books on hand, bring it along, as I want to give it to our friend. You'll meet her later, and will like her.

Stella is off on a tour (Pantages circuit) and will be gone till June, so I'm lonesome. No one can fill her place—my penalty for getting the best one in the bunch.

Beastly weather, isn't it? You'll be happier down in Belmont.

      Affectionately,   George.

[161] CAS to GS [ALS]

                       Auburn, Cal.,
                       Feb. 28th, 1917

Dear George:

I've had your letter lying by me for several days, hesitating as to how I could answer you. I'm sorry, but the sanitarium idea is as repugnant to me as ever. Besides, the expense would be so unnecessary; my health is already much improved, and people tell me that they never saw me looking so well. My real problem at present is the financial one—and a few months in the hospital wouldn't solve *that*. The mortgage on our place (a matter of seven hundred dollars, including unpaid interest[)], is due, and if not paid or transferred very soon, will necessitate our selling out to meet the debt. Possibly, tho, my people may be able to obtain a loan from someone in Auburn. Otherwise, we will certainly have to sell out.

I wish I could have a talk with you—also with the lady of whom you speak. I fear that I haven't explained matters fully enough to you before. A loan of $1500 or better still, $2000, to pay off the mortgage and give us a little capital to "go on", is about all that would really help me. I can take care of my health—my getting so run down at times has been partly my own fault, and partly a matter of too much emotional and nervous tension. You are mistaken, too, in thinking that I would, be happier at the sanitarium. I would fret and chafe all the time, balk at most of the rules, and be considered a cantankerous nuisance—Dr. Abrams, if you will remember, told me that I would probably not do well in a sanitarium.

Please believe that I am deeply gratified to you for all the trouble you have taken—also to the kind lady who has offered to help me. You make it so embarrassing, so difficult for me to refuse, as I feel that I *must* do.

Am I to return the check? I'm holding it till I hear from you again, since I can't use it for the purpose for which it was sent.

I wish you were here. The Spring has been coming on by leaps and bounds, these last few days. The almonds and plums are already beginning to blossom. I feel as if I could write a little now—I've hardly tried for a long time.

      Affectionately,
       Clark.

P.S. I'm sending you a copy of my book, for the lady of whom you speak. I suppose it's out of print now.

[162] GS to CAS [ALS]

                       Mch. 1st, 1917.

Dear Clark:

If you won't go to a sanatorium, why, you won't! And if your health is really improving, I don't see why you should not stay where you are.

I doubt greatly if I can raise such an amount as $1500. for you. Is the mortgage at some bank? If so, would they not let it run on if you paid $200. on the principal, and interest to date?

You are to keep the check, of course. Let me know how much more you need per mensem to run the household (including interest on mortgage), and I'll send it. This will go on until you are at least well, and probably indefinitely. When I see our friend again, I'll state your case more fully to her. So far, she is concerned mainly with your physical welfare.

I'd not try to do any writing yet, were I you. You need all your vitality to fight bacilli with. The kind of poem that "writes itself" will not hurt you, however.

I expect to go down to Carmel on Monday, so let me hear from you as soon as possible.

Affectionately,   George.

[163] CAS to GS [ALS]

Auburn, Cal.,
March 3rd, 1917.

Dear George:
                Your letter came yesterday, and I'm answering it immediately, to settle the business details. My parents think that the person who holds the mortgage on our place, would be willing to let it run on if the interest, (one hundred dollars), were all paid up. As to the amount per mensem for our household expenses, I hardly know what to say. Do you think $60 or $75. a month would be too much? Our bills are very light, and we could put aside capital for the poultry venture on such a sum.

I can't say how deeply indebted to you we all feel, for the trouble to which you have been. And will you not convey my gratitude to the lady who is willing to do so much for me? I shall certainly try to repay the debt when I get on my feet financially.

Don't worry about my health. I'm a lot harder to kill than most people seem to think (else I wouldn't be alive now)[.] My weight is back to normal, and I think that the temporary loss (due mainly to my not eating enough for a long time) was good for me rather than otherwise, thro the elimination of much effete matter and certain digestive poisons. I feel much more buoyant and cheerful, and my skin is much clearer than it used to be.

I wish you could come up some time during the spring. May or April would be the best month. Couldn't you make it? My father and I are planning a little trip to the mountains during the summer. How about coming along with us, if you can't make it earlier?

Affectionately,
                Clark—

P.S. Raine Bennet has offered to publish my next book without expense to me, if I'll give him the exclusive rights. What do you think of the idea? Robertson is so eternally slow and cautious, that, personally, I feel like accepting the offer. But of course, I shan't, if you advise me to the contrary.

[164] GS to CAS [ALS]

Mch. 5, 1917.

Dear Clark:

I enclose a check for $125., being $100. to pay up that interest, and $25. for the balance of the $75. for the month of March. This $75. will run on till you are well, and probably longer. But it is given that you may have plenty to eat, and I hope you'll not divert too much of it to poultry, which would do you no good in the trans-Styx region. I'm hoping too that your optimism isn't the fatal variety almost inseparable from tuberculosis. Don't take any chances with it.

I'd consult a physician before trying that Sierran trip. It may be that complete rest is better for you than so much exercise.

I'll pay you a visit in about a month.

I hardly know how to advise you about the book. I've a notion that R. will *never* get around to it. So perhaps you'd better take a chance on B.

Affectionately,   George.

[165] CAS to GS [ALS]

Auburn, Cal.,
March 16th, 1917.

Dear George:

I've been intending for the past week or more to acknowledge your letter, with the enclosed check. But, somehow, I've kept putting it off—more, I fear, from laziness than for any better reason.

I'll be awfully glad to see you, whenever you can come. The country is at its best in April, and most of the wild flowers are in bloom at that time. Nothing, tho, could be more perfect than the weather we've had during the last few days.

Please don't worry about my health. It isn't optimism that makes me say I'm growing better. Everyone speaks of it. I seem fated to live—even tho I've not wanted to live for many years past. I believe Dr. Abrams must have been mistaken about my condition—the slight lesion in my lung may be of longer standing than he thought. Nearly everyone has a touch of t.b. at some time in their lives.

I've not tried to do any writing. It might be better for me, tho, if I did. I feel so idle, and yet so restless—and you know the old adage about "idle hands."

Affectionately,
Clark—

[166] CAS to GS [ALS]

Auburn, Cal.,
April 14th, 1917.

Dear George:

This is a rather belated acknowledgement of your last letter, and the check; but I've had so little to write about, that, as usual, I've kept putting it off from day to day. So perhaps you'll excuse me, considering that you haven't missed much.

I keep in good health, physically, but, so far, I've not felt like doing any literary work. I fear the rest cure is making me lazy. I wrote a few tentative verses the other day, and then gave up, partly from discouragement, and partly, I am afraid, from sheer indolence.

Have you heard from Loveman lately? I've not had a letter from him for a month, and am beginning to wonder what is wrong. Letters miscarry, tho, sometimes—especially when they have to pass thru the Auburn postoffice.

Robertson writes me that he was mistaken about the sale of my book. Only **half** the edition has been sold, the other half still lying unbound at the printers'. How's that for a come-down? And so far, I've not learned anything definite about the publication of my new volume. Bennet hasn't even written to me about it yet—I merely heard that he **intended** to make me an offer of publication. I shall call the book "Ebony and Crystal"—if it ever is published. The title is appropriate enough, and is more to my taste than any of the floral titles proposed.

Have you read any of the books of Edgar Saltus? I've just been reading "The Philosophy of Disenchantment" —a fascinating and finely written exposition of the history and theory of pessimism. I'm trying to obtain another book by Saltus, entitled "The Anatomy of Negation." I've been reading a great deal lately—"De Profundis," the dramas of John Webster and Cyril Tourneur, the "Journal" of Marie Bashkirtseff, Dostoevsky's "Journal of an Author,"[1] James Thomson's "City of Dreadful Night", and two or three books by Lafcadio Hearn, among many others. Hearn, Wilde, and de Quincey (aside from Poe and Bierce) are the prose-writers to whom I seem to take most naturally.

> Affectionately,
> Clark—

1. Edgar Saltus (1855–1921), *The Philosophy of Disenchantment* (1885) and *The Anatomy of Negation* (1886), works of popular philosophy based largely on Schopenhauer; Oscar Wilde (1854–1900), *De Profundis* (1905), an account of his two years in Reading Gaol; John Webster (1578?–1632?) and Cyril Tourneur (1575?–1626), Jacobean dramatists; Marie Bashkirtseff, *The Journal of Marie Bashkirtseff* (1887; Eng. tr. 1890), a diary that caused a scandal for its sexual explicitness; Fyodor Dostoevsky (1821–1881), *A Writer's Diary* (1873–76).

[167] GS to CAS [ALS]

Apr. 30, 1917.

Dear Clark:

It's good to learn that you continue to feel well. As for not feeling much like writing, that's only natural, and, as I've told you before, I don't see why you should feel in any hurry. You are still young. *I'm* forty-seven, and don't feel in any hurry.

No—I've not heard from Loveman for much over a month. He owes me a letter; but I've found him a spasmodic correspondent, and am not worrying.

That *was* odd about your book, and shows what R. is as a business man! I have been trying since Jan. 1st to get my annual statement from him, but see no immediate prospects of succeeding.

I'll speak to Bennett about the new book, if you wish. You've a fine title for it.

I've read most of Saltus' books. "The Anatomy of Negation" is his best. I had it, but Mrs. Sterling owns it now. If you'll write to her at Piedmont, she'll be glad to lend it to you. His "Imperial Purple" is good, too.[1]

I've not been any busier than usual. I write sonnets whacking the Hun, mostly, and to my vast surprise sold one to "McClure's."[2] I sent you my "Revenge," didn't I?

Mrs. Clark has gone to N. Y.—not for long. I'm lunching with her sister on Thursday. She (Mrs. C.) still seems eager to have you try Dr. Rothchild's serum! When she returns, you must come down and let Abrams look you over again.

Affectionately,   George.

1. Saltus, *Imperial Purple* (1892), a series of impressionistic sketches of the Roman emperors.
2. "Germany in Belgium," a series of two sonnets.

[167a] CAS to GS [non-extant]

[Auburn, Cal.
c. mid-May 1917]

[168] GS to CAS [ALS]

May. 28th, 1917.

Dear Clark:

Don't let's apologize to each other for belated letters! We're both slow coaches when it comes to that.

How about the photograph you thought of sending? I'd be glad to have one, if only to prove to Mrs. Clark that you shouldn't go to a sanatorium. She is still in N. Y., I believe.

My Stella is now in Vancouver, and won't return for nearly a month more, as it's a twenty-week "tour."

I've not seen Bennett for some time, but will mention your prospective book to him when we meet. I fear he'll not be able to finance it, as it costs so much to bring out a book now-a-days.

Robertson thought he had sold out the 2000 edition of "The House of Orchids," but has discovered about 600 unbound copies! He's a wonder!

I don't see much prospect of getting up your way, yet. Here's that poem I spoke of.

Yes—I've read the "St. Anthony–Hearn" book.[1] It is a fine thing, as is everything else that Hearn put a hand to.

Affectionately yours.   George.

[Enclosure: "The Revenge."]

1. Flaubert's *The Temptation of St. Anthony,* translated by Lafcadio Hearn (1910).

[169] CAS to GS [ALS]

Auburn, Cal.,
June 17th, 1917.

Dear George:

I should have written sooner, but I've been a little under the weather for the past week. The first heat is devastating, after the uncommonly cool spring. Everyone is complaining of it—indeed, many people suffer far more from it than I do.

I like your "Revenge"—everything that you write is perfectly finished and effective. The phrase in the line next to the last is simply terrific—I can't get it out of my head.[1]

Sorry, but I've had no photographs taken as yet. I'm at outs with the only photographer in the town, since I refused the last work that he did for me. However, I'll try to get you something presently, even if it's only a snap-shot.

I've not written anything the last few weeks. I'll try to enclose copies of a few things that I wrote in May—nothing, I fear, that you will care for particularly.

I've had trouble with my feet lately—the arch of the right foot is threatening to break down, which makes walking more or less painful and difficult. The defect is remediable, tho, through the use of proper supports. I may need to have one specially made, on account of my high instep. I wouldn't be of much use on a long march, if I were in the army.

Affectionately,

Clark—

[Enclosures: "The Broken Lute," "The Tears of Lilith."]

1. "The Revenge," ll. 31–32: "I kiss no more the mouth and curdled eyes / Of her a fortnight dead."

[170] GS to CAS [ALS]

July 8th, 1917.

Dear Clark:

I've not written till now, because I had no money to send you. Mrs. C. told me, when I saw her late in June, that she'd send me another check, but she hasn't yet done so.

I'm not sure why she hasn't. Her husband is having very serious trouble with strikers at the United Verde mines, which he manages, and maybe that has made her forget—or given her reasons for economy. However, I'm hoping to hear from her before long. I'd "come through" myself, but have the Heron family still on my hands, none too strong.

I like "The Tears of Lilith"—a lovely lyric, though the word "aconite"[1] has been spoilt for me for ever, as I had to take aconite pills when a child. (Of course that's no reason for *your* not using it!) "The Broken Lute" is beautiful, too. "Smart Set" ought to take this sort of prose poetry.

I had first-hand news of you lately, from Dewing, who says he never saw you looking better. He's now in Yosemite, with some of our local "Bohemians," including two adventurous girls. The trip ought to be a success.

I was just reading an article that quoted Swinburne; he ranked the English poets thus: Shakespeare, Milton, Shelley, himself. Imagine imagining oneself a better poet than John Keats! Or Shell[e]y a better, for that matter.

The Book Club of Cal. has just printed 35 of my sonnets, *very* beautifully. I'd send you a copy, but the edition is limited and not for sale. They gave me a bronze plaque also; so I've not had "to die first!"

Stella is back, hard and rosy, from an 18 weeks dancing-tour, and I have little leisure. So good-bye for awhile!

Affectionately ever,   Geo.

1. "The Tears of Lilith," l. 3.

[171] CAS to GS [ALS]

Auburn, Cal.
July 26th, 1917.

Dear George:

I should have written long before this, had it not been for the long spell
of devastating and exhausting heat—the hottest July that I remember in many years.
To-day, for the first time, almost, the temperature has fallen precipitately, and there's a
cool wind, with an autumnal poignance in the air.

Don't worry about the money—we'll be able to get along, probably. I can get
work of some sort, at a pinch. We hope, tho, to negotiate a loan on our property.
There must be someone in Auburn with enough idle money.

My father has not been well, so I've given up the walking-tour that we planned.

I've not been able to write—every thing seems frozen at the source with me—a
matter of a broken heart that doesn't mend. Why should a hopeless and impossible
passion have power to disorganize and disrupt one's entire existence?

My name is on the draft list, so I dare say I'll have to appear for examination,
some time next week.[1] I almost wish they would take me—but there doesn't seem to
be much chance of that. The physical requirements are pretty stiff.

Affectionately,
Clark—

1. The United States entered World War I on 4 April 1917; President Woodrow Wilson a
signed a draft bill on 18 May, and the draft began on 5 June.

[171a] CAS to GS [non-extant]

[Auburn, Cal.
c. August 1917]

[Enclosures: "Ave atque Vale," "Impression," "Remoteness."]

[172] GS to CAS [ALS]

Sept. 19, 1917.

Dear Clark:

I hope you haven't thought I'm dead! I've come near wishing to be, for
the past month, what of tonsilitis, ulcerated teeth and a number of other maladies. I've
lost ten pounds, and don't feel well yet, but can write letters, anyhow.

I've written to Mrs. Clark several times since you last heard from me, and from
what she said in her last letter I thought she was about to come through with some
more money. I saw her personally, though, last week, and she didn't even refer to the

subject. So, when I see her again, which should be soon, I'm going to find nerve to bring up the matter orally, and pin her down. She has *loads* of money, and ought to help genius. I wish Mrs. Vanderbilt were here.[1] She has just fallen heir to $8 000 000. more, and maybe would pay off your mortgage.

Let me know as soon as you can how things are, and then I can talk with more conviction. Perhaps you don't want to be helped, but I'm determined you shall be— you or your parents.

I wish I could talk to you about your unhappiness. To think of your wasting a psychology such as yours on a thing so absurd as a girl—or woman! Wait till you're forty!

I liked the poems which you enclosed. "Impression" is absolute—very Gallic. "Remoteness" is good,[2] but of course not comparable to this big sonnet ("Ave atque Vale"). That's tremendous! Have you any especial reason for the extra foot in the last line? For "Leave fire and dust" etc. will do about as well.[3]

I'll be glad when I'm feeling better. It takes good health to face this groaning world, where I seem to attract misery as a magnet does iron-filings. It's my youngest sister now—and a dozen others, mostly women, of course.

Stoddard's poems are out: do you want the book?[4] It will disappoint you.

Let me hear from you soon, if you feel at all like correspondence.

Affectionately,   George.

1. GS refers to Margaret Emerson Vanderbilt, widow of Alfred Gwynne Vanderbilt (1877–1915), a son of Cornelius Vanderbilt whose estate was appraised in August 1917, more than two years after his death on the *Lusitania* (7 May 1915).

2. "Remoteness" appears to be non-extant.

3. The last line of the sonnet "Ave atque Vale" now scans properly ("Leave fire and dust from quenchless leagues of drouth"), so evidently CAS followed GS's suggestion for revision here.

4. *Poems of Charles Warren Stoddard*, ed. Ina Coolbrith (New York: John Lane Co.; London: John Lane, 1917). GS's poem "Charles Warren Stoddard" was included in the volume.

[173] CAS to GS [ALS]

Auburn, Cal.,
Sept. 24th, 1917.

Dear George:

I'm so glad to hear from you again, so sorry to know that you have been ill. I had worried a little about your not writing, but now I understand. I, too have been in no mood or condition for correspondence, but feel better, comparatively speaking, with the first cool weather. I've had a rotten summer of it, partly or chiefly through my own cussedness, and ought to be dead by all the laws of nature. I've had fever at times, and latterly have been troubled with a swelling of the jaws. I thought it was mumps at first, from the location of the swelling (in the salivary glands). I'm afraid now that it may be tubercular, unless it's from my teeth. You might ask Abrams about it, if you see him.

We have been trying to secure a loan here in Auburn, but so far, with no success. Personally, I don't care, but I wish my parents were provided for. Even if I were in better health, my earning-capacity would be negligible, or slight. At present I'm rather "up against it."

Glad you like the poems. I've nothing new to send, but hope to have, presently. My only salvation, physical, mental, and emotional, is in art, and I mean to begin work as soon as possible.

I saw a few quotations from Stoddard's volume, and thought them rather mild, to say the least. Of course, the book would interest me, in a sense; but don't trouble to send it.

Thanks for the inscription in your volume of sonnets! The last sonnet (on Life)[1] is one that I had never seen before, and I liked it very much. Surely there's no need for me to say what I think of the others.

I hope that this finds you in better health and spirits—also that you will carry **my** troubles lightly. After all, there's nothing in the whole d——d world that's worth worrying about.

Affectionately,

Clark—

1. "To Life" had appeared in *Sonnet* 1, No. 3 (1917): 2. CAS refers to *TfS*.

[174] GS to CAS [ALS]

Sept. 28, 1917.

Dear Clark:

We want you to come down here right away and have another examination. It can't hurt you and it may help you. Also the weather here is probably cooler than in Auburn.

Here is $50. to pay your expenses, and there will be more later on, if you'll only take an interest in your health.

Better come on Monday. But be sure to come. I'll answer your letter when I *see* you!

Affectionately,

George.

[175] CAS to GS [ALS]

Auburn, Cal.,
Oct. 1st, 1917

Dear George:

I'll be down Wednesday, on No. 9, which will get me into the city about 2.30 p.m. Can you meet me at the Ferry?

I won't be able to stay more than a day or two—just long enough to see the doctor.

Thanks—a thousand thanks—for the check. I'll have more to say when we meet.

Hastily,

Clark—

[176] GS to CAS [ALS]

Nov. 10, 1917.

Dear Clark:

I've been expecting to hear from you for ten days, as you said you'd write toward the end of October and let me know how you're progressing. As you don't write, I suppose I'm to assume you are not well.

I'm enclosing check for $50. After this it will be $75., as Mrs. Clark wants to be sure you have plenty of meat to eat. So don't stint yourself, please.

We think that if you don't continue to improve you ought to go to a sanatorium, and I hope you'll try to have an open mind as to this proposition. You'd find it pleasanter than you think.

Robertson is bringing out a little book of war-rhymes for me, mostly re-prints.[1] He wanted some such book for his Xmas trade.

Hoping to hear from you soon,

Affectionately,   George.

1. *BiB.*

[177] CAS to GS [ALS]

Auburn, Cal.,
Nov. 13th, 1917.

Dear George:

Your letter, and the check, came yesterday. Please pardon my silence—I have not been very well most of the time; also, I had expected to hear from you almost any day, or even to see you, since, when I was in the city, you spoke of the possibility of motoring up to Auburn with some friend, late in October. It seems to have been a case of waiting, on both sides.

We've had several good showers lately—enough rain to wash the dust out of the air. Today, the sunlight is dazzlingly clear, and fresh, and cool, and delightful. I feel very much better than for months past. I should be happier, though, if I could work; but I've neither the energy nor inspiration for *that*.

I wish you could see the orchards hereabouts—the autumn leaves have all the colours of flame this year. The peach-trees are especially beautiful and gorgeous.

My parents are both in better health. My mother, who has been lame so long from a bad fall, is now able to get around quite comfortably.

Give my best regards to Dewing, if you see him. I owe him a letter, and am not forgetting the fact.

I enclose a few grotesques. It amuses me to draw them, and I fancy that I've improved a little with practice.

Affectionately,
Clark

[178] GS to CAS [ALS]

Dec. 22, 1917.

Dear Clark:

I hope you'll not think I've entirely forgotten you! The truth is I've been waiting for Mrs. Clark to send your check, a thing she promised to do in a letter written to me two weeks ago. Why she doesn't send it I don't know. But she will, sooner or later.

Here's a review that mentions you. As it's by the toad-man, Herbert Bashford,[1] who loves to void his spite on Bierce (now that Bierce has gone), it's no especial compliment, tho true enough.

My little book of war-verse is out, and I'd send you a copy if I thought you'd care for anything in it. But you'd not, as it's verse and not poetry.

I'll write again soon, so don't bother to reply to this. And here's wishing you and your parents a happy holiday season.

> Affectionately,
>> George.

[P.S.] Stella is now in New York.

1. "Dr. Taylor as a Sonneteer," *Town Talk* No. 1304 (1 September 1917): [6–7].

[179] GS to CAS [ALS]

> Dec. 27, 1917.

Dear Clark:

> Here we are at last!

I'm wondering how you are. Better, I'm hoping, for cool weather braces one up.

I've no news, and haven't written anything for about two months. I'm vowing to reform at once, however, and get busy. I've a lot of things in *mind,* anyhow.

Stella hasn't landed a job yet, but seems to like New York, which is more than I do. It has been called "a Heaven for women and a Hell for me."

Let me wish you and your parents a happy New Year.

> Affectionately,
>> George.

[Enclosure] [ALS]

> [El Palomar, San Mateo]
> Dec. 26th, 1917.

Dear Poet:

> This is the cheque for our protégé. I am going to N. Y. on Sat., so I fear I will not see you for some weeks. I will just have time to see Dick before he sails.

We had a happy but exhausting Xmas—a huge tree, & all Tobins, great & small.

Every happiness & blessing for the New Year.

> Yrs. Sincerely,
>> C. C.

[180] CAS to GS [ALS]

> Auburn, Cal.,
> Jan. 5th, 1918.

Dear George:

> Both your letters, and the check, came "safely to hand." A thousand thanks! I should have written you before, but the holidays have rather disorganized me.

The weather is, and has been perfectly abominable, for weeks, on account of the fog and the cold—to me, the worst of all possible combinations. I keep pretty well, physically, but these blind, grey days, and long, cold, black nights are depressing. However, I seem immune to the ordinary winter ailments—I've not caught even a real cold, so far.

I'm ashamed to say that I've written nothing for months, and have not even cared to write. Am I getting old, or middle-aged? My 25th birthday is close at hand, so I feel quite ancient at times!

Andrew Dewing is up for a few weeks, so I'm not nearly as lonely as usual. I wish I were not so easily bored—it's an unenviable distinction, and nothing at all to [be] proud of. Most people tire me after the first, or at most, the second meeting.

Have you heard from Loveman lately? I've not had a letter from him for months.

Affectionately,
Clark—

[181] GS to CAS [ALS]

Feb. 16, 1918.

Dear Clark:

I hope you haven't been thinking I've forgotten you. I know you dislike to write often, so I've been waiting to hear from Mrs. Clark before letting you hear from me.

She returned from N. Y. a few days ago, and is now at the Fairmont here, ill. However, she was able to write and enclose the $75., which in turn I pass on to you.

How are *you*? Better, I hope, for the weather has been pretty good—here, at any rate. I've been doing all sorts of fool things since I last wrote you—a couple of one-act plays, a "popular" song (!) and a lot of "lyrics" for the next grove-play.[1] Anything to get ahold of some money, for almost all my friends seem to be up against it. If my song goes, and I see no reason why it shouldn't, I'll make short work of that mortgage on your place.

I heard from Loveman in November (I *think*) and haven't answered his letter yet! I owe lots of letters, and always shall, I suppose.

I *ought* to be writing a preface to your Book Club volume, and will, next week.[2]

Affectionately,
George.

1. Possibly two unpublished plays, *The Bluff* and *The Folding-Bed* (mss., San Francisco Public Library); the song may be "We're A-Going" (San Francisco, 1918) or one published in the revised edition of *Songs*, set to music by Lawrence Zenda (pseud. of Rosaliene Travis) (San Francisco: Sherman, Clay, 1928). For the grove play see letter 153, n.1.

2. GS wrote the preface to *OS* (1918). See Appendix.

[182] [ALS]

Auburn, Cal.,
Feb. 25th, 1918.

Dear George:

Many, many thanks for the check, which I should have acknowledged more promptly than this. I am sorry to hear that Mrs. Clark is ill, and hope that she is better by this time.

No news, in especial. I've written nothing, but have drawn a great deal, by way of avocation. I keep pretty well, and have gained considerably in weight, partly, perhaps, through lack of exercise.

Bender tells me that I've been made an honorary member of the Book Club. They've presented me with a beautiful bronze placque, of which, naturally, I feel very proud. But I shall feel even prouder of your preface for my book.

I've had two letters from Loveman during the past fortnight, with the promise of a third in a few days. He is certainly what you called him—"a spasmodic correspondent."

By the way, have you, or would you care to have, Symons' translation of Baudelaire's prose-poems?[1] I happen to possess an extra copy, and could turn it over to you just as well as not.

> Affectionately,
> Clark.

1. *Poems in Prose from Charles Baudelaire,* translated by Arthur Symons (1905).

[183] GS to CAS [ALS]

> Apr. 3, 1918.

Dear Clark:

I've been waiting to hear from Mrs. Clarke, before writing. At last I had to remind her.

No especial news. I finished "Lilith", to-day, at least in the rough. Probably I'll be tinkering at it till I get it published, which ought to be by October, if Alec will publish at all.

How do you feel? It was good news to know you've gained in weight—a fine sign.

Sure—I'd like to have that Baudelaire translation. Be sure to inscribe it.

Masefield has come and gone. He's a great poet, and interesting to see and talk with. But he was dog-tired and very depressed. He has written nothing since the first month of the War.[1]

Perhaps you've not seen the sonnets I enclose. The themes are certainly dissimilar! Here's my best ever to you!

> Affectionately,   Geo.

[Enclosure: ALS]

> [El Palomar, San Mateo]
> April 2ᵈ[, 1918]

Dear Poet:

I did not forget the cheque, but I have been too poorly to attend to anything. I am home again, & hope to be strong soon. Thank you for the lovely verses.

> Yrs. sincerely,
> Celia Clark

[Enclosure: "Infidels," one unidentified sonnet.]

1. Masefield visited San Francisco in March 1918.

[184] CAS to GS [ALS]

Auburn, Cal.,
April 8th, 1918

Dear George:

Your welcome letter, enclosing the check, arrived last week. A thousand thanks! I am sorry to hear that Mrs. Clark has not been well.

I mailed you the Baudelaire last Friday. Symons' translation is, of course, excellent, tho by no means superior (in my opinion) to that of Stuart Merrill, which I also possess.[1]

I've done a little writing lately; also a number of drawings, from which (even if they are valueless artistically) I get considerable amusement. I enclose two prose-poems and a sonnet.

I like both of the sonnets you send—"Infidels" best, even tho I agree with the dictum of the bonzes.[2] Even pleasure (from my experience) is not enough to redeem the wrong of existence.

Have you heard from Loveman lately? He has been drafted, and expects to be called up this month. Perhaps I may go yet!

I've been very good the last two months, and have kept unusually quiet, with no long walks or over-exertion of any kind. The trouble about the rest-cure is that one gets so infernally "soft." I feel tired and nervous most of the time, in spite of the gain in weight. The nervousness, however, may be due to digestive poisoning.

The flowers are beautiful now—pansies, popcorn-balls, shooting-stars, faun-lilies, wild hyacinth, and a score of others. I wish you were here to see them.

As ever, affectionately,
Clark.

[Enclosures: "Ennui," "The Princess Almeena," "Sepulture."]

1. *Pastels in Prose* (1890) by American poet Stuart Merrill (1863–1915), who also wrote poems in French. The book contains several translations from Baudelaire as well as other French poets. In 1925 CAS translated Merrill's "A Woman at Prayer" (unpublished).
2. The dictum is "Life is evil."

[185] GS to CAS [ALS]

Apr. 19, 1918.

Dear Clark:

Thanks for the Baudelaire translation! I can't say I care much for the stuff, though: I think *your* prose poems far better.

I've owed Loveman a letter for a long time, so naturally I don't hear from him. I have to write so many letters that I find it hard to write to persons I've never met, even though one may be a real poet, like Loveman.

It's too hot here to-day for work. I've finished "Lilith," at least roughly. I may tinker at it till Robertson can afford its publication: Christ knows when that'll be! Everything costs so heavily nowadays.

I don't think you're likely to be drafted; but it would be a great thing for you if you were.

I enclose my first draft of the foreword I've done for your Book Club volume. Forgive me for not expressing my *full* admiration: reserve is a valuable factor in such appreciations.

This "Ennui" of yours is a damned fine thing! I'm no admirer of victims of splanchnic neurasthenia, but that "has nothing to do with the case." If you don't care to send this beautiful thing to "Smart Set," will you not let me do so, with a written word to Mencken, with whom I correspond?

"The Princess Almeena" is good too. I never liked that word "ichor." It suggests an oozing sore to me!

By the way, it's "ecstasy," not "ecstacy." And it's "myrrh", not "myhrr." "Sepulture" is very, very beautiful. I'm sorry it has come too late to go in the book.

Is there a difference between "lotos" and "lotus?" It seems to me there is. One eats the lotos for forgetfulness, while the lotus is of the East, a symbol of immortality. It seems to me that the former goes better with "asphodel," being Grecian rather than Asiatic. But this is a mere detail.

My best to you ever, Poet!

Affectionately,   George.

[P.S.] I hardly expect to hear from Mrs. C. before the end of the month.

[P.P.S.] Did I ever send you a sonnet called "Caesar di Beccaria?"[1] I have no copy of it, but gave out several—to God-knows-whom!

G.

[Enclosure: "To Ruth Chatterton."]

1. Unpublished; no ms. appears to survive.

[186] CAS to GS [ALS]

Auburn, Cal.,
April 24th, 1918.

Dear George:

Thanks for your preface, which (despite the "reserve" of which you speak!) contains praise enough for any poet,—let alone *me!* Your remarks and criticisms are finely expressed, and all very much to the point. Certainly, I have small reason to fear the peril of popularity,—which is anything but imminent, in my case.

I like the beautiful sonnet you enclose ("To Ruth Chatterton").[1] No, you have never sent me "Caesar Beccaria". I should certainly like to see a copy of it.

I shall certainly avail myself of the distinction you make between "lotus" and "lotos." It's odd that I should make mistakes in spelling—I was a champion speller during my school-days. Latterly, I think that my aural memory has strengthened at the expense of the visual memory; and, of course, accuracy in English spelling depends upon remembering the *shape* of words as well as their *sound*.

I should be very grateful to you if you would recommend "Ennui" to Mr. Mencken. I seldom submit anything to the magazines, these latter days.

I enclose a few verses, including one or two poems written last autumn. You may have seen "Dissonance" before. Most of them are too monotonous and personal, I fear. I think of eschewing the subjective as much as possible henceforth. "The Seas of Saturn," poor as it is, gives an example of the style I should prefer to develop—one of objective beauty and material splendours dissociate from other than purely aesthetic emotion—in short, the Parnassian ideal.

As ever, affectionately,

Clark—

[Enclosures: "Anodyne," Dissonance," "Eidolon," "Haunting," "Image," "In November," "Memorial," "Palms," "A Precept," *"Requiescat in Pace,"* "Upon the Seas in Saturn," "Winter Moonlight."]

1. Ruth Chatterton (1893–1961) was a film actress.

[187] GS to CAS [ALS, Dartmouth]

May 3, 1918.

Dear Clark:

This is only a note, to go with the check. I'll reply to your good letter in a few days.

Affectionately,

George.

[188] GS to CAS [ALS]

May 12, 1918.

Dear Clark:

I'm glad to know my little preface was not unpleasing to you—the Lord He knoweth you deserve a better one!

I sent your "Ennui" on to Mencken, and had the nerve to make one small change, as the editors may even make others! For the name "Chan" seeming too *amiable*, as it were, to me, I went over a list of the Chinese emperors and selected a name that sounded like that of a dangerous man to offend: Seaou-Sin. I trust you'll not greatly disapprove, even if it has unbalanced your sentences a bit. "Chan" is quite too plump and mild, I think. The other name is serpentish.

I spoke of that "Caesar di Beccaria" sonnet of mine because I've given away such few copies of it as I had, and thought I might have sent one to you. I'm unable to remember just how it went. I've lost several war-sonnets the same way—if one may call that a loss.

I like all these poems you send me, tho some, naturally, more than others. The "Seas of Saturn" one seems to me the best. I like especially the sestet. But "Eidolon" and "Dissonance" are just as good. That 8th line in the latter is terrific. (I think you can better "arméd"—even "iron" is preferable, I think.) It's a pity you couldn't have written in Paris (and in the French tongue), some decades ago, for so few of our own speech are ever likely to care for your style. By the way, I don't care for that long

French metre you use in some of these poems (such as "Palms"), though the context is always poetry, d—— good poetry!

Let me know how you are—at your leisure.

Affectionately,   George.

[P.S.] This "Requiescat" is very beautiful, I think.

[189] CAS to GS [ALS]

Auburn, Cal.,
May 17th, 1918

Dear George:

I had meant to acknowledge your good letter and the check long before this; but I've had considerable care and worry, and have not felt so well as in April. My mother is ill at present. The local M. D. calls it a nervous collapse; but some of the symptoms are suspiciously like those of incipient paralysis; and paralysis appears to run in her family, since several have died of it.

Thanks for what you say about the poems. I'm not worrying much about their lack of popular appeal: what in Hades does it all matter, anyway? As to the style, that may be merely a phase of my work. If I continue to live and write, I may develop (and discard) half a dozen different styles.

The change of names in "Ennui" is certainly an improvement. "Seaou-Sin" is a marvel of fiendish and serpentine suggestion.[1]

I suppose Loveman has been called up by this time. I've not heard from him very recently. The European war is worse than a revolution in Malebolge.

Have you seen Andrew Dewing lately? Tell him to write me, if you happen to run into him. He owes me a letter.

I've nothing new to send, excepting a brace of sonnets in the metre you dislike. However, you may find ideas in them.

Affectionately,
Clark.

[Enclosures: "Mirrors," "Inferno."]

1. CAS, however, restored the reading *Chan* when he reprinted "Ennui" in *EC.*

[190] GS to CAS [ALS]

June 10, 1918.

Dear Clark:

Mrs. Clark has had a relapse, and had to go back to bed. However, she's better now, and is probably well "for keeps."

I motored past the place yesterday, but did not call. It's a beautiful one.

There's any amount of poetry in the two sonnets you enclose. The metre sets all my poetic nerves a-howl, as I've already said. And yet the French love it. Well, poetry was never their strong point.

I prefer "Mirrors" to "Inferno," and am sending it to Mencken.[1] A letter from him to-day speaks of his having received some poems from you. He didn't care for them so much as for your sonnet I sent him, though. You must learn to put up with the odd tastes of editors; that is, if you care to patronize them. They're not to be taken seriously. But take their checks and smile at their rejection-slips.

I hope your mother is better now. But your weather can't be very pleasant, as it's too hot even here.

I saw Andrew a few nights ago, in his usual haunt, the Bologna restaurant. He's not well, as he may have told you.

I've written very little for two months, but am on the wagon now, and should soon be raping the Muse once more. I've an order for a 4th of July "poem!"[2]

Reply at your leisure.

Affectionately,   George.

1. HLM apparently rejected "Mirrors," as it did not appear in the *Smart Set*.
2. "The Messenger."

[190a] CAS to GS [non-extant]

[Auburn, Cal.
early July 1918]

[191] CAS to GS [ALS]

Auburn, Cal.,
Aug. 10th, 1918.

Dear George:

I'm wondering if you received my last letter, written sometime in the fore-part of July. I've been expecting to hear from you any time, so your silence makes me think that my letter may have miscarried. However, there was nothing of importance in it.

I was terribly shocked to read of Mrs. Sterling's death, and fear what it may mean to you.[1] Mrs. Clark, in a letter I have just received, speaks of your feeling so keenly on the subject. She (Mrs Clark) is wonderfully kind to me, and I feel as if my debt were more than a matter of dollars.

Everyone seems to be dying, these days. Andrew Dewing's brother, Walter, died last month, of consumption—a shock and surprise to me, since he had not seemed any worse than usual. Andrew, as you doubtless know, has been drafted. He is coming back to Auburn for a visit, and I'll probably see him to-morrow.

Have you ever found time to write to Loveman? Even a note from you would mean a great deal to him, I think. His life in the training-camp is a hard and unhappy one, since his poor eyesight debars him from any prospect of service over sea.[2]

I have been better, on the whole, since my visit to the city, and think that it really did me good. My "Katzenjammer" was two-thirds physical exhaustion and lack of sleep. I take better care of myself now, though it's hard for me to make myself eat enough. However, I've gained a little, the last few weeks, and don't look quite so much like a starving Belgian as when you saw me.

Our weather is wonderfully cool and pleasant, on the whole. The thermometer stands at 70° as I write—early this morning it was down to 50°, or less. I never knew such weather in August among these dry foothills.

When do you expect to return? Can't you stop off at Auburn, when you come through? I'd love to have you, for any length of time you could stay, or would care to stay.

As ever, affectionately,

Clark—

1. Carrie Sterling committed suicide on 7 August. Her death was widely reported in the San Francisco papers; e.g., "Mrs. Geo. Sterling Suicide: Divorced Wife of Poet," *San Francisco Examiner* (9 August 1918): 1. She apparently was heartbroken over her separation from GS.
2. For much of the war and its immediate aftermath, Loveman was stationed at Fort Gordon in Georgia.

[192] GS to CAS [ALS]

August 21st, 1918.

Dear Clark:

I was about to write to you from N. Y. when the news of Carrie's death came, and I left at once for S. F., going through Auburn about noon, on Saturday.

It's good to hear from you and know you are improving in health. Do try to eat a lot: it will repay you. I know Andrew is still with you—do you know his ailment? I do.

I wrote nothing while in N. Y. It was too hot to write even a letter, and it was a triumph to exist at all. Truly a detestable place, which I hope never to see again. It is Heaven to be back in S. F., even with all I have to be remorseful for. I hope never to have to leave the west coast again—nothing is worth it.

I saw several celebrities while in N. Y., notably Carman and Dreiser. John Reed, Harry Kemp and Nina Putnam were lesser luminaries. They work hard and play hard there. Carman & Dreiser tried hard to steal the girl I had with me, but didn't succeed![1]

My best to you and to Andrew!

Yours ever,   Geo.

1. Theodore Dreiser (1871–1945), American novelist; John Reed (1887–1920), American journalist and poet; Harry Kemp (1883–1960), American poet, novelist, and dramatist.

[193] CAS to GS [ALS]

Auburn, Cal.,
Aug. 31st, 1918.

Dear George:

I should have written you before this, had it not been for the extreme heat. Even letter-writing is a severe mental effort, when the mercury is flirting with the hundred-mark. I do little but lie around and read, these days, though I feel much stronger than I did last month, in spite of the debilitating weather.

As usual, there's no news, in particular, unless it's the fact that I've actually sold a poem ("The Desert Garden") to Ainslee's Magazine.

Andrew is here, and expects to stay on the ranch for several months. What *is* his trouble? "Tobacco heart?"

I am extremely distressed, and very much puzzled, over the rumour concerning which you wrote to my mother. The income I have received (as she is writing you separately) has been more than ample for all our necessities, and even for a few luxuries. I can think of only one person from whom such a story might have emanated—a young musician in Red Bluff, with whom my mother and I both had some correspondence, anent the melodies he had composed for certain of my poems, and whose publication he wished me to finance, on a profit-sharing basis. This I declined to do . . . How anything that my mother said, or that I said, could have been construed into a profession of abject poverty, I am totally unable, or, at least, unwilling to imagine.

Can't you run up for a few days, when the weather grows a little cooler? I want very much to see you.

Affectionately,
Clark.

[194] GS to CAS [ALS]

Sept. 9th, 1918.

Dear Clark:

It was a relief to learn that all was well with you. That Pendleton person,[1] besides being variously a false alarm, is an irresponsible he-gossip, and should join some old ladies' knitting circle. Miss Coolbrith, to whom he did his talking, has given him a good scolding.

I'm glad you sold your "Desert Garden" to Roberts.[2] I spoke to him of you, early in July, during a conversation in which we agreed that if a magazine is to run verse at all, it may as well be poetry.

I'll tell you Andrew's malady, but you must protect *me* by telling no one else, even him. He has tuberculosis. However, he is such a husky chap that I'm sure he'll get over it if he takes any decent care of himself. He isn't telling even his folks what ails him.

Kilmer's death made me feel bad. I knew and liked him well. Not a very big poet, but a dandy chap. Seeger was a snob, on the other hand.[3]

I've done little work, since returning, besides writing a fool photo-play. I sha'n't be able to go to Auburn, at least for some time. For one thing, I've not even the fare!

Robertson can't afford to publish "Lilith" this year, so I'm offering it to Macmillan's, who asked me for it a number of times, through their reader, when I was in N. Y. But now they'll probably not be able to bring it out till the spring.

Thank your mother for me for her letter. I guess there's no need for me to reply to it. Even one extra letter is an effort to me.

What's Loveman's address? I'll be glad, of course, to drop him a line.

Take your time about answering.

Affectionately,   George.

1. Robert Emmet Pendleton (1887–1964), a composer who later set some of CAS's poems to music.
2. Walter Adolphe Roberts (1886–1964), editor of *Ainslee's* and a correspondent of GS.
3. Joyce Kilmer (b. 1886) died in a battle near Ourcq, France, on 30 July 1918; Alan Seeger

(b. 1888), American poet, died on 4 July 1916 in a battle at Belloy-en-Santerre, France, after enlisting in the Foreign Legion. He enjoyed a brief vogue with his poem "I Have a Rendezvous with Death" (*North American Review,* October 1916).

[195] CAS to GS [ALS]

Auburn, Cal.,
Oct. 13th, 1918.

Dear George:

I should have written you long before this; but there seemed to be nothing in particular to write *about;* and I know how burdensome and voluminous your correspondence has become. So I've spared you my tale of platitudes and trivialities till now.

Have you written much of late? I haven't. One sonnet (which I enclose) makes up the sum total of my work during August, September, and the present month. Nor have I been able to sell anything since the poem that found lodgement in Ainslee's. I've not felt like writing, and have been tired and depressed most of the time. I eat more than I did, and have gained in weight, but, somehow, not in strength.

I see Andrew fairly often, which breaks the monotony of my solitude. He told me himself (in secret) about his real malady. I'm not surprised (his elder brother died recently of the same disease) but I don't think that he stands in much danger of a breakdown . . . Still, one never can tell.

Loveman writes me regularly. He doesn't like the training-camp life, and seems to suffer greatly from depression. His address is: Corporal Sam Loveman, Co. H., 4th Infantry Replacement Reg't., Camp Gordon, Ga.

The news to-day is disgusting and appalling. But it hardly seems possible that we can make an armistice with Germany; to do so would be a crime against the whole future of civilization. However, our pusillanimous president, and his Congress of cowards, are capable of anything.

Give my best regards to Bender, if you see him. My parents wish to be remembered to you. Can't you manage to run up, some time? My parents join me in the most cordial of standing invitations.

Affectionately,
Clark.

[Enclosure: "The Chimaera."]

[196] GS to CAS [ALS]

Oct. 26, 1918.

Dear Clark:

As I have said before, it's never necessary for you to apologize for any protracted silence on your part, in the matter of correspondence. I shall understand.

You may not have written a great deal of late, but to have written the very powerful sonnet you send me ("The Chimaera") is a good deal to have done—more than to have composed several tons of the usual verse we find in the magazines of to-day. I wish you'd send this fine sonnet to Mahlon Leonard Fisher, of Williamsport, Pa. He gets out "The

Sonnet," and this one will, I'm sure, appeal strongly to him. He pays only 25¢ a line; but then, other magazines pay less than that, and some of them nothing at all!

No—I've not written very much since my return from N. Y. Lately I've felt more like work, however, and have ground out five or six things. I'll enclose copies of the few I've copies of.

I think you're too hard on Wilson, though I admit he has had me scared more than once. However, he always comes through in good shape, and Congress seems belligerent enough, at least to me; and you'll admit I'm no pacifist. I hope you'll be careful what you write to Loveman in this strain, as his (and your) letters may be seen—and even censored.

Here's hoping the influenza skips you and yours! *I am wearing a mask when I prowl abroad.*[1]

Affectionately,   George.

1. To protect against the flu epidemic of 1918–19, which killed 15 million worldwide and about 450,000 in the US. *AJ* for 21 November 1918 notes that citizens were required to wear masks in public.

[197] GS to CAS [ALS]

Nov. 12, 1918.

Dear Clark:

To-day I'm mailing you one of your books, which I wish you'd inscribe to a friend of mine, Phil B. Bekeart. He's a book-collector and good friend to writers and artists generally.

No especial news. I'm still recovering from yesterday's peace-celebration. San Francisco certainly "knows how!"

I hope you sent something to Fisher. He says in a letter to me that your "Smart Set" sonnet[1] is "a beautiful thing." And he's right. Also hard to please, as he has refused one or two of my own sonnets that I thought rather well of.

I'm writing a metrical satire on the free verse gang.[2]

Remember me kindly to Andrew and your folks.

Yours ever.   George.

[Enclosure: "Ocean Sunsets," one unidentified poem.]

1. I.e., "Sepulture."
2. See letter 206.

[198] CAS to GS [ALS]

East Auburn, Cal.,
Nov. 16th, 1918

Dear George:

I inscribed the copy of my book for Mr. Bekeart, and mailed it to you yesterday. I should have written you before, but, as usual, there was little or no news. I've been keeping to my hill-top pretty closely, since the mask ordinance went into effect (the wearing of one is a Chinese torture to me) and have only been in Auburn once or twice in the past month. So I've had a rather quiet and peaceful time of it.

I submitted a few sonnets to Fisher, who has accepted two of them ("The Mummy" and "In Saturn"). He returned "The Chimaera" and "Eidolon", both of which, in my opinion, are superior to "The Mummy."

I like the triad of sonnets you enclose ("Ocean Sunsets") but think the second one the best. Your river-poem is strong, like everything of the sort you have written.

Have you written to Loveman? He has been in hospital with a severe and protracted case of bronchitis, and had just been released when he wrote me last.

I haven't seen Auburn for nearly a fortnight, so you can surmise the completeness of my isolation. I don't feel any too well, and avoid walking and tiring myself any more than I can help. Physical exhaustion or over-exertion seems to hurt my nerves in a way that it didn't use to. I suffer from depression and insomnia when I fatigue myself too much.

To-day, I've been making clean and revised copies of some of my unpublished work. I shall go on, and put together everything that I care to have preserved in book-form, under the general title, "Ebony and Crystal." If anything were to happen to me, you'd have one hell of a time editing my mss. as they stand. I've been very careless in the past, and have even neglected to keep typewritten copies of some of my things.

> Affectionately, as ever,
> Clark.

[199] GS to CAS [ALS]

> Dec. 12th, 1918.

Dear Clark:

Accept my belated thanks, please, for the fine Christmas berries. It's two years since I've gathered any, and then it was down toward San Luis Obispo.

Yes—Fisher's tastes in poetry are not ours, but so long as he'll give me $3.50 apiece for sonnets that I can't possibly sell elsewhere, I'm for him! Caveat emptor!

I've written several poems lately, but have no copies to send you. I find it hard to get typing done gratis. Here's a "snap" of me, though. I was about to murder some innocent ducks.

No—I've not written to Loveman. I have to write so many letters that I'm cutting out all I can. I may get around to him some day, though. He's a poet, all right.

That's a good plan of yours to get your MSS in shape. Every writer should do so, knowing the precarious nature of this sour life. "Ebony and Crystal" is a wonderful title.

Tell me what book you'd like for Christmas.

> Affectionately,   George.

[P.S.] Tell him Heine is dead. My best to Andrew when next you see him.

[200] CAS to GS [ALS]

> East Auburn, Cal.,
> Feb 2nd, 1918 [i.e., 1919]

Dear George:

How is it with you, these days? I'm appalled to find how long it has been since I last wrote you. Time goes by so quietly, so imperceptibly, amid the purple depth and silence of these hills and canyons; and scarcely anything occurs to distinguish one day from another, beyond the alternations of temperature, of cloud and rain and sun. It surprised me yesterday to find the first wild flowers of the year; they made me realize, with a sort of shock, that I had not written to you since the early part of winter.

Have you managed to escape the plaguey "flu"? I have, so far, though Auburn is rotten with it. I keep out of the town as much as possible; we live, in point of isolation, at least, much like the people in Boccaccio.

My health has not been any too good, and I am still unable to work. Even the effort brings on extreme fatigue, and a host of unpleasant nervous symptoms. I've written only one sonnet during the winter, and have made a few drawings.

Loveman has been in the hospital again, this time with heart-trouble—myocarditis, I think he called it. They may keep him awhile for treatment, before discharging him.

I see Andrew occasionally. He seems in excellent health, and takes good care of himself, so I doubt if he's in much danger of a breakdown.

Have you written much of late? I liked your clever little comedy in "Smart Set."[1]

Give my best regards to Albert Bender when you see him. I wish I could drop down upon you all; but I don't know when it will be.

Affectionately,
Clark—

[Enclosure: "Forgetfulness."]

1. "The Dryad," a short prose play about a married man tempted by a dryad.

[201] GS to CAS [ALS]

Feb. 11th, 1919.

Dear Clark:

I'm sorry that your creative energy has not been at a higher level, this winter. Nevertheless, this exquisite sonnet that you send me is worth more than several books of poorer verse. It is as beautiful a thing as I've seen in many a day. Have you sent it to some magazine? I am sure "Smart Set" will take it, but I'd try some, first, that pay better. Be sure to send it to Mrs. Clark. I've not seen that nice lady since the autumn; I fear I'm forgotten.

I know how you dislike to write letters, so I don't write to you so often as I might otherwise. I'm pretty lazy myself. Have done nothing much since before Christmas. I enclose a sonnet. Have written a few "songs" for Lawrence Zenda.[1]

It's good to learn that Dewing is looking well. I have Dr. A. now attending a beautiful woman who has come here from N. Y. with the t.b. She is improving rapidly under his treatment, though she is careless about following out all of his instructions. I want you to see her, one of these days.

My mother, in Honolulu, has had a paralytic stroke, but is now much better.

I've a satiric poem in the Feb. "Century."[2] Nothing much, but it serves to present my regards to the modernist gang, in a playful way.

I sold my three "Ocean-Sunsets" sonnets to Harper's Monthly. I hope they'll print them by next autumn, as Robertson wants to bring out a book for me then. Boni & Liveright will also publish "Lilith" in the fall. I'll be known from Ukiah to Milpitas, yet.

Odd—Mrs. Clark just rang up! Wants me to go to dinner with her at the Fairmont, Sunday. But I've another date.

Yours affectionately,   George.

[Enclosure: unidentified sonnet.]

1. See letter 181, n.1.
2. "The Roman Wall."

[202] CAS to GS [ALS]

East Auburn, Cal.,
March 2nd, 1919

Dear George:

How is it with you these days? I saw your sonnet in Fisher's publication, opposite my own,[1] but have seen nothing else by you of late. Have you written much?

Glad you liked "Forgetfulness". I didn't care much for it myself, and hardly thought it would be salable. "The Sonnet" snapped it up, rather to my surprise.

I've little to complain of these days, excepting the climate; which is getting to be a pretty serious grievance, after a month or more without twenty-four consecutive hours of fair weather. This everlasting rain, fog, frost, ice, hail, mud, etc., would be a disgrace to Malebolge. I wonder if it's as bad in S. F. as here.

I had a visitor early in February,—a young poet from the Russian river country, named Robbins Lampson.[2] He spoke of having met you.

Loveman is back in Cleveland, and has had to go to work again, though he is not in the best of health. What hellish luck, after a year in a training-camp! However, there's many a poor devil that's even worse off. The I.W.W. will have no lack of new recruits.

By the way, can you get me a copy of the issue of "The Smart Set" containing "Ennui?" I'm told that it is out,—probably in the November, December, or January number,—but have not been able to obtain one. Also, I've lost or mislaid my only fair ms, and can't remember some of the final revisions.

I enclose a few more sonnets—my output for February. Do you think any of them salable? I never seem able to tell, myself.

I've not seen Andrew for two weeks or more, on account of this diluvial weather, which turns my hill-top into a sort of Juan Fernandez, or Devil's Island . . . He wanted to be remembered to you.

Affectionately,
Clark.

[Enclosures: "Laus Mortis," "To the Beloved," "Transcendence."]

1. CAS's "In Saturn" and GS's "Outward" appeared on facing pages of the January–February 1919 issue of the *Sonnet*.
2. I.e., Myrle Robbins Lampson (1900–?; later "Robin Lampson"), poet and novelist.

[203] GS to CAS [ALS]

Apr. 8th, 1919.

Dear Clark:

You may have seen Andrew by now, and received any such small news as I could give. It is rather from you that the news must issue, as I have been wondering what has become of May Greenwood and her husband, who went to Auburn a couple of weeks ago, and of whom I'd like to hear. I told them to call on you: have they done so?[1]

I know of no way of getting you the number of Smart Set with your "Ennui," except by ordering it from them—and I don't know which number to order. It's not in the January one. It seems to me it was in the December number, but I am very far from certain. Better drop them a line. You'll find it to be your final version. For me to hunt up the copy you sent me would necessitate a day's work!

The three sonnets you enclose seem very beautiful to me. I don't know just how good Baudelaire is in the original, but I've seen nothing in translations of him any better than this trio. The best of them has been stolen from me, probably when I showed them at the Bologna. I forget its name: I have "To the Beloved" and "Transcendence."

Heaven knows if these exquisite things will "sell!" It's like prof[f]erring orchids to a menagerie ape—he *might* take them. Anyhow, I'd try them on the best magazines.

I've written almost nothing for four months: too much dissipation. However, I've now been "good" for a week, and shall probably write, as soon as I've replied to a pile of letters. Here are two late sonnets, one on a hackneyed theme, but containing at least one good line.

Andrew says you're gaining in weight, for which I'm glad, as it's a good sign. I saw Charlie Clark in the St. Frantic yesterday. He said Mrs. C. is well. I've not had any news of her otherwise for over two months.

I've just written a letter to W. S. Braithwaite that will jar his Harvardized dignity. I'm attacking his taste in poetry, and telling him to leave me out of his anthologies in the future.[2]

Neihardt sends me his "Song of Three Friends," a fine accomplishment. It's not the sort of poetry you'd care for yet, or I'd lend it to you.[3]

Here is an "announcement" that may be of use to you. I am availing myself of it. I prophesy that the magazine will succeed, despite the hog-census.

See if you can't fall in love with May.

Affectionately,   George.

[Enclosures: two unidentified sonnets.]

1. May S. Greenwood was a friend (and probably a lover) of GS. Through his influence, she published some poems in the *Smart Set*.
2. The letter is dated 8 April 1919. See "George Sterling's Letters to William Stanley Braithwaite: The Poet versus the Editor," ed. Dalton H. Gross, *American Book Collector* 24, No. 2 (November–December 1973): 19–20.
3. Neihardt, *The Song of Three Friends* (1919), another volume in his series of epics of the American West.

[204] CAS to GS [ALS]

East Auburn, Cal.,
April 16th, 1919

Dear George:

You've come to the wrong shop, when you ask me for news—I'm nearly always out of that particular article. I've heard nothing at all of May Greenwood and her husband, excepting from you and from Andrew. I imagine they found Auburn unsuitable—the elevation is not very high (1300 feet) and went further into the hills, perhaps to Weimar or Colfax. There's a big tubercular sanatorium at Weimar, and Colfax is also a "popular" resort for t.b.s, with an elevation of 2000 feet. I should have been glad to see them, and glad to divvy up with all the fresh air on Indian Hill—it's d—d near the only thing that's neither taxed nor prohibited now-a-days.

Mrs Clark was in the Adler Sanatorium when she last wrote me. So she can't be very well. Nervous disorders are the most complex and difficult to cure, as I've reason enough to know.

Thanks for the "Thrill Book" announcement,—which I've already seen—The editor wrote, asking me to contribute, and accepted my sonnet, "Dissonance." He paid me seven dollars, and wrote me an enthusiastic letter. I imagine the periodical will succeed fairly well,—there's undoubtedly a growing demand for the rarer and more imaginative types of literature. Witness the B. & L. publications—the Modern Library announces a complete translation of "The Flowers of Evil" among its forthcoming additions![1]

I like the sonnets you send. The one of mine that you lost at the Bologna must have been "Laus Mortis". I enclose a fresh copy, in lieu of anything better to send you. Also, I enclose my "Ode to Peace", which, for obvious reasons, I neglected to submit in the Chronicle competition last fall. It may amuse you.

Braithwaite, I notice, never even mentioned my work in his index of magazine poems for 1918. It's quite a distinction, not to be mentioned by Mr. Braithwaite, and receive a poetic report-card with one or more stars. Such pedagogery would be intolerable if it weren't so ridiculous.

Can't you come up and visit me next month? I'll give you a job digging a wine-cellar if you will. Also, a half-interest in the cellar!

Affectionately,
Clark

[Enclosures: "Laus Mortis" (copy), "Ode to Peace."]

1. The Modern Library did not publish a complete translation of *Les Fleurs du mal*, but did publish a selection: *Baudelaire: His Prose and Poetry* (1919), ed. T. R. Smith (1880–1942).

[205] GS to CAS [ALS]

May 17th, 1919.

Dear Clark:

I was in error as to the whereabouts of May and her tuberculan: they were at Geyser Hot Springs, but have returned. He's much better, but she has left him, having found him to be a domestic tyrant! By the way, all small men become that: only the big ones (physically) can be bullied by wives.

I enjoyed your "Ode to Peace." Why not send it to "The Liberator"?[1] They even pay. I've been very lazy of late, merely helping Wilkes, the playwright, in two of his plays,[2] so I've no verse to submit—that is, of late production. I doubt if I do much metrical work before the state goes dry.

I gave Braithwaite such a panning that he did not venture a rejoinder, which was just as well for him. He has the esthetic tastes of Cotton Mather.

I'd only be jollying you if I said I'd try to visit Auburn soon. My girl doesn't want me out of her sight that long—and she usually has her way.

The last I heard of Mrs. Clark, she was at Adler's. I left "Lilith" at her home, in early April, as she wanted to read it. It was returned by mail, without comment. Mrs. Coryell has it now, and says she likes it. I rarely see her, but her husband comes to the Bologna now and then.

Remember me to your parents and to Andrew.

Your affectionately,
George.

[Enclosure: "The Modern Muse."]

1. The *Liberator* was a left-wing magazine founded by Max Eastman (1883–1969), absorbing the *Masses;* after two years as the *Workers' Monthly* (1924–26), it became the *New Masses* (1926–48).
2. Earnest Wilkes, playwright and owner of four theatres in the Bay Area. Some months earlier he had wished to produce GS's *Lilith,* but GS, thinking it a losing proposition, advised against it. See GS to HLM, 24 November 1918; in *FBB* 44.

[206] CAS to GS [ALS]

East Auburn, Cal.,
June 10th, 1919

Dear George:

I certainly enjoyed your satire on "The Modern Muse." Many of the stanzas are tremendously clever . . . The badness of much of the "new poetry," is almost unbelievable. Certainly, the Bolshevists have taken Parnassus, and the Muses have fled to some happier and more peaceful planet. Helicon is contaminated with filth and spittle.

I've tried to work, but with small success. However, I enclose the result—two prose-poems, a lyric, and a sonnet. I've sold a few things during the past month—one poem to "Ainslee's," one to "The Thrill Book",[1] and two more ("Palms" and "Flamingoes") to a beautifully printed geographical magazine entitled "Asia", which pays 50¢ per line. Oddly enough, three of these four poems were in the alexandrine form—the measure you dislike so much.

Things are quieter than ever, if possible. Andrew is serving a term of hard labour on the ranch, and I've not seen him for three weeks or more. I amuse myself in all ways that happen to be unavailable, i.e., the reading of unpopular fiction, the shooting of cottontails out of season (and without a license) and the manufacture of cherry wine. The last involves a double felony, since I'm making the stuff from stolen cherries.

I may come down for a few days, before the end of the summer. My health is improving, in spite of a mouthful of bad teeth. I weigh close to 130 lbs., and feel much stronger, in a physical sense. Mentally, I still feel as if I were dead and damned, but even that is improving.

I wish you could see the tiger-lilies—I gather them by the arm-full in the canyon. They fairly startle one at first sight, growing as they do on the dry hillsides. Their flowers are so exuberantly gorgeous and savage, that they give the impression of a more than vegetable vitality.

The wild black berries will begin to ripen in a week or so, and I expect to gather them by the bucket-ful, for preserves and wine. Also, I'm planning an expedition in search of wild goose-berries. Think of all the innocent rural pleasures that you're missing!

Affectionately,
Clark.

[Enclosures: "Quest," two unidentified prose poems, an unidentified sonnet.]

1. "In November" was accepted by *Ainslee's*. "Crepuscule" was accepted by the *Thrill Book*, but the magazine folded before the poem could be published. The magazine had previously accepted CAS's "Dissonance," which appeared in the issue for 15 September 1919.

[207] GS to CAS [ALS]

July 7th, 1919.

Dear Clark:

Nearly a month since your letter came, in which time I've been to the Jinks and seen the Great Drought come on the land.

The Jinks wasn't much. I miss London so much when there that it's all spoilt for me.[1] I spent much time in the river and at the bar.

The enclosures are good, as usual—full of that beauty which is its own excuse. My one objection is to the (to me) weakness of "undelaying mien" as a *last line*.[2]

I've written nothing myself but some weak and overpaid newspaper verse.[3] Shall do more, now that I can drink less. I've put in quite a lot of time going over Mrs. London's biography of her husband.[4]

It's *hot* here to-day, and we San Franciscans hate heat. Our dear friend Mrs. Clark is somewhat better, and may be able to go home in a few days.

"The Bellman" has ceased publication, and I'm "out" a good patron. But "Munsey's" prospers.

Try to keep cool!

Affectionately,   George.

1. JL had died (probably by suicide) in November 1916. Oddly enough, there is no mention of his death in GS's letters to CAS of that period.

2. "Quest," l. 29. (In *EC* the poem has 33 lines.)

3. The only poem GS is known to have published in a newspaper during this period is "Memorial Day, 1919."

4. Charmian London (1870–1955) had previously published *Jack London and Hawaii* (1918). Presumably GS was helping her with *The Book of Jack London* (1921).

[208] CAS to GS [ALS]

East Auburn, Cal.,
Aug. 28th, 1919.

Dear George:

Thanks for "The Hill of Dreams," the reading of which has given me considerable pleasure. Much of it is very beautiful and subtle. Am I to keep the book? . . . I have another of Machen's books, entitled "Hieroglyphics,"[1] one of the best things on literature and literary values that I have seen for a long time, apart from the writings of John Cowper Powys.

Have you written during the summer? I've not felt up to much, and have done nothing, with the exception of a few indifferent sonnets. I feel worn-out, after the long and tedious hot spell—the temperature here has risen above ninety every day for the past three weeks.

Nearly everyone seems to be sick, or ailing, these days. My father and mother are unwell, and so are Andrew's parents. You may see Andrew in a few days—his mother is in Oakland, and wants him to come down.

Loveman writes me pretty often. He, too, has been ailing—heart-trouble, perhaps, since he was laid up with something of the sort while in Georgia.

Thanks for the clipping from the "Bulletin", which I am returning at last. It must have been tremendous—that last and culminative night in the city.[2] I can't imagine what the place is like now, even with such oases, and "wells amid the waste"[3] as will continue to exist.

Here are the sonnets I mentioned. I wonder that I ever attempt to write—nothing of the sort seems worth while in these days. The whole world seems crumbling into chaos—I'm not even sure that you'll receive this letter,—I'm told there was no no [*sic*] mail from the city yesterday, on account of the railroad strike.

Affectionately,
Clark.

[Enclosure: "Heliogabalus" (two sonnets).]

1. Arthur Machen (1863–1947), *The Hill of Dreams* (1907); *Hieroglyphics: A Note upon Ecstasy in Literature* (1902).
2. Presumably a clipping relating to the onset of Prohibition on 1 July 1919.
3. From stanza 48 of the *Rubaiyat*.

[209] GS to CAS [ALS]

S. F.
Aug. 30, 1919.

Dear Clark:

You should worry about where the Muse has gone to! A searching-party will find her about a mile outside of Auburn.

Will write at greater length soon. Return the Machen book to

Leslie Nelson Jennings,
Rutherford, Cal.

Affectionately,
George

[210] GS to CAS [ALS]

Sept. 27th, 1919.

Dear Clark:

Have you been burnt out yet? From perusal of the daily press, I infer that most of rural California has been given to the flames.

As I intimated, your sonnets seemed very poetical to me, nor can I come on anything I'd care to see changed. I note you're wavering between "glad, intolerable" and "unimaginable." It seems to me the former is much preferable.

What on earth put you up to glorifying that idiotic pervert Heliogabalus? But since you don't mind the worst of that crowd, why not go on and write a series of sonnets on the *dark* emperors of Rome, just as Saltus did on various drinks? So far as poetry goes, it should be a fine affair.

I've written several poems this month, but doubt if I've copies at hand. Shall be tied down to some other work for the next three months.

If Andrew is back he has probably told you that the dry-law hasn't hurt S. F. much, yet. Anyhow, such Italian places as the Bologna go on selling booze openly. Likely enough the Govt. will land on them soon.

Yes—the world certainly seem[s] crumbling. Maybe Bierce's "Shadow on the Dial" or London's "Iron Heel" will yet eventuate.[1] Then, me for the Monterey hills with my rifle!

Good luck, poet!

Affectionately,   George.

[Enclosure: "The Queen Forgets."]

1. Ambrose Bierce's "The Shadow on the Dial," in *The Shadow and the Dial and Other Essays* (1909), is a warning of the dangers of socialism and anarchism. JL's novel *The Iron Heel* (1908) is a novel of the future in which an oligarchy ruthlessly suppresses a revolt of the people and institutes a rigid fascism.

[211] CAS to GS [ALS]

East Auburn, Cal.,
Nov. 1st., 1919

Dear George:

Have you been arrested yet? The Prohibition Enforcement act is so complete and all-comprehensive, that millions of people must be liable to prosecution under it. It'll be a case of "safety in numbers", I suppose, for people who have made wine or other liquor at home. However, there's no telling to what length these pestilential puritans may go in the future—they may establish an Inquisition, with racks and thumbscrews for anyone who is suspected or accused of knowing how to make wine!

The poem you send ("The Queen Forgets") is one of your best lyrics, in my opinion. You have caught the very essence of mystery, in a few lines as magically simple as those of "La Belle Dame sans Merci." I wish I had something to send in return—but I have felt, and still feel, totally unfit for work.

How are you coming on with "Lilith?" Andrew tells me you were at work on the proofs when he saw you last.

The Heliogabalus sonnets were written for Loveman, who has a tremendous admiration for the strangest and most "decadent" of the Roman emperors. I've no compunction or concern regarding the "ethical" aspect of the matter—ethics are an illusion, like everything else. Virtue and vice are but veils of Medusa . . . No, I don't care to write a series of sonnets on the Roman emperors—I'm tired of that vein of thought and imagery.

The t.b.s appear to have given me up—there's no loss of weight or strength, at least. Otherwise, I feel damnably unwell—my nerves, brain, eyes, teeth, and stomach are ill in a conspiracy against me. Perhaps a doctor would diagnose the trouble as common, everyday ennui—but that's bad enough. It isn't drink, at any rate, since I've been "on the wagon" for weeks, and have taken little enough at any time for a year past. I've manufactured more than twenty gallons of assorted vino during the summer and autumn, but my father is the principal consumer. Some of the stuff I've made is quite promising—it ought to be the real thing, if it gets a chance to age.

When are you coming up? I can give you a bunk, and something to eat and drink, at any time.

Affectionately yours,
Clark—

[212] CAS to GS [ALS]

East Auburn, Cal.
Dec. 17th, 1919.

Dear George:

Here are a few verses, written since my last letter to you. Please write me before so very long—I am swamped, inundated, smothered, eaten up, and altogether annihilated with sheer monotony and boredom.

Is there any news of "Lilith"? I am eager to see it again—when I read the ms., it impressed me as being one of the best things you had ever done.

Have you seen Arthur Waley's translations from the Chinese?[1] The stuff is too bald and literal, for the most part, to be considered as English poetry; nevertheless, it interests and pleases me more than anything I've read for a blue moon. The Chinese discovered the futility of life thousands of years before we did.

Affectionately,
Clark.

[Enclosures: unidentified poems.]

1. Presumably *A Hundred and Seventy Chinese Poems* (1918), or possibly *More Translations from the Chinese* (1919), translated by Arthur Waley (1889–1966), British poet and translator.

[213] GS to CAS [ALS]

Dec. 19, 1919.

Dear Clark:

Pardon me for not having written ere now! I had no idea my letters could [be] doing anything toward the relief of boredom. In fact, I've always supposed that they were a bit of a nuisance to you, on account of your distaste for correspondence. (I don't like to reply to letters either, though I like to receive them!)

I got some copies of "Lilith" in, a few days ago, and gave them *all* away. I'd have sent you a copy at the time, but thought there was no need of haste, for from something you said (or I thought you said) when you read the MS., I'd an idea you didn't care for the thing. That would have been natural, you see, for young poets do not care overmuch for dramatic verse—that's commonly a disease of their elders.

I'll have some new copies of the book in a day or two, and will forward one. It seems to me to *read better* in print. I had only 300 copies made, and am giving away 150 and selling the rest for enough to pay for 300. Alec. couldn't very well finance the thing, so I'm doing so, but have put his name on the book.

I've heard of that Waley book, and intend to get ahold of it. I'll admit the futility of life for everyone but myself! I usually manage to have a good time; and pleasure isn't "futile" when it's happening. But why discus the relative? It's everyone for himself.

All the poems you send are *absolutely first class*. They're sheer, pure, undiluted poetry. If I were to praise each line I like I'd have to specify each one, so you must accept this "blanket" critique. Indeed, you are so much my superior in this kind of poetry that I'd regard any strictures on it as almost an impertinence on my part, excusable only by reason of my venerable years. Bierce said something like that to me, once, and now I have to say it to you: I'm glad to say it.

Alec. was somewhat excited the last time I was in his shop, as he had just heard of some man in the East who declares (it may have been orally) that you're the greatest living poet. You certainly are, to one who desires pure poetry and nothing else, as I and a few others do. I wish we existed in greater numbers.

I've written nothing for weeks but some love-sonnets, and those I've not cared (nor dared) to show yet. So I've nothing to enclose. Take, though, my heartiest congratulations on your superb work, and my love to you and your parents.

Affectionately,   George.

[Enclosure: "The Face of the Skies."]

[214] CAS to GS [ALS]

East Auburn, Cal.
Dec. 27th, 1919.

Dear George:

My heartiest thanks for "Lilith," and a thousand congratulations! I am almost tempted to say that it is the greatest thing you have ever written; but I don't think the comparison between a long dramatic poem, and short, or comparatively short lyric or philosophic poems, would be proper or just. It is sufficient—incomparably sufficient—that you have written both. "Lilith" is certainly the best dramatic poem in English since the days of Swinburne and Browning. The work of Stephen Phillips is pale and thread-bare beside it. Your last scene—to mention nothing else—is unforget-table in its perfect beauty and terror—a complete symbol of life. The lyrics interspersed throughout the drama are as beautiful as any by the Elizabethans. They add enor-mously to the effect.

If you will let me pay for them, I should like you to send me a couple copies of the book. I want one of them for Samuel Loveman—would you mind inscribing it? There are d——d few who will appreciate "Lilith" as much as he . . . Let me know the price, and I will remit. By the way, I noticed a few slight misprints that escaped you. On page 52 the word "it" is omitted in the line "But (it) is told a dragon bars the way." On page 65, "the" for "thee" is printed in the line "Give thee more greatly." "Or" for "of" oc-curs on p. 78 in "Of dullness, for I weary of all things.["] On 94 "Impinged" is spelt "Impigned." You must have had one hades of a time with those yap printers!

I'm glad you found something in my verses. I don't care for them myself; but the toil of composition serves to inhibit the consciousness of myself and my surroundings for the time being.

I like the poem you enclose in your letter ("The Face of the Skies"). No, you've never sent me "Spring in Carmel" . . . That title awakens the happiest memories that I possess.

Doubtless the Eastern admirer of whom Robertson told you, was Frank L. Pol-lock.[1] He has written me letters of extraordinary praise. He thinks that I should submit my unpublished work to some of the big Eastern and English firms—John Lane for first choice. I may do so, if I ever get the damned stuff together. I'm not sanguine as to the result, however.

Here are some more of my verses. I wish the Omar ode were better—it seems a string of pessimistic platitudes. But life itself is a platitude—the supreme platitude of the universe.

Affectionately,
Clark.

[Enclosures: "Beyond the Great Wall," "The Ennuyé," "In Lemuria," "Omar," "Solu-tion."]

1. Frank Lillie Pollack (1876–1957), a minor science fiction writer.

[215] GS to CAS [ALS]

Jan. 20, 1920.

Dear Clark:

I should, I know, have written to you weeks ago and said how beautiful a thing I think the "Omar" ode is. You are extremely successful with your odes, and I hope you'll give more time to them.

I showed the ode to Lafler, who wrote to you at once about it. And since then I've shown it to several other good judges of poetry, notably E. F. O'Day, whose brief and inadequate notice of it (in the Oakland "Enquirer") I enclose. I lent him the whole en-velope, and find he also gave your opinion of "Lilith," a thing he wasn't authorized to do, though it gives me pleasure, naturally.

Thanks for your detection of the errors in printing! Surely you've an eagle eye! I read the poem many times without detecting them.

I utterly forgot your request for two copies, as I was alcoholized pretty thoroughly at the time. Now it's too late, as I've given away 165 of the books and the remaining 135 have been sold. I'm sorry. Anyhow, I'll have a second edition out before the year's over.

I think John Lane's just the publisher for you to send a MS book to. And I hope you'll send "Omar" out to a few of the magazines. Editors are hell, but some of them have lucid streaks.

I like these other poems too, though feeling that none of them touches "Omar." "Solution" is certainly a terror, and "In Lemuria" a gorgeous thing. I greatly like

"Pallid and pure as jaspers from the moon."

"The Ennuye" is good art, too, and "Beyond the Great Wall" is undiluted poetry.

This club is taking prohibition with an ill grace. As for me, I'm glad for a rest. I've booze here in my closet, but shall leave it alone indefinitely. I see a good deal of Dr. Abrams lately. He has come on some wonderful stuff—some of it one hardly credits even when seeing it. His telepathic experiments are now almost 100% successful.

Hoping your ennui is no worse, I remain, as ever,

Affectionately yours,

George.

[216] CAS to GS [ALS]

East Auburn, Cal.,
Jan. 29th, 1920.

Dear George:

Thanks for the clippings—O'Day's review of "Lilith" was very good, I thought. I'm glad he quoted my opinion, and am sorry I didn't say more,—as I might well have done.[1] The poem is packed with beauties—I find something new every time I take it up.

I don't think much of Cale Young Rice's classification of modern poets. I'm sick of classifications, anyway. . . . He'd call me a "romanticist", I suppose. Well, at a pinch, I'd rather be called that than a "realist"—it sounds much less offensive.

I enclose a philosophical fantasy "The Ghoul and the Seraph." Bender complains of the "pessimism" in it—which I can't "see". The philosophical thesis is a plain statement of scientific fact—the immortality of matter, and the evanescence and commutation of its forms.

I've been at work on a much longer poem, "The Hashish-Eater," but am "stuck" at the end of three hundred lines. It will take another hundred to finish the thing. I'm afraid it's too long and incoherent. It has some monstrous images—"Boulder-weighted webs of dragons' gut", "plagues of lichens" that overrun empires, "Continents of serpent-shaped trees, With slimy trunks that lengthen league on league", etc., etc. I've left the poor devil of a Hashish-eater in mid-air, fleeing on the back of some providential hippogriff, from a python as big as a river.

I suppose you're right about my odes. I've long meditated an ode in honour of Poe, and another for Swinburne. Also, an ode on the seven prismatic colours. I might "do" one in honour of Dionysus, too, for the delectation of our friends the prohibitionists.[2]

I enclose a note for Lafler, since I don't know his address. He surprised and naturally delighted me with his letter—I had scarcely expected anyone to become excited over "Omar.["]

Don't apologize for not answering my letters sooner. I know what your correspondence is like.

Affectionately,
Clark—

[Enclosure: "The Ghoul and the Seraph."]

1. Edward F. O'Day quoted from a letter by CAS in his column "Men and Women in the Mirror" (as by "The Clubman"), *Oakland Enquirer* (10 January 1920): 8.
2. In later years, CAS composed an entire cycle of poems that he titled *The Hill of Dionysus*.

[216a] CAS to GS [non-extant]

[Envelope only, postmarked East Auburn, Cal., Feb. 3, 1920.]

[217] GS to CAS [ALS]

Mch. 23, 1920.

Dear Clark:

I'd have written long ere this, had I not had a physical setback—injured one of my testicles and had to spend two weeks in bed—some of the time out at Mt. León hospital, which I recommend for its pretty nurses, wasted on *me*. Also my mother died.[1]

I like some of this new poem, "The Ghoul and the Seraph," very much. You strike a mighty deep note in that last soliloquy of the ghoul. Have you tried the poem on The Ladies Home Journal yet?

I'm greatly interested in the hashisch poem, and hope you've gone on with it. There are vast possibilities there. Don't worry about length or incoherence, which are both "in atmosphere" when it comes to that drug. Nothing, it seems to me, affords imagination a better excuse (if one be needed) for absolute licence.

I was elected, without being consulted, to membership in the American Academy of Arts and Letters. At first I accepted, but in looking over the list of members, I withdrew my acceptance in a letter that Robert Underwood Johnson (who proposed my name) says contained "unwarrantable language!"[2] I've written to him in much sharper language. Imagine a society that included Bob Chambers, Will Payne, Ned ("Chimmie Fadden") Townsend, Lefevre and C. B. Fernald![3] Mencken is filled with joy at my resignation, and writes: "The whole episode is rich and stimulating. At one stroke you have accomplished something permanently valuable. Old Johnson is an ass."[4] Mencken, by the way, is to be out here in June to report the Democratic convention— "the obscenity," he calls it.

I've written only one lyric, so far this year. I enclose it: a good deal in a few lines, I think. I have, however, just completed the first draft of another dramatic poem, the plot for which I found in "The Decline and Fall of the Roman Empire." It's a bloody thing. I'm calling in "Rosamund." I suppose Swinburne has no patent on that name, it being a "proper" one. But Rosamund was improper—and a murderess.[5]

Yours affectionately,

George.

[Enclosure: unidentified poem.]

1. GS's mother, Mary Havens Sterling (b. 1845), died on 23 February 1920.

2. Robert Underwood Johnson (1853–1937), American poet, editor, and secretary of the American Academy of Arts and Letters.

3. GS refers to the American writers Robert W. Chambers (1865–1933), popular novelist; Will Payne (1865–1954), popular novelist; Edward W. Townsend (1855–1942), novelist and short story writer best known for two volumes of dialect stories, *Chimmie Fadden, Major Max, and Other Stories* (1895) and *Chimmie Fadden Explains* (1895); Edwin Lefevre (1871–1943), journalist, novelist, and stockbroker who wrote stories about Wall Street; and Chester Bailey Fernald (1869–1938), short story writer who wrote about Boston's Chinatown.

4. See HLM to GS (15 March [1920]); *FBB* 83.

5. The story of Rosamond [*sic*], who murders her husband, Alboin, King of the Lombards, in revenge for the murder of her father, Cunimond, is told in chapter 45 of Gibbon's *Decline and Fall of the Roman Empire*. Swinburne's first book, *The Queen Mother; Rosamond* (1860), featured a verse drama, *Rosamund,* but not on the same subject as GS's. However, a later work, *Rosamond, Queen of the Lombards* (1899), is on the same subject as GS's play.

[218] CAS to GS [ALS]

East Auburn, Cal.,
March 29th, 1920

Dear George:

I hope you won't be overwhelmed by the bulk of the enclosure!—the draught of my interminable hashish-poem, which I've finished, after a fashion. Loveman, the only person who has read it so far, thinks it "the greatest imaginative poem in the language"—an amazing judgement. The poem is imaginative, but, to me, the technique is so intolerable that I can take no pride or pleasure in it. I would revise it, if I could; but for the past month, the nerves of my head and eyes have been so troublesome that I find it difficult to concentrate to any purpose.

I am sorry to hear of your mother's death, and sorry that you have been laid up. But you have not been idle, it would seem! I'm tremendously interested in that new dramatic poem you mention, and have a "hunch" that you've been doing some great stuff. You know my opinion of "Lilith." "Rosamund" seems all right as a title; Swinburne's drama of that name was an early and minor performance, anyway.

Your resignation from the American Academy of Arts and Letters, is the best bit of news that I've heard for a coon's age! Men[c]ken summed it up very felicitously, I think—the episode is certainly "rich and stimulating!" Possibly, some of these purveyors to Demos, these pandars of stupidity, may surmise that there is a difference between literature and hog-wash—Anyway, they will be forced to know that there are people in America who hold that such a distinction exists.

Sam Loveman intends to start a magazine in Cleveland—a sort of semi-private affair—for the publication of his own work and mine. He spoke of calling it "The Decadent;" but I've suggested "The Satanist" or better still, "The Saturnian", as alternatives.[1] I've no particular wish to be identified with any "school"—even the "Decadent"—a word that critics have forced to serve in too many senses, often contradictory or conflicting.

I'm pleased that you found something good in "The Ghoul and the Seraph." I planned a series of these fantastic dialogues, many years ago. "Asmodeus and the Gargoyles" was one of my titles. The scene is the Paris of Villon's time. Asmodeus, in his flight through the midnight heavens, pauses to chat with the gargoyles of Notre Dame, who tell him the news of the city, and receive all the current gossip of Hades in return. Perhaps I shall write it some day. A fine subject for an etching by Felicien Rops, or Meryon.[2] I don't think there is any living artist who could draw the scene to my taste . . . I had other titles, too, such as "The Colloquy of Christ and Belial," and "The Girl from Venus." All of the dialogues were to contain a philosophical import, under their guise of fantasy and grotesquerie.

I like the lyric you enclose very much. It **says** little enough, but **conveys** everything.

I had a nice letter from Leslie Nelson Jennings, some time ago. He wanted to suggest "The Nation" as a possible market for my sonnets!

As you say, there are tremendous possibilities in hashish. The subject has been touched upon very little, at least in poetry. Bailey Aldrich has a poem with the same title as mine, and Symons a lyric entitled "Hashish," the last stanza of which is truly great:

> "Who said the world is but a mood
> In the eternal thought of God?
> I know it, real though it seem,
> The phantom of a hashish-dream,
> In that insomnia which is God."[3]

A lot of Baudelaire's imagery is undoubtedly reminiscent of his visions and sensations while under the influence of the drug. But no one seems to have attempted anything on the order of my poem. Possibly, I'm at a disadvantage, in having no personal knowledge of the effect of hashish. But I remember your telling me that the effect was often disappointing, at least to Occidentals.

I hope all this doesn't bore you too much. I rarely see anyone that I can talk to, and must take out my loquacity in correspondence—when I feel loquacious, which is seldom enough.

Affectionately,
Clark—

[Enclosure: *'The Hashish-Eater; or, The Apocalypse of Evil.'*]

1. Loveman published three issues of the *Saturnian* (June–July 1920, August–September 1920, and March 1922). It contained no work by CAS or GS.
2. Felicien Rops (1833–1898), Belgian Symbolist engraver; Charles Meryon (1821–1868), French artist.
3. American poet and fiction writer Thomas Bailey Aldrich (1836–1907) wrote a poem entitled "Hascheesh" in *Pampinea and Other Poems* (1861). British poet and critic Arthur Symons (1865–1945) wrote "Haschich" in *Images of Good and Evil* (1899).

[219] GS to CAS [ALS]

June 10th, 1920.

Dear Clark:

It seems incredible that it's over two months since I've written to you! I'd a notion it was about a month, and I was going to write in a day or so. Now comes the "Saturnian" (a fine name!) to prick my conscience further. I've had time merely to glance at it, but can see it's all poetry. (If you kids really had any idea of Wilde's "soul," you'd think it resembled a long-dead fish more than an emerald!)[1]

"The Hashish-Eater" is indeed an amazing production. My friends will have none of it, claiming it reads like an extension of "A Wine of Wizardry." But I think there are many differences, and at any rate, it has more imagination in it than in any other poem I know of. Like the "Wine," it fails on the esthetic side, a thing that seems of small consequence in a poem of that nature. I could fill many pages telling you what I think of it, but prefer to wait till you're in S. F. again. By the way, the town is anything but dry—it's merely expensive.

Your ideas for new poems are most interesting. For Heaven's sake go on with them as soon as your climate permits! As for me, I've been loafing, as usual. Here are the only two poems I've written since finishing "Rosamund." *That* lady, by the way, should have made her debut by now, but Mrs. Reed has had hay-fever, not to mention other woes, and the thing is dragging.[2] But it should certainly be out this month. An early copy goes to you. I can't get any more copies of "Lilith," tho I'm offering $5. apiece for them. I suppose that "indicates," as the doctors say, another edition; but it costs so to publish now.

Be careful how you take hashish, should you get ahold of any. It won't kill you, but it will probably make you suffer horribly, as your vitality is low. Not suffer physically, but mentally, which is worse. Your former "gas" nightmare would be nothing to what you'd get.

Another thing about "Rosamund:" don't look for poetry in it, as in the case of "Lilith." I've tried merely to make it dramatic. The whole thing will leave a bad taste in the Philistine mouth, which will please you and me. No heroes nor heroines: only a rape and four murders! Hooray!

That resignation of mine from the Institute was so awful a thing that no literary magazine referred to it. Mencken saw, however, that it became well known. R. U. Johnson never replied to my answer to his letter of protest. Just as well for him!

Mencken will be here for a week, at the Democratic convention. My brother-in-law from Honolulu will also be here, as a delegate. So I'll have my hands more than full. I almost wish it were all over, and I up in the grove at Bohemia.

Remember me to your parents, please.

Affectionately,　　　　　　George.

[Enclosures: "To Louis Untermeyer" and two unidentified poems.]

1. GS refers to Loveman's poem "Oscar Wilde," *Saturnian* No. 1 (June–July [1920]): [6–7], containing the lines "His lips were spoken melody, / His soul an emerald" (ll. 5–6).
2. Anna M[orison] Reed (1849–1921), poet and editor of *The Northern Crown* (Ukiah, CA: Excelsior Press, 1904–1920). She printed *Lilith* for A. M. Robertson, and later *Rosamund.*

[220] CAS to GS [ALS]

East Auburn, Cal.,
July 10th, 1920.

Dear George:

I hope "Rosamund" is ready for her debut by now. Can you get me an extra copy of it? I've promised one to Loveman, and will gladly pay for it.

The second issue of "The Saturnian" will probably appear in August. Two of my drawings are to be reproduced as illustrations. Loveman is coming out to California in December, to take a position at Paul Elder's.[1] I imagine he will find S. F. much more congenial than Cleveland, in spite of Paul Elder.

I liked all the poems you sent me. The one to Untermeyer is terrible,[2] and the other two are filled with pure lyric beauty and melody. I wish I could send you something good in return; my blank verses on Nora May French appear tedious, rambling, and un-inspired. Pass them on to Lafler, if you care for them at all. Possibly they are not as bad as I think—I'm no competent or impartial judge of anything at present, since I feel dis-gusted with everything I have ever written. I've turned more seriously to drawing than ever before, and am working steadily at it. I illustrated the "H. Eater,"[3] among other things, and am making a set of designs for Poe at present. The Poe drawings are better than most illustrations of P. that I have seen—which isn't much of a brag, after all.

I'm sorry that people think "The H. Eater" a mere extension of "A Wine of Wiz-ardry". That's no mean compliment, however—The "Wine of Wizardry["] has always seemed the ideal poem to me, as it did to Bierce. But the ground-plan of "The H. E." is really quite different. It owes nearly as much to "The Temptation of Saint Anthony" as to your poem. But few American critics will prove sufficiently well-read and perspi-cacious to notice the former debt. After all, what's the diff? My literary ambitions are almost dead, and I may not write again, except in prose.

That Democratic convention must have been horrible. It sickened me to read the headlines in the papers. America is putrid to the point of utter dissolution—it reminds me of M. Valdemar, in the story by Poe. How long till the liquefaction of the corpse?

I don't know when I'll be able to visit S. F. I'm up against the money-problem, and am hesitating between bank-robbery and shortstory-writing.[4] I've a faint hope (perhaps without foundation) that I may be able to sell some of my drawings. It would be a case of reaching the right people,—people with a taste for the weird and the bi-zarre, and a **distaste** for conventional technique. "Rare birds," I dare say—I meet very few of them, and they never have money, by any chance.

Affectionately, as ever,
Clark—

P.S. Don't worry about my tampering with hashish. Life is enough of a nightmare without drugs, and I feel content to take the effects of h. on hearsay.

[Enclosure: "To Love," "The Whisper of the Worm," "To Nora May French."]

1. [David] Paul Elder (1877–1948), a well-known specialty publisher and bookseller in San Francisco.
2. Louis Untermeyer (1885–1977), well-known American poet and critic of poetry. GS's scathing satire "To Louis Untermeyer" (ms., Bancroft Library) is unpublished.

3. In the 1930s, R. H. Barlow obtained the paintings from CAS in order to publish an illustrated edition of the poem, but it never appeared.

4. In 1929, CAS embarked on a career as a short story writer, in order to support his parents.

[220a] CAS to GS [non-extant]

[Envelope only, postmarked Auburn, Cal., 16 August 1920.]

[221] GS to CAS [ALS]

August 26, 1920.

Dear Clark:

As usual, I'm late in replying to your last letter; but the Jinks has intervened, and a trip to Carmel, and, to crown all, the "shingles." It sounds like a somewhat comic ailment (such as measles or mumps), but can be truly hellish. I had but a mild attack, and am cured of that now, thanks to Abrams.

It is great news that Loveman is coming out here. I prophesy that he'll love S. F., if he can stand cities at all—as I can. He sends me the second number of the Saturnian, with some beautiful translations of Heine. I hope he can keep it going, and should be glad to help in any way, even financially.

I note you say you're "up against the money-problem." Isn't Mrs. C. sending you that $75. a month any more? I understood that that was to continue indefinitely. She is now in France (or Italy) with all her children.

You don't seem to care for your poem to Nora May French, but to me it seems a very lovely thing, and I'm sure Lafler will think the same of it as soon as I've shown it to him—a thing I've neglected to do, so far. The two sonnets are tremendous things, too, and I'm sure you greatly under-rate them. I've nothing but praise for the three poems, except to suggest that "evenings eager-starred" is perilously close to my "evenings early-starred," in "Lilith."

Poor "Rosamund" won't be out till next month, if she is then. The boy printer whom Mrs. Reed relied on to print it eloped (from Ukiah, of course) with a married woman! I'm not likely to get the book before Sept. 20th, and shall be sending you one promptly. I'll send one to Loveman. Did he get a "Lilith?" I'm offering $5. for a copy, and can't get one even at that.

Oh yes! The poem to Nora May is *solid poetry*. I wish I'd a signed copy to send to Roberts, late editor of "Ainslee's." He is a Nora May enthusiast, and would greatly appreciate it.

Loveman mentions that you may have an exhibition of drawings here. I am greatly interested, as the one you sent called "Pan" seems significant, and I'm wondering what the other artists will think of your work. They value technique so much more than inspiration, it seems to me. If you get a chance, show them to Herkomer. His advice should be valuable.

Yes, the convention was absurd. I didn't see it, though I had some tickets. But I had a good time with Mencken.

You can't say much about this country's putridity that I'll not agree with. But, as you remark, "What's the diff.?" We won't be here so much longer.

Affectionately,   George.

[P.S.] The Book Club of Cal. is printing an edition of 350 copies of "Lilith," to sell for $6.00 per!

[P.P.S.] I've been on the arid wagon for nearly three weeks!

[222] CAS to GS [ALS]

East Auburn, Cal.,
Sept. 5th, 1920.

Dear George:

I await "Rosamund" with eagerness, and hope there will be no further delay in its publication. . . . I shall begin hunting a publisher for "Ebony and Crystal" some time this month.

Wish I had something good to send to you, but I've written scarcely anything since May or June. Perhaps—you've not seen the enclosed lyric—it's the latest of my productions. I gave the summer to my drawing, and produced a lot of work, but seem to have small chance of unloading it. The proposed exhibition didn't "come off": Hargens, who runs the Old Book Shop near Paul Elder's, promised a friend of mine that he would put a few of my drawings on display. Instead of doing this, he held them pending the opinion of various artists (whose names I have so far been unable to ascertain) and these gentlemen proceeded to blackball (in effect, at least) me by telling him that my work was not **art**—whatever that is. He, and other dealers, have refused to handle it. I am far from agreeing with my critics (I had scarcely expected my work to appeal to the ordinary types of artists and art-patrons) and should **force** an exhibition of it if I had money or influence.

I've heard nothing from Mrs. C. since May, when she announced her intention of going abroad. I wish she could have gone on with the allowance; we may have a hard time of it this winter. There seems to be no sale for anything that I can produce, with the exception of firewood. And I'm not strong enough to stand a great amount of manual labour.

The "shingles" must be hell—I've heard of them before. Hives are bad enough; I suffer from them occasionally.

Loveman, too, has been unwell—some sort of bronchial trouble. I wonder how the climate of S. F. will agree with him. I'm glad you wrote to him; he mentions having received a letter from you.

Affectionately,
Clark—

[Enclosure: "Requiescat."]

[223] GS to CAS [ALS]

Sept. 10, 1920.

Dear Clark:

I showed your lyric "Requiescat" to Lafler yesterday, and we wondered if you realized how sheerly, purely beautiful a thing it is. I cannot conceive of a magazine refusing it. None would have, in the years before the war. But now the world has gone crazy, editors included, and any jewel is rejected, any dung accepted. I advise you, though, to send the poem to all the best magazines. I think "Scribner's" and "Harper's" are best to begin with.

No news and no "Rosamund." Next month, I suppose. The inconceivable and maddening slowness and delays of a semi-helpless old lady. There's no recourse.

I hope to see "Ebony and Crystal" out, but don't expect much from the publishing clan: it costs so hellishly to get a book out now. Try Knopf.

I'm sorry Mrs. C. has recanted. I can't see why she should, with all her money. Maybe she thought you too unorthodox: did you send her your later poems?

Affectionately,   George.

[224] CAS to GS [ALS]

East Auburn, Cal.,
Sept. 29th, 1920

Dear George:

I am sending "Ebony and Crystal" to Alfred A. Knopf; he seems as good a "chance" as any. However, I am not too sanguine. Brentano's, or Boni and Liveright, would be a good second choice, don't you think?

I am sorry that "Rosamund" is delayed. I look forward to it, and feel that there is still a pleasure in store for me.

I tried the "Requiescat" on several magazines, including "Harper's," but to no avail. I've sold exactly *one poem* during the past year![1] I've done better with my drawings—five or six of those have been disposed of, though at very trifling prices.

I, too, don't quite understand Mrs. C.'s action. I doubt if she could have been offended by the poems that I sent her—they were my most harmless ones. Probably she thought that I was well enough to shift for myself. Theoretically, I am; but if I work for a living, I will have to give up my art. I've not the energy for both. And I hardly know what I could do—I am "unskilled labour" at anything except drawing and poetry. To make matters worse, we have a mortgage that falls due in December. It's a small one, only five hundred dollars, and we may be able to raise this money in Auburn.

I've not written anything of late. I feel exhausted with work and worry, and am preyed upon more and more by this horrible monotony and isolation. One can work only so long, for the work's sake alone, and it seems to me that I've gone about as far as I can. Everything that I have ever really desired has been denied me by some hellish combination of circumstances. The starvation that I suffer is worse than a mere lack of food, and no less weakening, in the end. So you mustn't blame me for not being able to write.

Have I sent you "The Flower-Devil" before? I don't remember having done so.

Affectionately,
Clark

[Enclosure: "The Flower-Devil."]

1. Possibly a reference to "In Lemuria" (*Lyric West,* July–August 1921).

[225] GS to CAS [ALS]

Oct. 6th, 1920.

Dear Clark:

  In returning "Requiescat," the mag. editors reach a nadir of imbecility heretofore uninfested by them. Better try "Smart Set." Also try "S.S." with this strangely beautiful "Flower-Devil." It seems to me that is just the sort of thing they'd want.

  As to "Ebony & Crystal," I hope you'll steel yourself to disappointment, for it's almost impossible for a *poet,* almost *unknown* in *New York,* to have a book of poems brought out there with no cost to himself. If you visited N. Y., you'd know better what the chances are against it. Five million rats scrambling over one another in a caldron that gets hotter every day!

  (Boni & Liveright are the best second choice, not Bretano's. [*sic*])

  Were I in N. Y., maybe I could do something for you with the book-publishers, but here I couldn't get even Robertson to publish you! I think of having *my* next book of lyrics printed by a young Chinaman I've lately met!

  Truly you are dreadfully "up against it!" It's a great pity that Mrs. C. should have seen fit to drop out when she did. I suppose she thought she'd done her share—and one must admit she has. You are surely caught in a trap, and only death (not your own) can release you. I'll see what I can do. Have spoken to Albert, who'll do what he can (he has so many calls on him!), and I will have a talk with Phelan as soon as the obscenities of election are over.

  Don't hesitate to "give up your art" for more or less time, if you really *can* get anything to do up there. You've many years in which to write, and the world is clogged with great poetry as it is. Five years mean nothing in art.

  "Rosamund!" Ye gods! The damned book is *never* going to be out, I suppose!

    Affectionately ever,

      George.

[226] CAS to GS [ALS]

East Auburn, Cal.,
Oct. 19th, 1920.

Dear George:

  My congratulations on "Rosamund!" As you warned me, it lacks the poetic beauty of "Lilith;" but nevertheless, it is a great drama. What action! It should make a tremendous "film" if you don't mind my saying so: I don't mean that as a slam, in any sense. "The Iris-Hills" is very beautiful; in the setting in which it occurs, it is like a sapphire on a breast-plate of bronze.[1]

  I've nothing to send you this time; I can't create in my present mood—a mood in which no art, no creation seems worth the price one pays for it. You are right—the world is "clogged with great poetry." And I've written nothing that satisfies me at all;

and feel the impossibility of doing so in the strait-jacket that circumstances have made for me.

Knopf is "unable to consider the publication" of "Ebony and Crystal"—I doubt if they even *read* the poems. However, I'll try some of the other firms,—B. & L. and John Lane, anyway. Can you think of others worth trying?

I'm cutting fire-wood when the weather permits. Otherwise, there seems nothing that I can do, at present. I've an idea or two for short-stories, and may try to work them up.

I went out to see the Herkomers a couple of weeks ago, and showed H. a few of my drawings. Like most painters, he is horribly unimaginative, and could see nothing in them but their shortcomings from the stand-point of the usual studio-technique. I feel absolutely certain that some of my work possesses great imaginative value; but few people seem able to see it. As to "bad drawing"—they used to charge Beardsley with that. The indictment has been brought against almost every imaginative artist.

Are you writing?

Affectionately,
Clark—

1. "The Iris-Hills" is one of the songs in *Rosamund*.

[227] GS to CAS [ALS]

Dec. 17th, 1920.

Dear Clark:

It seems incredible that your last letter has been on my table for nearly two months, unanswered! I can only plead in extenuation of the offense the facts of my incurable laziness and aversion to letter-writing, and the absence of any news that would interest you.

I've none now, but want to enquire as to your exact condition physically and otherwise. Some chap from up your way, one Nicholl (?), rang me up a couple of days ago, and said you were sorely in need of medical care, etc. I've already "got to work" in the matter, but recalling a former canard, should like to be sure of my facts. So pray be frank with me . . . .

I'm glad you found something to like in "Rosamund." I agree with you that it would make a stirring film, and am even now trying to obtain D. W. Griffith's "real" address, as I've a notion he's the only big producer who'd risk such a picture, and produce it adequately.[1]

Ruth St. Denis, the dancer, had a talk with me last night.[2] She wants me to put "Lilith" into some such shape that she can use it. I've a notion I can do so without desecrating the poem; though I'd probably have to leave off the last act entirely. We shall see.

I'm sorry about "Ebony and Crystal." You mention the only firms (honest ones) I think it would have any chance with. As soon as the price of book-making comes down, as it's bound to before very long, I shall strongly urge Robertson to bring it out. I'd have Mrs. Anna M. Reed do so, but she has broken down in health (a cancer, which Abrams is trying to cure), and has given up her printing business. Her son may resume it, later on. Abrams has just cured *him* of the T.B.

The sanctified are "taking the joy out of life" more and more, though Bigin dispenses whiskey-highballs, furtively and at 60 cents per.[3] Poverty forbids me more than an occasional visit there.

As usual, I've written but little—the enclosed verses, mildly poetical, which the "Bulletin" gave me $15. for, and an ode of almost 115 lines, called "To a Girl Dancing." You might like the latter, a copy of which I'll send you when I can get it retyped gain.

Stella, in Copenhagen, has been owing me a letter for months. Her sis has lately heard from her, and infers from the tone of the missive that she's homesick and unhappy. However, I think she'll get over all that.

I've not heard from Loveman for a long time, but as I've not been correspondentially generous with him, I've hardly a right to complain.

The world is going crazy faster than ever. Everyone seems either ill or "up against it," and we've not even inexpensive liquor to help out. But "cheer up," etc.!

Affectionately yours,   George.

[Enclosure: clipping of "The Cool, Grey City of Love," *San Francisco Bulletin* (11 December 1920): 12.]

1. D[avid] W[ark] Griffith (1875–1948), celebrated and controversial film director.

2. Ruth St. Denis (1879–1968), American dancer who began her career in 1906 and founded the Denishawn School in Los Angeles with her husband.

3. Bigin's was a popular restaurant in San Francisco. It was repeatedly raided by Prohibition agents for serving alcohol.

[228] CAS to GS [ALS]

East Auburn, Cal.,
Dec. 27th, 1920.

Dear George:

        My illness was like the false report of Mark Twain's death—"much exaggerated." I *did* have a sort of breakdown (some temporary derangement of the sympathetic nerves) and spent a few days in bed. But at present, I feel as well as ever. The local M.D. could find nothing to account for my breakdown.

It must have been R. A. Nic[h]ol who rang you up. I believe you know his daughter Margaret, who is an artists' model . . . His wife was with me at the time of my collapse.

I think of sending my poems to Alice Meynell—she once offered to help me.[1] Her recommendation could mean a lot in London—if she cares to recommend anything so unorthodox as the "H. E." . . . . I'm afraid there's no chance on this side of the big Atlantic puddle . . . As to printing the poems here, I'd rather they were put out by Miss Reed or her son than by Robertson, whose business-methods I dislike. I'd print them myself, if I had a little money.

I may come to the city for a day or two next month, if the weather is at all settled. I need a little change—my illness was due to monotony more than to anything else, I think. One can't be healthy without a little pleasure—and pleasure is a proscribed article in this community of blue-noses . . . Is there anything to be found in the way of debauchery in S. F.? (I don't mean 60¢ highballs).

I like the poem you enclose . . . I've not been able to write for months.
Affectionately,
Clark—

1. Alice Meynell (1847–1922), British poet and essayist.

[229] GS to CAS [ALS]

Jan. 6th, 1921.

Dear Clark:

I'm glad to learn that your reported illness was no worse. The financial problem, of course, still remains. Bender tells me he has arranged for your immediate necessities, which gives me time to speak to some of our local rich men in regard to their doing a little for you on the 1st of each month. This I shall do unless you advise me promptly to the contrary. There is no valid reason why Phelan, Spreckels[1] and three or four others should not send you $10. a month, as they'd be glad to do. On account of your parents, you ought not to refuse such assistance.

Be careful what poems you send to Miss Meynell. She dropped out as a subscriber to "The Sonnet" on account of an irreligious sonnet I sold them—the one I called "Science."[2] She must be a frightful bigot, and easily antagonized intellectually. Still, London's the only place to have "Crystal and Ebony" published. It's a hopeless proposition in this hog-wallow.

Mrs. Reed won't be able, I fear, to do any more printing: Abrams has just cured her of cancer, but she still has gall-stones. Her son John is to have her "plant," in Petaluma, and may be able to give some of his time to such work. But at present "everything's up in the air," and not likely to come down for awhile. Otherwise, I'd be asking him to bring out a book for *me*. I've enough lyrics for two books.

I don't blame you for wanting to visit the city. As to "debauchery," I know nothing of the "scarlet side of things" here, any more. There are several approaciable [*sic*] young women who come to "Bigin's," but their favors are for love and not money. To win the former takes time, as a rule, for they have been spoiled and are hard to please. I'd stick to alcohol, which needs no devotion, charm nor persuasion!

I've been on the wagon for over a week, except for a few drinks at "Bigin's" on New Year's eve, and feel very energetic. So far, however, I've given all my pen-work to a pile of letters. I answer about ten a day, which is for me a bellyfull. I have written several love-sonnets lately, but I don't count those, as I don't purpose publishing them.

I hope I thanked you for the toyon and mistletoe. The latter was put to good use, at the home of English friends.

My nephew, late of the navy, is here, and has so far bled me for about $75. Thank Heaven, he sails for Guam on a lumber ship to-day!

Let me hear from you soon.
Affectionately,

George.

P.S. Yes—I know Miss Nichol: a **peach!**
G.

1. James D[uval] Phelan (1861–1930), mayor of San Francisco (1897–1902) and US senator from California (1915–21). GS also refers to Rudolph Spreckels (1872–1958), a son of Claus Spreckels, owner of a hugely successful sugar refining business and other commercial enterprises in California.

2. GS refers to the sonnet "To Science," whose concluding line refers to "the monstrous ghost of God."

[230] CAS to GS [ALS]

East Auburn, Cal.,
Jan. 31st, 1921.

Dear George:

I ought to have written you long before this—it seems incredible that I've let the month go by without answering your letter. I've not felt very well, most of the time; but that's a poor excuse. There's nothing definitely wrong with me; I'm inclined to blame my indisposition upon the weather.

The financial assistance of which you speak would be very welcome to me. There's nothing I can do at present to earn money. Even wood-cutting is impossible, because of the continual rains. Doubtless I'll be able to pick fruit in the summer; but there's little else available in the way of remunerative occupation.

I've written almost nothing. I began an "Ode to Aphrodite", but gave it up as being too conventional. I'm sick of the old subjects, the old images. They've been mauled, and thumbed, and slobbered over by so many million poets. Even blasphemy is trite,—God is a clichè.

I'm surprised at what you tell me about Mrs Meynell. I assumed that she was quite a liberal, from her praise of "The Star-Treader", which is pretty well saturated with agnosticism. Of course, some of my later things are more outspoken. I wouldn't have sent her anything if I had known what you tell me.

I doubt if I'll visit San Francisco. I don't feel that I can afford the trip; anyway, there wouldn't be much pleasure in it for me. I've sworn off on prohibition-booze, and have no time to bother with semi-virgins of the Bologna variety. Anyway, I never make love to girls. "Only married women need apply."

I've read some good books, lately. "A Bed of Roses", by W. L. George, is one of them. Do you know it? Also I've read a book by Somerset Maugham, "Of Human Bondage," which I found in the Auburn library. They had taken it off the shelves, though, as being "unsuitable for general circulation!" Of the two books, I prefer "A Bed of Roses."[1]

Affectionately,
Clark.

1. CAS refers to the work of two British novelists, *A Bed of Roses* (1911) by W. L. George (1882–1926), a novel that caused a scandal for its portrayal of a woman who turns to prostitution to support herself, and *Of Human Bondage* (1915), an autobiographical novel by W. Somerset Maugham (1874–1965).

[231] GS to CAS [ALS]

May 16th, 1921.

Dear Clark:

I've been on the joyless wagon for three weeks, and have begun to poetize again, also to reply to letters. For neglecting yours for so long, I can only plead "John Barleycorn," and hope for your pardon.

I *have* been bringing up the matter of your finances with several of my rich friends, five of whom promise to contribute $10. each per month; and you will hear from them on or just after the 1st, if they hold to their promises.

I'm wondering how your MS. fared in London. The English, being somewhat farther from barbarism than the Americans, ought to "eat it up." Robertson wants to issue a book of short poems for me, and may do so when printing costs go down. I can then avail myself of Macmillans' offer to publish a volume of "selected poems" for me. But I feel there's no hurry about such things, despite my advancing years. And how much less in your case!

Yes—I read the "Bed of Roses" when it came out. A gorgeous satire! His later "Caliban" is not nearly so good. Maugham's book is a really *greater* one, I think, but somewhat dull by comparison. I saw Maugham off for Singapore, last month. His last book, "The Magician," is a penny-dreadful.[1] He should be ashamed it have written it. But it was done with some reference to the movies, I think. I've fought shy of them, so far, but increasing poverty may drive me to them yet. Money's an hellish thing. If I could only live without women, I'd immure myself in the wilds of Monterey County!

Forgive this long silence, and don't imitate it!

Yours ever,

George.

[Enclosures: "Careless," "Distance," "His Own Country," "In the Valley," "Rainbow's End," "Sonnet on the Sea's Voice."]

1. George, *Caliban* (1920), a novel about a ruthless journalism magnate who becomes wealthy by giving the public what it wants; Maugham, *The Magician* (1908), a supernatural thriller with a character based upon Aleister Crowley.

[232] CAS to GS [ALS]

East Auburn, Cal.,
May 18th, 1921.

Dear George:

I was certainly glad to get your letter, along with that sheaf of lovely poems! I had thought of writing you, several times; but there seemed little enough to communicate.

I like all of these new poems—you seem to have "struck" a fresh vein! Please keep it up!

I, too, have been writing; but my compositions are all "personal"—some of them too much so, perhaps, for the official censors (the Anti-Vice Society!). I'll try to send you something with this.

My book never got to *any* of the English publishers: Mrs Meynell was too ill to read it (luckily for me, I dare say!) so the ms. was returned. I have just submitted it to Boni & Liveright. Of course, I haven't much hope . . . By the way, how much does it cost to put out a volume in the format of "Lilith"? I may have to print mine that way, if I can inveigle some one into putting up the money.

I have an exhibition of sixteen drawings at the "Art Department" of the Public Library in Los Angeles. They are "raising a riot," in the way of comment and questions; but I don't know whether it will lead to anything substantial or not. I wish I could manage an exhibition in S. F. The Hargens Book-Shop (which refused to exhibit my work last year) wants to get it back! But I can't forgive Mrs. H. for the "deal" she gave me—she *promised* to put my work on display, and went back on the promise.

I had another display, at an Art-Club in Sacramento, some time ago. The paintings were much praised. Women (it was a woman's club) seem to like my colouring. I attended a reception at the same club, later, and was the only man present! . . . But most of the ladies were too old . . . with the exception of the friend who took me there.

I spent a week in Roseville last month—the only vacation I've had in years. A "wild and wicked" time:—I encountered several new varieties of home-brew—not to mention a cellar-full of pre-prohibition vintages!

A thousand thanks for your efforts on my behalf! I'll certainly be grateful for that "financial assistance." I gave out at the wood-cutting. I've had several bad colds, and feel a bit "run down" at present . . . Please convey my cordial thanks to these gentlemen.

I'll probably see you next summer,—if not before. I expect to spend a few weeks in Northbrae.

Affectionately,

Clark—

[Enclosure: "Psalm" [= "A Psalm to the Best Beloved"].

[233] GS to CAS [ALS]

May 19, 1921.

Dear Clark:

I like the "Psalm" very much, and shall be glad to receive anything else of the kind—or, for that matter, any of your work, which is always good and sometimes great. Don't fear me as a "censor!" One in them may yet have *me* jailed.[1]

Between now and the 1st I will get after the men whom I referred to. They are Senator Phelan, Raymond Armsby, Rudolph Spreckels and Earnest Stent,[2] so far; and I hope to get two others—all at $10. a month. I've seen Stent already, and here is his June contribution. You might send him an autographed book. STENT.

I've some more poems to send you, but forget what ones I sent. Let me have their titles.

It cost me 50¢ each to have "Lilith" and "Rosamund" printed & bound. Of course that was a special rate, but I could get it for you were Mrs. Reed at work; but unfortunately she is dying. I'll put a bee in Robertson's bonnet, as soon as he gets out my next book ("Sails and Mirage"). He can afford to publish only 500!

This is a hell of a world for poets! "I should have kept a wine-shop." Then we'd both be in clover.

> Yours ever,
>
> George.

1. See further letter 289.
2. Raymond Armsby (1879–1971), an insurance agent in the Bay Area. Stent is unidentified.

---

[234] CAS to GS [ALS]

> East Auburn, Cal.
> May 27th, 1921.

Dear George:

Thanks for the ten! I'll remember Mr. Stent. I'm out of "Star-Treaders", and won't have any for another week, since Robertson has sold all the bound copies, and is waiting for a fresh consignment from the binders ... Will you give me Mr. Stent's address? Or shall I send the inscribed copy to you?

I've been "under the weather" for the past week; partly nerves, and partly an aftermath of the severe colds that I've had.

Here are some more of my verses—not all, by any means. They're the first writing I've done for a year. I question their literary value; but it doesn't matter. I am not writing them for literary purposes; and they are not meant for "general circulation."

By all means, send me some more of your poems. I was much taken with some of those in the last consignment. Their titles were: "Distance", "Rainbow's End," "In the Valley," "His Own Country", "Sonnet on the Sea's Voice", and "Careless." "Rainbow's End" and "In the Valley" were the ones I liked best.

> Affectionately,
> Clark

[Enclosures: "Ecstasy," "Nightfall," other unidentified poems.]

---

[235] GS to CAS [ALS]

> June 6th, 1921.

Dear Clark:

A letter from Sen. Phelan to-day informs me he has told his secretary to forward you $30. each quarter. Let me know if Spreckels, Armsby and Crocker[1] also "come through." They've promised to.

You may send the book for Earnest Stent to me. I'd like to have you send books also to the others:

> Hon. James D. Phelan,
>   Saratoga, Cal.
>
> Templeton Crocker,
>   Shreve Bld., S. F.
>
> Raymond Armsby,
>   Burlingame, Cal.

Rudolph Spreckels,
1900 Pacific Ave., S. F.

That is, if you hear from them.

Your poems are all peaches. I like that kind, which you do well in writing, as they add humanness to your other work. "Ecstasy" and "Nigh[t]fall" seem the finest to me, especially the former. But they're all fine work.

I'm glad mine were not unpleasing to you—and I'm a little surprised at your preferences, as I expected you to care most for "The Sea's Voice," as you once would have. It shows how our tastes change, and usually for the better.

Here are some more verses. I write a poem (?) every morning. Most of them are intended for sale to magazines. But I have made a start on my new dramatic poem "Truth", and hope that that will be worth while.

Let me hear from you when you feel energetic enough for letters. I hear no more from Loveman: how is he? *I* am well, having been on the wagon for seven entire weeks—a record for *me!*

Affectionately,

George.

[Enclosures: "Atthan Dances," other unidentified poems.]

1. [Charles] Templeton Crocker (1884–1948), scientist, explorer, and philanthropist residing in San Francisco.

[236] GS to CAS [ALS]

Saturday. [30 July 1921]

Dear Clark:

Please send this woman your book.

Mrs. Estelle P. Crane,
P.O. Box 36, Station H,
New York City.

Destroy the letter.

Yours ever,

George.

[237] CAS to GS [ALS]

East Auburn, Cal.,
Aug. 10, 1921

Dear George:

I mailed a copy of "The S. T." to Mrs. Crane, according to your instructions. Who is the lady, anyway? She sounds interesting.

I was in Roseville for a week after leaving S. F. The heat was dreadful, and the office-work even more tedious than I had expected. However, I shall go back in September, when Mrs. Hemphill returns from Berkeley. I don't know how long I'll be able to stay there: H. has a jealous disposition.[1]

I've had a letter or two from Loveman. He is still out of work, and has been ill to boot. What a tragedy!

I, too, have been more or less unwell. I've had a sort of bronchitis for the past month, and can't seem to get rid of it . . . And I've been in love since last March—with no prospect of a near recovery. I seem to have a facility for impossible love-affairs: The women who attract me are always unfortunate.

Newbegin[2] returned my drawings, after keeping them for two weeks. He thought I wanted to find a publisher for them! I've about decided to give up drawing. There's no public for the sort of work that I do. However, I may try a little sketching from life. But the models must be attractive!

I enclose a sonnet that I can't remember sending you before. I can't place anything—at least, with magazines that **pay**. I *gave* two poems to Frank Harris' magazine, "Pearson's."[3]

Are you still on the "wagon?" I don't blame you—when I think of the stuff at the Bologna! That South American absinthe was the best.

Please send me some more of your poems. Some of the last ones were very beautiful, particular "Atthan."

Give my love to Marie Parmeley.[4]

Aff.,

Clark

[Enclosure: "Secret Love."]

1. See letter 255.
2. John J. ("Jack") Newbegin, a well-known bookseller in San Francisco.
3. "Laus Mortis" (September 1921) and "Ecstasy" (October 1922).
4. Marie Parmalee, with whom GS had an affair for several years. Years later she was arrested on a charge of assault and batter for striking someone with a statue of Venus de Milo, in which she had hidden her letters from GS. The letters fell out and were immediately published (*Los Angeles Herald Express*, 7–9 December 1937).

[238] GS to CAS [ALS]

August 25th, 1921.

Dear Clark:

I suppose that by now you know more about Estelle Crane, as she writes that she has written to you: see enclosed portion of her letter. Please return it to me. She's a lovely thing, a sort of "Lilith," though she must be nearly forty years old. She's divorcing her husband at present, who threatens to bring in *my* name. I'd be "only too proud!"

Loveman would better come to S. F., if he can possibly afford it, and let Abrams cure him—I assume it's T.B. A. can cure that if it hasn't gone too far.

I'm sorry you gave any poems to F. Harris, variously a son of a bitch. He poses as a judge of poetry, but doesn't get it at all, really, just as Mencken doesn't. Almost all men approach poetry mentally and emotionally. The *magic* (Poe's "Ulalume" for example) utterly escapes them. They usually call the poetry "ornament!"

I was off the wagon for three days at the Jinks, but find that even good hooch poisons my nerves so much that it's not worth while to drink. So I'm "back on," until some grand "occasion," or until someone offers me champagne, which I love—or absinthe.

This sonnet, "Secret Love," is very beautiful—a splendid lyric. I'd not use "Carthage," though, as that city wasn't destroyed by Time, but by its own inhabitants, at the command of the victorious Roman. I think some Asiatic city would be better, though I can't suggest one.[1]

Tell your lady-love to be extra careful with your love-sonnets and letters, as husbands are resourceful and unscrupulous; and a woman *never* destroys such things, no matter how fervently she promises to.

Did T. R. Smith write to you? He's getting out an anthology of erotic verse—the kind one can't print oneself on account of the Vice Society. I gave him six of my things, and mentioned your name to him.[2] He's an old man—a New Yorker, and used to run a magazine syndicate. If he uses anything of yours, I'll tell him to pay you for it. Here's Stent's $10., which he overlooked on the 1st. I had to remind him. I hope to get Mrs. Spreckels on the list, when I next see her. Our trails don't often cross.

I suppose you saw about Marie's marriage. I brought it about. She and three other girls go about in Chinese costume now, in public!

Yours ever,   Geo.

[P.S.] I've written little since Jinks—my usual autumnal sterility.

[Enclosures: "Three Sonnets on Beauty," other unidentified poems.]

1. The poem now mentions Syria, not Carthage.
2. Smith used all six of GS's poems in *Poetica Erotica* (New York: Boni & Liveright, 1921–22; 2 vols.): "Infidels," "The Golden Past," "The Kiss of Consummation," "At Midnight," "Flame," and "Happiest." All but "Infidels" were previously unpublished. The anthology has no poems by CAS. See AB to GS, 9 September 1912: "I'd rather not hand 'The Golden Past' to a woman, and I hope you'll never hand it to the public, though it would doubtless delight the followers of Upton Sinclair. The conclusion is a trifle too graphic; you might as well have used 'the shorter and uglier word'" (*MMM* 226).

[239] CAS to GS [ALS]

East Auburn, Cal.,
Sept. 5th, 1921

Dear George:

I return the excerpt from Mrs. Crane's letter. Yes, I heard from the lady. She seems to have misunderstood me in more ways than one—which was perhaps inevitable ... Don't tell people that I am a cynic—it isn't more than half-true. I am incurably romantic—and prove it by falling in love every six months. ... But even cynicism might not protect one against *that*.

I have been very idle lately, and have seldom felt so listless and effortless. I am not very well—"nerves", eye-strain, and a disordered stomach. I don't know when I will go to Roseville—or whether I will go at all. "Everything is in the air."

I like the poems you enclose—particularly the sonnets on Beauty. I've nothing to send in return,—except a prose-poem written last spring.

No, I have heard nothing from T. R. Smith—which doesn't prove that he hasn't written me! The local post-office is run by a bunch of congenital idiots, and I get everyone's mail but my own. Two of "Cleopatra's" letters have gone astray.

I have not heard from Loveman for a long time. Had a letter from Leo Mihan[1] yesterday; he tells me that you have induced him to try Abrams' treatment. I wish I could have seen Abrams when I was in the city; but I'll be down again before the end of the year, if I have any luck.

Can you induce one or two others to contribute ten a month? It would be a great help. The forty dollars I receive now is barely enough; but we could get along on sixty.

I saw the notice of Marie's marriage . . . Marriage is an error I was never tempted to commit: I have not been in love with an unmarried woman since I was fifteen! Anyway, I object to marriage on moral grounds.

Ever yours,
Clark.

[Enclosure: "In Cocaigne."]

1. A friend of CAS and GS.

[240] GS to CAS [ALS]

Sept. 8th, 1921.

Dear Clark:

This is as beautiful as it is brief—this Cocaigne piece. It seems to me that "Smart Set" should take it. And have you ever tried sending love-poems to "Snappy Stories?" I've unloaded a few things on them, lately. The address is 37 W. 39th St., New York. Put the name "Miss McIlvaine" on the lower left-hand corner of your letter. She would like, I think, the "Cocaigne." I think it less disgraceful to be in "Snappy Stories" than in the "Atlantic Monthly."

I know that $40. a month isn't enough to live on, and have been expecting to run into two more local millionaires whom I shall ask to help out. I used to see them almost weekly. Now, just because I am eager to see them, we never meet! If I don't encounter them before Oct. 1st, I'll write to them, though that's not nearly so good a way.

Went on a grand two-day jag with Nina Putnam this week, and am still convalescent. It doesn't "pay;" but I'll never learn *that!*

Don't write till you feel quite like it.

Yours ever.   George.

[241] CAS to GS [ALS]

East Auburn, Cal.,
Sept. 26th, 1921

Dear George:

I may run down to S. F. for a day or two early in October. Could Abrams look me over? He might give me some advice about my nerves.

I've sold two of my drawings (to Mrs. Gregory, the novelist's wife).[1] But I've neither written nor painted for—months.

"Snappy Stories" used to buy my work. I've just sent them some of these new things. "Cocaigne," however, is not for sale—for more reasons than one.

I have been "off the wagon" several times of late. Some of the boot-leg hereabouts is excellent—and very cheap. The "grappa" they make down Auburn ravine is pure alcohol!—in more senses than one.

Life is not so dull as it has been. Auburn may yet become sufficiently demoralized to be habitable.

Affectionately,
Clark.

[Enclosures: "Alien Memory," "The Hidden Paradise," "Exotic," "Love Malevolent," "Sonnet."]

1. CAS refers to Lotus McGlashan Gregory. Jackson Gregory (1882–1943) was the author of popular westerns. CAS later wrote an introduction to *Shadow of Wings* (1930) by Gregory's sister, Susan Myra Gregory (d. 1939).

[242] GS to CAS [ALS]

Sept. 28th, 1921.

Dear Clark:

Of course life in fair Auburn must be highly conducive to grappa; but go light on that beverage: it will send all your bacteria into congressional conclave, and they'll pass all sorts of resolutions commending it.

I like your sonnet, as I like everything that you write. Its close is especially good. Seems to me "Smart Set" should want it. I've written little for a month, except love-poems, which "don't count." Have been up at Abram[s]'s clinic a good deal. He has entirely eliminated my congenital syphilis (we all have it, you know, though mine was not in the blood but the brain. Now I know why my poor dad had such terrible headaches.)

Of course Abrams will go over you if you come down. But would you follow his advice?

I've had two physicians from Honolulu there, lately. They were greatly impressed—as they should have been.

Yours ever,
George.

[Enclosure: "The Princess on the Headland."]

[243] CAS to GS [ALS]

East Auburn, Cal.,
Oct. 6th, 1921

Dear George:

I've given up my trip to S. F. for the present. For one reason, I am rather short of cash. I have had no luck at all in selling my poems.

Life in Auburn is not so dull as it was—even without grappa, in which I seldom indulge. However, I have almost gotten the cigarette habit, from smoking with ladies.

Andrew has just returned from the city. He spoke of seeing you.

I've no poems to send this time. . . . Your "Princess on the Headland" is very, very beautiful.

A letter from Loveman the other day. He is still sick—and out of work.

Ever yours,
Clark.

P.S. Stent has not remitted since August. Does he depend on you to collect for me?

[243a] GS to CAS [non-extant]

[San Francisco, Cal.
c. October 1921]

[Enclosures: "To the Moon," one unidentified poem.]

[244] CAS to GS [ALS]

East Auburn, Cal.,
Nov. 2nd, 1921

Dear George:

I'd certainly like to visit the city, and take in Abrams' clinic; but I don't feel that I can spare the cash just at present. Later, on, perhaps.

Have you tried "The Lyric West", the new Los Angeles magazine of poetry? They actually **pay**—five dollars a page on publication. The editor has accepted three of my poems, including the ode "To Omar."

I don't make a habit of smoking cigarettes, and never miss them between-whiles. I merely smoke them (for love's sake!) when I am with a certain woman.

I have written nothing at all, in the way of verse. I enclose a prose-poem, "The Litany of the Seven Kisses" (a very inadequate number!) which was written last spring.

Your poems are always excellent. I like the one to the moon; and the poem without sibilants is very ingenious as well as beautiful.

I am sorry that Stent "fell through", since we really need the money. I hope you *can* find some one else. I fear I must have done something or written something to offend Mrs C. But I can't help being immoral and irreligious!

Affectionately,
Clark—

[Enclosure: "The Litany of the Seven Kisses."]

[245] CAS to GS [ALS]

East Auburn, Cal.,
Dec. 17th, 1921.

Dear George:

I find many things that are new to me in your book,[1] and many that are very beautiful. I don't care quite as much for the title-poems, though, as I do for a number of others, such as "The Queen Forgets", "Saul," "The Secret Garden," "Hesperian," "The Rune," "Atthan Dances," ["]The Princess on the Headland," and ["]To a Girl Dancing." Among the sonnets, I like "Lost Colours", "The Wine of Illusion", "Vox Humana", the 2nd sonnet to Ruth Chatterton, and No. 6 "On the Sea's Voice." The twin poems, "The Morning Star," and "The Evening Star", are most lovely. In another vein, I like "Mammon",[2] "His own Country," and "The Passing of Bierce," and the sonnet, "Poe's Gravestone."

I've heard nothing about the fate of my own book, which is, or should be, in the hands of the Houghton Mifflin Co... The "literary shambler" of Keats' day (his own phrase)[3] wasn't a circumstance to that of the present. I have been reading Upton Sinclair's "Brass Check",[4] and feel more in sympathy with the Bolshevists than I have ever been before. I fear there's no chance for me. I could print a small edition myself, if someone would loan me a couple hundred dollars. There should be no difficulty in selling enough copies to pay for the cost of production. I wish something could be done: My inability to publish puts me in a false position, and disappoints the few people who care for my work. It has even affected my last love-affair:—the lady accused me of being a failure! If it weren't for my people, I'd hoof it out of this——! ——! ——! rotten country to-morrow, and stow away on a steamer for England or France. As it is, I may come to the city for awhile next spring: I've had nearly all I can stand of Auburn at one stretch.

Forgive this diatribe: it eases my mind a little.

The enclosed article, from an Auburn paper, may amuse you. It shows the estimation in which literature is held locally. The promising young journalist who wrote it, gives me a paragraph, and barely mentions Bierce. Gregory, who heads the list of luminaries, writes western tales of the Jesus-Christ-and-cowboys type. He isn't as bad as Harold Bell Wright,[5] and doesn't sell more than half as well.

I'll dig up some verses to enclose with this also. And next week I'll mail you two or three of my drawings (the ones you liked best.) I wish I had something better to send.

Affectionately,
Clark.

[Enclosure: "Placer County Scribes and Artists Shine Brightly Among the Stars of California's Literary Firmament," [Auburn] *Journal-Republican*, 15 December 1921, p. 8; one unidentified poem.]

1. *SM*.

2. There is no poem of this title in *SM*. CAS is evidently referring to "The Common Cult," which mentions Mammon in the opening line of every stanza.

3. Unidentified.

4. Sinclair, *The Brass Check: A Study of American Journalism* (1919), an exposé of the corruption of American newspapers.

5. Harold Bell Wright (1872–1944), a best-selling American novelist of the period.

[246] CAS to GS [ALS]

Auburn, Cal.,

Feb. 22nd, 1922.

Dear George:

How are things in the city? I've not heard from you since I was down. I might have written, myself, but had so little to communicate, in the way of news.

I'm going over my poems at present, preparatory to a fresh assault on the publishers. Can you give me the New York address of the Henry Holt Co? I think of tackling them next.

Here is my latest sonnet, the only thing that I have written so far this year. It isn't very good. Everything here has conspired to make me indifferent to poetry.

I long for Spring, as I have never longed before—the weather is beastly enough for Malebolge. There's "nothing doing" at present: I may have started one or two scandals (it isn't very difficult in a small town) but there's little enough in them. The few women I meet are all virtuous—or unattractive. I don't seem to fall in love any more—for which I am duly thankful.

Andrew and I are planning to visit Weimar to-morrow: A.'s friend, Dr. Bauch, has a position at the t.b. Sanatorium there.

Tell Louise Hansen that I'm in love with her! I wish I could get her up here, next time she has a vacation.

Ever yours,

Clark

[Enclosure: "Necromancy."]

[247] GS to CAS [ALS]

Feb. 26th, 1922.

Dear Clark:

I'd have written to *you*, had I anything to report. The numbers of the melancholy rich whom I keep hoping to meet, keep on the horizon, as if they feared my intentions! I can counsel only patience.

Things here are as dull as usual, though they flared up a bit, over two weeks ago, when my sister Marian and her husband came up from Honolulu. However, he died of the flu, and I got it myself and had to stay in my room for a week. Am all right now, and have begun to work again. Am also on the wagon, for the stuff one gets here now is sheer murder.

I've not been down in Bigin's for a month, nearly, and can't give "Jo" your message anyhow, as she went to El Paso several weeks ago, and intends, some one told me, to remain there—God knows why!

Holts' address is 19 W. 44th St., but I fear you won't have much of a chance with them, as Robert Frost is their adviser in matters of poetry! His style is the reverse of yours, as you know. Their man Robt. Cortes Holliday[1] has been after me for months for a book of my "selected" poems; but I wrote him lately that I feared we couldn't "get together," as I wouldn't stand for the way the N. Y. publishers advertise their wares.

Your sonnet is in the true Baudelairean vein, plus the richer beauty that goes into all you write. I have just written one myself, a thing I call "The Twilight of the Grape." Will enclose it. It's robust rather than beautiful. I've written five other poems since Monday, but haven't any typed copies. The girls get them! I wish they could understand them.

Yes—we've had a vile winter. The cold part of it, however, seems at an end, and I'm hoping for a trip to Carmel when the abalone law-limit expires.

Yours for the reform of God,
George.

[P.S.] My regards to Andrew.

[Enclosure: "The Twilight of the Grape."]

1. Robert Cortes Holliday (1880–1947), editor of the *Bookman* (1919–20) and literary adviser to Henry Holt (1921–23). He wrote about GS in the article "A Literary Lane" in his *Literary Lanes and Other Byways* (1925). They met in May 1920. GS did agree to compile a volume of his selected poems for Holt.

[248] CAS to GS [ALS]

Auburn, Cal.,
March 16th, 1922.

Dear George:

Of course, it's hardly worth while for me to try the Henry Holt Co., if Frost is their adviser. He would doubtless live up to his name, in respect to romantic poetry like mine. I'd better print the book myself, if any one can be found to finance it. As far as money goes, I'd make more out of it, anyway.

Your sonnet, "The Twilight of the Grape," is excellent . . . Speaking of wine, I had all that I cared to drink the other night! Andrew, Dr. Bauch, and I went to a party in Loomis. Our host brought out demijohn after demijohn of home-made vino, and we were all drunk enough to stand on our heads by midnight. Afterwards, we drove back to Auburn in a howling snow-storm!

I'm sorry "Jo" has gone away. She was the only girl in S. F. who interested me . . . I've had a grand row with my Auburn lady-love, and don't care much whether she ever forgives me or not.

I enclose a new lyric ("Satiety"). "The Motes"[1] was written years ago; but I can't remember sending it to you.

Aff.,
Clark.

[Enclosures: "The Motes," "Satiety."]

1. There are two extant mss. of "The Motes" at NYPL.

[249] GS to CAS [ALS]

Apr. 8th, 1922.

Dear Clark:

I dare say you're glad that winter is over. It has been a most unpleasant one, but I've managed to stay sober most of the time, and, as you know, have been delivered of more or less poetry, or verse. "Scribner's, " to my stupefaction, took a 204 line "Ode to Shelley."[1] I sent it out merely as a matter of routine, expecting ultimately to have to *give* it away.

Are you sending out anything? I know it's a semi-hopeless task for any of us, and particularly for a poet of your aloof and delicate timbre. But now and then the moronic editors *do* take a fancy to some poem; and it's a shame *not* to take the money. If you'll send me some of your stuff, especially the less daring love-verse, I'll send it personally to Mencken, Miss McIlvaine and one or two others.

You'll need the money. Mrs. Clark has skipped off to Paris again, without giving me a chance to see her. I'd have written to her had I known she was going. Mrs. Spreckels has gone to Paris also. And Armsby's "year" is up; so you'll hear no more from him. I have a few folk in mind, but can't broach the subject till I repay them what *I* owe.

I like the two poems, especially "Satiety." The other is very salable, by the way. Send me copies of each.

Yours in the Resurrection and the Life,

George.

[Enclosures: "The Gulls," CAS's "Satiety," other unidentified poems.]

1. Written for the centennial of Shelley's death.

[250] CAS to GS [ALS]

Auburn, Cal.
April 11th, 1922.

Dear George:

I like your new poems—especially "The Gulls". I wish **I** could turn things out whenever I want to.

Here are some extra copies of verses for you to send out; but I think most of them—except "Motes" and "Satiety"—have been out several times already. "The Lyric West" continues to buy my stuff, and "The London Mercury" (a "high-toned" monthly) took a sonnet some time ago.[1] Apart from that, I've had no luck. "Requiescat" which ought to sell, if anything of mine would, has been out six or seven times. "Smart Set" and "Snappy Stories" were among those who turned it down. The average editor seems to have the intelligent equipment of a guinea-pig.

One of the local printers has promised to bring out a volume of poems for me this summer—on credit. I hope to h-ll he keeps his word,—it will lift a load of worry from me to have the stuff between covers, no matter how small the edition.

I've planned a new book, which oughtn't to be so hard to dispose of. It will be made up entirely of love-poems, and the colouring will be sensuous rather than sensual. "Sandalwood" ought to be a good title, since the imagery and the setting will be largely exotic.

I'm sorry Armsby is going to drop out. I'll have to pick fruit this summer!

I seem to be more isolated than ever. Oh, h-ll—what a life! My "Cleopatra" has thrown herself into newspaper-work (in an effort to "forget") and her successor (?)

seems to [be] nursing a mortal grudge against me. I'll either have to leave the town—or steal Andrew's girl!

Aff., Clark

[Enclosures: unidentified poems.]

1. I.e., "Symbols."

[251] GS to CAS [ALS]

[Bohemian Club
San Francisco]

May 15th, 1922.

Dear Clark:

      I went on a two-week "bend" soon after you sent me those poems, and in consequence, they were not sent out (those that I did send: I refuse to send out free verse!) till about a week ago. But I should hear from them soon—or you: I asked Miss McIlvaine to write personally to you.

      I've been at the painful task of writing a short-story, lately. I hate the work, but have to have the money. Anyhow, I don't have to use my own name![1]

      Don't worry because your work doesn't get between covers immediately. It's sure to do so some day, even if I have to do it myself. No such poetry as yours can be lost, provided that copies exist.

      I've lately written a 25 stanza poem I call "The Voice of the Wheat," and one of the same length about trapping a mastodon![2]

      I like your idea for the new book of love-poems. Go to it! Love-poems are easy sellers, I hear. I've three hundred love-poems, but don't care to publish any till I am dead or otherwise impotent.

      I've sent Holt & Co. the MS. of my "Selected Poems;" there's enough to make a book of 190 pages. Their manager, Holliday, seems glad to get it; but I fear it will net his firm scant money. The public knows even less about poetry than editors do, if such be possible.

Yours ever,   George.

[Enclosures: "Beauty Dethroned,"[3] "The Midway Peace," and one unidentified poem.]

1. No short story as by GS was published at this time.
2. "The Trapping of Rung" (unpublished; ms. at Bancroft Library).
3. Probably the poem published as "Beauty Renounced."

[252] CAS to GS [ALS]

Auburn, Cal.,
June 11th, 1922.

Dear George:

      I have been working hard for the past month (at wood-cutting and cherry-picking) Hence my delay in answering your last letter. To-day is Sunday, and I am trying to clean up my correspondence. Nine hours of work on weekdays, leaves me too tired for any mental effort, even that of letter-writing. As to poetry or painting—I have forgotten all about them for the time.

Mencken took "Requiescat;" but I've not heard from any of the other poems. Were they returned to you?

The poems you sent me were admirable, as always. I hardly know which I liked best—"Beauty Dethroned", perhaps, for the thought, and the other two for music and lyric loveliness. . . . "Devachan",[1] as I understand it, is merely a temporary Paradise of beatific illusions—in which the discarnate soul is permitted to abide for a time before its return to mortal existence. The Buddhists have no conception of a *permanent* heaven, or "Eden." Their hells, too, are only temporary . . . The religions of the west are puerile compared to the esoteric doctrines of Buddhism.

I have a few new verses, and will enclose a sample or two.

I **am** anxious to have a book published—it might liven things up a little. People seem to think that I have done nothing.

Andrew spoke of seeing you in the city. Perhaps I'll be able to come down next fall, if I work all summer!

Aff.,

Clark.

[Enclosures: "Artemis," "Chance."]

1. The name is cited in GS's poem "The Midway Peace." CAS used it in "Enchanted Mirrors" (*S*).

[253] GS to CAS [ALS]

[Bohemian Club
San Francisco]

June 14th, 1922.

Dear Clark:

Forgive so prompt a reply to your letter! If I don't write now, I may not feel like it for weeks. And you don't have to reply for a long time, since you are working so hard.

I'm sorry you have to give all your energy to such toil. If ever I can get a-hold of Mrs. C. or Mrs. Spreckels I may be able to give you more leisure; but they're now in Europe—till autumn.

I like your two poems very much, especially the "Artemis," which is work of *very high quality*—a noble poem. Try it on the better magazines.

I find only one thing in it to complain of: that "apart" and "part" are similar in rhyme.

The sonnet is a bit awkward, or labored, but is full of fine stuff, and has impact both of beauty and thought. I am sending it to Mencken.

I sent out only two of the poems you gave me, for those two alone seemed salable to "Smart Set" and "Snappy Stories," the only two magazines where I've any "pull" at all. You must bear in mind that your work is "poets' poetry," and the vile editors fight shy of that kind, or print such drivel as "Poetry" and "The Dial" use.

I'm not doing much. I think I need a change. I've settled into a rut—a pleasant rut, what of wine, women and "song," but nevertheless a rut. I need a few months of loneliness.

I've signed my contract with Holt & Co., for the volume of "Selected Poems." They thought that title rather weak, so I've suggested that they use "Neglected Poems!" They may bring out the book in the autumn, but may do so next spring for all I care. One isn't in a hurry at my age. I only wish it were one of your books they were to issue. If I ever get to New York again I may be able to be of use to you; at this remove one can do nothing; and it's useless to prod Robertson. He is too much in debt to banks and printers, but when he is on his feet again, if ever he is, he'd willingly get out a book for you. By the way, it's now over five years since he has given me an accounting. I think he figures that *I* owe *him* money!

If you can send me down a few cherries by parcel-post, I'll remit what expense it may be to you. I want them for a nice girl.

Affectionately yours,

George.

[254] GS to CAS [ANS]

[Postmarked New York, N.Y.,
21 June 1922]

Mencken should soon be home from Europe. Do you want me to send him your fine "Artemis" and "Chance" when he is back? I especially admire the former, though "Chance" is damn good too. A trifle awkward.

George.

Leslie Jennings has at last gone to N. Y. He wants to be a sub-editor on some magazine there. Imagine such an ambition! I fear N. Y. will scare him back to California—a city of brass and steel!

Geo.

[Enclosures: CAS's "Cleopatra," "Mirrors," "The Tears of Lilith," "Impression," "Union," "The Motes."]

[255] CAS to GS [ALS]

Auburn, Cal.,
June 25th, 1922

Dear George:

I sent you a box of Lambert cherries by express last Friday. Hope you received them promptly, and made good use of them! Don't worry about *paying* for them—they didn't cost *me* anything apart from the expressage.

The cherry-picking will be over in a few days. I've been earning $3.50 per day at it. Plums are the next fruit; and I understand the wages are better for picking them. Of course, the work is a bore; but it's preferable to most other forms of wage-slavery. As to writing—I don't feel in a creative mood at present, anyway. I, too, am in a "rut,"—the opposite kind from the one of which *you* complain. Too much of the same thing is always deadly, I suppose.

If you want solitude, why not come up and spend a few days or weeks with me? You won't have to see *anyone* most of the time, if you don't want to. I haven't many friends; and they're all busy at present. And I'll be off at work most of the time, myself.

I *am* to have a book published at last! One of the local printers offered to do the job for me—on credit! They're setting up the type now; but I don't know just when it will be ready. The book will include nearly all the unpublished work that I care to preserve, aside from half-a-dozen of the more "daring" erotics. Those should have gone into T. R. Smith's anthology!

My friend Mrs. Hemphill (whom you met last summer) has published a book of short stories (mining tales of the days of '49.)[1] It came out in time for the '49 celebration at Sacramento, and sold very well, I believe.

There are two ex-bartenders on the cherry-picking "force" with which I work! Almost the only entertainment I've had lately, comes from over-hearing the reminiscences they exchange!

Aff.,

Clark.

P.S. Thanks for the check from Snappy Stories![2] It just came.

[Enclosures: "Plum-Flowers," "Song."]

1. Vivia Hemphill, *Down the Mother Lode* (Sacramento: Purnell's, 1922).

2. It is not clear what poem was paid for by *Snappy Stories* at this time. In letter 257 CAS notes that "Plum-Flowers" had been accepted, but its appearance in the magazine has not been located. "Poplars" appeared in the issue of 5 November 1922.

[256] GS to CAS [ALS]

[Bohemian Club
San Francisco]

Sept. 24th, 1922.

Dear Clark:

God He knoweth that I am, by all odds, "the least pleasing of the beasts of the field," as Bierce once put it.[1] But the combination of having no news and hating to write it if I had has been, as usual, too much for me.

I've been on the wagon for a month, however, with but one lapse, and have managed to write several poems (a few of which I'll enclose, if I have any carbons) and am catching up on my correspondence.

Bender showed me one of your letters lately, and it had the good news that your book is soon to appear. I think it will make a big hit with the discerning, and, incidentally, make Robertson sorry that *he* didn't publish it. Anyway, I hope so.

I got those cherries, all right. A hell of a date to be thanking you for them; but let me! I suppose your fruit-picking will soon be over: shall try to get a few millionaires' wives to come through. The ones I have in mind are still in the east or in Europe. Phelan is back, after an eleven month trip around the world.

Try to follow up the connection with "Snappy Stories." It's a punk magazine, but Kemp, Le Gallienne and I were in the last number!² So you'll have good company in whoring. Miss Ellan McIlvaine is the one to address. She would like this "Song." I do— also the "Plum-Flowers." Do you care if *I* send them to her, or elsewhere?

How are your love-affairs progressing?

Affectionately,   George.

[P.S.] How is the Rev. Andrew Dewing?

[Enclosures: "Ephemera," "Shelley at Spezia," other unidentified poems.]

1. AB, "An Insurrection of the Peasantry," *Cosmopolitan* (December 1907); rpt. *Collected Works*, 10.203. AB was referring to unimaginative critics.
2. Richard Le Gallienne (1866–1947), widely published British poet. The poem by GS in *Snappy Stories* has not been located.

[257] CAS to GS [ALS]

Auburn, Cal.,
Sept. 29th, 1922.

Dear George:

I know how hard it is to write, when one has nothing to write about. *I* haven't very much, myself; but I'm making a clean sweep of my correspondence, so here goes.

"Ebony and Crystal" *ought* to be ready before long. The type is all set up, and the paper has been ordered for it. The book ought to create something of a row, even if I *did* leave out a few of the most sensual love-poems. There are ninety-four poems and twenty prose-pastels in the collection. It will be printed on a good quality of rough paper, and bound in boards or cloth.

The poems you sent me are all good. I liked the sonnets best,—"Ephemera", and the one on Shelley.

Miss McIlvaine accepted "Plum-Flowers"; and "Song" and "Artemis" are included in my book. You might send "Chance" to Mencken, however. He never takes anything of mine unless *you* send it in!

I don't blame Jennings for going to New York, though his ambition is certainly a peculiar one! Here's wishing him luck, anyway!

Saint Andrew Dewing was quite o.k. the last time I saw him. He and Dr. Bauch turned up last Sunday with a bottle of hootch. Bauch has been offered a position in New York at $4,000 a year, and plans to leave pretty soon.

As to my love-affairs—the two that you knew about are over and done with. It's about time for another, now . . . A. and I are planning a wild picnic down in the river hills when my book comes out. I haven't decided who I'll pick for *my* partner in the affair. There are three "possibilities"—all safely married!

Here are my latest verses—a song for a projected play.¹

Aff.,
Clark

P.S. Yes, the fruit-picking is over. Wood-cutting is the hardest work that I'm doing now!

[Enclosure: "The Song of Aviol: From 'The Fugitives.'"]

1. I.e., *The Fugitives*. The play was not completed.

[258] GS to CAS [ALS]

[Bohemian Club
San Francisco]

Oct. 1st, 1922.

Dear Clark:

It's good to know that the book is so near to its advent. As soon as you receive copies, send me some for the papers here, and I'll present them to the literary editors and see that you get reviews. That is, if you care for reviews. It's true that they are usually inadequate, even moronic, and sell few books. But it at least lets the world know that you're on the map. I can take copies to the Call, Chronicle, Bulletin, News and Argonaut. The Examiner doesn't have book-reviews. One could also go to Eddie O'Day, for his page in each Saturday's Enquirer (Oakland.)

I see that Mrs. Clark is not to return to California this year. That's bad news. But Mrs. A. B. Spreckels will be home before long. She'll probably come through.

I like the lyric very much—had seen it at Bender's—and am greatly interested in the projected drama.

As soon as I've heard Mencken is back, I'll send in the poems. I'll enclose here a few more of mine.

Affectionately,   George.

[Enclosures: "A Critic," "Venus Letalis," other unidentified poems.]

[259] CAS to GS [ALS]

Auburn, Cal.
Oct. 17th, 1922

Dear George:

More delays—my printer has been ill with the flu! They are just beginning to print the book now. It's quite a job for a small country office; and I don't think the volume will be ready before the end of the month.

Bert Cassidy, my printer, suggested that I ask you to write a little preface or note of introduction (one or two pages would be enough.) Do you care to do this? It would certainly add to the value and interest of the volume. You could touch on the sonnets, "The H. E.," and the prose-poems, all of which you have seen, at one time or another. I'd type the preface, if you sent me a draft in ink or pencil. I hope you'll feel able to do this; but don't hesitate to refuse, if it's too much of a demand on your time. *I've* hesitated about asking you, and have only done so at the printer's request.

I think you would like Cassidy: He's an idealist of a rare type. His ambition is to make enough money so that he can devote himself to the publishing of books that are difficult or impossible to publish through the usual commercial channels!

Thanks for the new poems. I like them all—particularly "Venus Letalis". "A Critic" is good, in a different way. There's a wicked sting in the tail of it.

I have not written any more verse, myself. But the little drawings I enclose might interest you.

Aff.,

Clark

[260] GS to CAS [ALS]

[late October 1922]

Dear Clark:

An honor should always be a pleasure. So yr. preface is already under way. But I had a tooth pulled yesterday, and am now in one of J. Barleycorn's specially assorted hells, with jaw, forehead and belly an-ache. So no more now from

Yr. affectionate

George.

[261] GS to CAS [ALS]

[Bohemian Club
San Francisco]

Oct. 28th, 1922.

Dear Clark:

For two weeks I've had one hell of a time with a tooth, before and after pulling, and have been unable to write more than my signature. The pain has just quit, and I'll do the preface in the morning, hoping I'm not too late.

Yours ever,   George.

[P.S.] Thanks for those drawings!

[262] GS to CAS [ALS]

[29 October 1922]

Dear Clark:

Here's the preface—brief, it is true: but it seems to me I can "say more by saying less."

Verify that "misty mid-region."[1] I think it's "misty" and not "mystic." And let me have a proof of this and of the rest of the book when they're ready.

Yours affectionately,

George.

[Enclosures: "The Wings of Beauty," "Long Island Pebbles."]

1. Poe, "Ulalume" (1847), l. 7: "In the misty mid region of Weir." GS is referring to an erroneous citation of the Poe line in his preface to *EC;* it was not corrected (see Appendix, p. 290).

[263] CAS to GS [ALS]

Auburn, Cal.,
Nov. 1st, 1922

Dear George:
                    Thanks for the preface, which is a jewel of its kind! It was unnecessary to say more; one's poems have to stand for themselves, anyway.

I don't know when the d——d book will be ready. My printer swears the job will be done by the 20th of November. But I'll thank my stars if it's out in time to catch the holiday trade.

I have just had the "flu", or something very similar in effect; also, a violent attack of neuralgia at the same time. So I can sympathize with what you must have suffered from that tooth! . . . However, I'm a tough subject; I'm all right to-day, except for a sore throat. But I nearly fainted when I tried to get out of bed on Monday.

The poems are all good, especially "The Wings of Beauty," and that stanza in "Long Island Pebbles" beginning "Such globes the vine of sorcery might bear."

Has Loveman sent you his "Twenty-One Letters of Ambrose Bierce?"[1]

Here are some more drawings; also, eight more pages of my book. These are not proofs—only sheets that have been slightly spoiled or marked. I fear the book will have as many misprints as your "Lilith". But most of them are not *my* fault: I can't help it if the linotyper makes a fresh error when I set him to correct an old one!

I'll send you the sheets of the book as fast as I get them; also, a proof of your preface.
                    Aff.,
                         Clark.

1. *Twenty-one Letters of Ambrose Bierce*, ed. Samuel Loveman (Cleveland: George Kirk, 1922), containing AB's letters to Loveman, with an introduction.

[264] GS to CAS [ALS]

[Bohemian Club
San Francisco]

Nov. 3rd, 1922.

Dear Clark:
                    In figuring the date of a book's appearance, I've added, of late years, two months to the publisher's estimate, and not been "far wrong." If you have yours out by Dec. 15th, you'll be doing damned well. Getting out a book is an irritating business.

I'd like to have complete proofs. So far I've only pages 1 to 8 and 25 to 32, and note as follows:

Page 2: isn't it "verm*ei*l"?
          4: "   " "funer*ea*l"?
          8: "   " "*m*oonlight"?
          26: can't you dig up a better word than "enfraught"? It seems too artificial.
Page 31: to use "that is *I*" won't harm the rhyme.
You may have noticed most of these anyhow.

I won't say I care much for the way your printer uses stars—*****. They seem too large, and somewhat misplaced, and often unnecessary.[1]

No—Loveman didn't send me the Bierce letters, and I want them very much. See if you can obtain a copy from him, and then send it to me. He seems to have taken offense, long ago, because I was too lazy to correspond frequently with him, and now gets his revenge by ignoring *me!* Not that it can matter much to either of us. Get me more than one copy, if you can. Bender and Newbegin should have copies.

I'm closing. I want to say what a *magnificent* sonnet "Transcendence" is—surely one of the world's greatest!

Thanks for the drawings. And here's a poem or two more.

Yours ever,

George.

Remember me to the Rev. Dewing!

[Enclosures: unidentified poems.]

1. None of GS's suggested corrections were made. In *EC* the printer used asterisks to represent CAS's punctuational ellipses.

[265] GS to CAS [ALS]

[Bohemian Club
San Francisco]

Nov. 3rd, 1922.

Dear Clark:

I've just come on some pages (10 to 24) of your book. I'd overlooked them on my desk. I have these suggestions:

page 9: use period for colon in 9th line; no dash in 11th.
" 10: why not inset third line of each stanza?
" 11: "transcend*a*nt" is obsolete
" " : make it "wingéd"
" " : no comma after "glooms"
page 13: no comma after "unrecalled"
" 14: can't you find a better word than "olden?" *That* is implied in preceding stanza.
" 15: no comma after "loom"
" 16: use period instead of colon in 11th line
" 18: no dash after "close"
" 21: should not "her" be "thee", in 24th line.
" 22: make it "involvéd"
" " : "Eri*nn*a", not "E*rr*ina"
" 24: I greatly dislike that "marble-plungéd." It sounds forced, obscure and unnatural. The last line of the sonnet is *beautiful.*

I guess that's all for that bunch. But let me say that I think that "Belated Love" is a *very* lovely sonnet. Its last three lines are beyond praise. "Dissonance" is a big sonnet, too.

Oh—one more thing: use no hyphen in "pomegranate," page 23.[1]

I spoke to Leon Gelber, head of the book department of the White House, about you to-day. He'd like to meet you, and will push the sale of your book.

Good-night!

George.

1. None of GS's suggested corrections were made, except that a period follows *glooms* on p. 10. In published copies of *EC* CAS made the correction on p. 22 by hand.

[266] GS to CAS [ALS]

S. F. Nov. 20, 1922.

Dear Clark:

Received the proofs this noon, and find little to draw to your attention. But, for one thing, I don't "get" this capitalization of words after a colon, as in the 4th line on page 41. This occurs also in the 25th line of page 56 and 7th line, page 52. It may be customary, but I can't recall having seen it in *poetry*.

In the next to the last line on page 42, I'm not crazy about "trailing gown." It seems to me rather flat. I think the plain word "raiment" preferable.

On page 45 you use "beloved" (twice) without the accent. That is all right, though you've used it elsewhere *with* the accent. I prefer the latter way. Also, on this page "lilies" is spelt wrongly.

On page 47, the colon at the end of the 3rd line should be reset. And I think a comma is required after "lightly" (10th line.)

Page 49, last line: should be "ecstasy". This word is so often mispelled. [*sic*] I've done it myself.

Page 54, line 28: reset colon.

" 55. I'm just wondering if "Sabbath" couldn't be spelt "Sabboth." Seems to me I've seen it that way; and it looks weirder.

Good luck! And send me some more proofs as soon as they're ready.

George.

[Enclosure:]

Dear Clark:

There were some more printer's errors on the pages you sent, and I see you've caught some of them. If you care to correct others on books you send out, change (page 87) "abru*bt*" and insert "in" on the 4th line from the last, same page. And on page 94, first line, change "cemet*a*ry." That's all I've noticed so far. It's not much.[1]

George.

1. None of GS's suggested corrections were made, except that in published copies of *EC* CAS made the correction on p. 87 by hand.

[267] CAS to GS [ALS]

Auburn, Cal.
Nov. 23rd, 1922

Dear George:

These are finished pages,—not proof-sheets—that I am sending you!

Any alterations that I make now will have to be written in by hand. Sorry I didn't send you the galleys—I had such a h-ll of a time with misspelled words, omitted lines, etc., that I failed to give proper attention to the punctuation. My punctuation is rotten, anyway; but I don't think the linotyper improved it. Also, he repeated errors, and even made fresh ones, in attempting to correct! However, I suppose I am lucky to get this stuff into print at all.

Here is a proof of your preface, which you can send back at leisure. 90 pages of the book are done and folded ready for stitching; but I think it will take at least a fortnight more to finish the job. The binding will be done in Sacramento. . . . I enclose pages 57 to 80.

I have done all the folding myself, to expedite matters!! It's a lot of work; but, even at that, I keep up with the printers, and have time to call on one or two ladies besides.

Most of the blind-pigs in Auburn (eight or nine, at least!) were raided last Sunday and their proprietors consigned to the hoosegow! But they haven't done anything to the boot-leggers, who supply these places with hootch. I heard that one of the local Supervisors had made ten thousand by bootlegging, within the past year!

"Snappy Stories" has accepted a little prose-sketch of mine, entitled "The Flirt."[1] They pay 2 cents a word for prose. Maybe I'll do some more whore-mongering, at that price.

A. Dewing is as well as usual. One of my principal occupations consists in furnishing alibis for him. And occasionally he gets a chance to return the favour!

Affectionately,

Clark

1. The appearance of "The Flirt" in *Snappy Stories* has not been located, but a tearsheet exists among the papers of Genevieve K. Sully.

[268] GS to CAS [ALS]

[Bohemian Club
San Francisco]

Nov. 25th, 1922.

Dear Clark:

At least I won't be able to bother you any more about punctuation! But on page 63, line 23, you'll have to insert an "n" in "wyvers." And in the sixth line of page 59, you break the metre to commit the tautology of "tall" and "Titan." But that last can't be helped now, of course. But in line 23, page 59, you can insert the needed accent in "roofed."[1]

The progress of the book may seem slow to you, but you're getting on with it faster than *I* expected you would. It'll be a pity if you can't get it out for the holiday trade. As soon as you have complete copies for review, don't wait for them to be bound, but send me six for the newspapers and weeklies. And when you've the bound volumes, send me at least fifty immediately, and I'll see that they get into the bookstores, including the Emporium and White House. You'll probably have to follow them up at once with several more fifties: I'm not *sure*. We've no large poetry reading public.

One's tastes change with maturity, and I find myself liking your shorter and simpler poems (mostly the sonnets) best. But "The Hashish-Eater" is nevertheless an astounding creation, easily the most imaginative, *in its way*, in our literature. And even if one find it unpleasant, one isn't ever going to forget it! I want to discuss it with you much more fully, and hope to do so, some day. With ink isn't the way, life being short.

Stay with "Snappy"!

Affectionately,   George.

P.S. Mencken is back at last. As soon as I hear from him again I'll send him one of your poems. The last one I sent to Nathan[2] came back with the excuse that they were greatly overstocked.

George

[P.P.S.] Note change in the preface.

[Enclosure: "To a Stenographer."]

1. None of GS's suggested corrections were made.
2. George Jean Nathan (1882–1958), HLM's coeditor on the *Smart Set*.

[269] CAS to GS [ALS]

Auburn, Cal.
Nov. 26th, 1922

Dear George:

Your letter and the corrected proof of your preface came to-day. The book is going on much faster than I expected,—as you'll see from the sheets that I enclose. Probably I'll have some unbound copies for you by the end of the week. They're printing it faster than I can fold the sheets! The latter is one h-ll of a job.

"Wyvers" was intentional; I've seen the variant somewhere; and, referring to the dictionary, I find that Webster's gives it as alternative with the usual form.

It's good of you to take over the placing of my book with the stores! I thought of writing to several of them . . . I plan to sell the book for two dollars net, and am wondering what commission I should give the booksellers. The volume will cost me about a dollar per copy. It will contain 152 pages of text, and will be bound in a dark-green cloth.

I've written for some copies of the Bierce letters, and will send them to you as soon as they arrive.

"To a Stenographer" is clever!

Affectionately,
Clark.

[270] CAS to GS [ALS]

Auburn, Cal.
Dec. 3rd, 1922

Dear George:

I mailed you six unbound copies of "Ebony and Crystal" last night.

These six were made up from extra sheets, some of which were slightly marked or soiled. 550 were printed, in all.

The book goes to the binders to-morrow. It was impossible to get an **appropriate** binding.

I'll have some bound copies of the book for you by Friday or Saturday. Fifty will probably glut the market. The book **might** have been fairly presentable if the last half hadn't been hurried so much.

> Aff.,
> Clark.

[271] GS to CAS [ALS]

> [Bohemian Club
> San Francisco]
>
> Dec. 9th, 1922.

Dear Clark:

Your sample copies for review came at an evil hour, when I was in bed under a doctor's care, having been "bootlegged" by whiskey sold right here in this club! However, I was out in five days, and am all right again; but it has delayed having the book reviewed by a few days. Anyhow, I've taken it to all five newspapers and to the "Argonaut," making my spiel in each place, and the last review should be in print by the 17th.

The only value of these reviews is to let the dear public know your volume is out. You mustn't take them seriously otherwise, as your poetry is "caviar," and so much out of the prevailing fashion as to seem almost archaic to these reviewers, who can't view art in terms of centuries.

I think you underestimate the sale you'll have here, for with Gelber, Newbegin and Robertson "pushing" the book, as they've promised to, surely it should sell more than fifty copies! You'd better send me 200. Send them to Robertson's.

And tell me what I'm to do about Paul Elder. I'm not going to *leave* any there, for I hear he's in narrow straits, and at the best you'd have a hard time getting your money afterwards. You'd best authorize me to demand payment on delivery. As to what discount you're to give dealers, that's already a matter of custom, to which I advise you to conform, or they "won't play with you." One-third off, I believe. That won't leave you much profit; but such are the facts.

Bender says to send him five copies as soon as possible. That's not many, but he's sure to buy more, before Christmas.

When do I get the Bierce letters? Mencken writes me they're "hollow and polite," and that he's "slating" the book in "Smart Set," which is a pity.[1]

If I've anything more to say, it'll have to be said later.

> Affectionately,   George.

---

1. HLM harshly reviewed *Twenty-one Letters of Ambrose Bierce* in *Smart Set* 70, No. 1 (January 1923): 142.

[272] GS to CAS [ALS]

[Bohemian Club
San Francisco]

Dec. 11th, 1922.

Dear Clark:

I'm hoping you'll not mind this "funning" of the fool in the "Chronicle."[1] After my talk with its managing editor, I had no idea they'd spring any such stuff! But it's not a fiftieth of what I got on "A Wine of Wizardry," and, like that joshing, will be "forgotten in a day." So don't let it irritate you. I expected the "Chronicle" would refer to the book only in their literary columns, and I intended to let the "Examiner" use it as *news*, since they don't have book-reviews. Well, Anderson beat me to it, which is a pity, as now, I fear, Coblentz won't want anything second-hand.[2] And I could have made Coblentz run it decently. Damn all newspapers anyhow! They are dens of hyenas.

I've fixed the other ones, however, and Jones of the "News," Maslin of the "Call" and Douglas of the "Bulletin" will be good Indians—at least I infer so.[3]

No bound volumes have yet arrived, but as soon as they do so I'll shoot them out at the stores. And with the reviews in hand I'll tackle Mrs. Spreckels.

Affly.

George.

1. "San Francisco Poet Treads New Worlds: Earth Fetters Cast Off by Star Rover," *San Francisco Chronicle* (10 December 1922): 59.

2. Anderson (evidently managing editor of the *Chronicle*) is unidentified. Edmond D. Coblentz was managing editor of the *Examiner.*

3. Idwal Jones (1888–1964), Welsh-born American writer and journalist; E. Marshall Maslin, staff reporter at the *San Francisco Chronicle*. For Douglas, see letter 277, n. 1.

[273] CAS to GS [ALS]

Auburn, Cal.,
Dec. 13th, 1922

Dear George:

I've only received a few copies from the binders so far, but will probably get the rest in a day or two, and will send you a bunch of them in care of Robertson as quickly as possible. In the meanwhile, I am sending you a copy for yourself. You will note that the book has no fly-leaves, in addition to its other eccentricities! The printer only allowed for one at each end, and apparently it never occur[r]ed to anyone that the binders would have to paste these onto the cover!

I am also sending you the Bierce letters. Kirk, the publisher, only sent me two of them, though I **thought** I ordered three. I'll send the other to Bender. These two are about all my purse will stand, anyway, (they're $2.00 apiece) so if I get one for Newbegin, somebody else will have to pay for it. I insist on **giving** the other two.

The Chronicle's official jester is a fool in more senses than one. I don't mind. I hope, however, that some of the others will be fairly decent.

Aff.,

Clark.

[274] GS to CAS [ALS]

Dec. 15th[, 1922]

Dear Clark:

My words surely didn't fall on deaf ears in this case. I am writing Todd to thank him, and suggest that you do the same. It's really a splendid notice, much better than I expected he'd give.[1] I am sending you four more copies by 2nd class mail. George.—

[Enclosure:]

Dear Clark:

Will send you some more "Bulletins" later.

G.

1. Morton Todd, "Clark Ashton Smith's New Volume 'Ebony and Crystal' Marks Another Stage in the Development of a California Genius," *Argonaut* (16 December 1922): 387–88.

[275] GS to CAS [ALS]

[Bohemian Club
San Francisco]

Dec. 15th, 1922.

Dear Clark:

I'm glad to find you taking so sensibly the already-forgotten yawp of that Yahoo on the "Chronicle." I've registered my protest, and it seems that Anderson (managing editor) actually thought he was doing you a favor, by running the notice on the news-section of the paper (*even in that shape*) rather than on the "literary" page! They go on the principle that it's better to be joshed than not advertised at all; and they're not allowed to do the advertising unless they throw you, in a sense, to the lions—or rather the hyenas of the mob.

Well, it's only a fraction of what the poor old Wine of Wizardry got, and I've persuaded Coblentz (managing editor) to run it as news again in the Examiner, though it's warmed-over news now.[1] And it'll be done in a dignified manner, as will all the other reviews. Of course I can't tell how the reviewers, despite my talks with them, will take the book. Probably some of them won't care greatly for it, as they're addicted to modern verse rather than to pure poetry. Anyhow, one is not to take reviewers very seriously. "They who can, do; they who can't, teach." Or preach. Are you sending copies for review to eastern papers or magazines? Of all the "Sails and Mirage" that Robertson sent east, I got notice only in the "Bookman."[2] I suppose they review books published only by their advertisers. I can send one to "Smart Set" for you; but Mencken is not likely to care for your sort of work. He didn't review "Sails and Mirage" at all.

Thanks for "Ebony and Crystal"! Also for Loveman's book. I was surprised to find Bierce referring so often to me; but perhaps I was the only friend that he and L. had in common. I think L's preface is a good deal too cocksure for so young a writer; but he's in the swim with that. (Not that he overestimates Bierce; but some of the others aren't so bad.)

I'm sorry you insist on paying for the Loveman book. I'll have to get back at you some other way!

Don't forget to send me the mis[t]letoe and toyon, as usual. And hurry up with the consignment of "Ebony and Crystal!"

Affectionately yours,

George.

[P.S.] Bender says to mail him five copies of "Ebony and Crystal."

1. An unsigned notice did appear in the *Examiner:* "Boy Publishes More Poems," *San Francisco Examiner* (17 December 1922): 20.

2. An unsigned review of *SM* appeared in the *Bookman* 56, No. 1 (September 1922): 104. Actually, *SM* did receive another review in the East: William Rose Benét, "Sterling's Latest Poems," *Literary Review (New York Evening Post)* (11 March 1921): 487.

[276] CAS to GS [ALS]

Auburn, Cal.,
Dec. 17th, 1922

Dear George:

The d———d binders only sent up fifty of my books in the first consignment, and I needed most of these to fill advance orders, many of them local. I didn't receive any more till yesterday afternoon, and tried hard to get fifty of them ready in time to send off. But it took hours to number and autograph them, and correct the worst of the misprints, and the express-office had closed by the time I had them boxed up. They'll go down Monday morning, and I'll get off another fifty Monday afternoon. I'm addressing them to you in care of Robertson. I'm sorry about the delay; but, as you see, it was not my fault . . . Certainly, I'll authorize you to collect on delivery! I've paid my printer a hundred dollars, but I still owe him about four hundred more!

I was delighted with the Argonaut review—I hadn't expected anything half so intelligent and sympathetic from a San Francisco reviewer. **Thanks** for the extra copies! I'll write a letter of thanks to Mr. Todd.

I'm not sending any copies east, except to places where I **know** they will be reviewed. One will go to Canada, for a Professor Allison of the University of Manitoba, who reviewed The "S.-T." two or three years ago in a string of Canadian newspapers.[1] He was very enthusiastic. Also, a new correspondent and admirer of mine, Alfred Galpin, Jr., has been commissioned to write me up in "The New Republic!" Galpin (who is a college student at Madison, Wis.) must have a "pull" somewhere! Anyway, he is clever, and very appreciative, and will probably do the job quite well.[2]

No, I wouldn't bother Mencken with the book. I can't think of any one in New York who would be likely to do anything for it, with the possible exception of Beni Casseres.[3] He should be the man to appreciate it. Can you get me his address? . . . I haven't much use for "The Bookman." The editor wrote, asking me to submit some poems, and sent them back with the usual printed rejection-slip, after holding them for two or three months.

Don't forget to send me the "Examiner's" write-up! They may not put it in the "rural" edition of the paper. The "Chronicle's" little send-off was apparently confined to the city edition.

Affectionately,

Clark.

P.S. I'll send some mistletoe and toyon during the week.

1. Prof. William Allison's review has not been located.

2. The review of *EC* and *ST* by Galpin (1901–1983), a protégé of Lovecraft, appeared as "Echoes from Beyond Space," *United Amateur* 24, No. 1 (July 1925): 3–4 (as by "Consul Hasting"); rpt. in Lovecraft's *Letters to Alfred Galpin*, ed. S. T. Joshi and David E. Schultz (New York: Hippocampus Press, 2003), pp. 273–74.

3. Benjamin De Casseres (1873–1945), American critic and associate of CAS. See letter 295, n. 2. He later wrote the preface to CAS's *SP*.

[277] GS to CAS [ALS]

[Bohemian Club
San Francisco]

Tuesday, 8 A.M. [19 December 1922]

Dear Clark:

The books had not arrived up to five o'clock last night, but are here now, I doubt not; so I'll go down at once and distribute them. Elder is the only one I'll dare work the "cash on delivery" stunt on.

Here are some more "Bulletins." I dare say you'll find parts of Douglas' review severe, but when you're fifty you'll realize their justice. You have now been a writer for about twelve years (I think) and should be forming a style of your own. That's all he means.[1]

Idwal Jones' review has not yet appeared, but it ought to be out to-day—"Daily News."[2] That's somewhat of a proletarian sheet, but all the cognoscenti read it, as it tells the truth to a greater extent than the other papers.

You'd better send Todd an inscribed copy, as the unbound one I gave him is hardly adequate.

Don't forget those toyons!

Aff.

George.

1. [George Sterling,] "Recent Books of Fact and Fiction," *San Francisco Bulletin* (19 December 1922): 8. George Douglas was the paper's book reviewer, but GS wrote the review. See Appendix, pp. 290–91.

2. Jones's review, if published, has not been found.

[278] CAS to GS [ALS]

Auburn, Cal.,
Dec. 20th, 1922.

Dear George:

Hope you got the books. There were only 47 in the last box—a total of 97 in all. If the stores want any more, they'd better write to me—I didn't send any more this time, since it would be a lot of work for you to distribute them—more of a job than you expected, probably.

Thanks for the "Bulletin" reviews. I've no great quarrel with Douglas, since he really admits more (in spite of all his strictures,) than the others did.

I wrote to Morton Todd, and will certainly be glad to send him an inscribed copy. I have already received several orders from people who referred to his review. F. O'Brien[1] has just written me for five copies.

I am sending you a copy for Ernest Stent, since I don't know his address.

Affectionately,

Clark.

1. Frederick O'Brien (1869–1932), a Boston writer who later edited some CA newspapers. Author of *White Shadows in the South Seas* (1919), a book about his travels in the South Seas.

[279] GS to CAS [ALS]

[Bohemian Club
San Francisco]

Dec. 21st, 1922.

Dear Clark:

Your books didn't come till yesterday noon! It's a pity they weren't out three weeks ago: so many do their Christmas buying early. I've taken ten to the White House and ten to Newbegin (all they'd take to start in with), and shall try to have the Emporium use some.

I received the good news yesterday that Mrs. Clark is here. The first chance I get, I'll see if she won't join Crocker and Phelan. I saw the latter here in the club, yesterday, and told him of the "Argonaut" review; he said he'd look it up.

I told Bender you were hard up, and am sure you'll hear from him.

Getting out a book is a wearisome and thankless task, as you've doubtless found out. If we were sane we'd put it up to our heirs and assigns; but poets aren't sane!

I've seen no reviews in the "Call" or "Daily News" yet, and must investigate. They were promised.

Here's wishing you a wet holiday season!

Affectionately,   George.

[280] CAS to GS [ALS]

Auburn, Cal.,
Dec. 22nd, 1922

Dear George:

Got your letter this morning. I, too, am very sorry the book wasn't ready several weeks ago. Anyhow, I'm selling a few copies every day, myself; and I make a lot more money on these than I would have got from the booksellers. People continue to write here for the book.

Yesterday was a wild occasion! Hope you didn't mind Mrs. Lee and I ringing you up! We were both gorgeously stewed, from mixing gin and whiskey on an empty stomach. It was a crazy stunt,—for a small town, at least—since Mrs. L. will have to go and pay the telephone people for that particular item, so they won't charge it to her husband in the monthly account! We also rang up Leo Mihan.

Andrew is going to the city in a day or two, and I suppose he'll see you.

Hope you got the toyon and mistletoe. The berries ripened too early, and weren't so nice this year as usual.

I have a "hang-over" from yesterday.

No more now, from

Yours affectionately,
Clark

[281] GS to CAS [ALS]

[Bohemian Club
San Francisco]

Dec. 23rd, 1922.

Dear Clark:

I was very sorry not to be able to accept Mrs. Lee's generous invitation to come up to Auburn; but it was quite impossible, what of all my various engagements, and entanglements, here. Please thank her for me again. I couldn't hear distinctly over the wire, my hearing being none too good as it is, and perhaps I missed some of the things she said. And thanks for the greenery, too!

I caught Phelan in here, Thursday night, and put him to reading the "Argonaut" review. I must send one to Mrs. Clark, whom I hope to see before long.

I'm glad O'Brien "came through". I'd spoken to him, as I shall speak to many others, about the book. But it is necessarily such an exotic to the many that I don't dare ask a lot of my acquaintances to buy it! Yesterday, the White House, Robertson and Newbegin reported "fair" sales.

Merry Christmas!

Geo.

[P.S.] I gave Stent his copy.

[282] GS to CAS [ALS]

[Bohemian Club
San Francisco]

Dec. 27th, 1922.

Dear Clark:

I could tell, by your voices, that you and the fair one had a bit of a "glow" on, that day, and it is my regret that I could not have shared it. However, I've been on the wagon, all this month, and must so remain if I'm to do what I want to do—make a living, and remain an adequate lover!

I've not been down-town for three days, so don't know how the book is going. It will go, though, in time, though the 3rd edition of the "Testimony" has lasted 15 years already.

Mencken gives Loveman a pretty hot roast in the current "Smart Set," but I must say that it's not entirely undeserved. There's nothing in the letters to have warranted such a fuss having been made over them, i.e., publication.

In this connection, let me warn you to beware of the indiscriminate lavishness of

L's praise. The critical commendation of anyone under the age of forty is almost value-less. When you're as old as I am you'll see what I'm driving at.

I've written Wilkes for De C's address, but have had no reply. Probably W. is already in N. Y. He is the most unreliable of mortals, anyway.

Affectionately,   George.

[283] CAS to GS [ALS]

Auburn, Cal.,
Jan. 3rd, 1923.

Dear George:

Here's the latest review of my book. It appeared simultaneously in the Fresno "Bee" and the Sacramento "Bee", and was written by the assistant editor of the former, William Foster Elliot, who is also a poet and has written some uncommonly good stuff.[1]

No news at this end. I had a dull time during the holidays (everybody's husband was home, not to mention the children!) I think I'll begin looking for a childless widow—or a divorcee!

Andrew is just back from the city. He tried to see you, but you were out.

I wrote a sonnet the other day, but it seems pretty rotten. Maybe I'll send it in my next, if I can tinker it up a little.

I feel half-sick just at present: my nerves have gone to pieces, temporarily at least.

Aff.,
                     Clark.

1. [William Foster Eliot,] "News of Books: A California Poet. Clark Ashton Smith Reveals Unusual Talents in New Volume," *Sacramento Bee* (30 December 1922): 26; *Fresno Bee* (30 December 1922) 2C.

[284] GS to CAS [ALS]

[Bohemian Club
San Francisco]

Jan. 16th, 1923.

Dear Clark:

Here's one of O'Day's puffs, more complimentary to me than to you![1]

I return the "Bee" man's review, which is by much the most discerning and adequate of any you have (so far as I know) yet received. I could wish I'd written it for the preface of the book.

You got it to S. F. too late, as you're aware, to have much of a "Christmas sale," but it ought to have a sure and steady one. Remember that the 3rd edition of the "Testimony," issued 16 years ago, is not yet exhausted, and it was praised by a much bigger critic than any who has, so far, come across "Ebony and Crystal." But I go on drawing folks' attention to it, and you ought at least to be able to pay the printer, some day. I admit that this is no very gaudy prospect; but your Muse is for the few, yours being "music that scares the profane."[2]

I've been on the joyless wagon since Dec. 3rd, and emit occasional verses. Here's a poem that "Scribner's" gave me $50. for—and I was about ten minutes a-writing of it, to please a young woman! The ways of the editors are five times more mysterious than those of Providence. I dare say that this one accepted some girl's free-verse drivel within the same hour.

Jones promises to send me his review of "E. and C." as soon as the "News" runs it; and I'm calling again on the "Call" man in a day or so. The world is too much with me, as usual.[3] I still have my mornings, though!

Affectionately,   George.

[P.S.] Did I tell you May G. got married—to a man almost as old as I?

[Enclosure: "Wet Beaches."]

1. [Edwin F. O'Day], "The Clubman: Men and Women in the Mirror: A Lesson in Words." *Oakland Post-Enquirer,* (6 January 1923), p. 24 (unsigned).

2. Algernon Charles Swinburne, "Dolores" (1866), l. 198.

3. William Wordsworth, "The World Is Too Much with Us" (1807).

[285] CAS to GS [ALS]

Auburn, Cal.
Feb. 9th, 1923.

Dear George:

I hope you don't think I have fallen off the map! But I seem to have had nothing that was worth putting into a letter. I hope things are not so dull at your end of the line as they are here.

I haven't heard from anybody in S. F. None of the booksellers have deigned to write me, so I presume that my book is something of a "frost." There are no letters of appreciation, even, except from people to whom I have sent copies. Publishing poetry is a thankless business.

I haven't written anything, myself; but here is a story sent me by a correspondent of mine, H. P. Lovecraft, who is a friend of Loveman's. He writes in the Poe-Bierce-Dunsany style, and his best things are astoundingly imaginative. Please return "Dagon", and tell me what you think of it. The stuff is hard to publish, of course. One of Lovecraft's stories, "The Lurking Fear", is appearing as a serial in a magazine called "Home Brew"—which is somewhat on the order of "The Whiz Bang!" The editor (through Lovecraft) commissioned me to do eight drawings for the story—the first drawings that I've had published.[1]

My father is "laid out" with a lame back at present; and I'm suffering from eye-strain, and a bad case of the "blues." Life doesn't look very rosy: my "girls" are all married, and their husbands all have me on the black-list!

Phelan sent me his book, "Travel and Comment." I haven't read much of it (I've had to spare my eyes lately) but it looks interesting.[2]

Aff.,

Clark

1. Lovecraft, "Dagon," *Vagrant* No. 11 (November 1919): 23–29; rpt. *Weird Tales* 2, No. 3 (October 1923): 23–25. Lovecraft wrote "The Lurking Fear" for serialization in *Home Brew,*

a humor magazine edited by George Julian Houtain and E. Dorothy Houtain; it appeared in the issues of January–April 1923, with illustrations by CAS. CAS refers to *Capt. Billy's Whiz Bang* (1920f.), which described itself as "America's magazine of wit, humor and filosophy."

2. James D. Phelan, *Travel and Comment* (1923). Phelan quotes CAS's "Psalm" in the final section of his book.

[286] GS to CAS [ALS]

[Bohemian Club
San Francisco]

Feb. 13ᵗʰ, 1923.

Dear Clark:

I was about to write *you*, to ask if you had heard anything from Mrs. Adolph Spreckels. Despairing of ever running into her on the street, I finally wrote her a long letter, about 16 days ago, giving the facts in your case and enclosing the "Argonaut" review. Now I see you've heard nothing at all from her. It's shameful, as I intimated yesterday to Phelan! Our local rich are more indifferent to the artist than the wealthy of any other community, I think, though inclined to notice those whose work has intrinsic *value*, such as painters and sculptors. But you've heard from Armsby, have you not? He wrote me to that effect.

This story you enclose is very well written, and I enjoyed it decidedly. Its main fault is that it's an echo of former tales, *without* surpassing them, as *you*, in a similar manner, surpass Baudelaire (in English) and me. But that cannot, of course, be helped.

I've a suggestion to make—a valuable one, I think. The tale is disappointing at its climax, because there's not enough detail, enough suspense, enough action. It's all over in ten seconds, like a rabbit's amour. My advice is that he have the monster uprear, approach the monolith with horrible sounds of worship, and prostrate itself. Then have the mire quake and Dagon fall upon the monster, slaying it, just as other heads of its kind rise from the slime . . . .¹

Yes, "The Muse is an ungrateful bitch," as Bierce long ago wrote me.² It's the price you pay for appealing to the aloof few, who carry their aloofness into their correspondence.

Don't you think you ought to have your eyes examined? You probably need glasses.

Let me hear from you at your own convenience.

Yours ever,   George.

[P.S.] 72 days on the wagon now warrant my immediate canonizaton!

1. CAS conveyed this comment by GS to Lovecraft, who then cited it in a letter to Edwin Baird, editor of *Weird Tales*, with the comment that "poets should stick to their sonneteering" (published in the issue of October 1923). Lovecraft, who also criticized a story by Vincent Starrett in his letter, was mortified that Baird published the remarks, saying in a letter to Frank Belknap Long: "Grandpa'll have to be careful what he writes this Baird person, for the latter seems to have the repeating habit to a very alarming degree. If Starrett and Sterling don't start out after their Grandpa Theobald with stilettos and automatics, it'll be merely be-

cause they don't believe in bothering to swat small skeeters." *Selected Letters: 1911–1924,* ed. August Derleth and Donald Wandrei (Sauk City, WI: Arkham House, 1965), p. 254.

2. "I trust, however, you will not abandon the Muse, ungrateful bitch that she is." AB to GS (28 April 1900; ms., New York Public Library).

[287] CAS to GS [ALS]

Auburn, Cal.
March 7th, 1923—

Dear George:

No, I haven't heard from Mrs. Spreckels, nor from Armsby, either, though I have the letter you forwarded me, in which he announced his willingness to remit.

Thanks for the copy of "Laughing Horse." There were good things in it, especially the quotation from one of Bierce's letters.[1]

I haven't any news—at least, none that's good. My mother has been very ill for weeks with some sort of stomach trouble, and is likely to be laid up for several weeks more. And my best lady-friend (the one who rang you up at Christmas) has been sick three-fourths of the time lately. As for me, I'm trying to write verse and prose-fillers, in the hope that some of them, at least, will sell. I'm doing it absolutely without inspiration, with lacerated nerves and a sodden brain.

I haven't heard anything from the booksellers. I suppose the binding of my book (not to mention the printing) was enough to discourage the average purchaser.

This isn't a very cheerful letter. But, as you see, I've nothing very cheerful to write about.

Here are some of my latest verses.

Aff.,
Clark.

[Enclosures: "Don Juan Sings," "Song from 'The Fugitives.'"]

1. *Laughing Horse* No. 6 (1923) featured Willard Johnson's review of *The Letters of Ambrose Bierce* by (pp. [26–28]), which consisted chiefly of a long quotation from one of the letters. The issue also had GS's "Eidolon" (p. [18]) and CAS's "The Litany of the Seven Kisses" (p. [19]).

[288] GS to CAS [ALS]

[Bohemian Club
San Francisco]

Mch. 9th, 1923.

Dear Clark:

That's too bad about Armsby. His second letter to me, just before he left for Paris, asserted that he'd seen to it that "something was to go to" you. As for Mrs. S., she is shameless—though maybe she has a *sense* of shame, as she seems ashamed to reply to my letter. Some day I'm going to "do" an article on our Californian million-aires, who are easily the meanest on earth. Some of them will buy pictures and statues, *as furniture;* but otherwise they know nothing, and care as much, about art. Little Albert

Bender's worth the whole vile bunch of them. Well, I still have hopes of Armsby, for it was his own proposition.

I tried, a few days ago, to get T. Crocker to do more for you than his measly $10. a month, but found him unsympathetic. The next day he blew in several thousands on a pink ball at the Fairmont!

Are you sure that you're mother hasn't carcinoma? If there is no disciple of Abrams nearer to Auburn, Dr. McCubbin of Sacramento could give diagnosis and cure. Abrams is being hotly attacked nowadays in the magazines, but his enemies are wrong, not he. America's god, H. Ford, is the last to take a hand in hitting him.[1]

I'll tell Newbegin, the White House and Robertson to remit.

I like both these poems—the Don Juan one the more, as being maturer. If you'll send me a better copy I'll sell it to Mencken for you—if it's not sold already.

I'm now over three months on the wagon. Here are some of the sad results. Am at an essay just now.

Yours for the Second Coming,

George.

[P.S.] My essay is on the cosmos! Wait!

[Enclosures: unidentified poems.]

1. Henry Ford's paper, the *Dearborn Independent*, published several attacks on Abrams, including an article by A. Francis Morton, Jr., "The Latest Swindle: 'Psyching the Jack' Charlatan's New Game Prospers" (24 March 1923).

[289] CAS to GS [ALS]

Auburn, Cal.

March 15th, 1923

Dear George:

Thanks for the poems! There is no one else on earth who can equal you for quality combined with such amazing productiveness. I like all of them.

I sent my "Don Juan" to "Ainslee's." If they return it, I'll be glad to let you send it to Mencken for me. But, naturally, I would rather have 50¢ per line from "Ainslee's" than two-bits from "Smart Set"! The former price is little enough for poetry.

I have written at least one poem per day since the first of the month! I only hope that one out of four will prove salable! I'll be pretty short for money if they don't.

My mother is on her feet again, though none too strong.

"Ebony and Crystal" seems to have raised no end of a ruction locally. The poor old "Psalm" on p. 126 played havoc with the village proprieties.[1] I didn't know so many brick-bats were coming my way, till lately . . . I suppose that particular poem was the only one that the villagers could even partially understand. Your millionaires are princely, compared to what I am up against here in Auburn.

I enclose a few verses. It's not easy to go on working without hope and without inspiration.

Yours ever,

Clark.

[Enclosures: "Contradiction," "Dream," "On the Canyon-Side," "Semblance," "We Shall Meet," "The Witch with Eyes of Amber."]

1. "A Psalm to the Best Beloved" contains strongly erotic imagery. It appears on p. 121 of *EC*.

[290] GS to CAS [ALS]

[Bohemian Club
San Francisco]

Apr. 6th, 1923.

Dear Clark:

As usual, I find myself surprised at the swift passage of time, as I realize I've owed you a letter for nearly a month. Well, I hope time goes as fast for you.

I've completed, as least in the rough, my essay on the cosmos, and think you'll like it. I can see no logical escape from "the implications of infinity" that I call attention to in the writing.[1] It's now being typed, very slowly, and I won't be able to have it out as a pamphlet for over two months, I fear.

I like all these poems you send, and most of all the beautiful "On the Canyon-Side." You bid fair to be as successful at the human as at the demoniac. There seems to me to be no flaw in this poem.

"Contradiction" is mature, too. I don't see why you should feel depressed when you can do such work. Of course, your surroundings are not of the happiest; but you've only a few years to wait, and you'll be free to come and go as you please. Marriage will be your only pitfall, and you seem wise enough to avoid that.

"Semblance" is another "grown-up" poem, and in your best mood. When I note how much *wiser* you are than I was at your age, it makes me "smile a little sadly."[2] I was of slow growth, and have hardly matured yet—at least I hope I haven't!

Baudelaire (as translated) has nothing better than "We Shall Meet." I don't like that "flaffing," though—it seems an absurd word *in itself*. I'd keep off the ultra-obsolete.

And to conclude, let me say I like "The Witch with Eyes of Amber" immensely! A most luring and imaginative thing! I should think Mencken would fall on it with a whoop. Anyway, Poe would, were he now the editor of "Smart Set." You are not inferior to him at such stuff, though it is the world's way to give most of the credit to the *pioneer* of new styles of poetry. And even *he* doesn't get it while he lives! A delightful scheme of things.

I'm still in eruption with various verse, and shall be, I suppose, so long as I stay on the wagon (it's over four months now!) I've no copies of what I'd like most to send, but what I have may amuse for a few minutes.

Give my devoirs to your fair lady, and say I'm still sad because I couldn't join you in the holiday season. She should be very proud of the poems you write to her, even though you write for the poem, not its object.

Affectionately yours.   George.

[Enclosures: "A Lumberjack Yearns," other unidentified poems.]

1. The phrase "implications of infinity" does not occur in GS's essay "Pleasure and Pain,"

but is an encapsulation of its central idea (the infinity of the universe and humanity's consequent difficulty of fashioning meaningful criteria for existence).

2. Sara Teasdale (1884–1933), "Marianna Alcoforando" (1911), l. 43. GS corresponded occasionally with Teasdale.

[291] CAS to GS [ALS]

Auburn, Cal.,
May 10th, 1923.

Dear George:

Forgive me for permitting your letter to lie unanswered so long. I've been horribly discouraged and depressed, and didn't want to inflict the mood on anybody. But things look a little brighter now,—so I can clean up my correspondence without turning it into a jeremiad.

Your poems were all excellent, as usual. The "Lumberjack" poem certainly has a wallop! I'm glad you found something in my verses. I can't sell any of them to the magazines, and am letting the "Auburn Journal" print them.[1] I'll enclose a few new ones—I haven't done very much lately. Probably I could turn out several times as much, if I had more stimulus, more incentive. Discouragement is my worst enemy. You'd have to live here in Auburn for awhile, to realise just *why* I get discouraged.

Did I tell you that Armsby remitted? . . . I'm going to pick fruit again this summer, and will earn a hundred or two at that. The work is damnably monotonous, but I prefer it to working in an office or a store: I can always get an afternoon off, if I have a date with somebody.

I haven't seen my lady-friend (the one who rang you up) for some time: She's had her father on her hands for the past fortnight. Methinks I'll begin hunting for an orphan! I'm tired of having to watch my step when I go calling.

I've heard nothing from the booksellers. But I've managed to pay my printer the major part of what I owe him. The entire bill was $556, of which I still owe $180. That isn't so bad!

Affectionately,
Clark.

[Enclosures: "The Love-Potion," "The Secret," "Song of Cartha."]

1. CAS had begun "Clark Ashton Smith's Column" in *AJ* on 5 April 1923, in part to pay off the printer's debt for *EC*. The column contained a miscellany of verse and prose epigrams.

[292] GS to CAS [ALS]

[Bohemian Club
San Francisco]

June 5th, 1923.

Dear Clark:

Though I've my usual no-news, it's about time I wrote, if only to tell you how much these three lyrics ("Love-Potion," "Song of Cartha" and "The Secret") please me. Pure poetry, or I'm pure too! No one living can do such things better than you. At times I'm tempted to join the chorus of baser souls and beg you to begin to disavow your more archaic nouns, verbs and adjectives. But probably you'd not bother about the folk whom *they* bother—*I*'m not included in the number.

I trust you're less depressed than when you wrote. Don't let public indifference to poetry surprise or irritate you. It has always been, must always be. And remember that you're only a kid yet. Wait till you're 53! And at 53 I'm having "the time of my life." It beats "the glorious years of youth" all hollow.

I hope finances are not troubling you too much. A friend lately told me that Mrs. Spreckels said that she *had* "done something" for you. Is that true? I'm of a mind to doubt it.

I'm surprised that you've been able to pay so much to your publisher, and am delighted to find you want to be so honest in money-matters. You'll find that nothing else "pays" so well—to be prosaic. I'm amazed that you were able to pay so much. It looks as though you *did* sell a lot of the books. Remember that they'll all go in time. If ever I get a wad of bills, I'll buy a few hundred myself.

My own "Selected Poems" seem to be going well, as they've had good publicity. I didn't send you the book, for I have to pay $1.^{33} each for them, and you've seen everything in it. If you'll review the book for your Auburn paper, I'll have Holt & Co. send them one, and you may keep that—I suppose. Robertson ordered only five of the book! He sold them the day they came, and had to telegraph for more. The same thing happened to Gelber, who is now in business for himself at 331 Sutter St. Gelber ordered ten, though. I hear that the Sather Gate Book Shop sold 100 in less than a week. But that's only hear-say.

I'll enclose a few poems. Haven't written anything to matter for over a month, as I'm writing some real-estate ads. for my cousin! I don't like the work, but he begged so hard I gave in. After all, "I need the money," and the dear world would cheerfully let me starve, as it would you.

Remember me to your sweet friend, and come down here with her some day.

> Yours for the reform of God,
>
> > George.

[Enclosures: unidentified poems.]

[293] CAS to GS [ALS]

> [CLARK ASHTON SMITH
> AUBURN, CALIFORNIA]

> June 23rd, 1923.

Dear George:

No, I have heard nothing from Mrs. Spreckels. But I think I told you that Armsby remitted. And I have earned a few dollars by fruit-picking, so the bean-sack is never quite empty.

Your poems were all excellent, as usual. No one else can keep on turning out good work the way you do. I enclose some more of my own verses: There's no inspiration in them; but they're better than I could have done a few years ago without inspiration. Facility can be acquired, I suppose, if one keeps at it long enough.

There is a new magazine called "Weird Tales", which is publishing hell-raisers that no other periodical would print. They wrote asking me to send in some verse! "Dagon", the tale by H. P. Lovecraft that I showed you some time ago, was accepted by them.

Lovecraft tells me that I am mentioned in Braithwaite's last anthology.[1] Methinks the honour is a dubious one.

My mother is going to a family re-union in Monterey at the end of the month. Probably she will be in S. F. about the second week in July.

I don't know when I will be able to come down. But I don't care much at present: life promises to become a little more amusing than it has been. Perhaps I'll bring a *new* lady-love with me, when I do come, instead of the one you inquire about.

What do you think of the stationery? My printer gave me a whole ream of it for nothing!

Aff.,

Clark.

[Enclosures: "Alienage," "Moments," a clipping ("Clark Ashton Smith's Column" [*AJ*, 3 May 1923] containing "The Love-Potion" and "The Song of Cartha").]

1. CAS's "In Lemuria," "The Infinite Quest," "The Absence of the Muse," "Haunting," and "Rosa Mystica" were cited in "The Yearbook of American Poetry 1922" in William Stanley Braithwaite's *Anthology of Magazine Verse for 1922* (Boston: Small, Maynard, 1923), p. 328.

[294] GS to CAS [ALS]

[Bohemian Club
San Francisco]

June 29th, 1923.

Dear Clark:

These poems are both beautiful, and finely passionate, though I prefer "Alienage." One thing: I fear you'll have to make a change in the second stanza of "Moments". It's almost *comic* at the end—too literal; all one sees is the underwear.[1] The poem is too lovely to have even one flaw in it. This shift of yours from the demoniac and Baudelairian is pleasing; and you'll find lands even fairer beyond the island of Circe.

I hope you do well with "Weird Tales," though I fear they can't, or won't, pay much. However, they can't be much worse than "Smart Set!"

I warned Braithwaite, long ago, to leave me out of his anthologies, so now he merely lists such poems of mine as appear in magazines during his "poetic year." I imagine that's what has happened in your case. He's too pious for your kind of sin-fire! I gave him a bad roasting. Bynner told me, afterward, that he's a humble creature—which made me rather ashamed.

Here's a check for you. I hope you'll not blow it all in on a trip to S. F. with your new girl! Give some to the printer. When Mr. Lathrop returns to S. F. in the autumn, I'll have him join our $10. a month club. Next winter shall be made easier on you.

If you want to write him a letter of thanks, you may send it to me. *Don't* send him your book: he cares for only cheerful verse!

Your stationery is impressive: don't use it when writing your benefactors!

If I can do anything for your mother when she's here, let me know.

Affly.   George.

1. "From all the moments of our love / What moment would I first recall? . . . That hour, when . . . I found the fruits of my desire / Amid your garments' disarray?" (ll. 1–2, 5, 7–8). CAS did not revise it for subsequent publication.

[295] CAS to GS [ALS]

[CLARK ASHTON SMITH
AUBURN, CALIFORNIA]

July 16th, 1923.

Dear George:

Thanks for that extremely welcome hundred! I enclose a little note for Mr. Lathrop.

You may have seen my mother by this time. She has been in Oakland and S. F. for the past week. She writes me that Robertson has sold all the copies of "E. & C." that he had on hand.

Not much doing up here—except work. I picked plums all of last week. Yesterday, I went on a little jamboree with a lady-friend, but we had nothing stronger than Chesterfields and coffee.

"Weird Tales" accepted two of my poems.[1] They pay on publication; but I can stand that, when they take stuff no other magazine would print.

I sent "Ebony and Crystal" to de Casseres, who wrote me a nice letter about it. He intends to review the book in "Arts and Decoration", along with your "Selected Poems."[2] He wanted to be remembered to you.

I'll be glad to review "Selected Poems" for the Auburn Journal, if the publishers care to send them a copy. The review won't be worth much from an advertising standpoint. . . . I'd like very much to have the book.[3]

I'll see you some day; but I don't know just when. Probably not before September.

Affectionately,
Clark.

P.S. The stationery didn't cost me a cent; but of course, I don't use it for writing to benevolent millionaires; and I don't use it for billets-doux, either.

[Enclosures: "Change," "A Valediction."]

1. "Duality" (as "The Garden of Evil") and "Moon-Dawn" (as "The Red Moon"). The magazine's policy initially was to publish no poetry, but relented at Lovecraft's recommendation that it publish CAS's poems. It ultimately published many of CAS's poems and stories.

2. "And a Little Book Shall Lead Them," *Art and Decoration* 19 (August 1923): 47.

3. No such review ever appeared.

[296] GS to CAS [ALS]

[Bohemian Club
San Francisco]

Aug. 20th, 1923.

Dear Clark:

As usual, this letter is long since due, and written now mostly to thank you for the *very beautiful* lyrics, for I've no news.

Indeed, they are lovely, lovelier than you think, I imagine, especially "Change." I'm glad to see you leaving behind the demoniac, which you have done more justice to than any other poet, and turning to more important things, which include love. These lyrics are heart-piercing. How Bierce would have exclaimed over "A Valediction!" You came too late for him: he would have cared more for your work than for mine—at least my later work.

As soon as I'm out of my present state of financial zero, I'll buy and send you one of those books. Maybe when you're down here. By the way, I expect to be absent a good part of Sept., and again in Oct.

Let me know when de C. reviews our books. He should be especially sympathetic with *your* work.

I didn't go to see the grove-play. Too poor, and also, I didn't want to get to drinking. I've done my share!

Affectionately,   George.

[P.S.] I've written practically nothing for over three months.

[297] CAS to GS [ALS]

[CLARK ASHTON SMITH
AUBURN, CALIFORNIA]

Nov. 4th, 1923.

Dear George:

This is an unusual lapse even for me—it must be two or three months since I received your last letter. But I guess you'll forgive me: there has been little or nothing to write about, anyway.

De Casseres' review came out in September. It was very "brief mention", though favourable enough to *me*, as you surmised. I'll enclose it with this. . . . I sent a copy of "E. & C." to Arthur Symons some time ago, in care of his London publisher. I hope it will reach him in one of his lucid intervals.

I have not written any verse this fall, with the exception of the enclosed ("Barrier.") Latterly, I've amused myself by making a lot of epigrams, and am letting the Auburn Journal print the milder ones.[1] Many people think the stuff might easily be syndicated; certainly, I hope so: it's about the only *possible* way for me to ever make any money—unless I marry a rich wife. And I've known too many married women to think highly of marriage.

Life isn't so rotten as it was, apart from eyestrain, and having to milk the cow for my nearest neighbour's widow! I seem to be almost popular, of late, with the Auburn ladies. There's nothing like having a bad reputation!—at least, for a poet.

You **did** give me a copy of your "Selected Poems:" my mother brought it home from the city with her. The selection was excellent, for general purposes: Doubtless not nearly so many people would buy the selection I would make.

Andrew spoke of meeting you one night in the city . . . I'll *never* have a chance to come down again, unless I syndicate my "column"!

Aff.,

Clark.

[Enclosure: "The Barrier."]

1. Gathered in *The Devil's Notebook: Collected Epigrams and Pensées* (1990).

[298] GS to CAS [ALS]

[Bohemian Club
San Francisco]

Nov. 28th, 1923.

Dear Clark:

It was good to hear from you at last. I was beginning to suspect you'd been given six months in the city jail, without privilege of corresponding. That would be the natural result on Auburn of your epigrams, some of which are good enough to sting the booboisie.

Your picture shows you're maturing fast. I'd not be surprised if you grew into a regular "white hope" by the time you're 35. Ay di mi! I'll be 54, this Saturday! I wish God had a longer start on me.

I had a good laugh over De Casseres' review (?). He couldn't be farther wrong, for poetry was never farther from being dead than it is to-day. And for that matter, I wish folks would *not* "want to know" me after reading my verses! An uncomfortable number do want to, as evidenced by letters and the spoken word.

The trouble with De C. is that he's blasé, all burnt out, from a lifetime of drunkenness. For a long space of years he had to have a *quart* of whiskey in bed before he could get up. It has made him *numb* to all but ferocious stimulation, to the sharpest swords of the bizarre and unearthly. Imagine him taking any esthetic pleasure in Miss Reese's "Tears"!¹ It's unthinkable. Well, only some of his own imaginative work matters, and we don't have to take seriously his critical notions.

"The Barrier" is damned good! Too good for our more erotic periodicals; but why not try it on one of them. I don't know whether or not to send any more verses to "Smart Set," since Mencken's resignation.² I'm waiting to see the January number, first, which may give me a notion of what they want—if anything. I've written no poems, except some love-sonnets and that "Pony Express" thing, since April, but a fourth dramatic poem is brewing within me. I think I'll call it "In the Gardens of Caligula."³

"Truth" is nearly ready, at last. I've autographed the 285 pages. Should have it by Dec. 20th.

Yours in Christ,   Geo.

1. Lizette Woodworth Reese (1856–1935), "Tears," a sonnet included in her poetry collection, *A Wayside Lute* (1909).

2. HLM and Nathan resigned from *Smart Set* as of the December 1923 issue because the new publisher wished to slant the magazine toward a popular audience. GS sold it no more poems.

3. GS refers to an unpublished poem, "The Pony Express." He did not write any more

dramatic poems aside from revising *Truth* (1923) as a grove play in 1926.

[299] CAS to GS [ALS]

[CLARK ASHTON SMITH
AUBURN, CALIFORNIA]

Dec. 11th, 1923.

Dear George:

No, they haven't put me in jail—not yet. Doubtless a few, or a good many, would like to see me there; but on the whole, my popularity seems to be growing.

I've had one hell-tooter of a cold for the past week, but am recuperating in time to nurse the rest of the family. The weather is beastly—frost and ice every morning, and a north wind half the time.

Here are my latest contributions to the "Journal," which is still running, in spite of the epigrams. I run a poem every week now: I can't sell **anything** to the magazines.

There's nothing sensational in the way of news. I'm still unmarried; and I haven't joined the Episcopal church, either (there might be more inducement to join the Catholics, in my case!)

Mrs. Lee (who rang you up last Christmas!) left Auburn several months ago. I don't imagine she'll come back—not to live, at any rate. She was done to a turn by the local gossips: I never knew them to be so vindictive towards anybody. She was a "common adventuress," according to some of them; and she and her husband were both under police surveillance! "Interesting, if true."

De C.'s review wasn't much ... I wish *my* book could be reviewed by someone really adequate to the task. H. P. Lovecraft is giving me a send-off in some amateur magazine; but he seems to care only for the demoniacal and horrific.[1]

I wish I could come down; but there's no chance at present. I guess I'll never have any money!

Yours,

Clark.

[Enclosures: clippings from the *Auburn Journal*.]

1. Lovecraft's review appeared in *L'Alouette* 1, No. 1 (January 1924): 20–21; rpt. *Collected Essays* (New York: Hippocampus Press, 2004), Vol. 2, pp. 73–74.

[300] GS to CAS [ALS]

[Douglas Fairbanks]

Jan. 15, 1924.

Dear Clark:

I'm down here for a couple of weeks, writing the titles for "The Thief of Bagdad," Fairbank[s]'s new film.[1] As you know, I've a small opinion of the movies and their makers, but Fairbanks, like Chaplin,[2] is really an intelligent man, and this film will be a beautiful one. That it will be exciting goes without saying—you should see the sea-spider and the dragons! They got the latter by actually putting a carapace (probably papier mache) on a real live alligator! How it was done God He knoweth. They have the critter emit smoke from his artificial nostrils!

I have luncheon on "the lot" daily with Fairbanks and his wife (Mary Pickford).[3] I've been here 12 days, and she's the only actress I've seen, so far.

I get $25. a day and my fare to and from S. F. Not bad for a poor poet. Wish I could feel I was earning it: one can't put much into movie titles, though they're mostly scenery. I've lifted a few lines from "Rosamund," and am inserting a verse from "The Gardens of the Sea," though they may not use it. The Rosamund lines are for the love-scenes.

I didn't bring your letter with me, so can't comment on it or any enclosures; will do so when next I write.

I live in Hollywood, which isn't so bad. The Los Angeles are a God-forsaken mob, and the street-car system the meanest, slowest and most complicated on earth. Some time I'll take a day off to curse it sufficiently in.

I'll send you "Truth" as soon as I get back—next week.

"Good hunting!"

George.

1. *The Thief of Bagdad* (Fairbanks, 1924), directed by Raoul Walsh; starring Douglas Fairbanks, Snitz Edwards, and Charles Belcher. GS wrote about 300 "captions" (i.e., scene descriptions) to this *Arabian Nights* fantasy, but only 25 were used. See letter 307. American actor Douglas Fairbanks (1883–1939) was the most popular leading man in American film at the time.

2. Charlie Chaplin (1889–1977), celebrated British-born actor and director.

3. Mary Pickford (1893–1979), popular American actress who teamed with Chaplin, Fairbanks, and D. W. Griffith to form United Artists in 1919.

[301] GS to CAS [ALS]

[Bohemian Club
San Francisco]

Mch. 13th, 1924.

Dear Clark:

Which of us owes t'other a letter? If you're the debtor, maybe you don't care to write to one who has butted into the movies! Well, I promise not to *act!* It was a brief experience, not unpleasant; but I was fortunate in being with Fairbanks. Some of the other companies are the unholy limit.

I met but two of the movie queens: Mary Pickford, who was at luncheon on the "lot" almost daily, and Mary Miles Minter,[1] whose lover brought me to her home for dinner a few times. She had a lot of pre-Volstead[2] stuff she'd wheedled out of an elderly admirer. She's a beauty, but too plump now for the movies—is going into vaudeville.

I've not done much since my return. Was in Carmel two weeks ago, and got mussels on Pt. Lobos, being wet from hair to heels in the process. I visited the Gouverneur Morrises, who live in Monterey now.[3]

Your epigrams are damned good—many of them. I'm keeping them on my desk to show to Lafler, who is a long time in visiting me. He hopes to leave Los Angeles next year and have a colony below the Sur. I wish you could live there. I want to if my girl will also.

Remember me to yr. mother.

As ever,   George.

[P.S.] I neither sell nor write any more poems.

1. Mary Miles Minter (1902–1984), American actress whose career was damaged when she became one of the suspects in the murder of director William Desmond Taylor in 1922.
2. Andrew Joseph Volstead (1860–1947), US Congressman from Minnesota, author of Volstead Act (1919), which allowed for the enforcement of the Eighteenth Amendment.
3. Gouverneur Morris (1876–1953), popular American writer of short stories.

[302] CAS to GS [ALS]

[CLARK ASHTON SMITH
AUBURN, CALIFORNIA]

April 2nd, 1924.

Dear George:

     I was the one who ought to have written; but I've kept putting it off because of the usual paucity of subject-matter.

     Here are some new sonnets. One is printable, but the other isn't. I have almost given up the epigrams—there's no audience for those, either,—so I might as well write poetry. I don't expect people to understand or appreciate my poems.

     I have some new paintings—one or two of which you would like.

     I wish I *could* join Lafler's colony. Auburn is more of a hell-hole than ever: There's no one in the place who really cares for art. People of that kind always leave after a year or two. The Auburnites are the most god-forsaken crew of cheap snobs and four-flushers imaginable. I haven't many friends; and most of those are a bore.

     Have you read anything of Aldous Huxley's? Someone loaned me a copy of "Antic Hay," which gave me a whole evening of entertainment.[1]

     Dewing is busy on his fruit-ranch, and I seldom see him. I'm glad I haven't a fruit-orchard to worry about. The ranchers have been having one bad year after another.

     This isn't much of a letter. But there's little to write; and I've had a head-ache for days and days. The head-ache is unearned—which makes it worse!

As always,
Clark.

[Enclosures: "The Pagan," one unspecified poem {"Enigma," "Query"}.]

1. Aldous Huxley (1894–1963), British novelist and essayist. *Antic Hay* (1923) is a novel about cynical Bohemians in London.

[303] GS to CAS [ALS]

[Bohemian Club
San Francisco]

Apr. 9th, 1924.

Dear Clark:

     Was glad to learn you'd not acquired fame by death! These sonnets are great. I read them before I read your letter, and thought them translations from Baudelaire, so perfectly have you caught his spirit and used his material. I like them better than anything of his, however, especially "The Pagan." I'm not sure, but have a notion that "The Measure" would risk printing that.[1] Do you mind if I try it on them? Will send you a copy of the magazine soon.

Some of your epigrams are horribly good! I hate to see them wasted on Auburn, and can't see why they don't sell elsewhere. If you'll compile for me a list of about 20 as good, I'll try them on Mencken.

Yes—I've read all Huxley's books. An amusing cuss. If you like that sort of thing, try to get hold of Van Vechten's "The Blind Bow-Boy."[2] It's a scream! But I'm too vital to care much for the decadents. Imagine Swinburne having once been classed as one!

You've plenty of time to prepare to live in Lafler's "colony," for it will take him at least a year to free himself from Los Angeles realty. I've had no word from him since I was there.

About headaches: have you ever had a[n] x-ray of your teeth taken.[sic] I had, lately, and found that *seven* of them had abscessed, one having been that way for over ten years! It was no wonder I was beginning to feel lazy. Have severed connections with them, and have begun to pep up already. Even one abscessed tooth can slow a man down. So look to yours.

Have been notified that The Lyric Year gives me a hundred dollar prize for their best narrative poem in 1923.[3] I must have had but little opposition. Well, it comes in handy to pay for my bridge-work, which is to raise Hell for me soon.

I've not been to Bigin's for over a month. The place is crowded every night, I hear, but I'm damned if I'll try the present bootleg!

Do you care to have me send you "The Am. Mercury" every month?[4] It was a disappointment to me. I prefer the old "Smart Set." But it's better than nothing.

Great Christ! What a country!

In His name, George.

1. The poem referred to is unknown. CAS's "The Remorse of the Dead" (a Baudelaire translation) appeared in *Measure* (April 1925).
2. Carl Van Vechten (1880–1964), American novelist and critic. *The Blind Bow-Boy* (1923) is a satire on New York society.
3. It is not known what poem received the Lyric Year award.
4. HLM and Nathan had started a new magazine, the *American Mercury,* in January 1924. The magazine focused much more on articles on current affairs rather than on fiction or poetry. Nevertheless, GS published a few poems and several articles in it in 1924–26.

[304] CAS to GS [ALS]

[CLARK ASHTON SMITH
AUBURN, CALIFORNIA]

April 21st, 1924.

Dear George:

Here are some epigrams that you can send to Mencken, if you think it worth while. I am running short on that sort of stuff, having written few of them since last fall.

Thanks for the magazines. Yes, I'd be glad to have "The American Mercury," to read and pass on. A certain platonic friend of mine seemed to like the magazine.

The headache I spoke of seems to be of a nervous type: a sense of weight and oppression at the base of the brain. I haven't had it for some time,—and feel rotten enough without it, anyway.

I have had no luck of any kind this spring. I can't sell anything that I write; and the only woman who wanted to flirt with me was too much of a hell-cat for my taste!

Damn the Prohibitionists! Bilge-water and horse-piss would be too good for 'em.

As always,

Clark.

[Enclosures: epigrams "From the Devil's Notebook," "Adventure."]

[305] GS to CAS [ALS]

[Bohemian Club
San Francisco]

May 28th, 1924.

Dear Clark:

Here's a note from Mencken (you may return it) with his comments and advice as to the epigrams. I think he's dead wrong, but an editor *should* be wiser than an outsider, in such matters. [1]

I think "Adventure" very lovely—and *alive*, which is more than I can say for the sonnets I enclose. On the other hand, "The Little Hills," which may remind you of Auburn, is alive without being lovely!

I was in Yosemite, most of last week, and should have loved to motor over to see you, but I had to return to S. F. by train, a hot and tiresome trip. Lots of water in the falls, and I managed to work myself into a dangerous place, exploring, from which I returned with difficulty.

Your headache is in a bad spot: you ought to consult some *good* physician about it—though maybe it's gone now. Here's hoping.

I can't sell anything, either. We're out of date, son, and should join the Neo-Mongolian school! Am hoping for more work in the movies.

Yours for 30% beer.

George.

[P.S.] Sending you some magazines.

[Enclosures: "The Little Hills," other unidentified poems.]

1. See Introduction, p. 12.

[305a] [GS to CAS] [non-extant]

[Envelope only; postmarked San Francisco, Cal., 30 June 1924.]

[306] CAS to GS [ALS]

[CLARK ASHTON SMITH
AUBURN, CALIFORNIA]

July 21st, 1924.

Dear George:

You owed *me* a letter—but I'll forgive you. Thanks for the various notes from magazine editors that you forwarded me. I was surprised that any one would even consider "The Pagan." I tried Benet with "On the Canyon-Side" and "The Witch with Amber Eyes," but apparently they were too strong for him.[1]

Hope you received the "Ten Story Book" containing a storiette of mine.[2] I received $6.00 for it—on publication! But the story was rotten, anyhow—except for the spanking—which was what I **ought** to have administered, some time back, to a certain badly spoiled female person.

The magazines are always welcome. My lady friends get a great kick out of some of them—particularly "The Chicago Literary Times."

I ought to work, but I don't seem to get anything done in a literary way. Doubtless I'd be in better shape if I could afford a few hundred dollars worth of treatment from doctors, dentists, and oculists. As it is, I'm cutting live oak wood for a little money to live on next winter. Armsby seems to have dropped out again, though Phelan and Crocker keep on remitting . . . I'll have to go in for bootlegging or blackmail if I'm ever to make any money!

As ever,

Clark.

1. William Rose Benét (1886–1950) was an editor at the *Saturday Review of Literature*.
2. "Something New."

[307] GS to CAS [ALS]

[Bohemian Club
San Francisco]

July 30th, 1924.

Dear Clark:

Yes—the "10 Story Book" came, and I really enjoyed your sketch, though it's my experience that few women like the "cave-man stuff."

I've not received a "Literary Times" for about a month. Maybe they've got tired of writing it. As for other magazines, their editors seem to want only poems (?) that have a vital human application, and it's d—— hard to make poetry out of that. The younger poets, though, seem capable of a sort of acrid wisdom.

I wish I were rich enough to have you overhauled physically. As it is, I have to go around with sundry gaps in my teeth because I can't afford to patronize a dentist! Am loosing [*sic*] my faculty of *grinning!* Maybe, by next winter, I can get some more folks to make a monthly contribution to the cause of art. I've tried to see Mrs. Clark about you, but she is evidently willing to keep out of my way.

Poverty has driven me too to prose, and I've lately finished a short-story, and must soon begin another. I hate the work, but it seems my sole recourse, as my only other craft is to keep books, not make them.

I had to go down to Los Angeles this month, to be at the funeral of the wife of my old friend Roosevelt Johnson. Luckily he sent me the fare! While there I saw "The Thief of Bagdad", and found that Fairbanks had used but few of the titles I wrote for him. Some of his own were awful—imagine "Yourself hath done it!" That's a good indication of the calibre of the movie brain.

I should be up at the grove this week, but have about decided I can't afford the expense.

Pro Christo et Ecclesia,

Geo.

[Enclosures: "Farm of Fools," other unidentified poems.]

[308] CAS to GS [ALS]

[CLARK ASHTON SMITH
AUBURN, CALIFORNIA]

Aug. 25th, 1924

Dear George:

I liked the last poems you sent me—especially "The Farm of Fools." Sorry I've nothing to send in return; but I'm too tired for any serious mental effort, after a few hours on the wood-pile. I'll tackle some more fiction when the wet weather comes. Literary whore-mongering is distasteful to me; but I don't want to break my back, if I can help it, or tie myself down to a job, either. I'd rather starve than be a wage-slave for anyone in Auburn.

Thanks for the magazines. . . . M. L. Fisher may review my last book in "The Galleon." I sent some stuff to "The Chicago Literary Times", but never heard anything from it. "The American Mercury" is good, though by no means an improvement on "Smart Set." Too much solemnity, too much breaking of beetles on a wheel. "Clinical Notes" and "Americana" are the best things in it, as a rule.[1]

Success to fornication!

Yours,

Clark.

[Enclosure: water color sketch.]

1. "Clinical Notes" was a column (cowritten by HLM and Nathan up to July 1925, thereafter written by Nathan alone) of miscellaneous comment, usually of a satirical nature. "Americana" (a column begun in the *Smart Set* in 1923) was an assemblage of amusing newspaper clippings from around the country.

[309] GS to CAS [ALS]

Bohemian Club,
Sept. 14th, 1924.

Dear Clark:

It's too damn bad you're too tired for poetry! Can you let me have a poem (it has to be rather short) for "The Step-Ladder," the "organ" of the Bookfellows? I am editing their poetry, but Seymour hasn't sent me, so far, anything worthy of publication!

I too have to "tackle fiction" now and then. I wrote a 5200 word tale last month, and am to begin another to-morrow. I hate the work, but it pays, at least, and "one must eat," as Hiram famously put it.[1]

The Chicago Lit. Times seems to have gone out of business. I subscribed by the year, but no issue has come for weeks. I'm sorry, for it was a snappy sheet. You're dead right as to the "Mercury." It's pretty heavy, and its one theme of the awfulness of these U. S. tires finally, however true. As bad a case could be made out, even though on other lines, against any nation, I suppose. Humanity is humanity: one can say no more—nor worse.

I managed to get in the papers again for stealing pond-lilies, this time with a beautiful blonde. But we'd got our clothes on before the cops arrived. I've no clipping of the event or I'd send it; maybe you've already seen it.[2]

I've had two boils on my neck for two weeks, and it'll be ten days more before I'm rid of them. A ghastly experience. So I've written darned little verse lately. The world is rather too much with me,[3] despite my ailment, and I often long for a lodge in some vast wilderness, preferably south of the Sur.

Yours ever,   George.

[Enclosures: "Which Was, and Never Shall Be," other unidentified poems.]

1. GS did sell a short story, "The Old Wreck," to *Munsey's* around this time.

2. See "Poet and Girl Swim Unclad in Stow Lake," *San Francisco Examiner* (27 August 1924): 1, 3; "Poet's Back Aches After Night Swim for Lilies to Please 'Lady of the Moment,'" *San Francisco Bulletin* (27 August 1924): 1–2; "Sterling in Hospital After Lake Swim," *San Francisco Examiner* (29 August 1924): 16.

3. See letter 284, n. 3.

[310] CAS to GS [ALS]

[CLARK ASHTON SMITH
AUBURN, CALIFORNIA]

Sept. 21st, 1924.

Dear George:

I have found time to do a little scribbling; but the result is probably rotten. You can use one of the enclosed for "The Step-Ladder" if you like. Or, if none of them are suitable, I well send you something else.

Life seems to be made up of work, boredom, and depression, as far as I am concerned. Too bad you can't change with me, for awhile, if you want solitude. You would get enough of it here. Wild women never stay long in Auburn: The people here are so addicted to the Seven Deadly Virtues—foremost of which are chastity, sobriety, and industry. Attending to other people's business seems to be an essential portion of the latter, from the Auburn viewpoint.

Thanks for the poems—"Which Was, and Never shall be," had an especial appeal for me. An old love came to see me yesterday. But I was out, of course.

Ever yours,
Clark.

[Enclosures: three unidentified poems ("Consolation"(?), "The End of Autumn"(?), one other).]

[311] GS to CAS [ALS]

[Bohemian Club
San Francisco]

Sept. 28th, 1924.

Dear Clark:

Thanks very much for the poems! I hardly know which one I prefer, for all are very charming—first-class work. And the short one levels up with the others by reason of a deep poignancy. Unless you want to send any of them out, I'd like to have all three for the little monthly of The Bookfellows.

I'd not think you'd be depressed when you can do such work as that. I wish I could! Guess I'm too old for the lyric of pure beauty.

My two boils have gone, leaving but two scars to remind me that we are all but dust of the laboring earth.[1] I have, however, fallen into the hands of a painstaking (and making) dentist, whose final pang will be a big bill for bridge-work (at least $200.) "Ay di mi, Alhama!"

Have finished another story—10000 words this time. A boy-story that probably won't sell. Am starting on a third tale to-morrow. Damn dentists! They should pay *us*.

Yours in Xt.,   George.

1. Swinburne, "Atalanta in Cayldon" (1865), l. 331

[312] CAS to GS [ALS]

[CLARK ASHTON SMITH
AUBURN, CALIFORNIA]

Oct. 3rd, 1924.

Dear George:

Certainly—use all three poems for "The Step-Ladder," if you like.[1] I can't sell anything to magazines, and am tired of wasting postage.

I, too, ought to visit the dentist, among other things. My troubles—physical and otherwise—keep on accumulating.

I have written about 75 lines of a poem called "The Temptation", which will be unprintable outside of some such collection as "Poetica Erotica." Fatigue and depression have kept me from finishing it, so far.

The magazines are fairly amusing. But I got more of a kick out of the "Chicago Literary Times" than any of these others. Send them along, though: They divert my lady-friends.

Ever yours,
Clark.

1. *Step Ladder* published "Apologia" (February 1925) and "Estrangement" (March 1925). In May 1927, *Step Ladder* published a selection of 19 poems and translations of Baudelaire, along with a brief unsigned article, "The Poetry of Clark Ashton Smith" (p. 129).

[313] GS to CAS [ALS]

[Bohemian Club
San Francisco]

Oct. 16th, 1924.

Dear Clark:

I'm sorry that you're feeling so rotten! In this fine autumn weather, at that. I've a scenario "under consideration," and if the movie-lice ever take it, I'll see that your teeth are attended to. My own are now O.K., though I shudder when I think of the unpaid bill for bridge-work.

Thanks for letting me have the poems. I gave the shortest one to "The Wanderer."[1] Think of an editor sending back such a lyric!

I wish I could send some more "Chicago Lit. Times," but they quit publishing some time ago. The others are all I have to send. I've some "Mercuries" for you as soon as I can retrieve them from the person who borrowed them.

I ought to be starting on another short-story, but don't feel energetic enough for that, nor even for poetry.

My old home in Carmel burned down, but Hopper, who owned it, had lots of insurance on it: $5000! I don't see how he could get so much.

By vigorous proddings, I'm having Robertson make me out a statement—after a full 8½ years! I dare say he'll find *I* owe *him* money!

Affectionately yours,   George.

1. Apparently "The End of Autumn."

[314] CAS to GS [ALS]

Auburn, Cal.,
Oct. 27th, 1924.

Dear George:

Thanks for all those periodicals! The "A. M." is really a worthy magazine, though the "Americana" are often the most amusing things in it.

I hope your "movie" goes through! I dare say it's the quickest way to cop a lot of coin.

Here is what I have done of "The Temptation." You'll probably think it's enough! The poem is too indecent for anything but T. R. Smith's "Poetica Erotica". But I have the authority of Shakespeare and Chaucer for the "obscene" words that I used.

I haven't done much lately. I feel horribly middle-aged: The aftermath of too much mental and physical suffering, and too many love-tragedies. Maybe I'll wake up some morning, and find myself married.

Drew was to leave for S. F. to-day. Perhaps you'll see him.

Aff.,
Clark.

[Enclosure: "The Temptation."]

[315] GS to CAS [ALS]

[Bohemian Club
San Francisco]

Dec. 24th, 1924.

Dear Clark:

Ages since I've written, I know; but I had nothing to say that would be of interest. I've not now, but want to acknowledge the Xmas greens, which are always acceptable.

All our crowd—the "Telegraph Hill bunch"—liked "The Temptation" immensely. It seems, so far, to be written just about as Keats would have done it, had he tried to do something similar. Why don't you go on with it? We'd all like to see more in the same vein. It would be "indecent" only to "the booboisie."

I've heard nothing about my scenario yet, nor do I expect to. God long ago decreed that I was to live and die in poverty. None of my stories sells, nor do more than a few poems. If it wasn't for the Blesséd Bender's Xmas check, I'd sure be up against it this "joyous Yuletide!" He told me he did as much for you, Miss Coolbrith and one or two others. The Lord smile upon him, and not call for him too soon! We've none like him.

I hope this is merely a ghastly joke where you hint at getting married. Cut your throat first, unless indeed your marriage would mean an end of your money troubles. To be poor and married is as near to Hell as it is given most poets to arrive.

I didn't see Andrew when he was here—nor especially cared to. The dope of superstition is as unpleasant (to the spectator) as the other kinds.

I've not "let" much verse lately, except one unholy terror, which I'll enclose. The doctors tell me it is quite possible.

My best to you and yours. Stay sober, but not too sober!
Affectionately,   George.

[Enclosure: unidentified poem.]

[316] CAS to GS [ALS]

[CLARK ASHTON SMITH
AUBURN, CALIFORNIA]

Jan. 20th, 1925.

Dear George:

I have been laid up for the past week with an injured toe, and am learning to curse by more gods than you could find in a book of cross-word puzzles. I ought to be out cutting wood to help pay off the family mortgage! (which falls due next winter.) It's a merry life . . . Also, my best friend has left the neighborhood (including her husband) and things are upset, and likely to be more so.

Anyway, I have plenty of time for letter-writing and the composition of bum verses. Here are some specimens. I feel like tearing them up: nothing seems to read as it should.

As to getting married—you mustn't mind my wicked sense of humour! I wouldn't marry the Queen of Sheba,—not if I had to live with her all the time. A week-end marriage with a rich orphan might not be so bad; but I don't know any rich orphans—or any poor ones, for that matter. Women always seem to have a superabundance of relatives.

Your last verses were excellent, as usual. I've mislaid them, along with the letter.

If this d——d toe doesn't improve pretty soon, I'll have to have it amputated! It was bruised (not broken) by a falling block of wood; and a bruise of that sort is worse than a break, sometimes. I can't afford to be laid up for any length of time.

Aff.,
Clark.

[Enclosure: "Query."]

[317] CAS to GS

[Envelope only, postmarked Auburn, Cal., 6 March 1925. Contains: "Loss," "Maya," "Incognita," "Concupiscence," two columns ("Paradox and Persiflage"); no letter.]

[318] GS to CAS [ALS]

[Bohemian Club
San Francisco]

Mch. 8th, 1925.

Dear Clark:

My God, isn't that toe well yet? You must have kicked a boulder over your house! But don't worry too much about the mortgage. They can always be renewed if one cuts them down a bit, and before next winter I hope to get in touch with Somerset Maugham, whom I know well, and lay your case before him. He is establishing a fund out of his huge income from plays, for writers who're temporarily or permanently "up agin it."

You don't have even to *seem* to apologize for any of the verses you send me: they're all poetry, and damned good poetry. The only reason why you receive no more recognition is because so few folk (poets of a certain rank among them, even) "get" pure poetry. Also, tastes are always changing, whether or not for the better. The world will always be at least relatively a pig. This "Concupiscence" is especially fine. Baudelaire would have given a back tooth to have been its author. "Incognita" is *subtle*. I wish you'd try it on the "Dial." But change the "thou"—no magazine will take anything, any more, with "thou" and "thy" in it—the more shame to the time-serving swine!

"Maya" is excellent too. It reminds me of Saltus' "The chuckle of Satan in Chaos." And "Loss" is very beautiful. Of course "eloigned" would give any magazine-editor the Melanesian pip!

I wish I could send better magazines to you. The club now takes the "Mercury," so I don't buy it. As to cross-word puzzles, I know no more of them and their buyers than a dervish might. Of course you *would* be good at them, with your unparallel[le]d vocabulary.[1]

Whom do you think I've been knocking around with lately? De Casseres, of all persons! We became warm friends at once, for he's a loveable chap, though you'd never guess it from his work. He apologized for "panning" me, as he phrased it, and said many flattering things about my work. But probably his real opinion was that which he put into print, and of course I *am* too conservative in some ways to make a hit with so wild a poet—for poet he is.

He had to go to Hollywood finally, where he's to write movie-titles. That lupanar seems to yawn for us all, however belatedly or intermittently. At least it's the "easiest money" extant, including even crime.

I had him up at the Lafler's, and he got very drunk. We romped up and down Lafler's big room for two hours, our arms around each others['] necks, chanting various topical songs, mostly of ancient vintage—"a sight to make the angels weep!"[2] I'm still on the wagon (68 days now), and so have enough extra vitality to do such a thing with sincere joy and verve.

We had a "costume dancer" up there lately that was truly Babylonian. All one girl had on was a very scanty grass hula-skirt. Fortunately, her figure was flawless, even to the breasts. But absolutely *nothing* was left to the imagination. The girl who went in for pond-lilies with me was there too—a peach! My costume was a jock-strap and a scarlet velvet table-cover hung from one shoulder! I called myself Catullus, and my face was "made up," with painted lips and eyes. I made a great hit.

I had a horribly funny letter from Lee Mihan a while ago—he didn't mean it to be so funny, but was evidently quite drunk when he wrote it. Some day I'm going to return it to him.

I wish I had some poems to enclose that were the esthetic equivalents of yours. But I get closer to the earth every day, and farther and farther from the ivory tower. This evaluation of truth before beauty is all wrong, but being probably one of the diseases of aging powers is inevitable. May you die young and avoid it!

I've "let" a thing in free verse I think well of. It's not yet typed.

Affectionately,   George.

[Enclosures: "The Dreamer," other unidentified poems.]

1. CAS had designed at least one crossword puzzle around this time. See CAS to H. P. Lovecraft, 20 March 1925 (ms., JHL).
2. A paraphrase of Shakespeare, *Measure for Measure* 2.2.222.

[319] CAS to GS [ALS]

[CLARK ASHTON SMITH
AUBURN, CALIFORNIA]

March 15th, 1925.

Dear George:

No, I didn't kick a boulder over the cabin: I was sawing wood—and a block rolled off the pile, and struck me on the little toe. I'm still laid up—any effort to get around only sets me back; and Satan only knows when I'll be able to wear a shoe and set the village husbands to worrying again . . . But I guess poets are always more or less unlucky: Their ill-luck begins with the fact that they **are** poets, in a world of pigs and pawnbrokers.

Don't apologize for the magazines you send. The worse the merrier, from my viewpoint. I find a Satanic amusement in some of them,—especially Miss Monroe's monthly assortment of canary-droppings.

The confinement is "getting my goat," and I don't feel very creative. My latest diversion is paraphrasing a few of the Baudelaire translations by F. P. Sturm and others.[1] I don't know how close my versions come to the original; anyway, French verse (B. included) **seems** infernally banal, from what little I can make out . . . Probably I have superadded a good deal . . . Anyway, I have tried to avoid such pusillanimous banalities as "woman frail and weak"[2] in Sturm's translation of "The Remorse of the Dead." Compare the second half of his octave with mine:

> "And when the stone upon thy trembling breast
> And on thy straight sweet body's supple grace,
> Crushes thy will and keeps thy heart at rest,
> And holds those feet from their adventurous race—"

I've never seen the original; but it seems to me that my version is more *Baudelairian*. B. *might* have written something of the sort.

There isn't much news to record, as far as I know. Hardly anyone comes near me. I begin to think that the person who would most like to come is being kept in a room with barred windows! Drew was here the other day. He seemed to be on the sick-list, but was rather vague concerning the nature of his malady.

If you know any superfluous virgins, you might give them my address. But tell 'em to bring enough money for return fare!

Affectionately,
Clark

P.S.

I like "The Dreamer" best, of the new poems that you send. But the sonnets are all excellent, too. You have written more good sonnets than anyone else in the world.

P.P.S. How do you like my yellow paper? I got it from Montgomery Ward & Co for about 60¢ a ream, postage included! I invested in two reams, also a ream of good white paper. The local stationer won't have a chance to rob me for awhile.

[Enclosures: "Beauty (After Baudelaire)"; "The Passing of Aphrodite"; clippings from *AJ*.]

1. F[rank] P[earce] Sturm (1879–1942), *The Poems of Charles Baudelaire*, selected and translated from the French (London: Walter Scott Publishing Co., 1906).
2. "The Remorse of the Dead," p. 30. In his translation, CAS instead used the phrase "unslumbering wantons."

[320] GS to CAS [ALS]

[Bohemian Club
San Francisco]

Mch. 18th, 1925.

Dear Clark:

Tough luck! Tough luck! But at least you've no husband gunning for you.

I've written to Mr. Lathrop about your disability, and he is very likely to "come through."

Have you tried painting your foot with iodine? That is often a wonderful remedy. It's infallible in tonsilitis.

I don't like the French metres, but like immensely the part of that octave you give in your letter. The sonnets, too, seem as good as man can make them with our present vocabulary. Our age, of course, has turned a cold back to all the old sentiments, if not the old forms, but poetry outdated in its own day will not seem so much so in perspective, when regarded down a long vista of years. So, unless one wants recognition when one's alive, one may as well re-use and refashion the tropes and emotions of past days. I'd not do it myself, lacking your gift for it; but I like it in *you*.

I'd not send that skit to 'Arriet—she'd never get it, fine as it is. I'll send it to "The Measure."

Our Cal. anthology will be out late in April, I guess.[1] A copy will be sent to you.

In haste,   George.

1. *Continent's End: An Anthology of Contemporary California Poets*, ed. GS, Genevieve Taggard, and James Rorty (San Francisco: Book Club of California/John Henry Nash, 1925). The anthology contained two poems by CAS: "On the Canyon-Side" and "Transcendence."

[321] CAS to GS [ALS]

Auburn, Cal.,
May 21st, 1925.

Dear George:

Thanks for all those magazines! The more contemporary verse I read, the more highly I think of my own productions!

Have you written to me in the past two months? I've been losing mail, in addition to my other troubles.

Here are some more Baudelaires. I feel frightfully stale and uncreative—the natural result of being laid up so long. I get around a little on the ranch; but it may be months before I can walk to town without doing myself up. Of all the putrid luck—!!!

However, the village is still talking about me! One of my fair friends has brought suit for divorce; and some of the local tabbies seem to think that I have an interest in the case. In reality, no one is to blame,—except the husband, who is an ass of the first magnitude. But the lady and I have been seen together pretty often . . . There was one yarn going around, to the effect that we used to meet every day at the local post-office! That's a h-ll of a rendezvous!

Is the new California anthology out yet? I haven't heard anything about it.

I notice that Gelber is publishing books of verse. Does he do it at his own expense—or only in the customary way?[1]

As ever,

Clark.

[Enclosures: "Anterior Life (After Baudelaire)," "Causerie (After Baudelaire)," "L'Examen de Minuit (From Les Fleurs du Mal)," "Harmonie du Soir (From Les Fleurs du Mal)," "Moesta et Errabunda (From Les Fleurs du Mal)," "La Musique (From Les Fleurs du Mal)," "Rêve Parisien (From Les Fleurs du Mal)," "Semper Eadem (From Les Fleurs du Mal)," "A Woman at Prayer (From the French of Stuart Merrill)."]

1. The publisher Gelber Lilienthal of San Francisco, under the imprint of The Lantern Press.

[322] GS to CAS [ALS]

> [Bohemian Club
> San Francisco]
>
> June 18th, 1925.

Dear Clark:

Quite time that I replied to your letter! Also that I returned your "Yondo" prose-poetry, a magnificent exercise in imagination.[1] I don't advise you to devote much time to such things, however: the mind of man begins to smile at anything that is inherently absurd and outdated. Your faculties are far too fine to be wasted on such vacua. The Baudelarian poems are worth many pages of even "Yondo."

The anthology is out, but for financial reasons (the printer needs more money than has so far been given him!) cannot be distributed yet to the contributors. You may *buy* a copy!

Gelber doesn't bring books out at his own expense; but I think I have a publisher for you, at least for a small book. George Steele Seymour was with me for three hours yesterday, and I gave him a long talk about you. His organization, The Bookfellows (Chicago) brings out one or two books yearly, and though he has "signed up" for one for the Christmas season, he says he can handle another one, if it doesn't run over 75 pages. It would have to be something he could sell for a dollar. But printing isn't so expensive in the east as it is out here, and he could, I think, bring out a very tolerable little volume. So if you care to send him such a MS., you are at liberty to do so any time, as he left for home last night. Address, 1217 E 53rd St., *Chicago*.

I've written, like you, very little poetry for the past two or three months—had to turn my attention to bum short-stories, signed with a nom-de-plume! It's a nuisance, but better than bookkeeping, I suppose. It's several years since I've kept books. Such poems as I have written I've no copies of, for I have to pay to have the damned things typed, nowadays.

The Laflers are to be divorced, and *he* is building a stone house four miles below the Sur River. I may go there to live before winter—am thoroughly tired of city-life. But love would be a problem: girls in sparsely-settled communities are rifle-guarded!

> Yours ever,   George.

1. "The Abominations of Yondo."

[323] CAS to GS [ALS]

> [Clark Ashton Smith
> AUBURN, CALIF.
> P. O. Box 388]
>
> July 1st, 1925.

Dear George:

My copy of the B. C. Anthology arrived last week. Your preface is about the best thing it contains—from my point of view. Many of the poems are meritorious, or at least clever; but not one of them is **pure poetry**. Yours and Lafler's are probably the best. One of Scheffauer's was good, too.[1] But I don't "get" this vitalistic school. Some of their stuff is clever (but, lacking the preservative of fine art) it will look—and smell—like a lot of dead cabbages the day after to-morrow.

Here are some more Baudelaires. I have been digging the stuff out of the original French—and find it well worth the effort. Most of the poems are new to me (Sturm only translated about a third of them, and his rendering is a bit Bowdlerized in places ("flood" for "slime", "wanton" for "lecherous woman," etc., etc.) And I don't think he gives an adequate impression of the style and technical qualities. The manner is peculiarly formal, glacial, armor-like—but often with a red-hot content! There are many beautiful things,—and one, at least, that is ghastlier even [than] "The Corpse." It describes a room where a woman has been murdered (decapitated,) by her lover, who has left the naked body lying on the bed, and placed the head on the table! There is more than a hint of necrophilism in the poem—it is more awful than Poe's "Berenice."

I am so disgusted with everything and everybody, that I would write my own poems in French—or Latin,—if I knew either language well enough.

I walked to town yesterday, for the first time since January—and my feet are so blistered as a result that I can hardly toddle to-day! I'm certainly in no condition to pick fruit.

By the way, I'd be glad to type some of your poems for you if you'd care to send them up. I'd return them promptly—and you wouldn't have to pay a typist.

I'll send my new collection of verse ("Sandalwood") to Seymour in a few days. I've been holding it to polish up some of the Baudelaires; but my brain refuses to work in this devastating torridity. I hope this Seymour isn't a stickler for "modernity". Anyway, I'm leaving out all the lascivious ones. If he rejects the collection, I'll put 'em all in again, and send it to Pascal Covichi![2]

As ever,

Clark.

[Enclosures: "Ciel Brouillé," "Le Coucher du Soleil Romantique," "La Géante," "La Mort des Amants," "Sed Non Satiata (From Baudelaire)."]

1. The GS poems included in *Continent's End* were "Beyond the Breakers," "'Omnia Exeunt in Mysterium'" (Sonnets I–II only), "To a Girl Dancing," and "Autumn in Carmel." The poems by Lafler were "Wireless" and "The White Feet of Atthis." The poems by Scheffauer were "Disarmament" and "Man and the Mountains."
2. Pascal Covici (1888–1964), a publisher in Chicago known for publishing daring books, some of which were banned for obscenity.

[324] GS to CAS [ALS]

[Bohemian Club
San Francisco]

July 16th, 1925.

Dear Clark:

I hope, and think, that you'll have no friction with Seymour about the book. The only way you may be disappointed is that he may be able to afford only a small volume. He *isn't* addicted to ultra-modernity, by any means.

You'll care less for "pure poetry" and more for the "vitalistic" when you're grown up. I'd have written exactly as you do, at your age, of the anthology. But there is much negligible stuff in it: I was often over-ruled by Genevieve and Rorty.

I've a notion that you are doing for Baudelaire what he did for Poe. After all, only a poet can adequately translate a poet. Go on with the work, and maybe we can find you a publisher some day. It will mean fame for you, and perhaps even a little money. I can see he was "just *made*" for you—it's enough to make one believe in reincarnation! Anyhow, one has to have a gift for such work. Once I tried to put a French sonnet into English, and nearly went bughouse. I gave it up.

Of the poems I like best the "Reve Parisien." After forty-five, though one *should* be a little jaded, the poetry of the jaded has no very great appeal. One wants life as well as imagination. The other stuff always retains a flavor of the absurd.

Don't bother about typing my poems: I've found a girl up in Mendocino Co. who wants to do them. You are too fine a machine for anything but gem-cutting.

I go up to the grove for the week-end, to see the *alleged* "Cremation of Care."[1] If they only *could* cremate him! The club is to use my "Truth" for the 1926 grove-play.

Lafler is still at his stone house below the Sur. When you're free we'll go there to live.

Yours ever,   George.

[P.S.] Pascal-Covici failed; but there's some successor, I understand.

[Enclosure: A clipping of GS's "Sierran Dawn" in an unidentified reprint from *Yale Review* (July 1925).]

1. The "Cremation of Care" was an annual presentation at the Bohemian Grove.

[325] CAS to GS [ALS]

Auburn, Calif.
Aug. 2nd, 1925.

Dear George:

Here are some more Baudelaires. Probably they are not the worst that have been done; though "Rêve Parisien" is the only one that really satisfies me, so far.

Seymour returned my typescript. I enclose his letter. I had an intuition, somehow, that he wouldn't do anything with my stuff. I can't think of anyone else to try it on;— and the increase in second-class postal-rates is no joke, anyway.

Thanks for the magazines, etc. The symposium of great poetic lines is interesting; so many of the selections lean toward the didactic, which is just what one would expect! Personally, I am quite unable to select any particular line in English verse that seems more beautiful than all others. I think, however, that Keats is richer in fine lines than any other English poet. He was able to play on more than one string, too:—"Mid hushed, cool-rooted flowers fragrant-eyed;" "Savour of brass and poisonous metal sick"; "Her open eyes where he was mirrored small in paradise;" "Aea's isle was wondering at the moon," etc.[1]

If it were a question of French poetry, I might select one particular line—"Infinis bercements du loisir embaumé," (from Baudelaire's "Le Chevelure") which seems to convey all the enchantment, all the perfume, and all the infinite lazy rippling of a tropic sea. Other lines haunt me, too—"Encensoir oublié qui fume / En secret á travers la nuit,"[2] which gives me a weird and ghostly sensation of familiarity. I could believe that I had written, or, at least, read it in some past life!

Did you ever see "The Book of Jade?" An admirer in Milwaukee has loaned me a copy of it. About half the poems are based on the idea that everything and everyone is dead and rotten! Some of them are very good, though it's not easy to make much out of sheer corruption, in poetry.[3]

As ever,
Clark.

[Enclosure: clippings from *AJ:* "Rêve Parisien," "La Géante," others?]

1. The citations are from: "Ode to Psyche," l. 13; *Hyperion,* 1.189 ("Savour of poisonous brass and metal sick" in Keats); *Lamia,* 2.46–47; and *Endymion,* 3.415 ("Aeaea's" in Keats).

2. From "Hymne" (ll. 11–12), a poem added to the third edition (1868) of *Les Fleurs du mal.*

3. [David] Park Barnitz (1878–1901), *The Book of Jade* (New York: Doxey's, [1901]). The book was lent to CAS by Donald Wandrei (of St. Paul, not Milwaukee).

[326] GS to CAS [ALS]

[Bohemian Club
San Francisco]

Sept. 9th, 1925.

Dear Clark:

Doubtless you've seen this adolescent review. God knows where he got the notion that you are "careless of the rules of perfect art!" It's the one thing you are *most* careful of. In fact, I agree with almost none of his strictures, and *dis*agree with but one item of his praises.[1]

They're having some sort of a fool Jubilee down here. The sound of brass bands comes from a distance, and one can almost smell the sweat of the million morons who parade or look on.

As is usual with me in summer, I've not written much, though I've a couple of humorous (?) ballads you may like if ever I've copies to send you.[2]

Is "The Mercury" to be had in Auburn? You'll find my hastily written article on Bierce in the Sept. number.[3] I'm getting more praise for it than it than if I'd written "The Eve of St. Agnes!" Such is the world we inhabit.

My former fiancée, Stella, has been here for the summer, and I've seen a good deal of her. She has, to my surprise, developed a marvellous voice, and will be famous some day.

Affectionately yours,   George.

1. GS refers to the review of *ST* and *EC* by Alfred Galpin (see letter 276, n. 2).

2. "The Ballad of the Grapes" and "Ballad of the Swabs."

3. "The Shadow Maker."

[327] CAS to GS [ALS]

[Clark Ashton Smith
AUBURN, CALIF.
P. O. Box 388]

Sept. 14th, 1925.

Dear George:

Thanks for the review,—which, however, I have seen before. It was submitted to me in ms. by the author, a student at the University of Minnesota, named Alfred Galpin.[1] Some of his criticisms were quite amazing; but not all of them were sincere: he tried to get the article into "The Nation" (or "Freeman," I forget which) and qualified his praise in an effort to obviate suspicion. However, they refused to "bite."

I have had to break my back lately, to earn a few miserable dollars, and have done very little writing. Damn the economical system: I ought to have a rich mistress.

I am printing a small edition (250 copies) of "Sandalwood", myself. A new admirer—(in St. Paul, of all places—) very generously offered to assume half the expense; and the printer is willing to give me credit on the rest. The book will be bound in art-paper, tied with cord, and certainly ought to present a more attractive—and saleable—appearance than the last one. It contains 43 new lyrics and sonnets, and 19 of my French translations. I have taken the liberty of dedicating it to you.

No, the "Mercury" is not obtainable in Auburn. I don't imagine anyone in these parts would buy it, except me—and I'm too poor, at present.

Stella was a great girl! I'd like to have seen her—

Aff., Clark.

[Enclosures: "L'Aube Spirituelle (From Baudelaire)," "Interrogation," "Madrigal."]

1. CAS confuses Galpin with Donald Wandrei, who was the student at the University of Minnesota. Wandrei is the admirer mentioned below. See also letters 360f.

[328] GS to CAS [ALS]

[Bohemian Club
San Francisco]

Sept. 26th, 1925.

Dear Clark:

This is good news about "Sandalwood," and I'm glad you haven't had to wait a whole year for Seymour's convenience. I am honored by the dedication, which may be all I'll be remembered for two hundred years from now! Send me advance copies of the book as soon as you can, (say six of them), and I'll see you get good local reviews.

I forgot about the "Mercury," or you'd have had a copy ere now. Give me a little more time. The Oct. number is now out, with my "Ballad of the Swabs" in it. Can't you get your public library to take the magazine? It is readable almost in toto, as a rule.

Edgar Lee Masters sends me his Selected Poems, also a pessimistic letter that shows that he, like most poets, is galled by the economic yoke.[1]

As poetry-editor for The Stepladder I've just made a find, a girl named Phlegar (of all names) who lives in Virginia.[2] If she isn't a comer I miss a big guess.

Stella has come and gone, a radiant vision. Ay di mi! She's now on the Atlantic.

Yours in the Lord,　　　　George.

[P.S.] Look for your name in a Lit. Rev. I'm mailing to-day. (Markham).[3]

1. Edgar Lee Masters (1868–1950), *Selected Poems* (1925).

2. Thelma Phlegar Owens (1905–1987), author of children's books. As Thelma Phlegar she published a few poems in the 1920s.

3. In "The Judgment of Mr. Markham," *Literary Review (New York Evening Post)* 6, No. 3 (12 September 1925): 1, 6, an article on great lines in poetry, Edwin Markham wrote: ". . . I close with a hasty reference to Clark Ashton Smith of Auburn, Cal. Mrs. Chauncey Juday sends a line from his poems, but I like better this terrific one:

Were I God, [. . .]

What rapture it would be if but to watch

Destruction crouching at the back of Time.

This seems to me to be one of the highest reaches on the wings of imagination" (p. 6). The lines are from "Nero," ll. 52, 55–56.

[329] GS to CAS [ALS]

[Bohemian Club

San Francisco]

Sept. 29th, 1925.

Dear Clark:

I come on yr. letter of Aug. 2nd, in a foot-high stack of unanswered ones, and suppose I've not replied to it.

I don't care much for Baudelaire, who makes me think, sometimes, of a ghoul masturbating in the morgue, but I think you will have been by far his best translator, being a better poet than he. Of these translations I like "La Géante" the best; it's delightful.

I never read the "Book of Jade," but have seen some of its contents quoted and have heard it's [sic] author described—six feet high and weighing 110! The poor chap committed suicide at last. An imagination like his couldn't have been an agreeable guest.

I sent you the September "Mercury." When you're done with it you may cut out my article and send it back, as I'd like it for my scrap-book.

Sometimes I have the vision of some old lady in Auburn trying to read your "Ebony and Crystal!" God has certain put on *some* pageant for His earth! Send me a poem for the Overland Monthly.

In His name,　　　　George.

[330] CAS to GS [ALS]

[Clark Ashton Smith
AUBURN, CALIF.
P. O. Box 388]

Oct. 7th, 1925.

Dear George:

"Sandalwood" ought to be ready by November. I'll send you copies for the reviewers as soon as possible. As for the dedication—I wish I had something better to dedicate to you. However, the book may be more "popular" than the last—if that is any recommendation. It is mostly lyrical, and has a larger proportion of love-poetry,— without containing anything that might get me into jail.

If you see Robertson during the month, you might ask him if he cares to handle a few copies. The other booksellers can go to hell. The White House actually returned several copies of "E. & C.," with an intimation that they were unsaleable on account of the binding! If people really care for poetry, they ought to be glad to get it in any shape. But I dare say most people who buy verse at all, buy it for gift-books.

I enjoyed your article on Bierce: it gives some astonishing side-lights. I'll return the article when I get the magazine back from Drew, who wanted to read it. (I'm afraid the A. Library is too poor to take "The Mercury.")

Will "December" do for "The Overland?" I am not including it in "Sandalwood." However, you can use any of the other verses enclosed, if you prefer. No one will buy them.

I wrenched my back, lifting some heavy logs, a week or so ago, and have been feeling rotten ever since. I'm not even fit to do any wood-cutting. It's a hell of a life!

I could defend Baudelaire; but others have done it long since, and more ably than I could. You ought to read Gautier's memoir of B: it says all that need be said.[1] My only complaint against B. is, that he wrote too much that was realistic, and not enough that was purely romantaic. But I admire his courage—and his art . . . Incidentally, I fail to find the slightest resemblance to Poe. I think the critics are all "off their base."

To-day is my parents' wedding-anniversary.

As ever,

Clark

[Enclosures: "Enchanted Mirrors," "LXXX. Spleen," "December," other unidentified poems.]

1. Presumably Théophile Gautier (1811–1872), *Charles Baudelaire: His Life,* translated by Guy Thorne (London: Greening & Co., 1915).

[331] GS to CAS [ALS]

[Bohemian Club
San Francisco]

Oct. 9th, 1925.

Dear Clark:

Don't you ever worry about not having anything "better" to dedicate to me than "Sandalwood!" There's no man living who'd not be honored (whether he knew it or not) by *any* of your volumes.

I'll see Robertson about handling the book; but you'd better let me speak to New-begin, Gelber and the man in the White House (he's a new manager, and likes me.)

I'm very glad to have "December" for the Overland, but we don't want to use it till the Dec. number.[1] For the Nov. I want to run this exquisite "Enchanted Mirrors." The other poems are all up to your snowy level. That "sot" one of Baudelaire's hits me especially hard, as I'm just about back to normal, after a Gargantuan revel last week.[2] I know precisely the feeling.

It will not be long now before we can pay (even if mildly at first) for Overland material.

Too bad about your back! It's the worst of things to injure.

Here's some more stuff from De Casseres. I've not yet acknowledged the books he sent me last spring!

In the Prophet,   George.

[P.S.] Guess I sent you my humorous "Ballad of the Grapes."

[Enclosure: Advertisement from *Arts and Decoration* for De Casseres's *Mirrors of New York*.][3]

1. The poem did not appear in the *Overland Monthly*.
2. GS apparently refers to "L'Aube Spirituelle."
3. *Mirrors of New York* (1925), a collection of essays on life in New York.

[332] CAS to GS [ALS]

[Clark Ashton Smith
AUBURN, CALIF.
P. O. Box 388]

Oct. 14th, 1925.

Dear George:

Here are some sheets of "Sandalwood," which may be ready a little sooner than I expected. Most of the actual printing is already done, and the rest **may** be done by Saturday. There will be a few misprints, as usual—most of which are my own fault, since I failed to "spot" them in the galleys.

Speak to the other booksellers, if you like, though I don't care very much whether they sell the book or not. I will barely be able to pay the printer, after their commission and the heinous postage are deducted . . . Come to think of it, I don't remember that either Robertson or Newbegin has remitted anything from the sale of "Ebony and Crystal." You might ask them if they sold any! I would never have been able to pay the entire cost of the printing, if Cassidy hadn't knocked off over a hundred dollars from the bill, in consideration of my services to the "Journal".

Thanks for the "circulars" from De Casseres . . . No, you never sent me "The Ballad of the Grapes."

Aff.,
   Clark.

P.S. The index of "Sandalwood" will come at the end.[1]

[Enclosure: "October."]

1. CAS means the table of contents.

[333] GS to CAS [ALS]

[Bohemian Club
San Francisco]

Oct. 16th, 1925.

Dear Clark:

Yours with the loose pages arrived yesterday, and I got a real thrill of pride to see my name as dedicatee. I shall never find it in the front of better poems.

I've spoken to Gelber and Newbegin and Robertson. They want your *publisher's* name and address, that they may "do business" direct with him. To-day, if I've time, I'll speak to them about remitting for the "Ebony & Crystal" sales.

Robertson says you may send him 20 copies of "Sandalwood" at once, and he'll pay immediately. I'll see that he does.

Here's $50. that I've extracted from an admirer of yours. Don't thank *me*.

Here's my "Ballad of the Grapes". Of course you know I don't consider such things *poetry*, in its highest sense. As one grows older one takes pleasure in writing things that have a vital value, a human relationship, as apart from "the literature of escape." It isn't that one can't write the other kind, but—somehow the human holds more *kick!*

In the Name of the Prophet,   George.

[Enclosure: "The Ballad of the Grapes"; proof of an advertisement from *Arts and Decoration* about Benjamin De Casseres.]

[334] CAS to GS [ALS]

[Clark Ashton Smith
AUBURN, CALIF.
P. O. Box 388]

Oct. 18th, 1925.

Dear George:

Tell the booksellers they will have to deal with me, since I am the publisher of "Sandalwood." The Journal people are merely printing the stuff at my expense; and they don't care to be bothered with filling orders.

Since I am forbidden to thank *you* for that fifty, you must convey my best thanks and appreciation to the donor, whoever he or she is. The money will certainly come in handy.

"The Ballad of the Grapes" is delightful. I find nothing in it to quarrel with . . . As to the "poetry of escape—" it seems to me that anything that liberates or stimulates the imagination, might be called an "extension of life", rather than an "escape from life". However, I don't really object to the latter term. Perhaps **all** art,—"realistic" or romantic,—is an escape in one sense.

Here are some more sheets. The last one will be printed to-morrow. I'll send you some copies as soon as possible, for the newspapers. Let me know, if you want inscribed copies for anyone. The edition (as I may have told you) is limited to 250 numbered and autographed, and will sell at $1.00. I hope to clean it out within a reasonable length of time.

Do you like the compact way in which the stuff is printed? It might have been strung out to a hundred pages, if printed in the style of many modern books of verse.

                    Aff.,
                         Clark.

[335] GS to CAS [ALS]

                    [Bohemian Club
                    San Francisco]

                                        Oct. 30th, 1925.

Dear Clark:

            I have the book with its dedication—my great gratitude for such an honor!

I have too the six unbound copies, and have taken them to the Call, Examiner, Bulletin, Chronicle and Argonaut, in all of which you'll have reviews, I can't say *how* inadequate, though inadequate they are sure to be.

I'll try to get the last copy to the Daily News[1] some time to-day. Am writing my article on Miller,[2] so have not much time for letters, wherefore farewell!

            Yours ever,
                 George.

1. Apparently no review of *S* was published there.
2. "Joaquin Miller."

[336] CAS to GS [ALS]

                                        Nov. 10th, 1925

Dear George:

            Thanks for the clippings from the "Call" the only press-notice that I've seen, so far. It is quite amusing.[1]

Have you seen Robertson? I mailed him his twenty copies two weeks ago, but have heard nothing from him ... However, the book is selling pretty well, locally, doubtless because of the attractive binding and the low price ($1.00) I think of having a second edition of 250 run off, before the type is broken up. It won't cost nearly as much as the first 250.

I may have a chance to come down for a few days, before Christmas: some friends are planning a trip to the city.

Don't thank me for the dedication! No one else was worthier of it—or as worthy!

            Aff.,
                 Clark.

P.S.

I've been too busy to do much writing. The enclosed (in French!) may amuse you. Probably it isn't very good.

I'll return your Bierce article in my next. My mother wants to read it.

[Enclosure: unidentified poem in French.]

1. "Poet of Rockies in Debut Honors Sterling," *San Francisco Call and Post,* (30 October 1925): 6.

[337] GS to CAS [ALS]

[Bohemian Club
San Francisco]

Nov. 12th, 1925.

Dear Clark:

The reviews of "Sandalwood" will be out, this Saturday, in the Bulletin, Chronicle and Argonaut.[1] Idwal Jones was to have had something in the Examiner, but he has been ill. It will appear sooner or later. The Daily News will have a review, too, but I'm not sure of the day. I'll send you copies of all, as soon as they appear.

I think it's a good plan to have a second edition of "Sandalwood," if you can afford it, for it will sell sooner or later, and, as you say, the issue will be much less expense. I wish I'd had a second edition of "Lilith." It's with Macmillan's now, but God He knoweth what its fate will be. The New York publisher has only profits in view.

This lyric in French seems good to me, but I'm no judge. I think I'll send it to Hopper, who is that rara avis, a man who has equal knowledge of English and French, with is [*sic*] corollary of "word color" and atmospheric values.

Can't remember whether or not I sent you this Nora May poem, but will take a chance.

Shall speak to Robertson to-day.

Affly. ever,   George.

1. [George Douglas], "Mostly About Books: A Gentle Bard," *San Francisco Bulletin* (14 November 1925): 10; [Morton Todd], "The Bard of Auburn," *Argonaut* (14 November 1925): 9. For the *Chronicle* review, see letter 347, n. 1.

[338] GS to CAS [ALS]

[c. 12 November 1925]

Dear Clark:

Here's the "Bulletin" review—foolishly inadequate, as one might expect.

I expected reviews in the "Examiner," "Chronicle" and "News." They seem to be holding off for another week.

George

[P.S.] Your stuff is about as "gentle" as vitriol!

G.

[339] GS to CAS

[c. 15 November 1925]

[Enclosure only: *Argonaut* clipping: review of *S.*]

[340] CAS to GS [ALS]

Auburn, Cal.
Nov. 18th, 1925.

Dear George:

Thanks for the "Bulletin" review, which is quite diverting, at any rate. Did Douglas write it?

I may print a second edition of 150 copies. The sale is sure to slacken after the holidays.

No news. I am everlastingly bored, depressed, and worried . . . "Weird Tales" rejected my story, "The Abominations of Yondo," saying that it was "more of a prose-poem than a narrative." Would it have any chance with the "Overland?" I go out in the woods and swear for about ten minutes, whenever I try to think of magazines to which I could submit my work.

Is Armsby still at Burlingame? I want to send him a copy of "Sandalwood."

As ever,
Clark.

[341] GS to CAS [ALS]

[Bohemian Club
San Francisco]

Nov. 28th, 1925.

Dear Clark:

You are truly naïve in imagining that you could have the "Yondo" poem accepted by any magazine that *pays!* A few that *don't* pay might take it. Send it to me and I'll see what "Overland" thinks of it.

All highbrows think the "Yondo" material outworn and childish. The daemonic is done for, for the present, so far as our contemporaries go, and imagination must seek other fields. You have squeezed every drop from the weird (and what drops!) and should touch on it only infrequently, as I on the stars. The swine don't want pearls: they want corn; and it is foolish to hope to change their tastes.

Yes—Douglas wrote the "Bulletin" review, and Todd the "Argonaut" one. God knows why you've not had them yet in the "News" and "Chronicle"!

Armsby was in town a week ago, so you can address him at his home. I'm sending in my "The Pathfinders" for the "Nation's" annual contest, but editors' tastes are as weird is [*sic*] anything in "Yondo."

Yours ever,
George.

[342] CAS to GS [ALS]

Auburn, Cal.,
Dec. 1st, 1925.

Dear George:

Thanks for the Argonaut review—which, like the other, amused and disgusted, but did not surprise, me.

I sent "Sandalwood" to de Casseres, and he wrote me a letter shortly after mailing that card to you. His praise of "E. & C." is certainly munificent; and I don't know of anyone whose opinion I value more.

I can't agree with the high-brows that the "weird" is dead—either in poetry or anywhere else. They're all suffering from mechanized imaginations. But, I, for one, refuse to submit to the arid, earth-bound spirit of the time; and I think there is sure to be a romantic revival sooner or later—a revolt against mechanization and over-socialization, etc. If there isn't—then I hope to hell my next incarnation will be in some happier and freer planet. Neither the ethics or the aesthetics of the ant-hill have any attraction for me.

Here is my latest. I'm in no mood to write madrigals. Some of the fantasies I am planning will have an ironic undercurrent of the deadliest kind. The enclosed is mild.

Your poem *might* get the Nation's prize—good luck to it. I may be "naive"—but not sufficiently so to submit any of my verse in that contest! As to "Yondo"—Weird Tales (which pays ½ cent per word) **might** have taken it under the former editor, who actually published Lovecraft's "Dagon".[1] The present editor is more commercial; but he did take two of my Baudelaires, and will pay 25¢ per line for them on publication. I may write some shockers for him, with more action and less poetry than "Yondo". Lovecraft's tales are appearing in the magazine every month.

My mother has an injured hand, which may take quite a while to heal. The Lord certainly favours the poor!

As ever,
Clark.

[Enclosure: "The Envoys."]

1. *Weird Tales's* first editor (1923–24) was Edwin Baird (1886–1957). He was succeeded by Farnsworth Wright (1888–1940), who became editor in November 1924.

[343] GS to CAS [ALS]

[Bohemian Club
San Francisco]

Dec. 10th, 1925.

Dear Clark:

"The Envoys" is pure poetry: Poe would have hugged you for it—if he didn't stab you! I'm not sure I get the symbolism, and some of the words sent me to the dictionary. But that's no fault of *yours.*

I had a talk on the phone with Armsby, yesterday. *Let me know if you don't hear from him.*

I don't know why Small doesn't review "Sandalwood" for the "Chronicle." Have tried to get him on the phone several times, without success. You'd perhaps not like his reaction anyway. I don't know much about his tastes, though he's a cleverer person than the Mavity woman.[1]

By the way, I fear you can't get away with that "but *I*," in "The Envoys." But the couplet isn't especially poetic at that.

I'd like to see that "romantic revival," but fear things will get worse instead of better and poetry be given up entirely at last. The race is becoming too cerebral.

I'm going down to visit Jeffers at Carmel, next week, if it's not raining.

Too bad about your mother. Give her my sympathy.

Yours ever,   George.

1. Harold A[dams] Small (1893–?) was an editor at the *Chronicle*. Nancy Barr Mavity had reviewed GS's *SP* in the *San Francisco Chronicle* (27 May 1923): 5D.

[344] CAS to GS [ALS]

Christmas, 1925.

Dear George:

This is almost the first idle day I have had in weeks—I have spent much of the time chopping scrub oak into stove-wood, and have six tiers to show for my industry. The wood nets me about $4.75 per tier, after I've paid for the hauling. I certainly earn it!

Apparently the S. F. papers don't care about reviewing "Sandalwood." Perhaps they are wise at that!

Armsby wrote acknowledging "Sandalwood," and sent me a little Christmas gift of $25.00. By the way, I note Mrs C. is back. But I don't know whether to send her a book or not: she never acknowledged "Ebony and Crystal." "Sandalwood" may be pretty well cleaned out in a few months—I have only about sixty-five copies left now. But I don't feel rich enough to print another edition, and doubt if it would be worth while, anyway.

Who is this Jeffers? You gave him some extraordinary praise in the "Overland."[1] The specimen of his work in the Book Club Anthology didn't appeal to me very much—but, then, neither did most of the other stuff in that Anthology.[2] I didn't like the selections from my own work!

I enclose one part of a fantastic entitled "The Saturnienne," with which I hope to go on presently. It may run to a hundred lines. I enclose also an exercise in French—which, I am told, is no worse than some of Verlaine's French! A phrase like "desolée palais" is an infringement of the classic rules, I believe—all participial adjectives are supposed to come **after** the noun. . . . But I don't seem to get anything done: jewel-cutting requires leisure.

De Casseres has sent me his "Chameleon" and "Shadow-Eater," both of which I am enjoying immensely.[3] I have not read anything so genuinely inspired for centuries! I am so glad he has taken to my work—his estimate should help to counter-balance the Bynners and Douglases.

Here is "Yondo". The "Overland" can look it over.

Yours for the rape of Allah's houris,
Clark.

P.S. One copy of "Sandalwood" was sent to a convent. Hope to nuns will be edified!

[Enclosure: "The Saturnienne" (fragment); "The Abominations of Yondo"; clipping from the *Auburn Journal*. Unidentified poem in French ["L'Abîme"? "Un Couchant"?]]

1. GS, "Rhymes and Reactions," *Overland Monthly* 83, No. 11 (November 1925): 411.
2. The poems by Jeffers in *Continent's End* were "Continent's End," "The Cycle," "To the Stone Cutters," "Wise Men in Their Bad Hours," and "Invocation from Tamar."
3. *Chameleon: Being a Book of My Selves* (1922), a collection of essays; *The Shadow Eater* (1915; rpt. 1923), a collection of poems.

[345] CAS to GS [ALS]

Dec. 27th, 1925.

Dear George:

I hope you got my letter. I think I forgot to mention an alternative reading for the line you criticized in "The Envoys." Read—"The throng went by Encharneled 'neath an iron sky."[1] I can't think of anything better at present: anyhow, it obviates the grammatical error—

As ever,

Clark—

1. The text as finally revised (in CAS's *SP*) reads: "To Mammon vowed, the throng went by, / Charneled beneath an iron sky" (ll. 34–35).

[346] GS to CAS [ALS]

[Bohemian Club
San Francisco]

Jan. 5th, 1926.

Dear Clark:

You must have grown pretty husky, to have been able to chop all that wood! The last time that I saw you, you seemed at the sapling stage of effort.

This "Saturnienne" is in your best vein. As often, I had to consult the dictionary, and am by so much the wiser. I recall Bierce writing somewhere in praise of archaic words, commenting on their poetic value.

I'm disappointed that R. A. didn't "come through" more handsomely. From the way he spoke over the 'phone to me, I imagined you'd receive at least a hundred.

I went to see the "Chronicle" critic yesterday, and found his neglect to review "Sandalwood" was not inappreciation, but merely a combination of carelessness and overwork. He'll get busy, now, soon; but his review may seem very inadequate to you. Your "case" needs a "specialist" in poetry, not the average hack.

Mrs. Clark is back to the extent of being in N. Y. instead of Paris. I'm to see her brother Dick to-morrow, and if I can get her N. Y. address will let you know it: it might do no harm to let her have a copy of the book.

Jeffers is a Carmel poet, aet. 38. I meant all, and more, I said of him in the "Overland," but don't think you would care for his work on account of the medium he uses. If you can't get "Continent's End," for instance, the rest would not "register" with you.

I myself have rough-sledding with his form (such as it is), just as I used to have with Whitman, whom still I can't stomach except in very brief passages. Yet I must admit that W. is great, for the whole intellectual consensus of opinion so judges. Jeffers has much more form than W., and far more beauty and strength. I find myself often haunted by his great phrase about the sunset—or a certain sunset:

"the sad, red, splendid light."[1]

If you want to read "Tamar," I'll send it to you, but I don't want to argue about it. That would but serve to irritate us both.

I've sent your French "exercise" to Hopper,[2] to whom French is as English, and who has a true feeling for poetry. Will let you know what he thinks of it.

De Casseres writes now and then. I'm glad you've found someone so similar to you in tastes, for he cannot but be encouraging to you. He too has financial woes, and if not driven to the axe, like you, or to story-writing, like me, is at least subject to literary drudgeries far from his taste. Why not ask him to come to Auburn, and we'll have another try at that old shaft in your yard!

I'd have written before this, but was on a gorgeous boom from Dec. 24th to Jan. 1st. It took me three days in bed to recover!

I have signed contracts with the Macmillan Co. for the publication of "Lilith" in the spring, and for a volume of poems, selected and otherwise, to follow in six or twelve months,[3] and now, thank Heaven, I'll be able to lay hands on a "Lilith" without paying six bucks for a copy.

I'm getting ready for a new dramatic poem—have been reading up for it—but may not start on it for a month to come: too many other distractions.

As ever,   George.

[P.S.] I hear that Mr. Lathrop is pretty ill, in Miami, Fla.

[P.P.S.] I think Geo. Moore would like your work.[4] Why not try him?

1. Jeffers, "Point Pinos and Point Lobos" (1924), l. 125 (no commas in Jeffers).
2. James Hopper had spent a considerable period of time in France, hence would presumably be able to judge the accuracy of CAS's poems in French, which GS had apparently sent him.
3. No such volume of poems appeared.
4. George Moore (1852–1933), British novelist and essayist.

[347] CAS to GS [ALS]

Auburn, Cal.
Jan. 10th, 1926.

Dear George:

Yes, I've grown pretty strong. But I need to be, under the circumstances! However, I can't combine writing with manual labour: my verse takes *time* to compose, not to mention energy. I've no facility for reeling off stuff, like some poets.

I'll take your word for Jeffers' greatness. Don't bother to send me the book—I have sworn off on nearly all contemporary verse, "free" or any other kind. All I have read lately is a little French of the Parnassian period. Some of Leconte de Lisle pleases me; but Verlaine—at his best,—seems to get the most *poetic* effect out of the French language.

I saw the review in the "Chronicle" this morning.[1] Carramba! porca madonna! That bird takes the caraway-seed for literal-mindedness. Much of the verse in "Sandal-wood" *does* deal with "the monotony of things"—or, at least, of emotions. For all the strange colouring, the book is absolutely faithful in its rendering of certain erotic moods—But few people seem to notice this. . . . I suppose, too, from his comment on the Baudelaires, that he wants an absolutely *literal* translation in verse. All that I assume to do is to render the underlying conception, conserving [*sic*] as much as possible of the music and spirit. But I could do a literal version—in prose.

I've had no time to go on with "The Saturnienne."

I spotted several "slips" in that French exercise, when I came to give it a thorough overhauling. One can't take **anything** for granted—and I've a rotten memory for abstract rules. My worst error—the use of "palais" with a feminine noun—was due to a misprint—"une" instead of "un palais"—in a poem of Verlaine's. "Tous noirs", also, should have been "tout noirs"—though one would write "*toutes* noires" in the feminine! It's a wonderful language. Hopper will laugh, probably—if he doesn't weep.

I sent a "Sandalwood" to Mrs Clark.

Yours for the second Deluge,

Clark—

1. [Ben Macomber], "Clark Ashton Smith Soars High Again Upon His Hippogriff," *San Francisco Chronicle* (10 January 1926): 4D.

[348] GS to CAS [ALS]

[c. 11 January 1926]

You see! What's the use? The "younger set" either can't or won't get you.

If it's as cold in Auburn as it is in S. F. I'm sorry for you.

Geo.

[Enclosure: Review of *S* from *San Francisco Chronicle*.]

[349] GS to CAS [ALS]

[Bohemian Club
San Francisco]

Jan. 20th, 1926.

Dear Clark:

Here is a letter I got from Hopper. Soon afterward he came to S. F., and I had to go to Santa Rosa with him, to see Burbank. On the way up, he made the corrections in the poems as jotted down by me. I told you were aware of some of the errors, already. He too is strong for Verlaine.

The "Chronicle" critic is beneath contempt. I sent you his review (?) only that you might see what the criticism of such termites as he and Mavity is worth.

Mrs. Clark told me she'd received "Sandalwood." I suppose she'll write to you when she has leisure. Just now she's launching her daughter on the social sea, which is tempestuous but shallow.

I like the Baudelaire translation, as a "curiosity of literature." To dwell on it long with pleasure, though, would take more morbidity than I can summon when in a state of health. Just now, my poetry must suggest a naked girl running down a morning beach. I guess I sent you my "Wet Beaches."

By the grace of St. Mather Cotton, I am still on the wagon!

Yours ever,   George.

[350] CAS to GS [ALS]

Auburn, Cal.,
Feb. 19th, 1926

Dear George:

It must be months since I received your last letter—I'm afraid to look at the date! I came down with the "flu" about a month ago, and have hardly recovered from the effects of it even yet. My father and mother were ill at the same time, and I thought for awhile that we'd all "croak". I should hate to die in Auburn: the place isn't even fit to die in!

I've no poems to send you at present. The demon of drawing took possession of me when I was about half-recovered from the "flu", and I have done over a dozen new landscapes, two or three of which are my best, at least for colour.

Did you want Hopper's letter returned? I've mislaid it. I thought one of his criticisms a trifle meticulous. "Fané" means "faded" or "discoloured" as well as "withered" or "wilted": my phrase "sang fané" meant simply "faded blood."[1] His other comments were just enough—though he didn't spot *all* my slips.

Somebody sent me your article on Miller in the "Mercury." You seem to have a knack for that sort of thing: it was very entertaining. Miller was a picturesque figure; but I've never been able to read very much of his poetry. I don't know quite why; I've no particular objection to pose and pretence. I find Victor Hugo unreadable, too.

Mrs Clark hasn't acknowledged my book; but I suppose the rich are harried and badgered most of the time. I'd hate to be rich; but I would like to have enough to live on decently.

Can you give me George Moore's address? He should like many of the poems in my two last books.

"Sandalwood" will be sold out, sometime—I've only thirty-five or forty copies left, in spite of the "frost" in San Francisco. I had some orders from New York, including one from a bookseller.

As ever,

Clark—

1. The phrase occurs in the poem "Un Couchant."

[351] GS to CAS [ALS]

[Bohemian Club
San Francisco]

Mch. 1st, 1926.

Dear Clark:

Glad to hear from you at last! Don't bother about Hopper's letter: I didn't want it back.

I was in Carmel for nearly a week, last month, with "Main St." Lewis.[1] He was lit all the time, but was good enough company even at that.

I suppose Moore's address is in the English "Who's Who." The club has no copy, but I guess there's one in the Public Library, and I'll drop in there the first chance I get. I think he'd be delighted with much of your work—with all of it, perhaps—and ought to see it.

My "Pathfinders" failed to win the "Nation's" prize; it went to something much weirder, as you now know.[2] I have no regrets, as Mencken took it for "The Mercury," and I'd rather be in that, any day. Also he gave me $100. for it, about twice what I'd expected.

My girl and I went up to Inverness yesterday. It had been cracked up to me as more beautiful than Carmel, but I found that statement absurd. It's a pretty place, however. Went past San Geronimo, and was reminded of Leo, who is perhaps your staunchest friend. Wonder how his T.B. affects him. I once thought Abrams had cured him, but evidently not.

The "New Masses" will be out May 1st (39 W. 8th St.). They pay for poems, in moderation, and aren't afraid of daring ones.[3]

I got the megatherium[4] (Dreiser) to write a preface for "Lilith." I'm far from sure of his qualifications as a judge of poetry, but the folk that collect everything he writes will have to have "Lilith" too, and that will help sell the book. I'm not thinking of myself in the matter, except that I'd like to give Macmillan's a little surprise: they don't expect much of a sale for the book.

Where's Andrew now?

Yrs ever.   Geo.

[P.S.] Do you want to give me another poem for the "Overland"?

1. [Harry] Sinclair Lewis (1885–1951), American novelist, visited GS for two weeks in mid-February. He had briefly been a member of GS's literary colony at Carmel in 1909–10.

2. The winning entry was Babbette Deutsch's "Thoughts at the Year's End," *Nation* 122 (10 February 1926): 143–44; second prize went to Leonora Speyer's "Ballad of Old Doc Higgins," *Nation* 122 (17 February 1926): 179–80.

3. For the *New Masses,* see letter 205, n. 1. GS published one poem, "Grasshoppper," in the magazine.

4. GS addressed Dreiser in correspondence by names of various dinosaurs, presumably because of Dreiser's girth, or the length of his books.

[352] CAS to GS [ALS]

Auburn, Cal.

March 26th, 1926

Dear George:

I mailed you one of my coloured ink drawings early in the week, and hope it arrived safely. It illustrates the passage in "A Wine of Wizardry" about the "baleful cypresses," and the ghouls, "Whose king hath digged a sombre carcanet And necklaces with fevered opals set." Hope you will like the colour. I find figure-drawing—even ghouls!—difficult and uncongenial, and most of my new paintings are pure landscape, of a fantastic exotic type. Some of them would make good screen designs.

Sorry, but I've no new poems. You can have "The Envoys" for the Overland, however, if you think it will do. I'll make you a copy of it.

I have not been well since my attack of the grippe, and don't feel "up to much." Probably I need a change: I haven't been away from this pestilential hell-hole for about four years.

Saw Drew yesterday. He was on the last lap of his spring plowing, assisted by an old ex-stage-driver with a mule team. You should have seen the outfit—the old man had five mules and two wagons, one of them a prairie schooner. It was *some* picture when he departed, driving the wagons tandem-fashion, with the fifth mule tied at the rear! He also performed a weird stunt for our benefit, by putting his back to the hindquarters of one of the mules, and hoisting the brute sheer from the ground! Imagine it.

As ever,

Clark—

[353] GS to CAS [ALS]

[Bohemian Club
San Francisco]

Apr. 18th, 1926.

Dear Clark:

Yes—that drawing came in good condition. Thanks! It's even weirder than my own mental conception of the scene.

I too haven't felt up to par since the terrific cold I had about a month ago. I dare say it had a flu basis, for it put me in bed for a week—a thing that had never happened to me till then. But I'm beginning to buck up again, and have just finished a narrative poem in blank verse—about 260 lines—subjects, Lesbian love and incest![1] So it will have to be "for private circulation only." It's not yet typed, but I'll send you a copy some time. By the way, send me that copy of "The Envoys," for the "Overland." Your "Yondo" awoke many protests from the mentally infirm, I'm told.

"Lilith" isn't here yet, but ought to be in a few days more. I'll be glad to get copies for less than $6. This will cost $2., which is 50¢ too much.

Two weeks ago I went 30 miles up the Carmel valley, to recuperate on a ranch. The damned dogs and roosters made so much noise for four nights that I got but little sleep, and went home feeling worse than when I left! Guess the country's not for me any more. But it's very beautiful up the valley. They shoot quail & deer whenever they feel like it, and salmon, after they have spawned, with a 44 cal. rifle!

Dreiser wrote a flattering foreword for "Lilith." At that, he missed just what the poem is all about. Edgar Lee Masters wanted to write one, but I'd already asked Dreiser.

I hear from De Casseres right along. He's a wonder! God help God when Ben takes up his pen!

In nomine Patris et al.   Geo.

1. *Strange Waters,* a blatant imitation of Jeffers.

[354] CAS to GS [ALS]

Auburn, Cal.
May 8th, 1926.

Dear George:

Here is a copy of "The Envoys" for "The Overland." I hope it will get a few more goats. "Yondo" must have had a kick in it, after all, if it aroused so many protests.

Ben De C. has sent me his new book, "Forty Immortals."[1] It is great stuff, like everything else of his that I have read. I understand that he intends to do one some day on you, Jeffers, and myself, under the title of "Three California Poets." I appreciate the prospective honour, though, in my present mood, I feel inclined to deny that I am a Californian ... But I suppose one might as well be that as anything, since one can't emigrate to Saturn. ... Moronism, unhappily, is not confined to California.

I've gone back to the wood-pile, and may pick fruit later. Would have written before, but I get so beastly tired after a few hours' work. The "freak" rain-storms are giving me a day or two of respite. I got caught in a cloud-burst yesterday, coming home from the village. The cherry-crop must be pretty well ruined (by the rain) for commercial purposes: I'm glad I've no fruit to worry about.

Send me that new poem—the perverse one—when you have a copy ... You and Jeffers won't leave me anything to express, except a complete reaction against sex, à la Odo of Cluny.[2] The attitude should have a certain novelty, in this age of satyriasis! I have a perfectly plausible and defensible theory that we live and act in order to learn the worthlessness of life and action.

Don't forget to look up George Moore's address for me. Also, the address of any one else you can think of who might appreciate my stuff. I have about a hundred copies of "Ebony and Crystal" left—apparently unsaleable. My stock of "Sandalwood," though, has dwindled to about thirty.

Thanks for the clippings. I note that Lewis has refused the Pulitzer prize—but I'd refuse it, too, if my work sold as well as Lewis'.[3]

As ever,

Clark—

[Enclosure: "Bâillement."]

1. *Forty Immortals* (1926), a series of impressionistic essays on forty leading literary and artistic figures, contemporary and classic.

2. St. Odo (879?–942), abbot of Cluny, was noted for implementing reforms in the direction of asceticism.

3. Lewis was awarded the Pulitzer Prize for his novel *Arrowsmith* (1925), but declined it as a protest that the award was made for the best presentation of "the wholesome atmosphere of American life."

[355] GS to CAS [ALS]

[Bohemian Club
San Francisco]

May 15th, 1926.

Dear Clark:

Thanks for "The Envoys!" What a commentary on our "civilization" that such a poem shouldn't bring $10. a line!

I'm reading Ben's "Forty Immortals" now, though I don't think them all immortal. What a superb phrase-maker he is! Put the sentences into vers libre shape and they'd be poetry of a high order, and rhythmic to boot.

The idea that we live and act to discover the futility of living and acting is not an unreasonable one, for it usually results in that conviction with persons of intelligence. "Vanitas vanitatum!"[1] But life has its moments, usually those of the sex-orgasm.

Lewis told me he has $200000. salted down, mostly from the sales of "Main St." I'm glad he made that gesture. He didn't need the money, and he actually received $50000. worth of free-advertising.

I did go out to the Public Library and get the Moore address—and then I lost it! Shall try again. How about Machen[2] and Aldous Huxley too?

Here is my Lesbian poem. A poor copy, but I've none else to spare. It costs me $2. every time I have the thing typed.

I sent it to Mencken, the only hope of publication. He is extremely unlikely to use it, of course, for though it's modestly enough expressed, the theme is anathema maran-tha.[3] You might lend the poem to Leo, if you think he'd like it.

Visited Jeffers last week. A lucky man, with no money cares, a good-looking wife and marvellous twin-boys. He seems to have corraled *all* the luck!

Yours ever.   George.

[P.S.] "Baillement" is up to sample, which is going some.

[Enclosure: *Strange Waters.*]

1. "Vanity of vanities!" Eccles. 12:8.

2. Machen had written a belated review of *ST* in the *London Evening News* (12 February 1916): 4.

3. HLM returned the poem, writing: "it would simply get us bumped off again" (see HLM to GS, 11 May [1926]; *FBB* 231), referring the arrest of a magazine dealer for selling the April 1926 issue of the *American Mercury*, which included Herbert Asbury's story "Hatrack," about a prostitute. The court ultimately decided in favor of HLM and the *American Mercury*.

[356] GS to CAS [ALS]

[Bohemian Club
San Francisco]

Wednesday.
[postmarked 16 May 1926]

Dear Clark:

Here is Geo. Moore's address:

121 Ebury St.,
London, S.W.

I suppose he has gone to the country by this time; but of course he'd eventually get your book.

Yours ever,

George.

[357] CAS to GS [ALS]

Auburn, Cal.,
May 30th, 1926.

Dear George:

Thanks for George Moore's address. I have sent him copies of "Sandal-wood" and "Ebony and Crystal." Don't think he would care so much for the first book. It might be a good idea to send books to Machen and Huxley, also to Thomas Hardy, if you can get me their addresses.

I enjoyed your narrative poem. The idea is a wonder, and there are some fine lines, too.

De C. writes me that eleven of my pictures (maybe more by this time) have been sold in N. Y. Ten went to a carpet-dealer, one Christopher Sapanoff. Loveman, though, seems to have spoiled my chance of a good price by giving out that they were all for sale at the starvation-rate of $5.00 each. Some were worth more than that to **me**—and I had hoped to get $25. or $30.00! However, it's an opening, and proves what I have always contended: that there are people who would buy my stuff, if one could only reach them.

Maybe there will be an exhibition of my stuff in N. Y. next fall—a painter, Russell Iredell,[1] tried to get one for me, but galleries are all closing for the summer now. Leo thinks F. O'Brien might do something in Paris, which ought to be the **real** market for my exotic landscapes. Anyway, I'm going to do some more paintings—it's my only chance to make a dollar or two, and get out of this pestilential hell-hole. I want a chance to live among white people, before I'm too old to get any fun out of life.

I've been picking cherries for the past ten days—will have a couple days more next week. After that I'll paint for awhile.

How is Bender these days? Wish I could run down and see you both, but I don't feel like taking the money just now. Later, perhaps.

As ever,

Clark

1. Russell Iredell (1889–1959), American painter and illustrator.

[357a] GS to CAS [non-extant]

[Envelope only, postmarked San Francisco, Cal., 30 May 1926.]

[358] CAS to GS [ALS]

June 7th, 1926.

Dear George:

Note what "The Overland" did to my "Envoys." Of all the damnable misprints!—even the "Auburn Journal" never did worse.[1]

I return Bio De C's letter. It's interesting to see myself classed as a mystic—which is one thing that I am not . . . Also, my mode of life, though hard and unsatisfactory, is no more "sordid" than that of any one else.

Good hunting—if the chase still amuses you!

Hastily,

Clark.

1. Among other errors, the magazine printed CAS's "Cimmerii" (l. 7) as "Cimmreli." The poem was reprinted, with errors corrected, in the July 1926 issue.

[359] GS to CAS [ALS]

[Bohemian Club
San Francisco]

June 13th, 1926.

Dear Clark:

I've just got back from Carmel, after a week's visit. Got two sacks of mussels and a shot at a coyote. Otherwise nothing profitable.

You've a right to be indignant at the atrocious misprinting of "The Envoys." And after my raging at Miss Lee[1] for her bad proof-reading of my own stuff! As soon as I see her I'll tell her what I think of such ungrateful carelessness—also that I'll get her no more free poems! She seems quite unable to learn from experience, though as a partial excuse, she has much more work on her hands than any one person should be burdened with. That's because "Overland" is so poor.

Bio got you wrong, but I thought you might be interested in seeing what the kind but superstitious creature thought of you. Of course she mistakes the meaning of "sordid," thinking it a synonym for "poverty."

The next time I have a chance to visit the public library I'll get you those addresses.

This is interesting news about your pictures. I know Iredell very very well—a fine chap. As for O'Brien, he's a likable cuss, but irresponsible and *migratory*. He's in Paris now, but may be in Tokio, without warning, soon after!

Bender is in fine shape, and has recently invested in an automobile, a friend having suggested that he spend a little money on himself! I've not yet seen the car, but imagine it's a good one.

"Lilith" has so far received several good reviews (*none locally*), but I've no notion as to how it's selling. Bert Cooksley[2] has a friend who's going to print 200 "Strange Waters." I get half of them, and will send you one if he ever "comes through." I wonder if Sumner[3] will get after us!

Yours ever,   Geo.

1. B. Virginia Lee, editor of the *Overland Monthly*.
2. S. Bert Cooksley, poet and associate of GS.
3. John S. Sumner (1876–1971), head of the New York Society for the Suppression of Vice.

[360] CAS to GS [ALS]

Auburn, Cal.,
July 10th, 1926.

Dear George:

I have been picking plums for the past two weeks, on the ranch of a neighboring Swede. The work is hard and monotonous, but I get $3.50 a day for it, which is a little more than most fruit-pickers receive.

The sale of the paintings was somewhat exaggerated. Only four were really sold, it seems. I have been doing some lately on satin, or sateen. People think they might be used for cushion-covers! If they are, I hope the cushions will be put to an appropriate use. I am ordering some paints that are guaranteed to be proof against water,—and, I suppose, against other fluids.

Leo writes me that he is threatened with appendicitis. Everyone seems to be getting it: there have been eight or ten cases around here lately. I'll never get it—I don't like bakers' bread well enough.

Ran into a barb-wire fence last night, and raked my leg just above the knee. The leg is a trifle stiff to-day, in consequence. Luckily, I don't have to pick fruit again till Monday.

A correspondent of mine in St. Paul, one D. A. Wandrei, has written an article on my work.[1] I appreciate the article, but fear he'll have a hard time getting it published, except at his own expense.

Sorry, I've no verses to send. I will write some, when the fruit-season is over.

Good for Bender! I *hope* he bought a Chrysler, but fear it was only a Ford.

As ever,

Clark—

1. "The Emperor of Dreams," *Overland Monthly* 84, No. 12 (December 1926): 380–81, 407, 409.

[361] GS to CAS [ALS]

[Bohemian Club
San Francisco]

Aug. 8th, 1926.

Dear Clark:

I'd have written ere now, but the Jinks, followed by much work, has tripped me as a correspondent. I've had to write an article for W. S. Braithwaite's 1926 anthology, covering the western section of poetry. Am giving you as good a "send-off" as I've space for.[1] If your St. Paul friend can't get *his* appreciation printed, have him send it to me, and I'll get it in the "Overland," if it's not very long.

My "Strange Waters" is out, with eight bad misprints, as usual. What inconceivable asses most printers are! I'll send you one, if you want it. Did you ever read my "Truth?" The grove-play that I adapted from it was a huge success, but *I* think that most of the credit belongs to the men who managed the lights, designed the costumes and did the production.

I drank nothing whatever at the Jinks, to everyone's amazement. Did a lot of swimming in the Russian River. But the Jinks has been flavorless to me since London died, and I'm not sure I'll attend any more.

Masters was here for nine days, early last month, and we went to Carmel, as he wanted to meet Jeffers. A good time, but rather too much gin. He's a fine chap, and rather more Rabelesian than most poets. His "Spoon River" will live: I'm not so sure about the rest of his work. He considers his "Domesday Book" his magnum opus, but few will agree with him.[2]

Like you, I've not written much poetry this summer. Here are two or three things, all rather highbrow. Wrote a pretty fair sonnet this morning, but of course have no copies of it yet.

Good luck—and don't get sun-stroke at your fruit-picking.

As ever,   George.

[Enclosures: unidentified poems.]

1. "Poetry of the Pacific Coast—California." See the Appendix for the passage on CAS.
2. Edgar Lee Masters (1868–1950), *Spoon River Anthology* (1915), *Domesday Book* (1920).

[362] CAS to GS [ALS]

[CLARK ASHTON SMITH
P. O. Box 388
AUBURN, CAL.]

Sept. 4th, 1926

Dear George:

Pardon the stationery:[1] the printer must have thought I wanted to send out some bills. Unluckily, I have none that are collectible.

Your last sonnets are excellent, as always. I have nothing to send in exchange, since the pictorial muse won't leave me alone, when I have time for creative endeavour. I don't receive much encouragement for my paintings, but all the same, I am convinced of their value.

Leo passed on some verses you had sent him ("Items for the Christian Witness")[.] They are very clever, and have the true flavour of life in the "c(o)untery". I suggest that Mencken should publish them in "The Mercury", and hold a contest to decide the authorship, offering for prize a packet of French envelopes, or a whirling syringe, according to the sex of the winner. I am told that Mencken maintains they are Masters' work; but Leo says, "I see them as the spirit-work of Cardinal Newman." Following the pronouncement of two such great minds, I hesitate to offer my own theory.[2]

Thanks for the mention in Braithwaite's anthology. Wandrei (my St. Paul admirer) may send you his essay before long. He wanted to try "The Bookman" and "The Nation" first!! The essay runs to about 2500 words, including quotations.

I read "Truth" the last time I was in S. F. (four years ago) and admired it. I can see that it would be effective on the stage. The songs are among your best lyrics: two of them ("Atthan Dances" was one) still haunt me with ineluctable beauty and strangeness. There is nothing else like them in poetry.

I have not read very much of Masters' work. The "Spoon River" stuff has a kick, if nothing else. It has the merit of being true.

I wish I were in Abyssinia, or Sumatra, or Celebes—anywhere but twentieth-century America. I am bored, exasperated and afflicted by everything and everybody—no one was ever so alien and recalicitrant to the "time-spirit."

Had a nice letter from Miss Lee, of the Overland, some time ago. But I hear she's a blond—and I'm leary of blonds. Those I have known were either neurotic or lymphatic.

As ever,

Clark.

1. The stationery is a half-sheet of paper (8½″ × 5½″) with CAS's name and address printed horizontally at the top, resulting in a wide but short page.

2. It is not clear whether this poem was written by GS or by Masters. It does not appear to be extant.

[363] GS to CAS [ALS]

[Bohemian Club
San Francisco]

Sept. 12th, 1926.

Dear Clark:

I don't think your fruit-picking tires you more than prose-writing tires *me*. And within a month I had to write three articles, a short-story and three acts of a light opera.[1] So only one poem (it's hardly a poem, either), and no copy of that to send to you.

As regards your painting, I think you have immense imagination, as in poetry, but lack technical training. It's a pity you can't come to S. F. for that. Maybe Herkomer could help you.

Glad you liked those "Items." Leo writes me very brilliant letters, and I wish I'd time for longer and better ones in reply. He doesn't realize how large my correspondence is, nor how hard it is to escape from such a number of correspondents.

"The Bookman" might take Wandrei's essay. "The Nation" would be as likely to run the "Items"!

You surprise, not to say please, me by your unusual appreciation of "Atthan Dances" and "Egon's Song." You yourself have done far better. A good lyric has something of the quality of a diamond; a long poem is usually adobe or marble.

I understand your reaction to this awful country, which will become yearly more detestable. I fancy that all one can do, if too poor to emigrate, is to toughen one's hide. Of course it's sensitivity that counts, not environment.

Miss Lee is neither neurotic nor lymphatic; but she's no beauty.

In Christ,   George.

[P.S.] Percy Hutchinson [*sic*] says in the N.Y. Times that "Lilith" is "quite the finest dramatic poem published in America, and one of the finest in English literature."[2]

        Going some!

                        George.

1. The three articles were "Poetry of the Pacific Coast," "A First-Class Fighting Man" (on the boxer Pete McCoy, whom GS had known in his youth), and *Robinson Jeffers: The Man and the Artist*. The short story may have been "The Lovely Lady." The light opera is unidentified.

2. Percy A. Hutchison, "Poetic Drama Did Not Die with Stephen Phillips," *New York Times Book Review* (22 August 1926): 9, a review of *Lilith* and two other poetic dramas.

[364] CAS to GS [ALS]

                        Auburn, Cal.

                        Sept. 28th, 1926

Dear George:

        Thanks for the poems, and clippings. What P. Hutchinson [*sic*] says about "Lilith" is merely a modest statement of the truth.

        Too bad Mencken didn't run "Strange Waters." Being a poem, it might well have "gotten past" without action on the part of the moral police. Mencken is getting too respectable for me. The principal of the Auburn high school takes the "Mercury", and swears by it . . . Good night!

        Of course, I lack technical training, in the academic sense. But I don't care much more for the literalness of academic painting than I do for the geometrical abstractions of some of the modernists. What I am after is imaginative (some would say emotional) expression through organized design and colour with novel decorative values. Realism is not aimed at, and I reserve the right to paint in perfectly flat colours, if I wish. The decorative screens and panels of R. W. Chanler,[1] which show an Oriental influence, are more to my taste than the work of most American painters. As to getting instruction, I doubt if my ideals would be understood or sympathized with, by the average art teacher. I'll have to work it out in my own way. Certainly Herkomer, who is, or was, a portrait-painter, would be of little help in teaching me how to paint landscapes in Cocaigne, or Saturn, or Antillia. Like most people, he wouldn't get the idea at all.

        Not much news here. I sold a picture locally for ten dollars, which seems to be the top price. Two others went at five apiece, some time ago.

        I want to do some more poems this winter. Not love-poems, though—the subject is unbearably trite. Also, I've sworn off forever on sonnets and quatrain stanzas, except in translations.

        Leo takes the prize for letter-writing. I can't cope with him, either, since I am naturally incommunicative. Letter-writing is always more or less of a task for me.

        I enjoyed your last column in "The Overland," on the progressive dementia of the mob. You might have said that the world was going from general imbecility to absolute idiocy.[2]

        Miss Lee is safe, as far as I am concerned. What I want is an old-fashioned Persienne.

            As ever,

                Clark.

1. Robert Winthrop Chanler (1872–1930), American painter known for his portraits, murals, and wildlife paintings.

2. GS, "Rhymes and Reactions" (October 1926).

[365] GS to CAS [ALS]

[Bohemian Club
San Francisco]

Oct. 8th, 1926.

Dear Clark:

I've been on the wagon for 81 days, a record for me, I think! I'll probably remain there till Mencken reaches S. F., early in November.[1]

I've written nothing much but prose for the past two months—had to have the money. I can make $100. a week at prose, but I hate the toil. Now I have some leisure coming to me, and shall doubtless be delivered of sundry rhymes.

I think you're right, as to long poems. They seem to be the only kind that are *remembered*. To gain recognition (if one desire it) with short ones is like trying to fill up a lake by throwing pebbles in it. Anyhow, I'm wishing you leisure, and if my schemes eventuate, will contribute to it.

About Leo: do you know anything intimate about his present condition. His letters to me would indicate increasing paranoia. The last one was certainly the work of a deranged mind, and I'm seriously concerned over him. In fact, I'm going over to see him, the first free Sunday I have (I haven't many), as he refuses my invitations to have luncheon with me here in the club.

You probably have (you ought to have) a better notion than I as to where you stand in the technique of painting. Probably you're groping your way toward something new and significant. At least you've your vast imagination to rely on.

A matter has come up that worries me. Your friend Wandrei has sent me an essay on your poetry, perhaps with the intention of having it in some magazine. That would be impossible in any eastern one, for he is evidently a pretty young man, with a young man's unbridled enthusiasms, and has heaped such extravagant praises on you as not a combination of Shakespear, Coleridge and Keats could merit. So his adulation would awaken only derision in editorial bosoms, and laughter in readers', if published. I remember what I got in the case of "A Wine of Wizardry!"

However, if you don't mind the incredulity of lesser poets, I can have the essay run in "Overland," very probably. It would at least attract much attention to your work, and in itself is well-written, however open to argument some of its eulogies may be. Let me know your wishes, and they shall be complied with. Heaven knows you get little enough credit for your exquisite work, and if this will wake folks up, all the better.

   In Gawd,   George.

[Enclosure:] Do you get the Overland every month? I continue to contribute a page of prose and *verse,* as it gives me a chance to scold, and to work off rhymes otherwise unpublishable except in a book. I hear "Lilith" got a roast in the New Republic,[2] but then, most of the radicals have it in for me because I live in the Bohemian Club! They think of it as a stronghold of the rich, where they assemble and weave plots against the proletariat! And it's only a lot of poor old men playing dominoes!

George.

1. HLM did not arrive in San Francisco until 15 November, two days before GS's death.

2. *Lilith* was reviewed by the poet Léonie Adams (1899–1988) in *New Republic* No. 615 (15 September 1926): 99–100. Among other things, Adams wrote: ". . . this poem is nondescript. . . . The structure is limp, and except for a slight variation in the last act, of an appalling symmetry. . . . this grandiose effort betrays him [GS] to his worst side, to an almost wholly derivative verse, to all manner of rhetoric, the tawdrily pretty, the grotesque, the pompous."

[366] CAS to GS [ALS]

Auburn, Cal.
Oct. 11th, 1926

Dear George:

I agree with all that you say about Wandrei's essay; but after all, his "reaction" is obviously sincere, and it seems to me that he is entitled to a hearing. You might run the essay, if The Overland will stand for it. I won't mind the hee haws of the local tame asses. Anyway, W. means to print and circulate it at his own expense, if he can't get it into any magazine.

I always thought, and still think, that Bierce merely gave "A Wine of Wizardry" its just due. But good judges of poetry are almost rarer than poets, it would seem.

L. worries me, too. He is certainly a distressing problem, and I don't know what to make of him. He writes at times in a vein that seems to indicate unusual erotic obsessions or preoccupations, and, of late, imputes similar ideas to other people. Apparently he has been pouring it out on you, so you can doubtless infer as much as I know. I hope you can do something to help or straighten him out, if possible. He seems to be sane enough apart from this one thing. His life of idleness and isolation in San Geronimo is enough to put anyone mad. Incidentally, he may come up to see me during the month. I don't look forward to the visit with much pleasure.

As to my pictorial technique, I'll admit that it falls far short of my own ideal. However, I can't see that my pictures are so terribly rough, compared to much of the stuff that gets over nowadays. I may screw up courage to send some of my late work to Bender, with a request that he recommend it for exhibition somewhere, if he finds merit in it. Ray Boynton, who likes my stuff, would probably do something, even if Bender wouldn't. Do you ever see Boynton?[1]

Too bad you have to write prose. It's a beastly occupation. As to the length of poems, it seems to me that most brief ones don't have much driving-power. Too many people can write a good lyric, anyway. But few can write a hundred, or two hundred lines of sustained poetry.

As ever,
Clark.

1. Ray Boynton (1883–1951), California painter known for his town and landscape paintings and murals.

[367] GS to CAS [ALS]

[Bohemian Club
San Francisco]

Oct. 24th, 1926.

Dear Clark:

Miss Lee is "agreeable" toward using Wandrei's article, knowing that it will attract attention, from the very scope of its claims, not only to you but to her magazine. So I am writing to Wandrei for formal permission to use it. Since he really believes what he has written, he ought to stand by his words, even though they will be received with polite (and impolite) incredulity.

His address is on the article, now down in the office the "Overland," so, to save a day, I'm sending my letter to him by way of you. Read, address and mail it, please.

You must have given Leo a notion that I objected to the various indecency of his letters, for he writes apologizing for it. I did not mind it at all, but feared his preoccupation with it a bad sign, and have so informed him, in reply. He's an amazing chap, in his own rather pedantic way, and I hope he'll be long spared to us.

Boynton doesn't come in the club often, but I can ring him up and ask if he cares to do anything in the way of calling attention to your painting.

I now have an order to do an introduction to a book of Bierce's short stories, to be published by the Modern Library. And as soon as I've written that, I suppose another job will bob up and I'll fall for it on account of the "easy money." Guess I'm well adapted for brain-whoring!

I went up to a friend's ranch northeast of Santa Rosa last week-end for some quail-shooting, only to find when I got there that the season doesn't open till Nov. 1st! I had a good time, though, and drank so much thick cream that it made me bilious.

God guard you, Satan guide you!

Yours ever,   George.

[P.S.] Do you get the "Overland" monthly?

[368] CAS to GS [ALS]

Auburn, Cal.,
Oct. 27th, 1926

Dear George:

I forwarded your letter to Wandrei. He's a strange fellow, but is much more critical than you imagine. I don't know just how young he is; but it's only fair to say that there are men of middle-age (enough of them for a jury, almost!) who would back him up in his contention that my eventual place will be a very high one. He doesn't really contend that I am greater than certain other poets, and the excess of his essay is more in the manner than in the substance. Doubtful though I am, myself, I think that the people who will laugh at him are fools, and are deaf and blind to to [sic] all the lessons of literary history. Literary tastes and standards are in a state of perpetual flux, and the narrow, hide-bound "humanism" of the present may seem absurd in some future age. It **is** absurd to me, and to a few other free spirits. I've no quarrel with the slogan of "art for life's sake", but I think the current definition or delimitation of what constitutes life is worse than ridiculous. Anything that the human imagination can conceive of becomes thereby a part of life, and poetry such as mine, properly considered, is not an "escape", but an extension. I have the courage to think that I am rendering as much a "service" by it (damn the piss-pot word!) as I would by psycho-analyzing the male and female adolescents or senescents of a city slum in the kind of verse that slops all over the page and makes you feel as if somebody had puked on you.

I don't blame you for writing prose, if you can make money by it. But it's a hateful task, for a poet, and wouldn't be neccessary [*sic*], in any true civilization. Hell speed the ascendancy of the Japs and Hottentotts!

I gave Leo a lecture on my own account, not yours. He misunderstood me, and thought I was criticizing his ethics, when I was really more concerned for his aesthetics. He's a "card", all right; but I have the highest respect for his critical abilities, based as they are on a most remarkable erudition.

Don't bother to ring Boynton up at present. I'll "start" something somewhere, sometime, somehow in connection with the pictures. They provoke the same extremes of dislike and admiration as my poetry, though not always in the same people.

I've been reading some of Mencken's syndicated articles in the Chronicle. I predict that he will become almost as popular as Brisbane, if he goes on with that sort of stuff.[1]

> Yours, in the quest of the Holy Grail,
> Clark—

1. HLM's weekly articles on various literary and political topics of the day, written for the *Chicago Tribune* (1924–28), were serialized in newspapers across the country, including the *San Francisco Chronicle*. CAS also refers to Arthur Brisbane (1864–1936), a prolific journalist, chiefly for the Hearst newspapers.

[369] GS to CAS [ALS]

> [Bohemian Club
> San Francisco]

> Oct. 31ˢᵗ, 1926.

Dear Clark:

I wasn't trying to contend that you don't, according to my personal tastes in poetry, deserve a high place in it. I merely thought it uncritical of Wandrei to have you topping the heap, as his essay will lead every reader of it to infer that he believes. No one more than I would like to be able to entertain such hopes, since they involve to a large extent some of my own work, notably A Wine of Wizardry. But [it] is disquieting to observe that the whole intellectual (including of course the esthetic) trend is increasingly against admiration of the daemonic, the supernatural. Such elements now seem only to awaken smiles, as being childish in their nature and no part of the future vision of the race. I regret that this should be so, for it implies that I've wasted a good deal of creative energy; but only cranks and mental hermits now take my "Wine" seriously, and I feel futile when I use my imagination on "impossible" stuff, the element where it is best fitted to function. Maybe we'll have anarchy in America, some day, with the accompanying reversion to racial childhood. That will come too late for me, but perhaps not for you. For the present, my "blue-eyed vampire" is only an intellectual joke, and to call anyone a fool who smiles back at her is not to win the argument.

If Leo isn't mad, then his letters are no indication to the contrary. They're full of megalomania, insinuations and veiled insult, and I'll write to him no more. The very length of his screeds is egoistic, and a nuisance to the reader, and his habit of pasting irrelevant pictures on them is pretty fair evidence of paranoia.

When we find The Grail, it has in it "the coal black wine,"[1] Clark!

Yours ever,   George.

[P.S.] Now 104 days on the wagon!

1. Francis H. Noyes, "The Coal Black Wine" (1885), a song: "King Death was a rare old fellow and he sat where no sun could shine. And he lifted his hand so yellow and pour'd out the coal black wine."

[370] CAS to GS [ALS]

Auburn, Cal.,
Nov. 4th, 1926.

Dear George:

Why don't you write an essay on the prevailing trend in thought and aesthetics? You might call it "The Americanization of Intellect." I'd do the article myself, if I knew where Bierce had left his cat-o'-nine-tails.

I suppose I'm hopelessly "inadaptable;" but I simply can't attain to that faith in material values professed by the humanists and other Babbits. Many attempts have been made to convert me; but I still fail to see that the "impossible"—or problematical—is any more futile than anything else as a poetical topic. Indeed, my fondest dream is to find a Hyperborea beyond Hyperborea, in the realm of imaginative poetry. I have the feeling that my best and most original work is still to be done.

However, I didn't mean to start an argument by what I wrote. We both know the futility of argument. But—whenever you begin to feel that you have wasted your time in writing imaginative verse, remember that poetry such as yours and mine would have found as little favour in the 18th century as it does to-day. Dr. Johnson and the other Henry Seidel Canbys[1] of his time would scarcely have understood "A Wine of Wizardry." And I'll be damned if I can see that the present age, for all its scientific discoveries, psychoanalysis, etc., is any smarter or more sophisticated than the 18th. It is, however, equally cock-sure, and materialistic;—or more so. But the present orgy of materialism will exhaust itself sooner or later, and perhaps end in some great social *debacle*. After that—since history never does anything but plagiarize itself—there may be a revival of interest in imaginative literature, and a new Romantic epoch, like that which followed the French Revolution.

Yes, I get the Overland, and always look for your page in it. I'd appreciate an extra copy or two of the issue in which W.'s article comes out. Wandrei has a theory that the literature of the future, since purely human topics are pretty well worked out, will concern itself more and more with the fantastic and the cosmic. Hence, in part, his enthusiasm for my stuff. Of course, neither he nor I, nor any body else can **prove** anything about the literary tastes and trends of posterity.

Dam'me, I believe I'll do an article myself, in defense of imaginative poetry.[2] One could attack the current literary humanism, with its scorn of all that has no direct anthropological bearing, as a phase of the general gross materialism of the times. If imaginative poetry is childish and puerile, then Shakespeare was a babbling babe in his last days, when he wrote that delightful fantasy, "The Tempest." And all the other great Romantic masters, Keats, Poe, Baudelaire, Shelley, Coleridge, etc., are mentally inferior to every young squirt, or old one, who has read Whitman and Freud, and renounced the poetic chimeras in favour of that supreme superstition, Reality.

Ben says somewhere that poets pay their debts in stars and are paid, in wormwood. But I'll pay some of mine in nitric acid.

Affectionately,

Clark.

1. Henry Seidel Canby (1878–1961), American critic who founded the *Saturday Review of Literature* in 1926.

2. CAS, "In Defense of Imaginative Poetry," ms., John Hay Library.

[371] GS to CAS [ALS]

[Bohemian Club
San Francisco]

Nov. 9th, 1926.

Dear Clark:

I have utterly no quarrel with imaginative poetry, for as Bierce has said, imagination *is* poetry, or poetry imagination.[1] I'd merely want that imagination turned on such themes as have some relation to life, some vital significance, as in Adonais, the Eve of St. Agnes, Ulysses, Dolores, an many other great poems I could specify. I've no quarrel with such poems as my "Wine" and your "Hashish Eater," but cannot rank them as high as those I've mentioned. But, as you wisely say, argument is useless in matters of taste. And one's tastes change with advancing years. I only hope I won't find myself calling Whitman a Titan, as Ben De C. does!

I enclose a note from Phelan. To oblige him would do no especial harm. He has lately sent me a sonnet of his own—nothing remarkable, but far better than I imagined him capable of.

The Overland with Wandrei's article will be out late in the month. I'll see you get all the copies you want, as shall he.

Mencken won't be here till the end of the week. Some Hollywood cinema cat has her claws in him—Aileen Pringle, I think.[2]

I've quit writing to Leo, and hope he has quit writing to me.

Yours in the love of Aimee,[3]   George.

[Enclosure: newspaper clipping, "Mencken Again Poet's Woe."]

1. "Imagery, that is to say, imagination, is not only the life and soul of poetry; it is the poetry." AB, "An Insurrection of the Peasantry" (1907), *Collected Works*, 10.196.

2. GS was correct in believing that HLM was having an affair with the actress Aileen Pringle.

3. A mocking allusion to the popular evangelist Aimée Semple McPherson (1890–1944).

FATHER STERLING

e. a. d.

Appendix

To George Sterling

High priest of this our latter Song,
    Whose voice sustains her empery
    Far-fled beside the western sea,
With ocean-tones thy voice is strong;

And as the spirit of a height,
    Whose calm, majestic eyes behold
    The lower hills like waves outrolled,
And watch from vantages of light

The abysmal surge of heavenly wars,
    And know sidereal mirth and pain,
    Though call'st to me, who may not gain
Thy vast horizon of the stars.

Yet though I breathe a fainter tone,
    And bring to Beauty's deathless shrine
    A lesser offering than thine,
Whose blooms in loftier soil are grown,

Mayhap the note that I have sung,
    Obedent to the Muse's call,
    Is not in vain; the coronal
Of fragile flowers not voidly flung.

And this the recompense I find:
    To pass, a cadence of her lyre—
    A flame to feed her altar-fire—
And breath on some supernal wind.
                —*Clark Ashton Smith*

To George Sterling

What questioners have met the gaze of Time,
    Whose searchless eyes unyielding theirs denied,
    Till sank the casual monarch's baselsss pride,
And transitory fames of sword of rhyme!
What fames from gulfs monotonous shall climb,
    Whose eyes ephemeral, unverified,
    Shall that enduring scrutiny abide
As men that face the noontide sun sublime!

* * *

One after one the searchers stare and fall,
   Abased before its unabated scorn,
But this thy fame, in days eventual,
   'Mid ruins desolate shall stand unworn,
Confronting Time in vastness musical,
   Like Memnon's statue staring at the morn.
                    —*Clark Ashton Smith*

TO GEORGE STERLING

His song shall waken the dull-sleeping throng
   That dreams of sullen and of earth-bound things;
   He soars with Beauty where the Eternal sings,
And the Deep's insuperable chants prolong
The everlasting sovereignties of Song—
   Where caverned thunder from the mountains flings
   Its dirge o'er the dust of crumbled thrones and kings,
He stands defiant of Oblivion's wrong.

But ampler Liberty, divine and strange,
   Hums in the song of his Promethean lyre,
      An echo of lost Time's immortal ones;
The tangled webs of mortal Death and Change
   Perish before his chanting lyric fire
      That gleams in the paling light of sinking suns.
                    —*Clark Ashton Smith*

TO THE EDITOR OF *TOWN TALK*

Editor Town Talk, Sir:
   In a single day of last week all the daily newspapers of San Francisco published long eulogistic articles on the genius and work of young Clark Ashton Smith, the poet of Auburn. Some of them have repeated their raptures with further quotations from Mr. Smith's verses to justify the transports. That all these writers should be persuaded to see the light at once is obviously more than a coincidence, yet I think it does not imply the interested activity of a "press agent"—only the zeal of some fool friend more concerned for the glory of a discoverer than for the good of the discoveree. I call this "team work" and its instigation pretty "raw," and having myself a good opinion of Mr. Smith, his verses and his possibilities, am sorry to see him thrown to the lions of reaction from so many hands—one might almost say from several sides of the arena at once.
   In nearly all these eulogies I find myself credited with praises that I never uttered. One paper has me affirming Mr. Smith's "extraordinary genius," another "declaring" that his poems are "no way inferior to those of Keats," and so forth. These falsehoods have doubtless a common origin in the mind of the fool friend herein before mentioned but to me unknown.
   Several weeks ago I had from a correspondent a manuscript copy of Mr. Smith's

"Ode to the Abyss." It seemed to me uncommonly good work and a promise of better work to come. So I commended it—in just what words I do not recollect, but if I said any of the things recently attributed to me I beg my correspondent to cover me with shame and confusion by quoting them from my letter—and filing the letter in proof.

My correspondent is Mr. George Sterling.[1]

Sincerely yours,

—Ambrose Bierce.

Oakland, August 6.[2]

THE COMING SINGER

The Veil before the mystery of things
    Shall stir for him with iris and with light;
    Chaos shall have no terror in his sight
Nor earth a bond to chafe his urgent wings;
With sandals beaten from the crowns of kings
    Shall he tread down the altars of their night,
    And stand with Silence on her breathless height,
To hear what song the star of morning sings.

With perished beauty in his hands as clay,
    Shall he restore futurity its dream.
Behold! his feet shall take a heavenly way
        Of choric silver and of chanting fire,
    Till in his hands unshapen planets gleam,
        'Mid murmurs from the Lion and the Lyre.

—*George Sterling*

PREFACE TO *ODES AND SONNETS*

"The tendency of modern poetry" is against it, and the gaunt Muse of these lonesome latter years stammers with a greater facility than marks her singing. So many, however, are congenitally opaque to "the soul and inner light of song," and hence able to view it from only an intellectual standpoint, that she does not lack followers of her shambling "progress."

Those devotees of austerity will find little to appeal to them in the rich and spacious poems here presented. In fact, an even partial use of the intelligence that is their one asset will cause them to shrink from the stern conclusions involved in some of the

---

1. AB to GS, 11 August 1911, ms. NYPL: "Kindly convey to young Smith of Auburn my felicitations on his admirable 'Ode to the Abyss'—a large theme, treated with dignity and power. It has many striking passages—such, for example, as 'The Romes of ruined spheres.' I'm conscious of my sin against the rhetoricians in liking that, for it jolts the reader out of the Abyss and back to earth. Moreover it is a metaphor which belittles, instead of dignifying. But I like it.

"He is evidently a student of George Sterling, and being in the formative stage, can not—why should he?—conceal the fact."

2. *Town Talk* No. 1042 (10 August 1912): 10–11.

passages of this book—to turn from its terrible vistas. Clark Ashton Smith is unlikely to be afflicted with present-day popularity.

Nevertheless, one will find in the sheer imagination of the succeeding pages evidence and proof of a precocity vast and sublime in its range, and quite unequalled in English verse; for the greatest of these poems (most of them, indeed,) were written before their author had attained the age of twenty. At that age Pope had a certain hard cleverness (little more), and Rossetti had written, though not perfected, the beautiful "Blessed Damozel." But imagine either of them writing a thing at once so amazingly mature and imaginative as "Nero." It is unthinkable.

Chatterton is commonly held up as the criterion of literary precocity; yet he was, for all his strong personality, a babbling babe compared to Smith, so far as poetry is concerned. In fact, his "poems" are mere verse and not poetry, while in the pages that follow the discerner of pure gold will find it in heavy veins. Beside it, I can imagine nothing more ephemeral than the aridities and extravagances of free verse. In the new treason to beauty Clark Smith has had no hand. Let us be grateful for that, as the years to come will be grateful. And let California be proud that such a phenomenon exists within her borders.

—*George Sterling*

BOHEMIAN CLUB,
APRIL 17, 1918.

PREFACE TO *EBONY AND CRYSTAL*

Who of us care to be present at the *accouchement*[3] of the immortal? I believe that we so attend who are first to take this book in our hands. A bold assertion, truly, and one demonstrable only in years remote from these; and—dust wages no war with dust. But it is one of those things that I should most "like to come back and see."

Because he has lent himself the more innocently to the whispers of his subconscious daemon, and because he has set those murmurs to purer and harder crystal than we others, by so much the longer will the poems of Clark Ashton Smith endure. Here indeed is loot against the forays of moth and rust.[4] Here we shall find none or little of the sentimental fat with which so much of our literature is larded. Rather shall one in Imagination's "mystic mid-region,"[5] see elfin rubies burn at his feet, witch-fires glow in the nearer cypresses, and feel upon his brow a wind from the unknown. The brave hunters of flyspecks on Art's cathedral windows will find little here for their trouble, and both the stupid and the over-sophisticated would best stare owlishly and pass by: here are neither kindergartens nor skyscrapers. But let him who is worthy by reason of his clear eye and unjaded heart wander across these borders of beauty and mystery and be glad.

—*George Sterling*

RECENT BOOKS OF FACT AND FICTION

As a boy of sixteen or thereabouts, Clark Ashton Smith was discovered as "the Keats

---

3. Birth (literally, child-bed).
4. Matt. 6:19: "Lay not up for yourselves treasures upon earth, where moth and rust doth corrupt . . ."
5. See letter 262, n. 1.

of the Pacific Coast," and duly proclaimed as such by all the San Francisco newspapers. A great deal of water has passed in and out of the Golden Gate since then, but though we have heard less of the Keats, the bard has never ceased to woo the muse. His loves have changed and if unanimity were possible for a new label following publication of *Ebony and Crystal*, it would [be] "the Poe" or "the Baudelaire" of California.

Smith is a literary chameleon with a distressing facility for taking on the color of his poetic surroundings. At present these surroundings are Poe and Baudelaire with a little of George Sterling in the middle distance.

Baudelaire himself might have written such things as would make the Alexandrine sonnets "Inferno" and "Mirrors" read like perfect translations, while "The Land of Evil Stars" is so like Poe it might have been foisted on an innocent world as a long lost manuscript of our surest immortal. "The Hashish-Eater" outwizards "A Wine of Wizardry," for it more than speaks of the younger Sterling. It is a summing up of all possible weirdness and horror, a mosaic of a stupefying imagination. Yet it fails of that terror it was the evident purpose to suggest. To borrow from Gilbert it is sometimes merely "very terrible" and incites a smile.

Yet all in all this book is well stocked with splendidly imaginative lines. It is not for the general reader, but its craftsmanship will inspire either delight or envy in those that would rival it. A poet sings or croons to us in "Dissonance," "Transcendence," "Forgetfulness," and "The Harlot of the World"—the same being life.

The bard writes love poems, but he gives the impression of a poet with a mind more upon his own words than upon his lover's lips. He woos with artifice and not passionately: he presents jewels where he should give flowers. Evidently he has his own private dictionary from which all prose words have been expurgated. All is, as George Sterling says in a brief foreword, "pure and hard," and he might have added "without heart."

It is art in unhuman, almost unearthly form—a deliberate evasion of reality. But it is an art in which among living bards he stands alone.

—*George Douglas [i.e., George Sterling]*

POETRY OF THE PACIFIC COAST—CALIFORNIA

A younger and immensely imaginative singer is Clark Ashton Smith, the story of whose triumph with his neighbors, when hundreds of copies of his first book of verses were promptly bought up in a small California hill town, is a romance in itself. He is the author of *The Star-Treader, Odes and Sonnets, Ebony and Crystal,* and *Sandalwood.* His mood and writing are in sharp contrast to the realism of Sandburgian atmosphere. No idealization, in his woodland music, of the great machine of today, rather a turning away from industrialism and, as Max Nordau would say, the lies of civilization.[6] He sings:

> Let us leave the hateful town
> With its stale, forgotten lies;
> Far beneath renewing skies,

---

6. Max Nordau (1849–1923), Hungarian sociologist and author of *Die conventionellen Lügen der Kulturmenschheit* (1883; Eng. tr. as *The Conventional Lies of Our Civilization,* 1884), a study of religion and politics. Nordau is best known for his treatise *Entartung* (1892–93; Eng. tr. as *Degeneration,* 1895), a condemnation of the perceived morbidity of contemporary art that was widely ridiculed for philistinism and Puritanism.

> Where the piny slope goes down,
> All with April love and laughter—
> None to leer and none to frown—
> We shall pass and follow after
> Shattered lace of water spun
> On a steep and stony loom
> Down the paths of laurel-gloom.[7]

A disciple of Poe and Baudelaire, he has gone as far into the regions of the weird and terrible as either of the elder poets. For what is called "pure" poetry, one shall search for his equal in vain among contemporary poets.

—George Sterling

TO GEORGE STERLING: A VALEDICTION

1

Farewell, a late farewell! Tearless and unforgetting,
Alone, aloof, I twine
Cypress and golden rose, plucked at the chill sunsetting,
Laurel, amaracus, and dark December vine
Into a garland wove not too unworthily
For thee who seekest now an asphodel divine.
Though immaterial the leaf and blossom be,
Haply they shall outlinger these the seasons bring,
The seasons take, and tell of mortal monody
Through many a mortal spring.

II

Once more, farewell! Naught is to do, naught is to say,
Naught is to sing but sorrow!
For grievous is the night, and dolorous the day
In this one hell of all the damned we wander thorough.
Thou hast departed—and the dog and swine abide,
The fetid-fingered ghouls will delve, on many a morrow
In charnel, urn and grave: the sun shall lantern these,
Oblivious, till they too have faltered and have died,
And are no more than pestilential breath that flees
On air unwalled and wide.

III

Let ape and pig maintain their council and cabal:
In ashes gulfward hurled,
Thou art gone forth with all of loveliness, with all

---

7. CAS "Adventure," ll. 1–10.

Of glory long withdrawn from a desertless world.
Now let the loathlier vultures of the soul convene:
They have no wings to follow thee, whose flight is furled
Upon oblivion's nadir, or some lost demesne
Of the pagan dead, vaulted with perfume and with fire,
Where blossoms immarcescible in verspertine
Strange amber air suspire.

IV

Peace, peace! for grief and bitterness avails not ever,
And sorrow wrongs thy sleep:
Better it is to be as thou, who art forever
As part and parcel of the infinite fair deep—
Who dwellest now in mystery, with days hesternal
And time that is not time: we have no need to weep,
For woe may not befall, where thou in ways supernal
Hast found the perfect love that is oblivion,
The poppy-tender lips of her that reigns, eternal,
In realms not of the sun.

V

Peace, peace! Idle is our procrastinating praise,
Hollow the harps of laud;
And not necessitous the half-begrudgèd bays
To thee, whose song forecrowned thee for a lyric god,
Whose name shall linger strangely, in the sunset years,
As music from a more enchanted period—
An echo flown upon the changing hemispheres,
Re-shaped with breath of alien maiden, alien boy,
Re-sung in future cities, mixed with future tears,
And with remoter joy.

VI

From Aphrodite thou hast turned to Proserpine:
No treason hast thou done,
For neither goddess is a goddess more divine,
And verily, my brother, are the twain not one?
We too, as thou, with hushed desire and silent paean,
Beyond the risen dark, beyond the fallen sun,
Shall follow her, whose pallid breasts, on shores Lethean,
Are favorable phares to barges of the world;
And we shall find her there, even as the Cytherean,
In love and slumber furled.

—Clark Ashton Smith

GEORGE STERLING: AN APPRECIATION

Among the various literary fervors and enthusiasms of my early youth, there are two that have not faded as such things most often fade, but still retain in these latter years a modicum of their "fringing flames of marvel." Unique, and never to be forgotten, was the thrill with which, at the age of thirteen, I discovered for myself the poems of Poe in a grammar-school library; and, despite the objurgations of the librarian, who considered Poe "unwholesome," carried the priceless volume home to revel for enchanted days in its undreamt-of melodies. Here, indeed, was "balm in Gilead,"[8] here was a "kind nepenthe."[9] Likewise memorable, and touched with more than the glamour of childhood dreams, was my first reading, two years later, of "A Wine of Wizardry" in the pages of the old *Cosmopolitan*. The poem, with its necromantic music, and splendors as of sunset on jewels and cathedral windows, was veritably all that its title implied; and—to pile marvel upon enchantment—there was the knowledge that it had been written in my own time, by someone who lived little more than a hundred miles away. In the ruck of magazine verse it was a fire-opal of the Titans in a potato bin; and, after finding it, I ransacked all available contemporary periodicals, for verse written by George Sterling, to be rewarded, not too frequently, with some marmoreal sonnet or "molten golden"[10] lyric. I am sure that I more than agreed, at the time, with the dictum of Ambrose Bierce, who placed "A Wine of Wizardry" with the best work of Keats, Poe, and Coleridge; and I still hold, in the teeth of our new Didactic School, the protagonists of the "human" and the "vital," that Bierce's judgment will be the ultimate one regarding this poem, as well as Sterling's work in general. Bierce, whose own fine qualities as a poet are mentioned with singular infrequency, was an almost infallible critic.

Several years later—when I was eighteen, to be precise—a few of my own verses were submitted to Sterling for criticism, through the offices of a mutual friend; and his favorable verdict led to a correspondence, and, later, an invitation to visit him in Carmel, where I spent a most idle and most happy month. I like to remember him, pounding abalones on a boulder in the back yard, or mixing pineapple punch (for which I was allowed to purvey the mint from a nearby meadow), or paying a round of matutinal visits among assorted friends. When I think of him as he was then, Charles Warren Stoddard's fine poem comes to mind. I take pleasure in quoting the lines:

TO GEORGE STERLING[11]
"The Angel Israfel, whose heartstrings are a lute, and who has the
sweetest voice of all God's creatures."[12]

Spirit of fire and dew,
Embodied anew.

* * * * *

---

8. Jer. 8:22.

9. Poe, "The Raven" (1845), l. 83. The phrase "balm in Gilead" appears in l. 89.

10. Poe, "The Bells" (1849), l. 20 (hyphenated in Poe).

11. *Sunset* 20, No. 5 (March 1908): 502 (in "Concerning Books of the West and the Men and Women Who Are Making Them") rpt. Henry Meade Bland (ed.), *A Day in the Hills* (San Francisco: Privately printed, 1926), pp. 53–54.

12. The epigraph is also the epigraph to Poe's "Israfel" (1831), a quotation from the Koran.

Vital and virile thy blood—
> Thy body a flagon of wine
> Almost divine:
Thou art a faun o' the wood,
A sprite o' the flood,
Not of the world understood.

Voice that is heard from afar,
Voice of the soul of a star.
From thy cloud in the azure above
'Tis thy song that awakeneth love—
Love that invites and awe that retards—
Blessed art thou among bards!

My astral is there where thou art,
Soul of my soul, heart of my heart!

Thou in whose sight I am mute,
> In whose song I rejoice;
> And even as echo fain would I voice
With timbrel and tabor and flute,
With viol and lute,
Something of worth in thy praise—
Delight of my days—
But may not for lack of thy skill—
For the deed take the will:

Unworthy, ill done, incomplete,
This scroll at thy feet.[13]

Always to me, as to others, he was a very gentle and faithful friend, and the kindest of mentors. Perhaps we did not always agree in matters of literary taste; but it is good to remember that our occasional arguments or differences of opinion were never in the least acrimonious. Indeed, how could they have been?—one might quarrel with others, but never with him: which, perhaps, is not the poorest tribute that I can pay to George Sterling. . . . But words are doubly inadequate, when one tries to speak of such a friend; and the best must abide in silence.

Turning today the pages of his many volumes, I, like others who knew him, find it difficult to read them in a mood of dispassionate or abstract criticism. But I am not sure that poetry should ever be read or criticized in a perfectly dispassionate mood. A poem is not a philosophic or scientific thesis, or a problem in Euclid, and the essential "magic" is more than likely to elude one who approaches it, as too many do, in a spirit of cold-blooded logic. After all, poetry is properly understood only by those who love it.

Sterling, I remember, considered "The Testimony of the Suns" his greatest poem. Bierce said of it, that, "written in French and published in Paris, it would have stirred

---

13. Charles Warren Stoddard, "To George Sterling," *Sunset* 20, No. 5 (March 1908): 502.

the very stones of the street."[14] In this poem, there are lines that evoke the silence of infinitude, verses in which one hears the crash of gliding planets, verses that are clarion-calls in the immemorial war of suns and systems, and others that are like the cadences of some sidereal requiem, chanted by the seraphim over a world that is "stone and night." One may quote from any page:

> How dread thy reign, O Silence, there!
> A little, and the deeps are dumb—
> Lo, thine eternal feet are come
> Where trod the thunders of Altair!
>
> Crave ye a truce, O suns supreme?
> What Order shall ye deign to hark,
> Enormous shuttles of the dark,
> That weave the Everlasting Dream?

In the same volume with "The Testimony of the Suns" is a blank verse poem, "Music," in which the muse Terpsichore was hymned as never before or since:

> Her voice we have a little, but her face
> Is not of our imagining nor time.

Also, there is the gorgeous lyric "To Imagination," and many chryselephantine sonnets, among which "Reincarnation," "War," and "The Haunting" are perhaps the most perfect.

As I have already hinted, I feel a peculiar partiality for "A Wine of Wizardry," the most colorful, exotic, and, in places, macabre, of Sterling's poems. (This, however, is not tantamount to saying that I consider it necessarily his most important achievement.) Few things in literature are more serviceable as a test for determining whether people feel the verbal magic of poetry—or whether they merely comprehend and admire the thought, or philosophic content. It is not a poem for the literal-minded, for those lovers of the essential prose of existence who edit and read our *Saturday Reviews* and *Literary Digests*. In one of the very last letters that he wrote me, Sterling said that no one took the poem seriously any more, "excepting cranks and mental hermits."[15] It is not "vital" poetry, he said, as the word "vital" is used by our self-elected high-brows (which probably, means, that it is lacking in "sex-kick," or throws no light on the labor problem and the increase of moronism). I was unable to agree with him. Personally, I find it impossible to take the "vital" school with any degree of seriousness, and see it only as a phase of materialism and didacticism. The proponents of the utile and the informative should stick to prose—which, to be frank, is all that they achieve, as a rule. Before leaving "A Wine of Wizardry," I wish, for my own pleasure, to quote a favorite passage:

> Within, lurk orbs that graven monsters clasp;
> Red-embered rubies smoulder in the gloom,
> Betrayed by lamps that nurse a sullen flame,
> And livid roots writhe in the marble's grasp,

---

14. AB, "The Passing Show" *New York American* (27 December 1903): 32; *San Francisco Examiner* (10 January 1904): 44.

15. See letter 369.

As moaning airs invoke the conquered rust
Of lordly helms made equal in the dust.
Without, where baleful cypresses make rich
The bleeding sun's phantasmagoric gules,
Are fungus-tapers of the twilight witch,
Seen by the bat above unfathomed pools,
And tiger-lilies known to silent ghouls,
Whose king hath digged a sombre carcanet
And necklaces with fevered opals set.

No, "A Wine of Wizardry" is not "vital verse." Thank God for that, as Benjamin de Casseres would say.

Notable, also, in Sterling's second volume, is the lovely "Tasso to Leonora" and "A Dream of Fear." His third volume, *A House of Orchids*, is compact of poetry; and, if I were to name my favorites, it would be equivalent to quoting almost the entire index.[16] However, the dramatic poem, *Lilith*, is, I believe, the production by which he will be most widely known. One must go back to Swinburne and Shelley to find its equal as a lyric drama. The tragedy and poetry of life are in this strange allegory, and the hero, Tancred, is the mystic analogue of all men. Here, in the conception of Lilith, the eternal and ineluctable Temptress, Sterling verges upon that incommensurable poet, Charles Baudelaire. In scene after scene, one hears the fugue of good and evil, of pleasure and pain, set to chords that are almost Wagnerian. Upon the sordid reality of our fate there falls, time after time, a light that seems to pass through lucent and iridescent gems; and vibrant echoes and reverberant voices cry in smitten music from the profound of environing mystery.

One might go on, to praise and quote indefinitely; but, in a sense, all that I can write or could write seems futile, now that Sterling is "one with that multitude to whom the eternal Night hath said, I am." Anyway, his was not, as Flecker's,

The song of a man who was dead
Ere any had heard of his song.[17]

From the beginning, he had the appreciation and worship of poetry lovers, if not of the crowd or of the critical moguls and pontiffs.

Of his death—a great bereavement to me, as to other friends—I feel that there is really little that need be said. I know that he must have had motives that he felt to be ample and sufficient, and this is enough for me. I am totally incapable of understanding the smug criticism that I have read or heard on occasion. To me, the popular attitude concerning suicide is merely one more proof of the degeneracy and pusillanimity of the modern world: in a more enlightened age, felo-de-se will be honored again, as it was among the ancients.

In one of Bierce's books is a trenchant article entitled, "The Right to Take One's Self Off." Here is the final paragraph:

"Why do we honor the valiant soldier, sailor, fireman? For obedience to duty? Not at all; that alone—without the peril—seldom elicits remark, never evokes enthusiasm.

---

16. I.e., the table of contents.
17. James Elroy Flecker (1884–1915), "Felo de se," ll. 1–2.

It is because he faced without flinching the risk of that supreme disaster—or what we feel to be such—death. But look you: the soldier braves the danger of death; the suicide braves death itself! The leader of the forlorn hope may not be struck. The sailor who voluntarily goes down with his ship may be picked up or cast ashore. It is not certain that the wall will topple until the fireman shall have descended with his precious burden. But the suicide—his is the foeman that never missed a mark, his the sea that gives nothing back; the wall that he mounts bears no man's weight. And his, at the end of it all, is the dishonored grave where the wild ass of public opinion

> Stamps o'er his head
> But cannot break his sleep."[18]

—*Clark Ashton Smith*

George Sterling: Poet and Friend

My sixteen years' friendship and correspondence with George Sterling began, like so many human relationships, through another friendship. In 1911, when I had reached the age of eighteen, Miss Emily J. Hamilton, late of Oakland, was teacher of English literature at the Auburn High School. Though not one of her pupils (since my formal schooling was already finished) I had been showing her my verses for some months. These verses she was so good as to criticize and, on occasion, praise. One day she said: "Why not send some of your poems to George Sterling?"

The suggestion both delighted and dismayed me. It seemed rather like venturing to address a demigod, and I was a little doubtful whether the deity could even be reached through a medium so mundane and prosaic as the mails. Since my fifteenth year I had sought, read and admired with almost acolytish fervor everything published by Sterling in current magazines, together with his two early volumes of poetry. It was anomalous, even fabulous that such poetry could be written by a contemporary. How could I find the presumption to approach this Apollonian being with my own Marsyas-like crudities?[19]

My friend reassured me. The demigod not only had a local habitation but was, she hinted, very human—almost, if anything, too human. He was gracious, kindly, helpful, to the novices of the Muse. She had known him in his Piedmont days, with Jack London, Joaquin Miller, Herman Whitaker, Herman Scheffauer. If I wished, she would write him a letter introducing my verses and me.

This began a correspondence that was to end only a week prior to Sterling's death in November, 1926. From the first, his letters showed the interest of a master in a promising pupil; and soon they were tinged with the affection of an older brother writing to a younger. I believe he regarded me as standing, in relation to him, somewhat as he had been in relation to Ambrose Bierce; and sought to pass on, in his turn, the critical help, encouragement and praise he had received from Bierce. His letters were rich in technical instruction and correction, though perhaps over-encomiastic. They chronicled his movements, the poems he wrote, the people he met; they flashed with incisive observations, admonitions, touches of gentle humor, epigrams of pagan philosophy or

---

18. See letter 150, n. 1.

19. In Greek mythology, Marsyas was a satyr who, having found a flute thrown away by Athena, challenged Apollo to a musical contest. Apollo won the contest and tied Marsyas to a tree, flaying him alive.

timely comment. They were marked by unfailing solicitude and thoughtfulness. They contained snatches of self-revelation that were boyishly frank. Unconsciously, they sketched the outlines of a character brave, noble, generous in the antique manner; self-forgetful to a fault; modest for himself but eager to proclaim a friend's worth; responsive to beauty in every living nerve, whether the beauty was that of an ocean sunset, a line of poetry, a mountain, or a woman's face.

My first meeting with Sterling was delayed till late in June, 1912, when, at his long-repeated invitation, I went down to spend a month with him in Carmel. I remember well the circumstances. Sterling had come with a horse and wagon to meet my train in Monterey but had somehow missed me at the station.[20]

Giving him up after a few minutes' wait, I decided to walk the four miles over the ridge to Carmel, and started in the thickening dusk through a country that was thrillingly new and strange to me. Some dweller on the outskirts of Carmel steered me vaguely in the general direction of Sterling's house. The road ran obscurely through a black forest starred with infrequent lights, and seemed to end at the last visible light. A woman (Mrs. Michael Williams, I believe) redirected me. I had only to cross a wooden footbridge and follow a narrow, winding path down the ravine. There, in the pine-fragrant darkness, I came to the blurred outlines of a cabin and a house; I knocked on the cabin's door. A high, cracked, New England voice sang out, "Come in, Clark Ashton Smith!"

The cabin's kerosene lamp revealed a figure which, after all the years, and after the very silence and absence of death, seems much more presently alive and vital than many that walk the earth today. About him there was something of the world's youth, something of kinship with its eternal life and the agelessness of the sea. His fine brown acquiline [sic] features, his strange mingling of grace and vigor, made one think of a beardless Sylvan or Poseidon. Somehow, in spite of its modernness, his very costume contributed to the impression of viability: he wore golf clothes and stockings of dark green, with a green bow tie and brown canvas shoes. In lieu of a leopard-skin, of wreath of vine-leaves or sea-wrack, the garb was not too inappropriate.

His first gesture, after our greetings and explanations, was the pouring of a joint libation from a wicker-covered gallon demijohn filled with muscatel. The spicy golden wine was indeed the nectar of Parnassus. It was made, I believe, in Monterey; but no muscatel of these latter seasons has ever had quite the same savor and potency.

Thus, for me, began a month of rare companionship and happiness. At that time Carmel consisted merely of one main street and a woodland in which the scattered houses were mostly lost to sight. On one side, between Sterling's house and the main street, the pine forest stretched unbroken, peopled only by jays and quail and rabbits. Here Sterling could hunt game or collect pine-knots and logs for fuel. The sea, though hidden from view, was not far distant; and its murmur mingled always with the murmuring of the tree-tops. It was a milieu of enchantment for a boy who had lived wholly heretofore amid inland hills.

---

20. NB: CAS was told by the train conductor to get off at San Jose, and had to purchase another ticket to Monterey, to get a later train, or so he confided many years later to his wife. He had delayed accepting GS's invitation until GS finally understood the delay, and sent him ten dollars to pay train fare. The cost of the second ticket took the remainder of his money. He never, of course, told Sterling that he'd walked to Carmel because he'd had no money left, nor of why he was late. [Editor's note in original appearance.]

Robinson Jeffers has written of Sterling's Indian-like familiarity with the coast about Carmel.[21] Truly, he was the genius of that scene and nothing escaped his observation and knowledge. I remember the hidden sea-cavern that he showed me below Point Lobos; the places where wild strawberries grew the thickest; the abalone-reefs; and the furtive incursions of a strange lurid red fungus that he pointed out to me on the Lobos cypresses. This fungus, in latter years, has increased so much it seems to illume the boughs and boles of certain trees as with the reflection of hellish fires; but in 1912 it was confined to a few scattered thumbnail patches.

Like all who love life greatly, Sterling loved the sea: its changing moods and colors and voices; and the things that lurked in its ultramarine depths or were cast up on its tawny beaches. Almost it seemed at times that he was native to that third element, like one of the Swimmers in his own weird and lovely poem.[22]

At the time of my visit, Sterling had given the use of his house to John Kenneth Turner, author of *Barbarous Mexico*, and Turner's wife and children, Turner being in temporary financial difficulties. Sterling was occupying the little cabin he had built for Nora May French; but, turning this over to me, he moved into a little tent for the duration of my stay.

He spoke often of Nora May French, that strange and tragically gifted girl who had ended her life with poison in the same bed in which I slept nightly. She had, it seems, previously attempted to shoot herself with his revolver and had brought him a tress of her ashen-blonde hair clipped away by the bullet. He showed me the very spot beside the path up the ravine where this attempt had occurred, according to her statement. But, oddly, there had been no powder marks on her hair. I do not recall that he attributed her suicide to unrequited love for James Hopper; but there had been other reasons . . . perhaps sufficient ones.

She was, he said, the most changeable person he had ever known: incredibly radiant and beautiful at times; at others, absolutely dull and colorless in her appearance. One day he brought out a manuscript of hers dictated during the delirium of illness. It was full of an otherworld weirdness; but I can remember nothing of it, but that it was "such stuff as dreams are made of"[23] and therefore immemorable as dreams.

On one occasion, I recall that George told me to keep the cabin door shut at night. "If you don't," he warned, "the cat will come in and jump on the bed. You'll think it's Miss X—— trying to climb into bed with you, and you'll be scared." "Oh, no," I rejoined, "I'll probably think it's Nora May's ghost, and I won't be scared at all. I'm sure that her ghost would be a lovely one." "You certainly have an imagination," he commented, half admiringly, half deprecatingly.

Sterling was alone then; his wife Carrie (who[m] I never met) being in Oakland. I have said that he was the *genius loci* of that coast: he was also the presiding genius among the artists in Carmel, who included Fred Bechdolt, Michael Williams, Herbert Heron, Redfern Mason, John Northern Hilliard, Grace McGowan Cook, and Chris Jorgensen. George was their leader in a standing feud with the forces of realty and "civic progress," headed by Perry Newberry, who wished to urbanize Carmel and pro-

---

21. See Robinson Jeffers, "A Few Memories," *Overland Monthly* 85, No. 11 (November 1927): 329, 351.

22. See letter 88, n. 1.

23. Shakespeare, *The Tempest* 4.1.156–57 ("on" for "of" in Shakespeare).

mote a boom in lot-buying and house-building. The war was fought lustily and bitterly; and the two factions were scarcely on speaking terms.

Life, however, seemed simple and leisurely there. Almost every morning, if I recall rightly[,] George took me on a round of calls, often distributing surplus game among his friends. There were wagon-rides up the Carmel valley, along the 17 mile Drive to Point Lobos, and a sea-fowl haunted spot several miles below Lobos where we pic-nicked with the Turner family. There were mussel-stews and incredibly complicated "mulligans" cooked amid the white sand-dunes; there were walks to Pebble Beach and in the woodlands carpeted with yerba buena and wild strawberry plants.

Also, there were rituals to be observed, such as the pounding of abalone steaks with a big wooden mallet on a boulder in the back yard; and the making each afternoon of a huge pitcher of punch, compounded subtly with Bourbon and soda, sliced pine-apple and mint from the meadow-bottom below the house. I was privileged to purvey the mint. George often commented on my temperance, since I would never exceed a fourth glass of that delectable brew.

I do not recall any excessive drinking on George's part; unless the term can be ap-plied to his consumption of numerous bottles of beer at a beach picnic. Later he apologized, saying that beer was a swinish drink. But the Saxons (he believed himself to be mainly of Saxon blood) had always been prone to it. Either on this occasion or some other, he maintained the superiority of the Saxon over the Gaelic peoples. Per-haps he had this prejudice in mind when he wrote the lines of that splendid lyric, "The Princess on the Headland."

Anyway, his prejudices were always strongly held and stoutly supported. Among others, he frankly despised the men of mere affairs and money-making divorced from all else. "They are mutts," he said, "That's what their women call them. . . ."

Regarding women, his advice was often sage, and often exquisitely raffish. . . . "Don't ever let a woman get the upper hand of you," he counseled. "Rule them with a rod of iron!"

His physical fitness was remarkable but he told me that he had not always been as robust. He brought out a photograph taken during his Piedmont period—"Look how thin I was then!" Indeed, the picture was all profile—an esthetic-looking shadow. He attributed the improvement in his health to a system of exercises devised by Sanford Bennett, a San Francisco business man who claimed to have rejuvenated himself when past fifty. The exercises were based on a principle of alternate tension and relaxation; and one in particular involved massage of the abdominal muscles under tension. It was supposed to strengthen the digestive powers.

Many years later I began to experiment with Bennett's system myself, and can tes-tify that its claims are far from exaggerated.

At the end of my Carmel stay, Sterling accompanied me to San Francisco, from which city I returned shortly to Auburn. We spent a night in Oakland as the guests of George's friend, Roosevelt Johnson, who seemed as distinctly an incarnation of the old Roman world as George was of the Greek.

A. M. Robertson, Sterling's publisher, had agreed to bring out my first volume of verse, *The Star Treader and Other Poems*.

George was indefatigable in assisting me with the endless correction of galley and page proofs exchanged by mail. Previously, he had advised me in the choice of poems for the collection. The numerous letters that he wrote me at this time, as well as these in regard to my subsequent volumes of verse, testify eloquently to his unbounded generosity and helpfulness toward a fellow-aspirant to the Muses' laurels.

Our next meeting occurred early in 1914, just prior to Sterling's departure for New York after his final separation from Carrie. After visits to Colt Bierce and Jack London, he stopped in Auburn and spent some time with my parents and me—I remember that he was "on the wagon" at the time but had brought along an immense box of chocolate candy, most of which he consumed himself, with the result of a sleepless night! During that brief visit he endeared himself greatly to my parents.

He was vastly interested in a mining-shaft which my father and I had started, and often referred to it in his subsequent letters from the east. He sent me from New York the ms. of a mining story he had written, and asked me to revise it in regard to the correct legal points of claim-staking and filing. These details my

Here the manuscript stops short. It resumes on p. 11.

[Sterling also assisted me in choosing the poems for *Odes and Sonnets,* published by the] Book Club of California for which Sterling wrote the preface. Three years later he was to write the foreword for my third volume, *Ebony and Crystal.*

I made occasional visits to San Francisco during those years, and George was always my companion and cicerone. He was then domiciled permanently at the Bohemian Club. Many of my memories of him are associated with the Club, and with such favorite latin restaurants as the Trattoria Bolognese (more familiarly known as the Bologna) presided over by the affable Bigin. Here, as elsewhere in San Francisco, the spirit of Bohemia was not unduly subdued by the devastations of the Volstead Act.

I recall, too, that George took me on charming visits to Mrs. Travis (Lawrence Zenda) and the tall, statuesque blond Mrs. Warlock, whom he called "Boadicea."

One day, in that den of silence and solitude, the Bohemian Club library, he gave me the manuscript of *Lilith* to read.

Either I did not wholly grasp the play's tremendous import and poetic opulence at that first hasty reading, or else I was backward in expressing my appreciation; for, after its publication, he seemed surprised at the enthusiasm with which I wrote of it in a letter. Truly, it is a magnificent thing, and without parallel in modern literature, apart from the poetic plays of Swinburne and D'Annunzio.

I like to recall those evenings at Bigin's, which have about them the charm of a time irretrievably vanished and remote.

George, a little grey, was still master of the revels. Stella was gone, but there were other dancers in that world such as Marie Parmalee, and the two Nic[h]ol girls, Margaret and Amaryllis, whom I had known during their childhood in Auburn.

George Sterling died in 1926 *[burn]* [The last] time that my friend and I met face to face was during _____, between Christmas and New Years. He was ill in bed at the Bohemian Club: the result of an over-successful Yuletide celebration. I remarked then at the semi-monastic bareness of his room, aside from the pictured constellations of feminine beauty on the walls. There were few books. He told me that he no longer cared to accumulate many possessions. Long since,

Here the manuscript ends in burned fragments.

—Clark Ashton Smith

To George Sterling

And I too found the seaward way.
  —*Venus   Letalis.*[24]

Deep are the chasmal years and lustrums long
Since, following that dark Venus of thy dream,
Thou camest to the lulling foam's extreme. . . .
But, safely builded beyond change and wrong,
And past "the fleeting plaudits of the throng,"[25]
With blazons blown on some ethereal stream
In crystal and in haliotis gleam,
Crag-founded, thine aeolian domes of song.

Yet, ah! the vanished voice we shall not hear!
Alas! thy footsteps ending on the sand
By doubtful seas and skies not understood. . . .
Strange shells are found along that silent strand:
Thou too hast often held them to thine ear
And heard the baffled murmur of thy blood.
                    —*Clark Ashton Smith*

PAN

---

24. GS, "Venus Letalis" (1923), l. 24.
25. GS, "To Xavier Martinez, Painter," l. 7.

VENUS

C·A·S·

CHLOE

C·A·S·

Glossary of Names

Abrams, Dr. Albert (1863–1924), a quack doctor in San Francisco, inventor of "radion-ics." GS long remained devoted to him, believing him capable of curing almost any disease. GS long urged CAS to be examined by him, to which CAS eventually consented.

Baudelaire, Charles Pierre (1821–1867), French "decadent" poet whose *Les Fleurs du mal* (1857) CAS undertook to translate nearly the whole.

Bender, Albert Maurice (1866–1941), San Francisco businessman, patron of the arts, benefactor and friend of GS and CAS. CAS dedicated "Memnon at Midnight" to him.

Bennett, Raine (1891–1987), publisher of *Bohemia* and literary patron in San Francisco.

Bierce, Ambrose (1842–1914?), short story writer, poet, satirist, fabulist, and feared journalist who long worked for William Randolph Hearst's *San Francisco Examiner* (1887–1906) and later his *Cosmopolitan* (1905–1909). He was GS's poetic mentor.

Braithwaite, William Stanley (1878–1962), noted African American critic and anthologist, literary editor of the *Boston Evening Transcript,* and editor of the annual *Anthology of Magazine Verse* (1913–29).

Bynner, [Harold] Witter (1881–1968), poet; co-founder with Arthur Davison Ficke of the mock poetic school of Spectrism.

Clark, Celia, wife of Curtis W. Clark, the mining magnate, and occasional benefactor of CAS.

Coolbrith, Ina (1841–1928; née Josephine D. Smith, niece of the Mormon prophet), early editor of the *Overland Monthly,* librarian in Oakland, and the first poet laureate named in the US (1915–28).

Dewing, Andrew (1897–1977), friend of CAS from Auburn.

Dunlap, Boutwell (b. 1877), San Francisco lawyer and historian and formerly consul for Argentina who in 1911 brought CAS to San Francisco, where he was interviewed by the press, so that Dunlap could be recognized for "discovering" the poet.

Fisher, Mahlon Leonard (1874–?), poet and editor of the *Sonnet.*

French, Nora May (1881–1907), poet who committed suicide at GS's home in 1907 at the age of 26. Her *Poems* (San Francisco: The Strange Company, 1910) was published by George Sterling, Jack London, Harry Lafler, and Porter Garnett.

Garnett, Porter (1871–1951), San Francisco literary figure and a leading figure in the Bohemian Club's annual Jinks.

Herkomer, Herman Gustave (1865–1935), Californian painter of portraits and interiors.

Heron, Herbert (1881–1968) and Opal, friends of GS in Carmel. GS carried on an affair with Opal for a time.

Hopper, James (1876–1956), short story writer and a member of GS's literary colony in Carmel.

Jeffers, (John) Robinson (1887–1962), poet. His third (self-published) book, *Tamar and Other Poems* (1924), brought him immediate fame. He was a friend of GS and the subject of GS's *Robinson Jeffers: The Man and the Artist* (1926).

Jennings, Leslie Nelson (1890–1972), poet and friend of GS, best known for his poem "Lost Harbor."

Lafler, Henry Anderson ("Harry"), San Francisco businessman, poet, and friend of GS.

Lathrop, Barbour (1847–1927), internationally known botanist and philanthropist.

London, Jack (1876–1916), fiction writer and journalist; one of GS's closest friends. GS claimed that he knew London better than his second wife, Charmian, did. London modeled the character Ross Brissenden in *Martin Eden* (1909) on GS.

Lovecraft, H[oward] P[hillips] (1890–1937), writer of weird fiction who corresponded with CAS beginning in 1922.

Loveman, Samuel (1887–1976), poet and longtime friend of AB, GS, CAS, Hart Crane, and H. P. Lovecraft; author of *The Hermaphrodite* (1926) and editor of *Twenty-one Letters of Ambrose Bierce* (1922).

Markham, Edwin (1852–1940), a colleague of AB and GS who gained celebrity with the publication of "The Man with the Hoe" (1899).

Mencken, H[enry] L[ouis] (1880–1956), journalist and essayist; coeditor of the *Smart Set* (1914–23) and the *American Mercury* (1924–33) and longtime correspondent of GS.

Miller, Cincinnatus Hiner (Joaquin) (1837–1913), California poet and longtime friend of AB. He attained fame in England upon the publication of his *Songs of the Sierras* (1871).

Neihardt, John G[neisenau] (1881–1973), Nebraska poet who later gained celebrity as the author of *Black Elk Speaks* (1932). He and GS corresponded extensively.

James Duval Phelan (1861–1930), banker, mayor of San Francisco for three terms, and US senator for one term; he was one of CAS's financial benefactors.

Robertson, A[lexander] M[itchell] (1855–1934), San Francisco bookseller; publisher of most of GS's poetry and also of *ST* (1912).

Schauffler, Robert Haven (1879–1945), poet, music critic, and friend of GS.

Scheffauer, Herman George (1878–1927), California poet, playwright, and translator, and AB's leading disciple until the emergence of GS. He later moved to Germany, where he wrote numerous tracts condemning America's involvement in World War I. He achieved celebrity as one of the earliest English translators of Thomas Mann.

Seymour, George Steele (1878–1945), secretary of the Bookfellows of Chicago.

Sinclair, Upton (1878–1968), novelist and social commentator who, along with his wife, Mary Craig (Kimbrough) Sinclair, were longtime friends and correspondents of GS.

Smith, Fannie (Gaylord) (1850–1935. CAS's mother.

Smith, Timeus (1855–1937). CAS's father.

Sterling, Carolyn (Rand) ("Carrie") (d. 1918), GS's wife; they divorced in 1913 and she committed suicide five years later.

Turner, John Kenneth (1879–1948), journalist and magazine writer. In 1913 he was briefly imprisoned by Diaz's troops while he was in Mexico.

Wandrei, Donald A[llen] (1908–1987), poet and author of weird and science fiction. He and August Derleth founded Arkham House to publish the work HPL; they ultimately published numerous books by CAS.

Wilson, Harry Leon (1867–1939), fiction writer, journalist, and friend of GS.

List of Extant Enclosures

This appendix lists extant manuscripts (and a few clippings) of the poetry of George Sterling and Clark Ashton Smith that had accompanied their correspondence. All (save where indicated otherwise) are in the Henry W. and Albert A. Berg Collection of English and American Literature, New York Public Library. The library owns many more manuscripts of Smith's poems than are listed in Donald Sidney-Fryer's *Emperor of Dreams: A Clark Ashton Smith Bibliography*, pp. 253–55. The manuscripts long ago had been separated from the corresponding letters, and so now it is impossible to determine with certainty the enclosures to each letter. In addition, each poet occasionally passed enclosures received on to others. We have indicated in the text proper, as best we can from internal evidence, the enclosures that likely accompanied certain letters. Comparison of the listings below with annotations to letters will show that some of the titles listed cannot be associated with any particular letter and, conversely, that the letters contained enclosures for which the original enclosure has not been found. The letters of Smith to Samuel Loveman indicate that he gave many of the Sterling poems to Loveman. Also, it is known that Smith gave two items to R. H. Barlow.

George Sterling

"The Aeroplane." TMS and carbon.

"After Sunset." TMS.

"Altars of War." TMS.

"Amber." TMS (carbon).

"At the Grand Cañon." TMS (carbon).

"Bombardment." TMS (carbon).

"The Caged Eagle." TMS (carbon).

"The Caravan." TMS (carbon).

"The Coming of Helen." TMS (carbon).

"Conspiracy." TMS (carbon).

"Coup de Grace." TMS (carbon).

"The Cynic." TMS (carbon).

"Discord." TMS (carbon).

"Disillusion." TMS (carbon).

"A Dog Waits his Dead Mistress." TMS (carbon).

"The Dreamer." TMS (carbon).

"The Dweller in Darkness." TMS (carbon).

"Eidolon." TMS (carbon). [GS note: Yours is worth a thousand of this.]

"Exile TMS (carbon).

"The Flag." TMS (carbon). [GS note: (To be sung to the air of "March of the Men of Harlich")]

"The Fog-Sea." TMS (carbon).

"From the Mountain." TMS (carbon). [GS note: Can you give me a list of the poems I've sent you since you left here? Then I can fill in the gaps. I may have sent you *this*.]

"The Gleaner." TMS.

"The Grizzly Giant." TMS.

"Henri." TMS (carbon). [GS note: Perhaps I've already sent this to you. It was in the "Delineator." I got $40. for it, but there's d—— little poetry in it! G.]

"High Noon." TMS (carbon).

"Hostage." TMS (carbon).

"The Hunting of Astarte." TMS (carbon).

"In the Market-Place." TMS (carbon).

"Indian Summer." TMS (carbon).

"The Last Man." TMS (carbon).

"The Last Mirage." TMS (carbon).

"Lilies of Lethe." TMS (carbon).

"Lineage." TMS (carbon).

"The Master Mariner." TMS (carbon).

"The Meteor." TMS (carbon).

"Miocene." TMS (carbon).

"The Muse of the Incommunicable." TMS (carbon).

"Night on the Mountain." TMS (carbon).

"Old Anchors." TMS (carbon).

"An Old Indian Remembers." TMS.

"On Certain Verses." TMS (carbon). [GS note: (in the "Dial.")]

"Once." TMS.

"On Fifth Avenue." TMS (JHL).

"The Pathfinders." TMS (carbon).

"The Pathway." TMS (carbon).

"The Pirate's Grave." TMS (carbon).

"Poe's Gravestone." TMS (carbon). [Originally titled "Poe's Tombstone"; changed by GS in pencil.]

"The Quest." TMS (carbon).

"Reason." TMS (carbon).

"Repartee." TMS (carbon). [GS note: In lieu of poetry!]

"Respite." TMS (carbon).

"Return, Romance! TMS (carbon).

"Scrutiny." TMS (carbon).

"The Setting." TMS (carbon).

"Sierran Dawn." Clipping.

"Silence." TMS (carbon).

"Stars." TMS (carbon). [GS note: Maybe I never sent you this. G.]

"The Thirst of Satan." TMS (carbon).

"Three Sonnets on Sleep." TMS (carbon).

"To Charles Warren Stoddard." TMS (carbon). 20 lines.

"To Europe." TMS (carbon).

"To the Allied Arms." TMS (carbon).

"The Tracker." TMS (carbon). [GS note: Perhaps I've already sent you this.]

"The Voice of the Wheat." Clipping (JHL).

"What Porridge Had John Keats." TMS (carbon). [GS note: An imitation of Browning.]

"Willy Pitcher." TMS (carbon). [GS note: This is the poem "The Atlantic" took.]

"The Wings of Beauty." TMS.

"The Young Witch." TMS (carbon).

CLARK ASHTON SMITH

"The Absence of the Muse." TMS. [Originally titled "To an Absent Muse"; changed by CAS in pen.]

"Adventure." TMS.

"Afterwards." TMS.

"Alchimie de la Douleur" (From Baudlaire). Clipping.

"Alien Memory." TMS. [CAS note: For George.]

"Alienage." TMS.

"Anodyne." TMS.

"Anterior Life" (After Baudelaire). TMS.

"Artemis." TMS.

"L'Aube Spirtuelle" (From Baudelaire). TMS.

"August" [= "Septembral"]. TMS.

"Autumn Orchards." Clipping. With "Points for the Pious."

"Ave atque Vale." TMS.

"Bâillement." TMS.

"Le Balcon" (From Baudelaire). Clipping.

"The Barrier." TMS.

"Beauty" (After Baudelaire). TMS.

"Before Sunrise." TMS. [Signed "C. Ashton Smith."]

"Beyond the Great Wall." TMS.

"The Blindness of Orion." TMS. [Originally titled "Orion"; changed by CAS in pen.]

"The Broken Lute." TMS. Prose poem.

"Brumal." TMS.

"Brumal." Clipping. Includes "Points for the Pious."

"The Butterfly." TMS. [Extensive comments by GS.] [GS note: This is full of poetry—a "poem for poets," if you know the phrase. I like also the unity of thought.]

"The Caravan." TMS. Prose poem.

"A Catch." TMS.

"Causerie" (After Baudelaire). TMS.

"Ceil Brouille" (Les Fleurs du Mal). TMS.

"Chance." TMS.

"Change." TMS.

"The Chimaera." TMS.

"The City in the Desert." TMS. [CAS note: These lines are remembered out of a dream.]

"Cleopatra." TMS.

"The Clouds." TMS.

"Cocktails and Creme de Menthe." Clippings. *AJ*, 11 October 1923; 18 October 1923; 8 November 1923; 22 November 1923.

"Cocktails and Creme de Menthe." Clipping. Includes "Nightfall."

"Cocktails and Creme de Menthe." Clipping. Includes "December."

"Cocktails and Creme de Menthe." Clipping. Includes "The End of Autumn," "Diversity," and "Departure."

"Companionship." TMS.

"Consolation." TMS.

"Contradiction." TMS.

"The Corpse and the Skeleton." TMS. Prose poem. [With extensive revisions by CAS.]

"Le Coucher du Soleil Romantique" (From Les Fleurs du Mal). TMS.

"Crepuscule." TMS.

"December." Clipping. Includes "Cocktails and Creme de Menthe."

"Departure." Clipping. Includes "Cocktails and Creme de Menthe," "The End of Autumn," and "Diversity."

"Disillsionment." TMS. With "Ode to Peace." [CAS note: Satires.] As by "Arzè Dnüöp."

"Dissonance." TMS.

"Diversity." Clipping. Includes "Cocktails and Creme de Menthe," "The End of Autumn," and "Departure."

"Don Juan Sings." TMS.

"Dream." TMS.

"The Dream-Bridge." TMS. [GS note: This is a fine little lyric. You'll think more of such things as you grow older.]

"Echo of Memnon." TMS.

"Ecstasy." TMS.

"Eidolon." TMS.

"The End of Autumn." Clipping. Includes "Cocktails and Creme de Menthe," "Diversity," and "December."

"Enigma." TMS.

"The Ennuye." TMS. [CAS note: Variatoin of "Ennui."]

"The Envoys." TMS.

"Epigrams." Clipping. *AJ*, 4 October 1923.

[Epigrams (untitled).] Clipping. *AJ*, 27 December 1923.

"The Eternal Snows." TMS. [GS notations keyed to attachment to letter 3.]

"L'Examen de Minuit" (From Les Fleur du Mal). TMS.

"Exchange." TMS.

"Exotic." TMS.

"The Fanes of Dawn." TMS.

"The Flower Devil." TMS. Prose poem.

"A Fragment." TMS.

"From the Crypts of Memory." TMS. Prose poem.

"From the Devil's Note-Book." TMS.

"From the Persian." AMS. [Signed "C. Ashton Smith."]

"The Garden and the Tomb." TMS. Prose poem.

"La Géante" (From Les Fleurs du Mal). TMS.

"The Ghoul and the Seraph." TMS.

"Harmonie du Soir" (From Les Fleurs du Mal). TMS.

"The Hashish-Eater." TMS. [Note: Does not include familiar subtitle.]

"Haunting." TMS.

"Heliogabalus." TMS. [Two sonnets.]

"Les Hiboux" (From Baudelaire). Clipping.

"The Hidden Paradise." TMS.

"The Hope of the Infinite." TMS.

"Horreur Sympathetique" (From Baudelaire). Clipping.

"Hymne à la Beauté" (From Baudelaire). Clipping.

"Illusion." TMS.

"Image." TMS.

"Imagination." TMS. [Numerous marginal notations by GS.]

"Impression." Two TMSs.

"In Cocaigne." TMS. Prose poem.

"In Lemuria." TMS.

"In November." TMS.

"Incognita." TMS.

"The Incubus of Time." TMS.

"Inferno." TMS.

"Inheritance." AMS.

"Interrogation." TMS.

"The Last Night." TMS. [Marginal notations by GS keyed to letter 3.]

"Laus Mortis." TMS.

"Lemurienne." See "Tankas."

"The Litany of the Seven Kisses." TMS. Prose poem.

"Loss." TMS.

"Love Malevolent." TMS.

"The Love-Potion" (From *The Fugitives*). Clipping. Includes "The Song of Cartha."

"Madrigal." TMS.

"Maya." TMS.

"A Meeting." Clipping.

"Memnon at Midnight." TMS.

"The Memnons of the Night." TMS. Prose poem.

"Memorial." TMS.

"Minatory." Clipping.

"Mirage." TMS.

"Mirrors." TMS.

"The Mirrors of Beauty." TMS.

"Moesta et Errabunda" (From Les Fleurs du Mal). TMS.

"Moments." TMS.

"Moon-Dawn." TMS.

"The Moonlight Desert." TMS. [GS notatoins keyed to enclosure to letter 3.]

"The Morning Pool." TMS. [GS note: Good.]

"La Mort des Amants" (From Les Fleurs du Mal). TMS.

"Le Mort Joyeux" (Les Fleurs du Mal). TMS. [CAS note: A literal version of one of B's sonnets.]

"The Motes." Two TMSs.

"Mouths." TMS. [Author unidentified.]

"La Musique" (From Les Fleurs du Mal). TMS.

"The Mystic Meaning." TMS. [GS note: A fine lyric! Have you tried to place this? It seems to me eminently saleable—by which remark I don't intend to decry it!]

"Narcissus." TMS. Prose poem.

"Necromancy." TMS.

"New Teeth for Old Saws." TMS.

"Nightfall." TMS.

"Nightfall." Clipping. Includes "Cocktails and Creme de Menthe."

"Nocturne." TMS. [GS notations keyed to enclosure to letter 3.]

"October." Two TMSs.

"Ode." Clipping.

"Ode to Peace." TMS. With "Disillusionment." [CAS note: Satires.]

"On Re-reading Baudelaire." TMS. With "Tankas."

"On the Canyon-Side." TMS.

"The Orchid of Beauty." TMS.

"The Pagan." TMS.

"The Pageant of Music." TMS. [GS notations keyed to enclosure to letter 3.]

"Palms." TMS.

"Paradox and Persiflage." TMS.

"The Passing of Aphrodite." TMS. Prose poem.

"A Phantasy of Twilight." TMS.

"Plum-Flowers." TMS.

"Points for the Pious." Clipping. With "Brumal."

"Points for the Pious." Clipping. With "Autumn Orchards."

"A Precept." TMS.

"Psalm" [= "A Psalm to the Best Beloved"]. TMS.

"Psalm to the Desert." TMS.

"Query." TMS.

"Query." Clipping.

"Quest." TMS.

"Reclamation." TMS.

"Reclamation (rev.)." TMS.

"Remoteness." TMS. Prose poem.

"Requiescat." TMS.

"Requiescat in Pace." TMS.

"The Return of Hyperion." TMS.

"Reve Parisien" (From Les Fleurs du Mal). TMS.

"Rosa Mystica." TMS.

"Satiety." Two TMSs.

"The Saturnienne." TMS.

"The Secret." TMS.

"Sed Non Satiata" (From Baudelaire). TMS.

"Semblance." TMS.

"Semper Eadem" (From Baudelaire). TMS.

"The Shadow of the Unattained." TMS.

"A Sierran Sunrise." TMS.

"Solution." TMS.

"Song" (= "Love Is Not Yours, Love Is Not Mine"). TMS.

"Song" (from *The Fugitives*). TMS.

"The Song of Aviol" (From *The Fugitives*). TMS.

"The Song of Cartha" (From *The Fugitives*). Clipping. With "The Love-Potion."

"Sonnet" (= "Duality"). TMS. [CAS note: For George.]

"LXXX Spleen" (From Baudelaire). TMS.

"The Statue of Silence." TMS. Prose poem.

"Strangeness." TMS. [Original title obliterated.]

"The Sun and the Sepulchre." TMS. Prose poem.

"Symbols." TMS.

"Tankas." TMS. Contains "The Lemurienne," "Transmutation," and "You Are Not Beautiful." With "On Re-reading Baudelaire."

"The Tears of Lilith." Two TMSs.

"The Temptation." TMS. [With extensive revisions by CAS.]

"The Titans in Tartarus." TMS.

"To a Northern Venus." TMS.

"To Love." TMS. With "The Whisper of the Worm."

"To Omar." TMS.

"To the Chimaera." TMS.

"Transcendence." TMS.

"Transmutation." See "Tankas."

"The Traveller." TMS. Prose poem.

"Union." TMS.

"Upon the Seas of Saturn." TMS.

"A Valediction." TMS.

"Le Vin des Amants" (From Les Fleurs du Mal, by Charles Baudelaire). Clipping.

"The Voice in the Pines." TMS.

"The Voice of Silence." TMS. [GS notations keyed to enclosure to letter 3.]

"We Shall Meet." TMS.

"The Whisper of the Worm." TMS. With "To Love."

"Winter Moonlight." TMS.

"The Witch with Eyes of Amber." TMS.

"A Woman at Prayer" (From the French of Stuart Merrill). TMS.

"You Are Not Beautiful." See "Tankas."

BIBLIOGRAPHY

I. WORKS BY GEORGE STERLING

A. BOOKS

After Sunset. [Edited by R. H. Barlow.] San Francisco: John Howell, 1939.

Beyond the Breakers and Other Poems. San Francisco: A. M. Robertson, 1914.

The Binding of the Beast and Other War Verse. San Francisco: A. M. Robertson, 1917.

The Caged Eagle and Other Poems. San Francisco: A. M. Robertson, 1916.

The Evanescent City. With Nine Illustrations After Photographs by Francis Bruguiere. San Francisco: A. M. Robertson, 1915.

From Baltimore to Bohemia: The Letters of H. L. Mencken and George Sterling. Edited by S. T. Joshi. Rutherford, NJ: Fairleigh Dickinson University Press, 2001.

The House of Orchids and Other Poems. San Francisco: A. M. Robertson, 1911.

Lilith: A Dramatic Poem. San Francisco: A. M. Robertson, 1919. San Francisco: Book Club of California, 1920. New York: Macmillan, 1926 (preface by Theodore Dreiser).

Ode on the Opening of the Panama-Pacific International Exposition. San Francisco: A. M. Robertson, 1915. (Also in *San Francisco Examiner,* 20 February 1915, p. 65.)

The Play of Everyman. Based on the old English morality play. New version by Hugo von Hofmannsthal. Set to blank verse by George Sterling in collaboration with Richard Ordynski. San Francisco: A. M. Robertson, 1917.

Robinson Jeffers: The Man and the Artist. New York: Boni & Liveright, 1926.

Rosamund: A Dramatic Poem. San Francisco: A. M. Robertson, 1920.

Sails and Mirage and Other Poems. San Francisco: A. M. Robertson, 1921.

Sonnets to Craig. New York: Albert & Charles Boni, 1928.

Strange Waters. [San Francisco: Privately printed, 1926.]

The Testimony of the Suns and Other Poems. San Francisco: W. E. Wood, 1903. San Francisco: A. M. Robertson, 1904, 1907.

The Thirst of Satan: Poems of Fantasy and Terror. Edited by S. T. Joshi. New York: Hippocampus Press, 2003.

Thirty-five Sonnets. San Francisco: Book Club of California, 1917.

To a Girl Dancing. San Francisco: Printed by Edwin and Robert Grabhorn for Albert M. Bender, 1921. (Also in *San Francisco Bulletin,* date unknown. In *ThS.*)

Truth: A Dramatic Poem. Chicago: Bookfellows, 1923. Rev. ed. as *Truth: A Grove Play.* San Francisco: Bohemian Club, 1926.

Yosemite: An Ode. San Francisco: A. M. Robertson, 1916. (Also in *San Francisco Call and Post,* 22 October 1915, p. 13.)

B. POEMS

"The Abandoned Farm." *San Francisco Call and Post* (17 January 1914): 11. In *BB.*

"The Aeroplane." *Town Talk* No. 1231 (25 March 1916): 7 (as part of "Sonnets on the War"). In *CE.*

"After Sunset." *Smart Set* 70, No. 4 (April 1923): 54. In *AS.*

"After Vacation." *Munsey's Magazine* 52, No. 5 (September 1914): 784.

"Afterward." *Bookman* (New York) 37, No. 6 (August 1913): 682. In *BB*.

"Altars of War." *Bellman* No. 663 (29 March 1919): 356.

"Amber." *Step Ladder* 7, No. 2 (July 1923): 17.

"The Ashes in the Sea: N. M. F." In *HO, SP, ThS.*

"At the Grand Canyon." *Poetry* 1, No. 3 (December 1912): 76 (as "At the Grand Cañon"). In *BB, TjS, ThS.*

"At the Last." *American Magazine* 79, No. 3 (March 1915): 14.

"Atthan Dances" [from *Truth*]. *Smart Set* 66, No. 2 (October 1921): 87. In *SM, SP.*

"The Ballad of the Grapes." *Overland Monthly* 83, No. 10 (October 1925): 384.

"Ballad of the Swabs." *American Mercury* 6, No. 2 (October 1925): 140–41.

"Beauty Renounced." *All's Well* 2, No. 5 (April 1922): 78.

"Beyond the Breakers." In *BB. Collier's* 57, No. 26 (9 September 1916): 57 (as "Past the Breakers"). In *SP.*

"Bombardment." *Town Talk* No. 1188 (29 May 1915): 12. In *CE.*

"The Caged Eagle." *McClure's Magazine* 46, No. 37 (January 1916): 14. In *CE.*

"California." In *CE.*

"Careless." *Bookman* (New York) 53, No. 6 (August 1921): 520.

"The Caravan." *Voices* 5, No. 2 (November 1925): 49. In *ThS.*

"The Coming of Helen." Unpublished.

"The Coming Singer." In *BB. Literary Digest* 49, No. 19 (7 November 1914): 903. In *TjS, ThS.*

"Conspiracy." In *CE, SP, ThS.*

"The Cool, Grey City of Love (San Francisco)." *San Francisco Bulletin* (11 December 1920): 12. In *SM.*

"Coup de Grace." *Sunset* 57, No. 3 (September 1926): 18.

"A Critic." *Gently, Brother* 1, No. 1 (March 1924): [21].

"The Cynic." In *AS.*

"Discord." *Town Talk* No. 1119 (31 January 1914): 8. In *BB.*

"Disillusion." *Bookman* (New York) 60, No. 4 (December 1924): 429. In *ThS.*

"A Dog Waits his Dead Mistress." In *CE.*

"Distance." *Smart Set* 67, No. 1 (January 1922): 2.

"The Dreamer." Unpublished.

"Duandon." *Pacific Monthly* 24, No. 3 (September 1910): 266–71. In *HO, SP.*

"The Dweller in Darkness." *American Parade* 1, No. 4 (October 1926): 61. In *ThS.*

"Eidolon." *Laughing Horse* No. 6 (1923): [18]. In *ThS.*

"Egon's Song" [from *Truth*]. *Laughing Horse* No. 5 (1923): [29].

"Ephemera." *All's Well* 3, No. 2 (January 1923): 5. In *ThS.*

"The Evening Star." *All's Well* 1, No. 9 (August 1921): 186. In *SM. SP.*

"Exile." Unpublished.

"The Face of the Skies." *Smart Set* 66, No. 1 (September 1921): 130. In *ThS.*

"The Fall of the Year." In *CE.*

"Farm of Fools." In *AS, ThS.*

"Father Coyote." *Saturday Evening Post* 185, No. 1 (6 July 1912): 51 (as "Our Western Brothers"). In *BB, SP.*

"57." *All's Well* 2, No. 2 (January 1922): 24–25.

"The Fish Hawk." *Youth's Companion* 88, No. 49 (3 December 1914): 668.

"The Flag." See "Our Flag."

"The Fog-Sea." *Lyric West* 2, No. 10 (February 1923): 5. *Literary Digest* 76, No. 10 (10 March 1923): 38. *Current Opinion* 74, No. 5 (May 1923): 607.

"The Forty-third Chapter of Job." *San Francisco Examiner* (29 March 1911): 8. In *HO*.

"From the Mountain." *North American Review* 199, No. 5 (May 1914): 746. In *BB*.

"The Gardens of the Sea." In *HO. Sunset* 27, No. 1 (July 1911): 69. In *ThS*.

"Germany in Belgium" (2 sonnets). *McClure's Magazine* 49, No. 3 (July 1917): 18 (Sonnet I only). In *BiB*.

"The Gleaner." In *CE*.

"The Golden Past." In T. R. Smith, ed., *Poetica Erotica* (New York: Boni & Liveright, 1921–22), Vol. 2, p. 317. In *ThS*.

"Grasshopper." *New Masses* 1, No. 1 (May 1926): 29.

"The Grizzly Giant." *Sunset* 53, No. 5 (November 1924): 23. *Overland Monthly* 85, No. 3 (March 1927): 68.

"The Gulls." *Nation* No. 2959 (22 March 1922): 345.

"Henri." *Delineator* 86, No. 3 (March 1915): 19. In *CE*.

"Hesperian." In *SM, SP*.

"High Noon." *Step Ladder* 8, No. 3 (February 1924): 76.

"His Own Country." In *SM*.

"Hostage." *Lyric* 4, No. 11 (November 1924): 1. In *AS*.

"The House of Orchids." *Town Talk* No. 904 (25 December 1909): 18–19. In *HO, SP*.

"The Hunting of Dian." *Smart Set* 42, No. 2 (February 1914): 8 (as "The Hunting of Astarte"). In *BB, SP*.

"In the Market-Place." *Smart Set* 41, No. 3 (November 1913): 56. In *BB, SP*.

"In the Valley." Unpublished.

"Indian Summer." In *CE, TfS*.

"Infidels." *Smart Set* 55, No. 4 (August 1918): 386. In *SM, SP*.

"Kindred." *Poetry* 1, No. 3 (December 1912): 77. In *BB, TfS*.

"The Last Man." *All's Well* 5, No. 12 (December 1925): 12.

"The Last Mirage." Unpublished.

"The Last Monster." *Smart Set* 41, No. 4 (December 1913): 130. In *BB, ThS*.

"Lilies of Lethe." Unpublished.

"Lineage." *Bookman* (New York) 36, No. 5 (January 1913): 534. In *BB*.

"The Little Hills." In *AS*.

"Long Island Pebbles." *Argosy-Allstory* 153, No. 2 (28 July 1923): 180.

"Lost Colors." *Sonnet* 1, No. 8 (May–June 1918): 1. In *SM*.

"A Lost Garden." *Scribner's Magazine* 63, No. 2 (February 1918): 229. In *SM, SP*.

"A Lumberjack Yearns." Unpublished.

"The Master Mariner." *Smart Set* 40, No. 4 (August 1913): 8. *Literary Digest* 47, No. 8 (23 August 1913): 294. *Current Opinion* 55, No. 3 (September 1913): 202. In *BB, SP*.

"Memorial Day, 1919." *San Francisco Examiner* 105, No. 150 (30 May 1919): 22.

"Menace." *Century Magazine* 87, No. 6 (April 1914): 915. In *BB*.

"The Messenger." *San Francisco Chronicle* 112, No. 170 (4 July 1918): 1.

"The Meteor." *Verse* 2, No. 2 (October–November–December 1925): 16. In *ThS*.

"Miocene." *Saturday Review of Literature* 1, No. 33 (14 March 1925): 593.

"The Modern Muse." Unpublished.

"Moloch." In *CE*.

"The Muse of the Incommunicable." *North American Review* 197, No. 2 (February 1913): 234. In *BB, TfS, ThS*.

"Night on the Mountain." In *BB*.

"Night Sentries." *Harper's Monthly Magazine* 126, No. 3 (February 1913): 408. In *BB*.

"Night Sounds." *Munsey's Magazine* 53, No. 3 (December 1914): 513.

"Ocean Sunsets." *Harper's Monthly Magazine* 138, No. 6 (May 1919): 765. In *SM, SP*.

"Ode on the Centenary of Robert Browning." *Boston Evening Transcript* (4 May 1912): Sec. 3, p. 3. In Ferdinand Earle, ed., *The Lyric Year: One Hundred Poems* (New York: Mitchell Kennerley, 1912), pp. 235–41. In *BB, SP*.

"Ode to Shelley." *Scribner's Magazine* 72, No. 1 (July 1922): 69–72. In *AS*.

"Of Yesterday." *Cosmopolitan Magazine* 45, No. 2 (July 1908): 131.

"Old Anchors." *Literary Review (New York Evening Post)*, 21 June 1924, p. 833. *Argonaut* No. 2468 (12 July 1924): 4. *Current Opinion* 77, No. 3 (September 1924): 358–59.

"An Old Indian Remembers." *Southwest Review* 12, No. 1 (October 1926): 28–29.

"'Omnia Exeunt in Mysterium'" (3 sonnets). In *BB, TfS, SP* (Sonnets I and II only). In *ThS*.

"'On a Western Beach.'" *Sunset* 33, No. 1 (July 1914): 64. In *BB*.

"On Certain Verses." *American Parade* 1, No. 2 (April 1926): 30. In *AS*.

"On Fifth Avenue." *Munsey's Magazine* 54, No. 1 (February 1915): 41.

"Once." *San Francisco Bulletin* 138, No. 122 (27 August 1924): 1 (abridged). *Buccaneer* 1, No. 4 (December 1924): 29–30.

"Our Flag." As *The Flag (Dedicated to the 81st Field Artillery)*. San Francisco: A. M. Robertson, May] 1918. *Munsey's Magazine* 65, No. 3 (December 1918): 441.

"Outward." *Sonnet* 2, No. 2 (January–February 1919): 3. In *ThS*.

"The Passing of Bierce." *Reedy's Mirror* 25, No. 30 (28 July 1916): 491. In *SM, ThS*.

"Past the Breakers." *See* "Beyond the Breakers."

"The Path of Portola." *San Francisco Call* (unlocated). *Town Talk* No. 1159 (7 November 1914): 10.

"The Pathfinders." *American Mercury* 8, No. 2 (June 1926): 144–47.

"The Pathway." In *SM*.

"The Pirate's Grave." *All's Well* 3, Nos. 7–8 (June–July 1923): 7 (as "The Pirates Grave").

"Poe's Gravestone." *Nation* No. 2931 (7 September 1921): 259. In *SM*.

"The Princess on the Headland." *All's Well* 2, No. 1 (December 1921): 8. In *SM, SP*.

"The Queen Forgets." *Smart Set* 62, No. 2 (June 1920): 64. In *SM, SP*.

"The Quest." *San Francisco Water* 7, No. 3 (July 1928): 11.

"Rainbow's End." *Ainslee's* 48, No. 6 (February 1922): 136.

"Reason." In *SM*.

"Repartee." *San Francisco Review* (January 1926). In *AS*.

"Respite." *International* 8, No. 3 (March 1914): 89. In *BB, TfS*.

"Return, Romance!" *Independent* No. 3836 (17 February 1923): 126. In *AS*.

"The Revenge." *Contemporary Verse* 5, No. 1 (January 1918): 5. In *ThS*.

"The Roman Wall." *Century Magazine* 97, No. 4 (February 1919): 576. In *SM*.

"The Rune" [from *Truth*]. In *SM*.

"Said the Wind." *Poetry Journal* 2, No. 2 (February 1914): 49–50. In *BB*.

"Saul." *Bellman* No. 674 (14 June 1919): 661. In *SM, SP*.

"Scrutiny." In *BB*.

"The Seasons." *Delineator* 85, No. 2 (August 1914): 4.

"The Secret Garden." In *SM, SP*.

"The Secret Room." *Town Talk* No. 1129 (11 April 1914): 6. In *BB*.

"The Setting." In *BB*.

"The Shadow of Nirvana." In *CE, ThS*.

"Shakespeare." *Boston Evening Transcript* (22 April 1916): Part III, p. 4. In *CE*.

"Shelley at Spezia." *Step Ladder* 6, No. 3 (February 1923): 33. In *ThS*.

"Sierran Dawn." *Yale Review* 14, No. 4 (July 1925): 682 (a reprint; original appearance not found.).

"The Sibyl of Dreams." *Pacific Monthly* 23, No. 6 (June 1910): [frontispiece]. In *HO, ThS*.

"Silence." *Saturday Review of Literature* 3, No. 6 (4 September 1926): 81.

"The Slaying of the Witch." *Munsey's Magazine* 56, No. 4 (January 1916): 548–49. In *CE, SP*.

"The Sleepers." In *BB*.

"Sonnets on the Sea's Voice" [6 sonnets]. *Pacific Monthly* 21, No. 6 (June 1909): [frontispiece] (Sonnet I only; as "The Sea"). In *HO, TjS* (Sonnets I–IV). *Bookman* (New York) 58, No. 4 (December 1923): 438 (Sonnets V–VI). In *SM* (Sonnets V–VI).

"Spring in Carmel." In Jessie B. Rittenhouse, ed., *The Second Book of Modern Verse* (Boston: Houghton Mifflin, 1919), pp. 48–50. In *SM, SP*.

"Stars." Unpublished.

The Testimony of the Suns. In *TS, ThS*.

"'That Walk in Darkness.'" *International* 8, No. 2 (February 1914): 62. In *BB, TjS, ThS*.

"Then and Now." *Harper's Weekly* No. 2992 (25 April 1914): 23. In *BB*.

"The Thirst of Satan." *International* 8, No. 1 (January 1914): 26. In *BB, TjS, ThS*.

"Three Sonnets on Beauty." *All's Well* 1, No. 11 (October 1921): 235.

"Three Sonnets on Sleep." *Poetry Journal* 4, No. 5 (January 1916): 182–84. In *CE, TjS*.

"'Tidal, King of Nations.'" *Town Talk* No. 1118 (24 January 1914): 8. In *BB*.

"To a Stenographer." Unpublished.

"To Charles Warren Stoddard." In *HO*. *Town Talk* No. 1236 (29 April 1916): 8.

"To Europe." See "To Germany."

"To Germany." *New York World Magazine*, 16 August 1914, p. 2 (Sonnets I–III; as "To Europe"). *Literary Digest* 49, No. 11 (12 September 1914): 465 (Sonnets I–III; as "To Europe"). *Town Talk* No. 1160 (14 November 1914): 8 (Sonnets I–III; as "To Europe"; as by "George Stirling"). In John Erskine, ed. *Contemporary War Poems*. New York: American Association for International Reconciliation, 1914, pp. 28–29 (Sonnets I–III; as "To Europe"). *Town Talk* No.1231 (25 March 1916): 7 (Sonnets I–III; as "To Europe"; as part of "Sonnets on the War"). In *CE* (Sonnets I–V) (pp. 122–26); *BtB* (Sonnets I–VI) (pp. 16–21).

"To Life." *Sonnet* 1, No. 3 (1917): 2. In *TjS, SM, ThS*.

"To Margaret Anglin: In the Greek Tragedies." In *A Group of Sonnets Called Forth by Miss Anglin's Productions of Greek Tragedies in the Greek Theatre* (Berkeley: University of California Press, 1915). In *CE, TjS*.

"To Ruth Chatterton." *Ainslee's* 44, No. 5 (December 1919): 152 (as "The Masque of Dream: To Ruth Chatterton"). In *SM*.

"To Science." *Sonnet* 2, No. 5 (July–August 1919): 1. In *ThS*.

"To the Allied Arms." In *CE, BtB*.

"To the Mummy of the Lady Isis." In *CE, TjS, ThS*.

"To Xavier Martinez, Painter." *Lantern* 1, No. 9 (December 1915): 278. In *CE*.

"The Tracker." *All's Well* 2, No. 8 (July 1922): 121.

"Transmutation." *Harper's Monthly Magazine* 133, No. 4 (September 1916): 573. In *AS*.

"The Twilight of the Grape." *Smart Set* 68, No. 2 (June 1922): 56.

"Venus Letalis." *Smart Set* 70, No. 3 (March 1923): 98.

"The Voice of the Dove." *Century Magazine* 85, No. 6 (April 1913): 950. In *BB, SP*.

"The Voice of the Wheat." *Overland Monthly* 84, No. 4 (April 1926): 110–11.

"Vox Humana." In *Midsummer Music of Bohemia* (San Francisco: Bruce Brough, [1921]), p. 19. In *SM*.

"War." *Town Talk* No. 1113 (20 December 1913): 7.

"Wet Beaches." *Scribner's Magazine* 74, No. 5 (November 1923): 585–86. In *AS*.

"What Porridge Had John Keats." *New Republic* No. 470 (5 December 1923): 39. *Literary Digest* 79, No. 13 (29 December 1923): 32. In *AS*.

"Which Was, and Never Shall Be." *Wanderer* 2, No. 11 (November 1924): 148.

"White Logic." Unpublished.

"White Magic." In *HO, ThS*.

"Willy Pitcher." *Atlantic Monthly* 111, No. 6 (June 1913): 811. In *BB, SP*.

"The Wind." *Bellman* No. 523 (22 July 1916): 177. In *SM*.

"The Wine of Illusion." In *SM*.

"A Wine of Wizardry." *Cosmopolitan* 43, No. 5 (September 1907): [551–56]. In *WW, SP, ThS*.

"The Wings of Beauty." *Munsey's Magazine* 78, No. 4 (May 1923): 640.

"You Never Can Tell." *Smart Set* 43, No. 1 (May 1914): 8. In *BB*.

"The Young Witch." *Century Magazine* 106, No. 4 (August 1923): 588–91. In *AS, ThS*.

C. OTHER WORKS

"The Dryad." *Smart Set* 58, No. 2 (February 1919): 81–86.

"A First-Class Fighting Man." *American Mercury* 10, No. 1 (January 1927): 76–80.

"Introduction." In Ambrose Bierce. *In the Midst of Life*. New York: Modern Library, 1927, pp. i–xvi.

"Joaquin Miller." *American Mercury* 7, No. 2 (February 1926): 220–29.

"The Lovely Lady." *Munsey's Magazine* 90, No. 1 (February 1927): 90–94.

"The Old Wreck." *Munsey's Magazine* 84, No. 3 (April 1925): 511–18.

"Pleasure and Pain!" *Resources for American Literary Study* 3, No. 2 (Autumn 1973): 234–48 (edited, with introductory comment [pp. 230–34], by Joseph W. Slade; as "The Testament of an American Schopenhauer: George Sterling's 'Pleasure and Pain!'").

"Poetry of the Pacific Coast—California." In William Stanley Braithwaite, ed., *Anthology of Magazine Verse for 1926* (Boston: B. J. Brimmer Co., 1926), pp. 84–103.

Preface to *Odes and Sonnets* (San Francisco: Book Club of California, 1918), pp. iii–iv.

Preface [to *Ebony and Crystal*. (Auburn, CA: Auburn Journal,1922), p. ix.

"Rhymes and Reactions." *Overland Monthly,* November 1925–December 1926.

"The Shadow Maker." *American Mercury* 6, No. 1 (September 1925): 10–19.

The Vision of Portola. Town Talk No. 1139 (20 June 1914): 9 (excerpt). *San Francisco Water* 6, No. 2 (April 1927): 14–16.

II. WORKS BY CLARK ASHTON SMITH

A. BOOKS

The Abominations of Yondo. Sauk City, WI: Arkham House, 1960.

Burden of the Suns. Glendale, CA: Roy A. Squires, 1977.

The Dark Chateau and Other Poems. Sauk City, WI: Arkham House, 1951.

The Devil's Notebook: Collected Epigrams and Pensées. Edited by Donald Sidney-Fryer and Don Herron. Mercer Island, WA: Starmont House, 1990.

Ebony and Crystal: Poems in Verse and Prose. Auburn, CA: Auburn Journal, 1922.

The Fanes of Dawn. Glendale, CA: Roy A. Squires, 1976.

Grotesques and Fantastiques. Saddle River, NJ: Gerry de La Ree. 1973.

In the Ultimate Valleys. Glendale, CA: Roy A. Squires, 1970.

The Last Oblivion: Best Fantastic Poems. Edited by S. T. Joshi and David E. Schultz. New York: Hippocampus Press, 2002.

Nero and Other Poems. Lakeport, CA: The Futile Press, 1937.

Odes and Sonnets. San Francisco: Book Club of California, 1918.

Out of Space and Time. Sauk City, WI: Arkham House, 1942.

The Palace of Jewels. Glendale, CA: Roy A. Squires, 1970.

Planets and Dimensions: Collected Essays. Edited by Charles K. Wolfe. Baltimore: Mirage Press, 1973.

Poems in Prose. Sauk City, WI: Arkham House, 1965.

The Potion of Dreams. Glendale, CA: Roy A. Squires, 1975.

Sandalwood. Auburn, CA: Auburn Journal, 1925.

Seer of the Cycles. Glendale, CA: Roy A. Squires, 1976.

Selected Letters. Edited by David E. Schultz and Scott Connors. Sauk City, WI: Arkham House, 2003.

Selected Poems. Sauk City, WI: Arkham House, 1971. Prepared in the late 1940s.

A Song from Hell. Glendale, CA: Roy A. Squires, 1975.

Spells and Philtres. Sauk City, WI: Arkham House, 1958.

The Star-Treader and Other Poems. San Francisco: A. M. Robertson, 1912.

Strange Shadows: The Uncollected Fiction and Essays of Clark Ashton Smith. Edited by Steve Behrends, Donald Sidney-Fryer, and Rah Hoffman. Westport, CT: Greenwood Press, 1989.

To George Sterling: Five Poems. Glendale, CA: Roy A. Squires, 1970.

The Tartarus of the Suns. Glendale, CA: Roy A. Squires, 1970.

The Titans in Tartarus. Glendale, CA: Roy A. Squires, 1974.

B. POEMS

"The Absence of the Muse." *Lyric West* 1, No. 6 (October 1921): 14. In *EC, SP.*

"Adventure." *AJ* 24, No. 18 (14 February 1924; 30 lines only): 6. In *S, SP, LO.*

"Afterwards." *AJ* 23, No. 44 (16 August 1923): 6. In *S, SP.*

"Alchemy of Sorrow" [translation of CB]. *AJ* 25, No. 49 (17 September 1925): 4 (as "Alchimie de la Douleur"). In *S* (as "Alchimie de la Douleur"), *SP.*

"Alchimie de la Douleur." See "Achemy of Sorrow."

"Alien Memory." Original title of "Exotic Memory" (q.v.).

"Alienage." *AJ* 23, No. 38 (5 July 1923): 6. *Wanderer* 1, No. 6 (November 1923): 4. In *S.*

"Amor Aeternalis." In August Derleth, ed. *Fire and Sleet and Candlelight.* Sauk City, WI: Arkham House, 1961, p. 186. In *SP.* Original title: "To Love."

"Anodyne." See "Mors."

"Anterior Life" [translation of CB, "La Vie Anterieure"]. *Arkham Sampler* 1, No. 4 (Autumn 1948): 81. In *SP, S&P.*

"Apostrophe." In *SP.* Original title "Bâillement."

"Arabesque." In *EC, SP.*

"Artemis." In *EC, SP.* Written 16 May 1922.

"L'Aube Spirituelle." See "The Spiritual Dawn."

"August." See "Septembral."

"Autumn Orchards." *AJ* 24, No. 5 (15 November 1923): 6. *Buccaneer* 1, No. 2 (October 1924): 3. In *S, SP.*

"Autumn Twilight." [Probably = "Autumnal" in *EC*.]

"Ave atque Vale." In *OS, EC. Step Ladder* 13, No. 5 (May 1927): 136. In *SP.*

"Averted Malefice." In *ST, SP, LO.*

"Bâillement." See "Apostrophe."

"Le Balcon" [translation of CB]. *AJ* 25, No. 50 (24 September 1925): 4.

"The Barrier." *AJ* 23, No. 48 (13 September 1923): 6. In *S. Step Ladder* 13, No. 5 (May 1927): 130. In *SP.*

"Beauty" [translation of CB, "Le Beauté"]. *AJ* 25, No. 22 (12 March 1925): 4.

"Before Sunrise." Unpublished.

"Belated Love." In *OS, EC. Step Ladder* 13, No. 5 (May 1927): 132. In *SP.*

"Beyond the Great Wall." *Asia* 24, No. 5 (May 1924): 359. In *EC, SP, LO.*

"The Blindness of Orion." *Arkham Sampler* 1, No. 2 (Spring 1948): 20. In *SP, S&P.*

"Brumal." 24, No. 3 (1 November 1923): 6.

"The Butterfly." In *ST, SP.*

"A Catch." *AJ* 24, No. 51 (2 October 1924): 6 (as "Song"). In *S, SP.*

"Causerie" [translation of CB]. *AJ* 25, No. 30 (7 May 1925): 4.

"Ciel Brouillé." See "Doubtful Skies."

"Chance." *AJ* 23, No. 35 (14 June 1923): 6. *Bloodstone* 1, No. 2 (November 1937): 4. In *SP, LO.*

"Change." *AJ* 23, No. 39 (12 July 1923): 6. In *SP.*

"The Chimaera." In *EC, SP.*

"The City in the Desert." In *EC, SP, LO.*

"The City of the Titans." *Challenge* 1, No. 2 (Fall 1950): [12]. In *SP, LO.*

"Cleopatra." In *EC, SP, LO.* First title: "Anthony to Cleopatra."

"The Clouds." Unpublished.

"Coldness." In *EC, SP.*

"Companionship." Unpublished. Written 1910.

"Concupiscence." In *SP.*

"Consolation." *Step Ladder* 13, No. 5 (May 1927): 130. In *S, SP.*

"Contradiction." *AJ* 23, No. 31 (17 May 1923): 6. In *S, SP.*

"Le Coucher du soleil romantique" [translation of CB]. *United Amateur* 25, No. 2 (May 1926): 6.

"Crepuscule." In *EC* (as "Crepuscle"), *SP.*

"The Crucifixion of Eros." In *OS, EC. Step Ladder* 13, No. 5 (May 1927): 132. In *SP.*

"Cyclopean Fear." Extant?

"The Death of Lovers" [translation of CB]. *AJ* 25, No. 42 (30 July 1925): 4 (as "La Mort Des Amants"). *United Amateur* 25, No. 3 (July 1926): 6 (as "La Mort Des Amants"). *Arkham Sampler* 2, No. 4 (Autumn 1949): 80. In *SP.*

"December." *AJ* 24, No. 8 (6 December 1923): 6. *Poetry* 33, No. 3 (December 1928): 123. In *SP.*

"Demogorgon." Unpublished.

"Departure." *AJ* 24, No. 7 (29 November 1923): 6. In *S.*

"The Desert Garden." See "Song of Sappho's Arabian Daughter."

"Desire of Vastness." In *EC, SP, LO.*

"Desolation." In *EC, SP, LO.*

"Disillsionment." In *SP, S&P.*

"Dissidence." *AJ* 24, No. 7 (29 November 1923): 6 (as "Diversity"). In *SP*.

"Dissonance." *Thrill Book* 2, No. 6 (15 September 1919): 149. In *EC, SP, LO*.

"Diversity." See "Dissidence."

"Don Juan Sings." *AJ* 23, No. 30 (10 May 1923): 6. *Wanderer* 2, No. 3 (March 1924): 30. In *S, SP*.

"The Doom of America." Unpublished.

"Doubtful Skies" [translation of CB]. *AJ* 25, No. 34 (4 June 1925): 9 (as "Ciel Brouillé"). In *S* (as "Ciel Brouillé"), *SP*.

"Dream." See "The Nymph."

"The Dream-Bridge." In *ST, LO*.

"Dream-Mystery." See "Lunar Mystery."

"Duality." *WT* 2, No. 1 (July–August 1923): 69 (as "The Garden of Evil"). *AJ* 24, No. 20 (28 February 1924): 6. In *S, SP*. First title: "Sonnet"; second title: "The Garden of Evil."

"Echo of Memnon." In *EC, SP*.

"Ecstasy." *Pearson's Magazine* Vol. 48 No. 10 (October 1922): 32. In *EC, SP*.

"Eidolon." In *EC, SP*.

"Enchanted Mirrors." In *S. AJ* 26, No. 4 (5 November 1925): 4. *Overland Monthly* 83, No. 11 (November 1925): 407. In *SP, LO*.

"The End of Autumn." *AJ* 24, No. 7 (29 November 1923): 6. *Wanderer* 2, No. 11 (November 1924): 153. In *S* and *SP*.

"Enigma." *AJ* 25, No. 18 (12 February 1925): 4. In *S, SP*.

"Ennui." *AJ* 25, No. 14 (15 January 1925): 5. Later recast in alexandrines: *WT* 27, No. 5 (May 1936): 547. In *S, SP, LO*. First title: "The Ennuye."

"The Ennuye." See "Ennui."

"The Envoys." *AJ* 26, 13 (7 January 1926): 4. *Overland Monthly* 84, No. 5 (June 1926): frontispiece. *Overland Monthly* 84, No. 6 (July 1926): 230 (corrected version). In *SP, LO*.

"The Eternal Snows." In *In the Ultimate Valleys*.

"Evening Harmony" [translation of CB]. *AJ* 25, No. 47 (3 September 1925): 6 (as "Harmonie du Soir"). In *S, SP*.

"Examination at Midnight" [translation of CB, "L'Examen de Minuit"]. *AJ* 25, No. 40 (16 July 1925): 2 (as "L'Examen de Minuit"). In *S, SP*.

"Exchange." *AJ* 23, No. 34 (7 June 1923): 6. *Buccaneer* 1, No. 5 (January 1925): 17.

"Exotic Memory." In *SP.* First title: "Alien Memory."

"Exotique." In *OS, EC, SP*. Variant title: "Exotic."

"The Fanes of Dawn." In *The Fanes of Dawn*.

"Fire of Snow." *Poetry* 6, No. 4 (July 1915): 178. In *SP*.

"Flamingoes." *Asia* 19, No. 11 (November 1919): 1134. In *EC, SP*.

"The Flight of Azrael." *Fantastic Worlds* No. 1 (Summer 1952): 15. *SP*.

"Forgetfulness." *Sonnet* 4, No. 2 (May–June 1919): 2. In *EC, SP*.

"A Fragment." In *EC. Step Ladder* 13, No. 5 (May 1927): 134. In *SP*.

"From the Persian." Unpublished juvenilia.

"La Géante." See "The Giantess."

"The Ghoul and the Seraph." In *EC, SP, LO*.

"The Giantess" [translation of CB]. *Arkham Sampler* 2, No. 3 (Summer 1949): 82 (under "Two Poems after Baudelaire"). In *S* (as "La Géante"), *SP*.

"Gothic Nightmare." *See* "Nightmare."

"The Harbor of Dead Years" (= "The Harbour of the Past"? Unpublished.)

"The Harlot of the World." *Town Talk* No. 1179 (27 March 1915): 5. *Town Talk* No. 1361 (21 September 1918): [15] ("Golden Gate Literary Number"). *OS, EC, SP*. Variant title: "To Life."

"Harmonie du Soir." See "Evening Harmony."

"The Hashish-Eater; or, The Apocalypse of Evil." In *EC, SP, LO*.

"Haunting." *Lyric West* 1, No. 9 (February 1922): 6. In *EC, SP*.

"Hecate." Extant?

"Heliogabalus." In *SP*.

"Les Hiboux." See "The Owls."

"The Hidden Paradise." In *EC, SP*.

"The Hope of the Infinite." In *EC, SP, LO*.

"Horreur Sympathetique." See "Sympathetic Horror."

"Hymn to Beauty" [translation of CB]. *AJ* 25, No. 48 (10 September 1925): 8 (as "Hymne à la Beauté"). In *S, SP*.

"Hymne à la Beauté." See "Hymn to Beauty."

"Illusion." Unpublished.

"Image." In *EC, SP*.

"Imagination." In *LO*.

"Impression." In *EC, SP*.

"In Lemuria." *Lyric West* 1, No. 4 (July–August 1921): 6. In *EC, SP*.

"In November." *Ainslee's* 44, No. 5 (December 1919): 121. In *EC*.

"In Saturn." *Sonnet* 2, No. 2 (January–February 1919): 2. In *EC, SP, LO*. Original title: "Upon the Seas in Saturn."

"In the Wind." *Poetry* 6, No. 4 (July 1915): 178. In *SP*.

"Incognita." *AJ* 25 No. 25 (2 April 1925): 12. *Step Ladder* 13, No. 5 (May 1927): 137. In *S, SP*.

"The Incubus of Time." In August Derleth, ed. *Fire and Sleet and Candlelight*. Sauk City, WI: Arkham House, 1961, p. 184–85. In *SP, LO*.

"Inferno." In *EC, SP, LO*.

"Inheritance." In *EC, SP*.

"Interrogation." In *S. WT* 10, No. 3 (September 1927): 414. In *SP, LO*.

"The Land of Evil Stars." In *EC, SP, LO*.

"The Last Night." In *ST. Town Talk* No. 1304 (1 September 1917): 5. In *SP, LO*.

"Laus Mortis." *Pearson's Magazine* 47, No. 3 (September 1921): 100. In *EC, SP*.

"The Lemurienne." *AJ* 24, No. 10 (20 December 1923): 6 (as "The Lemurienne"). In *SP*.

"A Live-Oak Leaf." In *ST*.

"Loss." *United Amateur* 25, No. 2 (May 1926): 8. In *S, SP*.

"Love Is Not Yours, Love Is Not Mine." In *EC*.

"Love Malevolent." In *EC. Step Ladder* 13, No. 5 (May 1927): 134. In *SP*.

"The Love-Potion" from *The Fugitives*. In *S. AJ* 23, No. 29 (2 May 1923): 6. *Step Ladder* 13, No. 5 (May 1927): 135. In *SP*.

"Luna Aeternalis." *WT* 42, No. 4 (May 1950): 43. In *SP, DC, LO*.

"Lunar Mystery." In *S, SP*. First title: "Dream-Mystery."

"Madrigal." In *Seer of the Cycles*.

"A Masque of Forsaken Gods." In *ST, SP*.

"Maya." *AJ* 25, No. 23 (19 March 1925): 4. In *S. Step Ladder* 13, No. 5 (May 1927): 135. In *SP, LO*.

"The Meaning." In *ST* (as "The Mystic Meaning"), *SP*.

"The Medusa of Despair." *Town Talk* No. 1113 (20 December 1913): 8. In *OS, EC, SP, LO.*

"The Medusa of the Skies." In *ST, SP.*

"A Meeting." *AJ* 24, No. 12 (3 January 1924): 6. In *S.*

"Memnon at Midnight." In *OS, EC, SP, LO.*

"Memorial." In August Derleth, ed. *Fire and Sleet and Candlelight.* Sauk City, WI: Arkham House, 1961, pp. 185–86. In *SP.*

"The Messengers." Previously unpublished.

"Minatory." *AJ* 25, No. 29 (30 April 1925): 6. *Raven* 2, No. 3 (Autumn 1944): 17. In *S, SP, LO.*

"Mirage." In *EC, SP.*

"Mirrors." In *EC, SP.*

"The Mirrors of Beauty." In *EC, SP.*

"Moesta et Errabunda" [translation of CB]. *AJ* 25, No. 44 (13 August 1925): 4. In *S. Step Ladder* 13, No. 5 (May 1927): 140. In *SP.*

"Moments." In *SP.*

"Moon-Dawn." *WT* 2, No. 1 (July–August 1923): 48 (as "The Red Moon"). *AJ* 24, No. 15 (24 January 1924): 6 (as "The Red Moon"). In *S, SP, LO.*

"The Moonlight Desert." In *LO.*

"Morning on an Eastern Sea." In *The Palace of Jewels.*

"The Morning Pool." In *ST.*

"Le Mort des Amants." See "The Death of Lovers."

"Le Mort Joyeux." Unpublished.

"Mors." Original title: "Anodyne." In *SP.*

"The Motes." In *EC, SP, LO.*

"The Mummy." *Sonnet* 4, No. 2 (May–June 1919): 3. In *EC, LO.*

"Music" [translation of CB]. *AJ* 25, No. 38 (2 July 1925): 3 (as "La Musique"). In *S.*

"La Musique." See "Music."

"The Mystic Meaning." See "The Meaning."

"Namelessness." Extant?

"Necromancy." *Fantasy Fan* 1, No. 12 (August 1934): 188. *WT* 36, No. 10 (March 1943): 105. In *SP, S&P, LO.*

"Neptune." Extant?

"The Nereid." *Yale Review* 2 No. 4 (July 1913): 685–86. In *EC, SP, LO.*

"Nero." In *ST, OS, Nero, SP, LO.*

"Nightfall." *AJ* 24, No. 13 (10 January 1924): 13.

"Nightmare." In *EC, SP, LO.*

"Nocturne." *International* 6, No. 4 (September 1912): 76 (as "Nocturn").

"Nocturne." In *EC.*

"The Nymph." In *SP.* Original title: "Dream."

"October." *Westward* 4, No. 5 (May 1935): 5. In *SP, S&P.*

"Ode." *AJ* 26, No. 8 (3 December 1925): 14.

"Ode to Beauty." See "To Beauty (a Fragment)."

"Ode to Music." *Placer County Republican* 42, No. 23 (26 September 1912): 1. In *ST.*

"Ode to Peace." Unpublished.

"Ode to the Abyss." In *ST, OS, SP, LO.*

"Omar." See "To Omar Khayyam."

"On Re-reading Baudelaire." *AJ* 24, No. 9 (13 December 1923): 6. In *S, SP, LO.* First title: "On Reading Baudelaire."

"On the Canyon-Side." *AJ* 23, No. 50 (27 September 1923): 6. In *SP*.

"The Orchid of Beauty." In *EC* (as "The Orchid"), *SP*.

"The Owls" [translation of CB]. *AJ* 25, No. 51 (1 October 1925): 4 (as "Les Hiboux"). *Step-Ladder* 13, No. 5 (May 1927): 138 (as "Les Hiboux"). In *SP*.

"The Pagan." In *SP, S&P*.

"The Pageant of Music." In *The Tartarus of the Suns*.

"The Palace of Jewels." In *The Palace of Jewels*.

"Palms." *Asia* 20, No. 3 (April 1920): 330. In *EC, SP*.

"A Phantasy of Twilight." In *The Potion of Dreams*.

"Plum-Flowers." *L'Alouette* 1, No. 2 (March 1924): 44. In *S*.

"A Precept." *Lyric West* 3, No. 9 (January 1924): 4. In *SP*.

"A Psalm to the Best Beloved." In *EC, SP*. [Not to be confused with "Psalm," also in *EC*.]

"Psalm to the Desert." In *Klarkash-Ton and Monstro Ligriv*. Saddle River, NJ: Gerry de la Ree, 1974, pp. [26–27].

"Query." *AJ* 25, No. 26 (9 April 1925): 4. In *EC. United Amateur* 25, No. 2 (May 1926): 7. *Step Ladder* 13, No. 5 (May 1927): 131. In *SP*.

"Quest." *AJ* 22, No. 10 (22 December 1921): 4. *Step Ladder* 13, No. 5 (May 1927): 133. In *EC* and *SP*.

"Reclamation." In *Grotesque and Fantastiques*.

"The Refuge of Beauty." In *OS, EC. L'Alouette* 1, No. 3 (May 1924): 66. In *SP, LO*.

"Remembered Light." *Poetry* 1, No. 3 (December 1912): 78–79. In *EC, SP, LO*.

"The Remorse of the Dead" [translation of CB, "Remords Posthume"]. *Measure* No. 50 (April 1925): 9 (as "by" [not translated by] Clark Ashton Smith).

"Requiescat." *Smart Set* 68, No. 4 (August 1922): 102. In *EC, SP*.

"Requiescat in Pace." *Midland* 5, No. 5 (May 1920): 46–47. In *EC, SP*. Original title: "Dirge."

"Retrospect and Forecast." In *ST, Nero, SP, LO*.

"The Return of Hyperion." In *ST, SP, LO*.

"Rêve Parisien" [translation of CB]. In *S, SP* (as "A Parisian Dream").

"Rosa Mystica." *Lyric West* 1, No. 8 (December 1921): 7. *EC, SP, LO*.

"Satan Unrepentant." In *OS, EC, SP, LO*.

"Satiety." In *EC, SP*.

"Saturn." In *ST, SP, LO*.

"The Saturnienne." *WT* 10, No. 6 (December 1927): 728. In *SP, LO*.

"The Sea-Gods." *AJ* 23, No. 36 (21 June 1923): 6. In *Burden of the Suns*.

"The Secret." *AJ* 23, No. 27 (19 April 1923): 6. In *S, SP*.

"Secret Love." In *SP, S&P*.

"Sed Non Satiata" [translation of CB]. *Arkham Sampler* 2, No. 3 (Spring 1949): 24. In *SP*.

"Semblance." *AJ* 23, No. 26 (12 April 1923): 6. *AJ* 23, No. 27 (19 April 1923): 6 (corrected version). *Wanderer* 1, No. 2 (July 1923): 7. In *S, SP*.

"Semper Eadem." *AJ* 25, No. 36 (18 June 1925): 8. *Step Ladder* 13, No. 5 (May 1927): 137. In *SP*.

"Septembral." *AJ* 23, No. 47 (6 September 1923): 6. First title: "August."

"Sepulture." *Smart Set* 57, No. 2 (October 1918): 122.

"The Shadow of the Unattained." Unpublished.

"Shadows." Extant?

"A Sierran Sunrise." In *The Ultimate Valleys*.

"The Sierras." *Munsey's Magazine* 43, No. 6 (September 1910): 781.

"Solution." *WT* 3, No. 1 (January 1924): 32. In *EC, SP, LO.*

"Song." See "Love Is Not Yours, Love Is Not Mine."

"The Song of Cartha" (from *The Fugitives*). *AJ* 23, No. 29 (3 May 1923): 6. *Wanderer* 2, No. 8 (August 1924): 103. In *S* and *SP.*

"A Song from Hell." In *A Song from Hell, LO.*

"Song" from *The Fugitives. AJ* 23, No. 33 (31 May 1923): 6. *Wanderer* 2, No. 1 (January 1924): 1. In *S, SP.*

"The Song of a Comet." In *ST, Nero, SP, LO.*

"The Song of Aviol." *AJ* 23, No. 25 (5 April 1923): 6. *Lyric West* 3, No. 9 (March 1924): 28. In *S, SP.*

"Song of Cartha" from *The Fugitives. AJ* 23, No. 29 (3 May 1923): 6. *Wanderer* 2, No. 8 (August 1924): 103. In *S, SP.*

"Song of Sappho's Arabian Daughter." *Ainslee's* 43, No. 1 (February 1919): 80 (as "The Desert Garden").

"Sonnet." See "Duality."

"The Sorrow of the Winds." *Poetry* 1, No. 3 (December 1912): 80 (as "Sorrowing of Winds"). In *EC, SP.*

"The Spiritual Dawn" [translation of CB] *AJ* 25, No. 53 [*sic*] (15 October 1925): 4 (as "L'Aube Spirituelle"). In *S, SP.*

"Spleen" [translation of CB]. *WT* 7, No. 2 (February 1926): 254. In *SP.*

"The Star-Treader." In *ST, SP, LO.* First title: "The Sun-Treader."

"Strangeness." *Bohemia* 2, No. 4 (May 1917): 3. In *EC, SP.*

"Symbols." *London Mercury* No. 33 (July 1922): 245. *EC, SP, LO.*

"Sympathetic Horror" [translation of CB]. *AJ* 25, No. 46 (27 August 1925): 6 (as "Horreur Sympathétique" [*sic*]). *WT* 7, No. 5 (May 1926): 664 (as "Horreur Sympathique"). In *SP.*

"The Tears of Lilith." In *EC, SP, LO.*

"The Temptation." Unpublished.

"The Titans in Tartarus." In *The Titans in Tartarus, LO.*

"The Titans Triumphant." Extant?

"To a Northern Venus." Unpublished.

"To Beauty (a Fragment)." *SP.* Original title: "Ode to Beauty."

"To George Sterling" (High priest of this our latter Song,). In *To George Sterling.* Written c. 1910.

"To George Sterling" (What questioners have met the gaze of Time). In *To George Sterling.*

"To George Sterling" (His song shall waken the dull-sleeping throng). In *To George Sterling.*

"To George Sterling" (Deep are the chasmal years and lustrums long). In *To George Sterling.*

"To George Sterling: A Valediction." *Overland Monthly* 85, No. 11 (November 1927): 338. In *SP* and *To George Sterling.*

"To Love." See "Amor Aeternalis."

"To Nora May French." In *EC, SP, LO.*

"To Omar Khayyam." *Lyric West* 5, No. 8 (May–June 1926): 216–17. In *EC, SP, LO.* Original title: "To Omar."

"To the Beloved." In *EC, SP.*

"To the Chimera." *AJ* 24, No. 25 (3 April 1924): 6. *United Amateur* 23, No. 1 (May 1924): 7. *WT* 40, No. 6 (September 1948): 79. In *S, SP, LO.*

"To the Sun." In *ST, SP.*

"Transcendence." In *EC, SP, LO.*

"Transmutation." *AJ* 24, No. 16 (31 January 1924): 6.

"Union." In *EC.*

"Upon the Seas in Saturn." See "In Saturn."

"Uriel." Extant?

"A Valediction." *AJ* 23, No. 43 (9 August 1923): 6. *Buccaneer* 1, No. 1 (September 1924): 12. In *S, SP.*

"Le Vin des Amants." See "The Wine of Lovers."

"The Voice in the Pines." In *In Memoriam: Clark Ashton Smith* (August 1963).

"The Voice of Silence." In *The Palace of Jewels.*

"We Shall Meet." *AJ* 23, No. 28 (26 April 1923): 6. *Wanderer* 2, No. 5 (May 1924): 60. In *S, SP.*

"The Whisper of the Worm." In *SP.*

"The Wind and the Moon." In *ST.*

"Wind-Ripples." Previously unpublished.

"The Wine of Lovers" [translation of CB]. *AJ* 25, No. 42 (30 July 1925): 4 (as "Le Vin des Amants"). In *S. United Amateur* 25, No. 3 (July 1926): 6 (as "Le Vin des Amants"). *Step Ladder* 13, No. 5 (May 1927): 139 (as "Le Vin des Amants"). In *SP.*

"Winter Moonlight." In *EC, SP.*

"The Witch in the Graveyard." In *EC, SP, LO.*

"The Witch with Eyes of Amber." *AJ* 23, No. 32 (24 May 1923): 6. *Epos* 1, No. 4 (Summer 1950): 14. In *SP, DC.* Original title: "The Witch with the Heart of Amber."

"A Woman at Prayer" [translation of Stuart Merrill]. Unpublished.

"The Years Restored." In *The Potion of Dreams.*

"You Are Not Beautiful." *AJ* 24, No. 10 (20 December 1923): 6. In *S, SP.*

C. OTHER WORKS

"The Abominations of Yondo." *Overland Monthly,* 84, No. 4 (April 1926): 100–101, 114, 126. In *AY.*

"The Broken Lute." In *EC, PP.*

"The Caravan." In *EC, PP.*

"Cocktails and Creme de Menthe." *AJ,* 23, No. 52 (11 October 1923): 6; *AJ,* 24, No. 1 (18 October 1923): 6; *AJ,* 24, No. 4 (8 November 1923): 6; *AJ,* 24, No. 6 (22 November 1923): 6; *AJ* 24, No. 7 (29 November 1923): 6; *AJ,* 24, No. 8 (6 December 1923): 6; "Cocktails and Creme de Menthe." *AJ* 24, No. 13 (10 January 1924): 13. In *The Devil's Notebook.*

"The Corpse and the Skeleton." In *PP.* Written 5 April 1915.

"The Demon, the Angel, and Beauty." In *PP.*

"The Devil's Notebook." See *The Devil's Notebook* above.

"Ennui." *Smart Set* 56, No. 1 (September 1918): 32. In *EC, PP.*

"Epigrams." *AJ* 23, No. 51 (4 October 1923): 6. In *The Devil's Notebook.*

[Epigrams (untitled).] *AJ* 24, No. 11 (December 1923): 6. In *The Devil's Notebook.*

"The Flirt." *Snappy Stories?* In *Strange Shadows.* Written 22 December 1921.

"The Flower-Devil." In *EC, PP.*

"From the Crypts of Memory." *Bohemia* 2, No. 3 (April 1917): 27–[28?]. *Fantasy Sampler* No. 4 (June 1956): 12–13. In *EC, Out of Space and Time, PP.*

"The Garden and the Tomb: A Prose Pastel." In *EC. Phantagraph* 4, No. 3 [June 1936]: [12]. In *PP.* Written 9 June 1915.

"George Sterling: An Appreciation." *Overland Monthly* 85, No. 3 (March 1927): 79–80. In *Planets and Dimensions.*

"George Sterling: Poet and Friend." *Mirage* 1, No. 6 (Winter 1963–64): 19–24. In *Planets and Dimensions.*

"In Cocaigne." In *EC, PP.*

"The Litany of the Seven Kisses." In *EC. Laughing Horse* , No. 6 (1923): [19]. In *PP.*

"The Mahout." *Black Cat* 16, No. 11 (August 1911): 25–30. In *OD.*

"The Memnons of the Night." *Bohemia* 2, No.1 (1 February 1917): 27 (as "Memnons of the Night"). In *EC, Phantagraph* 4, No. 2 (November–December 1935): [9]; as "The Memmons of the Night." *PP.*

"Narcissus." In *PP.*

"New Teeth for Old Saws." *AJ* 24, No. 20 (28 February 1924): 6. In *The Devil's Notebook.* [Note: TMS contains thirteen items, of which only five were published. Appearance in *AJ* contains one item not in TMS.]

"Paradox and Persiflage." *AJ* 25, No. 21 (5 March 1925): 8. In *The Devil's Notebook.* [Note: *AJ* appearance contains one additional epigram not in the TMS.]

"The Passing of Aphrodite." *Fantasy Fan* 2, No. 4 (December 1934): 59–60. *Acolyte* 1, No. 4 (Summer 1943): 4–6. In *AY, PP.*

"The Peril That Lurks Among Ruins." *Acolyte* 1, No. 2 (Winter 1945): 3. In *PP.*

"Points for the Pious." 24, No. 3 (1 November 1923): 6; *AJ* 24, No. 5 (15 November 1923): 6. In *The Devil's Notebook.*

"The Princess Almeena." *Smart Set* 61, No. 1 (February 1920): 1. In *EC, PP.*

"The Raja and the Tiger." *Black Cat* 17, No. 5 (February 1912): 12–18 (as by "C. Ashton Smith"). In *OD.*

"Remoteness." In *EC, PP.*

"Something New." *10 Story Book* 23, No. 6 (August 1924). In *OD.*

"The Statue of Silence." In *EC, PP.*

"The Sun and the Sepulchre." In *PP.*

"The Traveller." In *EC, PP.*

SECONDARY

Benediktsson, Thomas E. *George Sterling.* Boston: Twayne, 1980.

Ferlinghetti, Lawrence, and Nancy J. Peters. *Literary San Francisco: A Pictorial History from Its Beginnings to the Present Day.* San Francisco: City Lights Books/Harper & Row, 1980.

Gross, Dalton Harvey. "The Letters of George Sterling." Ph.D. diss.: Southern Illinois University, 1968.

Hart, Jerome A. *In Our Second Century: From an Editor's Note-book.* San Francisco: Pioneer Press, 1931.

Sidney-Fryer, Donald. *Emperor of Dreams: A Clark Ashton Smith Bibliography.* West Kingston, RI: Donald M. Grant, 1978.

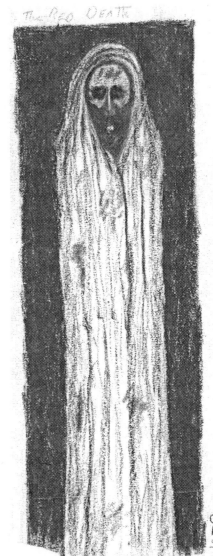

INDEX